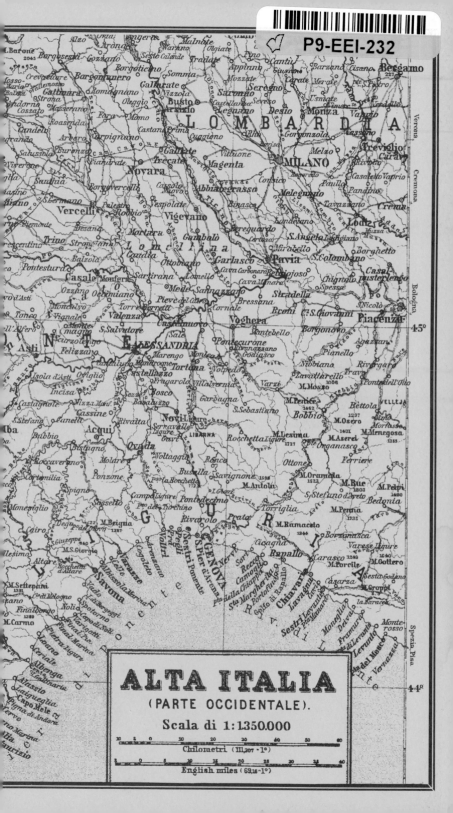

ALTA ITALIA

(PARTE OCCIDENTALE).

Scala di 1:1.350.000

Chilometri (111,307 = 1°)

English miles (69,16 = 1°)

Memoirs of the Oratory of Saint Francis de Sales

from 1815 to 1855

THE AUTOBIOGRAPHY OF SAINT JOHN BOSCO

Translated by Daniel Lyons, SDB

With notes and commentary by
Eugenio Ceria, SDB
Lawrence Castelvecchi, SDB
and Michael Mendl, SDB

DON BOSCO PUBLICATIONS
NEW ROCHELLE, NEW YORK
1989

Translated from *Memorie dell'Oratorio di S. Francesco di Sales dal 1815 al 1855*, ed. Eugenio Ceria, SDB. © 1946, Società Editrice Internazionale, Turin, Italy

English edition by Don Bosco Publications, New Rochelle, New York.
© 1984, 1989, Salesian Society, Inc. All rights reserved.

Printed in the United States of America

Maps of Piedmont and of Turin on the endleaves reproduced from Baedeker's *Italy. First Part: Northern Italy*, 1906, by courtesy of Simon and Schuster, Englewood Cliffs, New Jersey.

Map of Italy on p. lix reproduced from *The Makers of Modern Italy* by Sir J.A.R. Marriott, published by Oxford University Press, 1931. © 1931, Oxford University Press.

Map of the Turin–Castelnuovo area on p. lx reproduced by courtesy of SEI from *Don Bosco* (p. 234) by Leonard von Matt and Henri Bosco, trans. Carlo De Ambrogio. © 1965, Società Editrice Internazionale, Turin, Italy.

Maps of the Oratory on pp. lxiv–lxv reproduced by courtesy of SEI from *L'Oratorio di Don Bosco* (tav. 2 and 4) by Fedele Giraudi. © 1935 Società Editrice Internazionale, Turin, Italy.

Maps of the Castelnuovo Don Bosco–Becchi area and of Chieri on pp. lxi–lxii reproduced by courtesy of the Salesian Department of Formation, Rome, from *Sulle strade di Don Bosco* (pp. 8–9, 26–27). © 1983 Salesian Society, Inc.

Map of the Wandering Oratory on p. lxiii reproduced by courtesy of LDC from *Qui È Vissuto Don Bosco* (p. 147) by Aldo Giraudo and Giuseppe Biancardi. © 1988, Editrice Elle Di Ci, Turin, Italy.

Library of Congress Cataloging-in-Publication Data

Bosco, Giovanni, Saint, 1815–1888.
   [Memorie dell'Oratorio di S. Francesco di Sales dal 1815 al 1855. English]
   Memoirs of the Oratory of Saint Francis de Sales from 1815 to 1855: the autobiography of Saint John Bosco / translated by Daniel Lyons; with notes and commentary by Eugenio Ceria, Lawrence Castelvecchi, and Michael Mendl.
   Includes bibliography, maps, illustrations, and index.
   1. Bosco, Giovanni, Saint, 1815–1888. 2. Christian saints — Italy — Biography. I. Ceria, Eugenio, 1870–1957. II. Castelvecchi, Lawrence, 1925–1987. III. Mendl, Michael, 1948– . IV. Title.
BX4700.B75A3 1989   271'.79 — dc20 [B]   89-36115 CIP

ISBN 0–89944–135–1 perfect-bound cloth edition
      0–89944–139–4 Smyth-sewn deluxe cloth edition

With affection and esteem

the Salesians dedicate

this English edition

of the

Memoirs of the Oratory

to

POPE JOHN PAUL II

꩜

A Note on References

꩜

A selected bibliography is offered at the end of the book. Sources frequently cited are referred to by author, sometimes with an abbreviation of the work:

BM   Lemoyne et al., *The Biographical Memoirs of Saint John Bosco*
BN   T. Bosco, *Don Bosco: Una biografia nuova*
EcSo   Stella, *Don Bosco nella storia economica e sociale*
LesMem   Desramaut, *Les Memorie I de G.B. Lemoyne*
LW   Stella, *Don Bosco: Life and Work*
MB   Lemoyne et al., *Memorie biografiche di S. Giovanni Bosco*
Mem   G. Bosco, *Memorie*, ed. T. Bosco
MO   G. Bosco, *Memorie dell'Oratorio*, ed. Ceria
NCE   *New Catholic Encyclopedia* (New York: McGraw-Hill, 1967), 15 vols.
ReCa   Stella, *Don Bosco nella storia della religiosità cattolica*, vol. 2
SouAut   J. Bosco, *Souvenirs autobiographiques*, Desramaut commentary
SP   T. Bosco, *Don Bosco: Storia di un prete*
SpLife   Desramaut, *Don Bosco and the Spiritual Life*

See the bibliography for complete bibliographic information.

CONTENTS

ಬಿಂಬಿ

Memoirs of the Oratory of Saint Francis de Sales

from 1815 to 1855

LIST OF ILLUSTRATIONS

ꠀꠀꠀ

FOREWORD

The Importance of the *Memoirs* for the Salesian Family

ꠀꠀꠀ

by the Very Reverend Egidio Viganò
Rector Major of the Salesian Society

I t gives me great pleasure to write this foreword for the first English edition of the *Memoirs of the Oratory* of Don Bosco. This jewel of Salesian literature will be a great help toward a better knowledge of Don Bosco's personality in the first forty years of his life (1815–1855); it will make for a better understanding of the early, inspirational apostolate at Valdocco, its evolution, and its steady growth despite difficulties on all sides.

The *Memoirs of the Oratory* is simply written, engagingly intimate, warmhearted; and there is a touch of humor in it too. I hope the few thoughts in this foreword will help readers to benefit much from the profound spirituality that finds its natural seedbed in these writings of our founder. But apart from any reflections this foreword may engender, the thing that will really and truly help Salesians understand the heart of Don Bosco will be the great love we have for him and our firm resolve to know him better, so that at this point in mankind's history we may be able faithfully to continue his mission and spirit.

The renewal of our Salesian holiness, of which I have spoken often, must begin with these memoirs. They have a very special place, a particular significance among Don Bosco's writings. When his memoirs are read in terms of Don Bosco's sanctity — which is essential to understand them fully — they reveal a substance that is quite surprising.

xi

The word "holiness" is hardly found in the text, but Don Bosco's holiness is evident throughout the *Memoirs*. He reveals, for example, a keen awareness that God was using his humble person to establish a great project for the salvation of innumerable young persons, especially the friendless ones.

Pondering what use his *Memoirs* would be, Don Bosco concluded that it "will be a record to help people overcome problems that may come in the future by learning from the past. It will serve to make known how God himself has always been our guide."[1]

These considerations are basic; they prompt me to focus on three contemporary concerns and what Salesians can learn about them in this classic document so abounding in inspiration and foresight, so personally relevant. These concerns are the relationships of tradition and novelty, pastoral charity and ascetical discipline, and spirituality and action.

1. *Fidelity to Don Bosco in an Age of Novelty*

We must face the fact that our generation is totally enthralled by the latest trends. But these novelties do not constitute the whole of reality. In the future there is God, of course; but God does not belong solely to the future — "Christ yesterday and today and forever" (Hebrews 13:8).

The Salesian of our times is still a contemporary of Don Bosco, for yesterday was the beginning of tomorrow! To act as though the Salesian charism were merely the result of the signs of the times would be sheer philosophical immanence without faith. It would be tantamount to substituting for the founder an impersonal, ambiguous, and relative gnosis, disguised with a facelift dictated by fashion.

The true Salesian must anticipate the new times. If he shuts himself off from them, he becomes a mere curiosity in a museum; if he allows himself to be engulfed by them he destroys himself. If, however, in their midst he emerges as a bearer of a permanent charism of the Holy Spirit, then he is indeed true to his vocation.

The Salesian of Don Bosco moves into the new times from a platform of traditions; for him there is no future

without fidelity to the past. The Salesian will lose his identity if he does not guard the traditions of his vocation, does
not explore their depths, does not develop them. And this
demands a "return to the sources" if there is to be any true
renewal. The Second Vatican Council tells us that "renewal
of the religious life involves . . . a continuous return to the
sources of all Christian life and to the original inspiration
behind a given community and an adjustment of the community to the changed conditions of the times."[2]

For many people the concept of tradition is distasteful.
They feel that anyone invoking tradition is applying the
brake rather than pressing the accelerator. Nevertheless,
remaining faithful to tradition is the only way we can deal
with the signs of the times and preserve our identity. An
identity card carries a photograph and specific data, after
all, not vague directional promises.

Christianity also makes its promises, but it founds its
future on fidelity to its traditions. Once again, Vatican II
reminds us: "In his gracious goodness God has seen to it
that what he had revealed for the salvation of all nations
would abide perpetually in its full integrity and be handed
on to all generations."[3] And again: "Therefore the apostles,
handing on what they themselves had received, warn the
faithful to hold fast to the traditions which they have
learned either by word of mouth or by letter, and to fight
in defense of the faith handed on once and for all."[4]

Assuredly tradition is not static and entombed: it makes
progress within the Church with the help of the Holy
Spirit. The signs of the times do not merely "occasion" superficial external modifications; they actually present a
new dimension that must be understood as genuine progress. For this reason it is a mistake to hold that everything
was crystal clear in the beginning, and that in practice
there is nothing important to be changed. The greater
thoughtfulness and human sensitivity that mark the new
age do not constitute merely an external way of life. Indeed
they bring with them genuine values hitherto unknown.
We are not lacking in loyalty when we say that these values do not begin with Don Bosco or the Gospel, but arise
from the contemporary human situation.

It is only by grasping the realities of the signs of the times that we can speak of "living traditions" that contain their permanent Gospel values as a salvation message for mankind in the various stages of its development. Truly, tradition must be living. And this brings us to the nub of the matter: to accept new values and still conserve an authentic tradition, we simply must return to the Gospel through the insights and spirit of Don Bosco. Our striving for relevance, our new attitudes and methods, our decentralization, our debunking of certain moral observances that are no longer valid — all these efforts are of no earthly use to us if we forget the Gospel and the way Don Bosco did things.

For the Salesian of this new world, the signs of the times are particularly important. It is of vital concern, however, for him to turn back to the Gospel through Don Bosco, if he is to preserve his identity and grow in the future. Hence the importance of knowing and deepening our understanding of our origins, of studying the Salesian spirit, of pondering the depths of our Salesian Preventive System. Unless we return to our founder and study him profoundly, we undermine the dialog between God and the world proper to our vocation, for we are sent by God himself to the young people of the new age.

2. Two Pillars of Salesian Holiness

We take it for granted that our lives as Salesian religious cannot possibly be separated from the very real presence of God, from the demands of holiness. This holiness of the new age must be solidly based on two pillars that uphold our vocation: pastoral charity and ascetical discipline. These virtues were not lived fully only by Don Bosco; they are the two principal marks of every disciple of Christ, no matter what his vocation.

A. *Pastoral charity* is described in our renewed Salesian Constitutions as the sum and center of our spirit.[5] It is our heritage from Saint Francis de Sales, doctor of charity, from whom we take our Salesian name.[6] Such charity demands from each of us a heart like Don Bosco's; he said,

"I have promised God that I would give of myself to my last breath for my poor boys."[7] "The Salesian spirit finds its model and source in the very heart of Christ, apostle of the Father."[8] Since, in the first place, our mission is entrusted to the community,[9] the community must be based on charity, and our vows will be at its service; "brotherly love, our apostolic mission, and the practice of the evangelical counsels are the bonds which form us into one and constantly reinforce our communion."[10]

It is charity that spurs our Salesian community to undertake its joint pastoral work. "By the charity to which they lead, the evangelical counsels join their followers to the Church and her mystery in a special way,"[11] says the conciliar Constitution on the Church. Speaking of the universal call to holiness (chapter 5), that Constitution reminds us that "the first and most necessary gift is that charity by which we love God above all things and our neighbor because of God."[12]

It is not through any ideological system but through charity lived publicly according to a practical ideal expressed in their vows that religious (as distinct from the Church's hierarchy and laity) "give splendid and striking testimony that the world cannot be transfigured and offered to God without the spirit of the beatitudes."[13]

Pastoral charity is too vast and important a topic to be treated in these brief lines. Here I have been content to emphasize it as one of the most radical and indispensable conditions for a Salesian of the new age. It is not enough for confreres to be well versed in humanities and the sciences. We shall never build for the future if we are not motivated by the charity of the Holy Spirit, that charity by which love of our neighbor is the fruit of love of God. Indeed, the unifying quintessence of charity lies in the fact that our love for our neighbor must depend on our love for God.

B. The second distinctive mark is *ascetical discipline*. We think of the parable of the salt in the Synoptic Gospels (Mark 9:49–50; Matthew 5:13; and Luke 14:34–35). Jesus speaks of his disciples as the salt of the earth. The three evangelists comment on the Lord's words; they describe the disciple and his essential make-up. A careful scrutiny of the text makes it clear that the salt is the spirit of sacrificial renunciation indispensable for any disciple.

Oscar Cullman, a Protestant exegete and observer at Vatican II, has made a close study of these texts and has written on the enlightening metaphor of the salt:

> Salt gives life, purifies; but it has this quality only because it is also caustic and causes pain. In this sense the disciple's suffering is great, but for this very reason it confers on him the strength to fulfill his lofty mission as disciple. Now we know that the function of a disciple depends completely on the spirit of sacrifice and total renunciation he must possess. To be a disciple without renunciation and suffering is a contradiction — like the salt that has lost its essential elements. The essential quality of a disciple is inseparable from the function he must carry out for mankind, and vice-versa. To be a disciple means to be always a disciple for mankind. And since being a disciple demands the spirit of sacrifice, the world needs the disciple who is willing to suffer, renounce himself, and make sacrifices.[14]

Let us not deceive ourselves: if the salt loses its flavor, what use is it? I doubt that those responsible for forming the Salesians of the new age will be found among the leaders shouting fashionable slogans and playing down Gethsemane and Calvary; waxing eloquent in favor of the poor from the comfort of their armchairs; continually thinking up new forms of prayer but rarely speaking with God; relentlessly proclaiming the outdatedness of sexual taboos while calmly accepting amusements and friendships that put their purity of heart at risk; parading as paladins of social justice by playing politics instead of spreading and living the Gospel; downgrading authority in favor of brotherliness, yet neglecting the spirit of sonship we owe to the Father; and accepting neither the obedience of the cross nor self-sacrifice for the good of their confreres.

Let us never forget that our Salesian future must walk the way of holiness; it will require confreres who daily practice *pastoral charity* and genuine *ascetical discipline*. This will help us avoid chasing the will-o'-the-wisp, especially when we honestly discuss and examine the future together. History teaches us that it is the holy people who truly open up for the Church the frontiers of new eras.

3. *The Basis of Salesian Spirituality*

The final aspect on which I wish to touch is one that is basic to Salesian vitality in the new times. Indeed, on it hinged Don Bosco's own holiness—that spiritual characteristic of being able to achieve a vital union of being and action, consecration and mission, love of God and neighbor, prayer and work—that is, the "grace of unity."[15] This is a characteristic of the apostolic holiness of the active life to which "the Salesian for all seasons" must witness.

When Don Bosco speaks of his vocation and that of his co-workers, he means it to be realized in a saving mission for the young and the working classes. He was called by God to be active in the Church and was put in charge of a group of people characterized by activity—work, work, work!

Thus it is vital for us to seek a sanctity that is enhanced and perfected by apostolic action. The active life is part and parcel of our vocation; this is recognized and proclaimed by Vatican II in the famous number 8 of *Perfectae caritatis*. The active life belongs to the very nature of our religious life. Our vocation imbues us with a "holiness in activity."

Not all religious vocations are the same; there are quite a number of institutes of the contemplative life. We too must be contemplatives—in action.[16] We have much to learn from pure contemplatives, then, for our different vocations are complementary in the unity of the Body of Christ.

Of course there really is a distinction, but it does not necessarily mean separation. Such a distinction, however, does provide more than sufficient grounds for different vocations. It is a historical fact that certain vocations concentrate publicly on those specific areas of the Church's sacramental reality that have more to do with either being or activity, and it is in both of these that the Salesian vocation is to be found. For a Salesian, belonging to the

Church means ecclesial action, wherein witness is realized in a specific service.

The distinction does not aim to make any essential division between one aspect and the other, but rather to unite in different forms the various elements that give a characteristic tone to the variegated unity in the Church. Assuredly being part of the Church is, per se, more important than ecclesial action. Between witnessing and service there is certainly a distinction; however, one way of giving witness (and it cannot be called vague or useless!) consists in rendering a service.

It should be abundantly clear that the Salesian called to carry out such a service must never lose sight of the fact that he must carry it out as a *witness*; to do otherwise would falsify his vocation, since the whole Church exists and works as a "universal sacrament of salvation."[7] To witness in his service, the Salesian must possess and daily cultivate the "grace of unity" — which is *pastoral charity* deep in the heart, enthusiastic and mystic. Don Bosco expressed this intimate and ardent unity in his *Da mihi animas, caetera tolle*, which defines the essence of his spirit.

All these requirements will oblige the Salesian of the new era to search into the way of the Gospel traced out by his founder, to play his proper part in human history, to study pastoral practice and the subtle meaning of action. Thus his heart will be steeped in the spirit of Don Bosco's Valdocco Oratory; he will perfect an authentic theology of the active life and discover in it both the riches of holiness and the visible dimension of the sacraments as he pursues his mission to the young and the working classes.

Notes

1. Preface.
2. *Perfectae caritatis*, 2 (Abbot ed.).
3. *Dei verbum*, 7.
4. Ibid., 8.
5. *Constitutions of the Society of St Francis de Sales* (Rome, 1985), article 10.

6. Ibid., 4.
7. Ibid., 1; MB XVIII, 258.
8. *Constitutions*, 11.
9. Ibid., 44.
10. Ibid., 50.
11. *Lumen gentium*, 44.
12. Ibid., 42.
13. Ibid., 31.
14. Oscar Cullman, *La fe y el culto en la Iglesia primitiva* (Madrid: Studium, 1971), pp. 307–308.
15. *Acts of the Superior Chapter*, no. 127.
16. *Constitutions*, 12.
17. Cf. *Lumen gentium*, 1.

INTRODUCTION TO THE ENGLISH EDITION

by Michael Mendl, SDB

Before one begins reading Don Bosco's autobiography, it is helpful to know something about the circumstances of its composition, and it is essential to know why and for whom he was writing it. In his foreword, Father Egidio Viganò has explained why familiarity with the *Memoirs of the Oratory* is important for the men and women of Don Bosco's Salesian Family. This introduction suggests the value of the *Memoirs* to educators, scholars, and general readers. Finally, one cannot fully understand Don Bosco's activity and thought without understanding his world; so there is an extensive description of the historical and social background of the *Memoirs*.

I. *Origins of the Text*[1]

In the *Memoirs of the Oratory of Saint Francis de Sales* we have a precious and unique document. It is not so much the story of an institution as it is the story of a man and his vocation.

Yet it is not a story that has come to us easily. It is true that Father John Bosco often spoke to his first disciples about his origins and the origins of his works. When they wrote his biography for the same period (1815–1855), they filled four volumes (2516 pages).

What is unique about the *Memoirs* is that in these few pages the man himself speaks to us. In some instances, they are the only source from which we know particular episodes of his life or how he understood certain events. What is precious about them is not only their uniqueness but our good fortune in having them at all. Don Bosco wrote 148 textbooks, biographies, rule books, position papers, and devotional books, as well as thousands of letters. But he never meant to write an autobiography. He did so only under obedience, and even so never completed it. And he tried to prevent wide distribution of what he did complete.

When Pope Pius IX met Don Bosco for the first time, in 1858, he already knew a great deal about the boys' priest of Turin. But he wanted to hear Don Bosco's story directly, especially any part of his story that might be considered supernatural. After Don Bosco had told him everything, the Pope urged him to record his experiences, especially his dreams. Such an account, the Pope thought, would be a perpetual family heirloom and inspiration for the congregation which Don Bosco hoped to found.[2]

Don Bosco was both busy and modest. He ignored Pope Pius's recommendation. When they met again in 1867, the Pope asked whether he had obeyed. Realizing the insufficiency of his recommendation, the Pope commanded.

> Well, then, I not only advise you, but order you to do it. This task must have priority over everything else. Put aside the rest and take care of this. You cannot now fully grasp how very beneficial certain things will be to your sons when they shall know them.[3]

Even so, Don Bosco did not obey at once: he had so many journeys to make, so many problems to handle; and a grave illness in 1871–1872 nearly killed him.

The only external evidence as to just when he composed this mini-autobiography comes from a conference which he gave to the superiors of all the Salesian communities in 1876. He insisted that they should all keep chronicles concerning their communities. He had already set the example: "I have already summarily jotted down various items concerning the Oratory from its beginnings until now; in fact, I have detailed many things up to 1854."[4] This seems to mean that the *Memoirs* was finished in 1876.

External evidence points to revision of the text between 1878 and 1881, with his secretary Father Joachim Berto recopying most of it at that time. In January 1879 Father John Bonetti (1838–1891) began publishing his *History of the Oratory* in the *Salesian Bulletin*, one chapter a month. (He later revised this history into the book published in English as *St. John Bosco's Early Apostolate*.) In the January 1882 issue of the *Bulletin*, he used material taken substantially from the last twenty-two pages of Don Bosco's manuscript; so those last few chapters were certainly completed no later than November 1881.[5]

The internal evidence leads us to believe that he wrote it between 1873 and 1875 and revised most of it after 1878. In Don Bosco's manuscript are two pointers to the 1873 starting date. In chapter 10 of this English edition, he referred in the first draft to Father Joseph Gazzano as "still living in Upper Moltado in this year (1873)." When he revised the text, he eliminated the reference to the year and inserted a variant without a date. In chapter 43, Don Bosco speaks of his recovery from a near-fatal illness in 1846 and remarks, "For the next 27 years I had no need of either doctors or medicine."

There are likewise two indications as to when Don Bosco finished the first draft. Chapter 45 alludes to the current episcopal dignity of two prelates; in the original manuscript he puts "1875" in parentheses there. In chapter 56, but this time in Father Berto's copy of the manuscript, "1875" was added next to the reference to the Oratory's chapter of the Saint Vincent de Paul Society.

Since there is at least one reference to an event in 1878 in a note added later (in chapter 47 on the Church of Saint John the Evangelist), Don Bosco did at least some of the revision after that year.

Internal evidence also indicates that Don Bosco intended to continue the *Memoirs of the Oratory* by writing a history of the Salesian Society. He says so in chapter 48 when speaking of the first spiritual retreat offered at the Oratory.

Did Don Bosco himself mean to write such a history? In the above-mentioned 1876 conference, after asking the directors to keep community chronicles, he outlined the advantages of doing so and laid down guidelines. Such records, he said, would be invaluable sources for later historians of the Salesian Society. He referred to what he had written about the beginnings of the Oratory, and continued:

> From [1854] on we concentrate on the Congregation, and the subject matter becomes considerably vaster and more complex. I see this work as very useful to those who will follow after us and as redounding to God's greater glory. Hence, I shall strive to continue writing.[6]

Unfortunately, he failed to carry out his resolution. The relentless pressure of expanding and financing his work and the infirmities of age made it impossible. He was satisfied that he had done the minimum that Pius IX had ordered him to do.

The original autograph manuscript, preserved in the Salesian Central Archives in Rome, fills 180 pages in three large exercise books (29.5 x 20.4 cm).[7] These pages are closely written but have a generous left-hand margin which is sometimes filled with additions and corrections. The manuscript, except four passages, is entirely in Don Bosco's handwriting, and so are the additions and corrections. The last pages of this manuscript contain some additions and changes in another hand, but these were copied exactly from those made by Don Bosco in Father Berto's copy.

Father Berto made a second copy of the manuscript.[8] (He was skilled at deciphering Don Bosco's "terrible, awful, miserable" script, as the saint himself described it.[9]) The copy, most likely, was for Father Bonetti to use in preparing his series of *Salesian Bulletin* articles.[10] Father Berto accurately incorporated all of Don Bosco's marginal notes, filling six more 29.5 x 20.4 cm exercise books. Since he left every other page blank, Don Bosco had ample room to make further revisions and add fresh material — which he did in abundance through the first 143 pages of the text, i.e. as far as chapter 50. He did not revise the last thirty-seven pages of the copy because Father Berto did not complete them until 1913,[11] long after Don Bosco's death.

The Italian text which Father Eugenio Ceria (1870–1957) published for the first time in 1946 is based on Father

Sample of Don Bosco's manuscript of the Memoirs: *the conclusion of chapter 31 and the title and beginning of chapter 32 (Part II, chapters 15–16 in the original numbering)*

The same portions of the Memoirs *as copied by Father Berto and further revised by Don Bosco*

Berto's copy as revised by Don Bosco, after a meticulous comparison with Don Bosco's original manuscript.

2. *Contents of the* Memoirs

As important as the *Memoirs* is as a spiritual and historical document, it is not a polished, carefully written essay. Nor is it in any sense the kind of soul-baring autobiography to be found in writers like Saint Teresa of Avila or Saint Thérèse of Lisieux. It is a down-to-earth, matter-of-fact account of events, inner moods, hopes, and frustrations.[12]

Don Bosco, here as much as anywhere in his correspondence, speaks as a spiritual father to his sons. He has spent a lifetime establishing the Salesian Society. Now an old man nearing sixty, he has experience to pass on to them, the family story of ups and downs, heartache and triumph, fatigue and, above all, the mystery of God's grace. These are memories for his beloved sons to treasure and learn from.

To his children a father speaks freely and informally, from the heart. So does Don Bosco in these recollections. Even if he had wanted to speak more formally, to refine his style, he simply did not have the time. He seems to have written his 180 pages in fits and starts, whenever he could snatch a free moment at his desk. His thoughts flowed easily and he wrote hurriedly, without pausing to wait for just the right word to come. As in his letters, Piedmontese words and expressions fell readily from his pen — something he avoided when writing for publication.

Don Bosco never kept a diary. To recall his youth, his education, and his early apostolic efforts he had only his own memory, a few notebook pages (e.g. retreat resolutions), plus an occasional document that Father Berto located for him (a chancery rescript or an earlier publication).

So we are not surprised to find frequent errors of dates and first names, misspellings, omissions of words, and similar slips in details of lesser importance, even in the revised copy. These will be noted in the commentary, not to question the chronicler's authority or reliability but to aid his memory, as it were.

The mood which runs through this story does not dazzle

and excite the reader; rather, it gives limpid clarity and calmness. The writer makes the events unfold undramatically, just as they did when they were happening. The language is plain, frank, and unadorned. For this reason, some who have used the *Memoirs* have tried to serve Don Bosco by polishing his words. The only trouble with that is that the words are no longer his.

Don Bosco's aim was to record the events concerning the beginning of the work of the festive oratories, from which sprang the Salesian Society. Following two chapters on his boyhood (1815–1825), he presented his efforts in three periods: his early education (1825–1835), seminary training and the wandering Oratory (1835–1845), and planting firm roots in Valdocco (1846–1856). He wanted to show how each decade saw a striking development in his career and his apostolic work.

Intimately related to the Oratory's development and the birth of the Salesians are details of the founder's lowly origins, his family, his schooling, his vocational growth, and his priestly training. These are the main thrust of the first part of the *Memoirs*. The providential work which Don Bosco initiated is the focus of the second and third parts. God encouraged him, but one obstacle after another was raised in his path. Against the odds of poverty, misunderstanding, and political turmoil he not only persevered but finally succeeded in anchoring his work in a secure place, by God's grace. He is already beginning to gather permanent helpers about him — the young future first members of his religious family — when the narrative breaks off.

His broad aim of recording the significant events of the Oratory's beginnings had two more immediate ends. First, it was to be instructive, to provide examples whereby his sons might see the marvellous hand of God at work and from which they might learn: "It will serve to make known how God himself has always been our guide. . . . It is always to be hoped that the sons will draw from these adventures . . . some spiritual and temporal advantages." Second, it was to be entertaining, to tell a good yarn with many a touch of humor: "It will give my sons some entertainment to be able to read about their father's adventures. . . . A father delights in speaking of his exploits to his dear children."[13]

Don Bosco certainly has not told us everything about himself, his experiences, or his accomplishments. In some cases he seems simply to have forgotten something. For example, his title to chapter 3 includes "Bird nesting," but he gives that topic just a few phrases in the text. The diaries of Fathers Dominic Ruffino (1840–1865) and John Bonetti show that he spoke of it in much greater detail.[14] In other cases, omissions appear to be deliberate, e.g. the two and a half years that he spent at the Moglia farm.[15]

Even after all the research of Fathers Giovanni Battista Lemoyne, Michele Molineris, and Pietro Stella, among many others, much about him remains unknown, especially from his boyhood, youth, and early manhood. What Don Bosco has given us here is what he considered to be the most significant persons and happenings in his life, together with some individual occurrences illustrative of a number of events or a period of time. His biographers have fleshed these out tenfold. But in these *Memoirs* Don Bosco supplies what no biographer ever could: a look into his own heart.

3. *Publication History*

The first publication of the *Memoirs of the Oratory* was controversial. Don Bosco said expressly in his preface, "I am writing for my beloved Salesian sons; I forbid that these things be made public during my lifetime or after my death." To reinforce this prohibition, at the beginning of each of the three parts he wrote, "For Salesians Only."

This ban had several causes. First, Don Bosco was modest in speaking about himself. Second, the *Memoirs* lacked that literary polish which Don Bosco liked to give to his publications. It was his habit to submit his work to others for editing and always to revise, revise, revise. Third, some people still living might have been been embarrassed by publication.

The constraint of the founder's ban was enough to discourage the early publication of the *Memoirs*. On the other hand, so many authors drew on the manuscript or quoted from it, often without any acknowledgment, that a stage was reached when, in one form or another, the whole text had been published piecemeal. That alone seemed not only to justify publication but even to demand it, entire and authentic.

By 1946, more arguments in favor of publication had been brought forward. The lack of polish in the *Memoirs*, far from detracting from it, leads the reader to appreciate the author's spontaneity. The Salesians had become a worldwide congregation, and few members could go to Turin to see the manuscript.

Father Ceria (and the Salesian superiors of 1946) also felt that they had to justify publication in the eyes of the beloved author. Don Bosco's words, taken at face value, meant clearly that the contents of the manuscript were not to be revealed to any but the Salesian Family. Don Bosco wrote about himself and his adventures for a very limited readership, his own Salesians, a prohibition emphasized by repetition. Those who had known him, like Ceria, like the rector major Father Peter Ricaldone (1870–1951), would not lightly violate his wishes.

Father Ceria turned Don Bosco's own words against his ban. At the directors' meeting in 1876, Don Bosco had recalled the events that marked the birth of the Salesian Society. When he spoke of the need to prepare material concerning its history, he said:

> Many things must be heralded unto God's greater glory, the salvation of souls, and our Congregation's broader expansion. . . . We may say that nothing has happened which was not known in advance. Our Congregation took no step that had not been suggested by some supernatural occurrence, and approved no change, improvement or expansion that was not prompted by God. . . . We could have recorded everything that has happened even before it occurred, in every detail and with preciseness.[16]

He foresaw the objection that nobody could retell these events in detail without involving him:

> This matter brooks no opposition from Don Bosco or anything else. Since Don Bosco's life is bound up with that of the Congregation, let us speak of him. . . . Don Bosco does not matter in this regard. What do I care if people talk well or ill of these things? What does it matter to me if people judge me one way

or another? Let them say what they will.... It matters little
to me, and I shall be not one whit more or less than what I
am now before God. But God's interventions must be made
manifest.[17]

Thus one can say that as early as 1876 Don Bosco himself indirectly approved the publication of his *Memoirs*.
Two years later he was revising it and making it available
to Father Bonetti; so, indirectly, Don Bosco himself super-
vised its publication, almost from beginning to end, in the
Salesian Bulletin.

Publication of the *Memoirs* in 1946 marked two significant centennials, as well. One was the permanent foundation of the Oratory of Saint Francis de Sales in the beat-up
building belonging to Francis Pinardi. The other was the
election of Pius IX as Pope. Salesians are ever grateful to
that venerable Pontiff as to a cofounder of their family—
and to one wise enough to command that these memoirs
be recorded. It was to him that the Salesians dedicated that
1946 edition.

The basic text for this first English translation is Father
Ceria's 1946 annotated edition, which is not, in the technical sense, a critical edition.[18] But it is a reliable and careful
one. We have also consulted the French version translated
by Father André Barucq and annotated by Father Francis
Desramaut, and the modern Italian version by Father
Teresio Bosco, both of which follow Father Ceria but are
helpful with certain obscure words and with their notes.

Clearly an English edition, by the very fact of being a
translation, removes the reader one step from Don Bosco's
own written word. The translator and his editors have
tried to be faithful to that word, as well as to his flavor,
without sacrificing fidelity to idiomatic English.

4. *The Text and the Commentary*

As we said, Don Bosco introduces his *Memoirs* with two
chapters on his boyhood and then divides the rest into
three parts, or decades. Each decade was divided into chapters, which Don Bosco titled and numbered, except the last

six. He numbered them starting from 1 in each part. Father Ceria followed that system.

This edition has kept the threefold division and Don Bosco's titles as being integral to the text. But we have made two changes. First, we have followed the modern style of providing a unifying chapter title for most chapters, turning Don Bosco's titles into subtitles. Those chapters lacking subtitles have Don Bosco's original title. Second, we have numbered all the chapters consecutively. Appendix III offers chapter equivalencies for the benefit of anyone who may consult a different edition.

We have left Don Bosco's original text in its human simplicity; we have not corrected even his obvious mistakes, e.g. the spelling of proper names. Wherever possible, we have retained his italics, numbering, abbreviations, personal titles, etc. We have likewise tried to preserve Don Bosco's ability to play on words, as well as certain usages, such as his almost random use of *giovani* (boys, youths, young men), *giovenetti* (youngsters), *fanciulli* (children), and occasionally, *ragazzi* (boys, kids). Where either Father Ceria or the translator has had to insert a word or phrase, this has been put in brackets.

A particular difficulty in translating for an international readership is English usage. The general principle in this edition has been to follow a "British" style in the translation, since that is Father Lyons's style. The commentary, on the other hand, follows an "American" style.

To run a commentary alongside Don Bosco's text might seem to detract from the simplicity of his style, or worse, from what he has to say. He is not a lofty theologian like Saint Thomas Aquinas, nor is he far away from our time and culture like the scriptures. The extensive commentary offered here corrects errors of fact; clarifies the now-distant memories of our Salesian beginnings and makes them more intelligible to new generations who did not live with Don Bosco; explains various points of Italian history, geography, or culture; familiarizes the general public with matters of Saint John Bosco's and the Salesians' history, spirituality, and methodology that the Salesians themselves take for granted; and identifies Catholic practices for readers who may not be familiar with them.

5. *Importance of the Text*

A document like the *Memoirs* is valuable for more than one reason. Besides everything else, it presents us with precious autobiographical and psychological documentation concerning a major figure in the history of the Catholic Church, Church-State relations, and education in the nineteenth century. Pope John Paul II has said:

> Don Bosco is a landmark in Church history. In fact, he has left behind him a concept, a teaching, an experience and method which have become part of our heritage. In the words of my venerated predecessor Paul VI, he was "a renowned genius of modern pedagogy and catechesis but, above all, a genius of holiness. . . ."[19]

His memoirs are an indispensable primary source for what he did, why he did it, how he did it.

Who might be interested in them? First and most obvious are the members of Don Bosco's Salesian Family. Second are educators at all levels and in all types of schools. Third are scholars interested in nineteenth-century Europe, Church history, or the development of religious congregations. This edition has been prepared with these audiences in mind. The more general reader may certainly profit from the text.

John Bosco was a doer, the founder of the Salesian Family, one of the largest in the Church. It includes the Society of Saint Francis de Sales (Salesian Congregation), the Daughters of Mary Help of Christians (Salesian Sisters), the Salesian Cooperators, the Don Bosco Volunteers, and (as of 1989) eight congregations of sisters inspired by his charism. He sent missionaries to the far corners of the world to preach the Gospel and to educate the young as he had done in Turin.

The Catholic Church ranks Don Bosco as a "hero," a model for imitation, a canonized saint. His memoirs reveal his humanity; his struggles with himself, with others, with his environment; his human and his spiritual development. They reveal his mother's role as his first and best earthly teacher.

In his simplicity, the saint confesses some of the defects

of his youth. He condemns rather severely some of the outbursts of his as yet uncontrolled, generous energy. He speaks of his surrender to vanity and his occasional inconstancy. Such faults are like sparks or flashes here and there showing that he is still on the pilgrim road of obedience to divine grace.

What is the best lesson to be learned from these memoirs? Don Bosco himself tells us that his chronicle "will be a record to help people overcome problems that may come in the future by learning from the past." It is true that he had the Salesians in mind, but the statement itself is more wide-ranging. His life story tells of the difficulties that impeded the journey of a great saint but did not stop him from reaching the goal set for him by Divine Providence. His example is a lesson to all who must overcome hardships to reach an appointed or a chosen goal.

The *Memoirs of the Oratory* bears witness not only to a saint's spirituality and to the beginnings of a great apostolic enterprise but also to an exciting, formative period of European history. Scattered throughout the *Memoirs* are reflections on the political and religious personalities and questions that marked a challenging period of Italian history. In these pages we witness the beginnings of the urbanization and industrialization of Italy, and the currents of nationalism and anticlericalism that produced a united Italy in Don Bosco's lifetime.

Don Bosco does not focus on these events as such. But the social changes were the reason for his work, and the political changes could not help affecting it. His few candid observations on statesmen and the Church-State conflicts of his time are the more telling because of the dispassionate mood of his writing. That very dispassion helps to explain why he could, on at least four different occasions, have been called upon as a reliable intermediary between the Sardinian-Italian government and the Vatican. (He proved so discreet and trustworthy a channel that it is nearly impossible to trace his steps.)

The *Memoirs* is the autobiography of a great modern educator who is hardly known in the English-speaking world. He is not a theoretician but a practitioner. His few directly pedagogical writings — the little treatise on the Preventive System, an essay on punishment, confidential advice to directors, and a circular letter on the spirit that animated the Oratory in its pristine days — are more practical than theoretical, based not on some philosophical or psychological premise but on his years of experience.

The *Memoirs of the Oratory* recounts that experience. It is not purely anecdotal, for it tells us why Don Bosco did what he did and attempts some analysis of the success or failure that resulted. The first part, especially, abounds with material about guidance, peer pressure, moral formation, and methodology. The *Memoirs* describes, and in a sense embodies, the essential groundwork of an educational project that, one hundred years after their author's death, involves 17,650 Salesian priests and brothers working in 1572 youth centers, schools, parishes, mission stations, and publishing houses in 99 countries; 17,144 Salesians Sisters in 1508 centers; and countless Salesian Cooperators and alumni.

Don Bosco's educational ideas and method — his Preventive System — are proven by more than their anecdotal success or the huge family that is his most apparent legacy. His ideas and his method produce saints. One may point, if one is so inclined, to the number of his priests, religious, and Cooperators whose causes of canonization are under study: besides himself, one saint, three blesseds, six venerables,[20] and ninety-eight "servants of God." One could point to those who came under his influence: Saint Leonard Murialdo, Blessed Louis Orione, and Blessed Louis Guanella.

But the greatest proof of the efficacy of Don Bosco's educational method comes from its pupils. Many have led edifying lives — and the Church herself has said so by recognizing the sanctity of three of them. She has canonized Dominic Savio, beatified Laura Vicuña, and declared venerable Zeferino Namuncurá, all of them students no more than nineteen years old when they died.

The founder of so vast and so successful a project has something to say to educators everywhere: Christian or non-Christian, in public or private schools, in kindergarten or university. The method of reason, religion (or, at least, fundamental moral values), and loving kindness transcends boundaries, cultures, and age.

6. *Historical Background to the* Memoirs

A. *The French Revolution*

At the end of the eighteenth century the political, social, and economic order of Western Europe was ready to explode. Unrest in Paris in 1789 became a revolution, and the revolution became the spark that changed the world forever.

Italy in 1789 was a political, social, and economic backwater that Metternich would later dismiss as "just a geographical expression." But it too was ripe for change. The Church and a few wealthy and noble families controlled the peninsula, as they had since the Middle Ages. There was no middle class of any significance; an aristocracy ruled, though Genoa and Venice were nominal republics.

It was the small middle class of Paris that touched off the French Revolution. At its start it was not a democratic movement; it was an attempt by the middle class to get a share of the power and prestige enjoyed by the nobility and the clergy. The Declaration of the Rights of Man stressed the rights of property as much as it did liberty.

But the middle class did not control the streets of Paris. The lower class, the great mass of the people, began its own revolution alongside the middle class's, and it was far more radical. For the masses, all of the upper classes, the Church included, were the oppressors and became the targets of the revolution. The middle class provided the leadership, but the people provided the power that radicalized the French Revolution and brought on the Republic, the Reign of Terror, and the executions of the king, the queen, and thousands of nobles, clergy, and private citizens. Christianity itself (apart from such abuses as individual churchmen committed) was rated as an enemy of the people — of "liberty, equality, and fraternity." The goddess

Reason replaced Christ. A new calendar, dating 1792 as Year I, replaced the Christian calendar. A new political order, the republic of all the citizens, replaced the *ancien régime* of king, Church, and nobility.

The monarchs of Europe took note and were alarmed for themselves and their own nations. They declared war on the French Revolution. Europe was to be at war from 1793 till 1815, one side trying to export the Revolution (or later, Napoleon's tyranny), the other side trying to stomp it out.

It was the threat to the Revolution that propelled Napoleon to power. Before he was thirty, he was a general with a proven ability to defeat France's enemies and a charismatic ability to inspire the troops. His first victories were won in northern Italy at the expense of the Austrians and their Piedmontese allies. From 1796 until 1814 the French controlled northern Italy. They proved to be hard masters, depleting the country of money, art, livestock, produce, and able-bodied men. At least forty-five thousand Italians died in Napoleon's Russian and Spanish campaigns. But the French also brought something for Italy: change.

Napoleon linked the city-states of northern Italy into the form of a republic. The form was artificial and temporary, but the ideas of unity and of shared political power were planted. Later, when France took over the government of the whole peninsula, the traditional bureaucratic government was shaken up. Aristocracy was tossed out, and merit was led in; an efficient government administered justice, built roads and bridges, and supported education. The internal customs barriers came down, diverse legal systems were codified, the remnants of feudalism were abolished, and so were aristocratic and ecclesiastical privileges. Vast estates belonging to the Church were confiscated, broken into parcels, and sold. Therefore, wrote Sir J.A.R. Marriott, "among the makers of modern Italy, Napoleon holds a foremost place."[21]

The French Revolutionary and Napoleonic influences on Italy, northern and central Italy particularly, produced a movement that embodied nationalism and economic and social reform. It also included anti-Christian elements; but initially these did not dominate it, nor was the movement's eventual anticlericalism inevitable. This complex movement took the name *Risorgimento* ("Resurgence"), and it lasted from the Congress of Vienna until the capture of Rome by Italian forces in 1870. One could even say that it lasted until 1918, when the postwar settlement awarded the Trentino and Istria to Italy at the expense of the defunct Austro-Hungarian Empire, or until 1929, when the Lateran Treaty at last resolved the relationship between the new Italian State and the Papacy.

The Risorgimento stood for a unified national state for all Italians; the elimination of foreign domination, whether by the French or the Austrians; the modernization of the economy; universal education; a broadening of the base of political power by enfranchising the educated middle class of merchants and industrialists, professors, writers, minor clergy and military officers, and civil servants, if not all classes of the people; recognition of fundamental civil rights such as freedom of speech, of the press, and of religion; and a reduction of the economic, social, and political power of the Catholic Church.

The British, Prussian, Austrian, and Russian alliance brought Napoleon down in 1814 and then assembled its diplomats in Vienna to try to put Europe back together. The Congress of Vienna met from November 1814 until June 1815. In March, Napoleon fled Elba, returned to power in France, and was finally crushed at Waterloo in June.

B. *The Restoration of the Old Order*

The Congress of Vienna was dominated by its host, Austrian foreign minister Prince Metternich (1773–1859). Metternich, in turn, was dominated by two ideas: restoring the pre-1789 European order, and maintaining the balance of power among the European states, i.e. the four victorious allies and France. Lesser states such as Piedmont, Spain, and the Papal States would have to respect the wishes of the major powers. No power should grow either too powerful or too weak. The Revolution and all its fruits must be obliterated. Republicanism meant mob rule, terror, and war; the Old Regime meant order, peace, and prosperity.

And so the statesmen of Vienna decreed that the genie should return to its bottle. Royal dynasties and old borders should be restored, with due compensations being made to the victors, of course.

The Austrians reclaimed their former province of Lombardy; the better to secure it — and to obliterate a reminder of 1789 — they also grabbed the ancient republic of Venice and incorporated it into their empire. These two provinces were the economic and strategic prizes of all Italy. From them the Austrians could ensure that the rest of the Italians behaved. In the next forty years, the two provinces would provide the Austrian Empire with about one-third of its revenues, though they were only about an eighth of its territory. Austrian puppets were established in the duchies of Parma, Modena, and Tuscany.

The papal government of Pius VII (reigned 1800–1823) was restored in the States of the Church, but the Austrians kept garrisons in Ferrara and Bologna. The Bourbons returned to the Kingdom of the Two Sicilies (Sicily and southern Italy, with Naples as capital). And the house of Savoy, under King Victor Emmanuel I (reigned 1802–1821), returned to the Kingdom of Sardinia, which included Savoy, Piedmont, Sardinia, and Nice, with Turin as the capital. To complete, nearly, the abolition of any trace of republicanism, Liguria was also granted to Sardinia, and Genoa's centuries-old independence came to an end. (The insignificant republic of San Marino survived the massacre, as it later survived the Risorgimento; for that, stamp collectors are ever grateful.)

Into this world John Bosco was born eight weeks after Waterloo. He grew up in the religious and social world of the Restoration. The first twenty-nine years of his priestly ministry in the Sardinian capital were spent in the feverish world of the Risorgimento, and the last eighteen coped with its effects in Church and State (as well as with the tensions of French politics in the Third Republic).

Victor Emmanuel resolved on a thorough restoration. If powdered wigs and tricorn hats were worn in 1789, so they would in 1815. If the French had reformed the laws, their laws would be annulled. If the French had built bridges, their bridges would be blown up. (One bridge over the Po was spared; the queen used it to drive to the royal summer house.) If the Church had been robbed of its rights and its lands, the rights at least would be given back (not much land was). Competent civil servants under the French, such as Michele Cavour (see chapters 37 and 41), had to go, and the king's men had to come, regardless of their incompetence. The nobility required royal permission to read foreign newspapers. Protective tariffs went up again.

Some of the more liberal Piedmontese intellectuals chose exile over such a stifling environment. Massimo d'Azeglio and Silvio Pellico, for instance, found even Austrian-ruled

The Church of the Great Mother of God, built on the east bank of the Po between 1818 and 1831 to celebrate the restoration of King Victor Emmanuel I in 1814.

Milan preferable. Others like Cesare Balbo, Luigi Provana, and Santorre di Santarosa laid low until better times should come. Younger army officers were alienated by royal interference and the preference given royal favorites.

But the Piedmontese were generally tolerant of the royal nonsense. Indeed, in Piedmont as elsewhere in Europe, people were ready for peace, order, respect for religion, and an end to French taxation and conscription. But Metternich was not fooled into complacency. "Of all the Italian governments," he wrote to his emperor in 1817, "the Piedmontese is indisputably the one which calls for the most anxious attention. This country unites in itself all the different elements of discontent."[22] It was only a matter of time before the educated men of the middle class realized that the Restoration meant economic and social stagnation and their own exclusion from political power.

The Church, having been restored to its traditional powers and privileges, fully supported the restored monarchs and the ancient order. The Church had its own legal system for trying clerics (regardless of the alleged crimes) and for handling various matters such as marriage. The Church controlled education. Both Church and State censored the press and the stage. The State used its political power to support the Church, and the Church used its moral force to support the State.

Besides this wedding of throne and altar, the Church enjoyed a privileged social position. In 1854 Sardinia had a population of five million. There were forty-one dioceses, five hundred religious houses, fourteen hundred canonries, and eighteen thousand monks and nuns. All in all, one person in every 214 was an ecclesiastic.[23] The Napoleonic era notwithstanding, the Church held vast lands, from which it drew an annual income of about 9,000,000 lire; to that the State added generous subsidies totalling 11,000,000 lire more. All that wealth, however, was not enough to lift the average parish priest out of misery; the government felt compelled to supplement his salary of about 500 lire per year with 250 more just so he could survive.

Between political conservatism and economic feudalism, there was plenty of fuel for anticlericalism in Italy even if the Papal States had not existed as a stumbling block to nationalism.

C. *The Revolutions of 1820–1821*

By 1820 popular unrest was evident throughout southern Europe, particularly in the army, among students, and in the small merchant class. Secret societies were formed to advocate political reform and/or national unification. The Freemasons were the chief of these; in Italy there were also the Carbonari.

Revolution broke out first in Spain. In March 1820 Ferdinand VII was compelled to accept a constitution he had earlier rejected. Written constitutions limited monarchs, established representative government, and specified civil rights. Similar situations (with local variations) followed in Portugal, Naples, and Piedmont. Metternich convened the powers, and after a great deal of discussion an intervention by the Austrians was permitted. They smashed the Neapolitan revolution early in 1821.

In March 1821 the army garrison at Alessandria in Piedmont rose in rebellion, hauled down the blue flag of Savoy, and raised the green, white, and red tricolor of Italy. A regiment marched on Turin, hoping to get Victor Emmanuel to grant a constitution and lead a war to drive the Austrians out of Italy. The soldiers had solid middle-class support; both they and the businessmen wanted the power that until then only the nobility enjoyed.

But the soldiers failed to stir popular support. Two smaller Piedmontese garrisons joined their Alessandrian comrades, and there was an anti-Austrian rising in Milan;[24] but otherwise the Alessandria garrison was isolated. The old king, for his part, lacked the nerve to face the situation and abdicated in favor of his brother, Charles Felix. Charles Felix was in Modena; his twenty-three-year-old nephew Charles Albert became regent.

Charles Albert displayed the tendency to "waffle" that would be his downfall also in 1848–1849. He was caught between his uncle's rights, public pressure, and personal inclination. After some hesitation, he granted a constitution based on Spain's.

Charles Felix was not pleased. He repudiated his nephew's act, exiled him, and invited the Austrians to help him quell the uprising. They were more than willing. The new king swiftly and ferociously suppressed liberalism wherever he found it. He wrote to his brother the former king, "All those who have studied at the University are corrupt. The bad are the educated; the good are the ignorant."[25] For ten years he was a model of the absolute monarch.

Next it was Spain's turn. This time a French army supplied the muscle. By April 1823 "legitimate government" had been restored to all of Europe once more, except Greece, where a rebellion continued against Turkish overlords. That national revolution would eventually involve the great powers but would drag on into the 1830s.[26]

Charles Felix issued new education regulations in 1822. Under these rules, which were in force when John Bosco was a student, every commune was to establish and support an elementary school. The clergy was to do the teaching and approve all the books. Prayer, catechism, and religious services were as mandatory as instruction in reading, writing, and arithmetic.

The king also returned the Jews to the ghettos from which Napoleon had liberated them. Criminal and military punishments were stiffened and the use of capital punishment and of torture broadened.[27]

D. *The Revolutions of 1831*

Charles Felix died in April 1831. He had wished to disinherit his nephew as unreliable; but Charles Albert was the legitimate heir, and Metternich required that legitimacy be honored. So unlucky Charles Albert became king. In the meantime revolution had burst across Europe again. This time, as in 1789, it began in Paris. King Charles X was overthrown in July 1830 because of his absolutist tendencies, and a monarchy under King Louis Philippe, more responsive to the middle class, installed. Rebellions ensued in Belgium (for independence from the Netherlands) and Poland (for independence from Russia), and in the central Italian duchies and the Papal States (for better government).

Britain and France would not allow Austria, Prussia, and Russia to intervene in Belgium though the Dutch requested it; and so Belgian independence was recognized in 1831. The Poles and the Italians were not so fortunate. Russian troops in the first case, and Austrians in the second, quickly restored their versions of order. Meanwhile, the Greeks had successfully established their independence from the Ottoman Empire (1830), which Austria and Russia found acceptable because it weakened a powerful neighbor.

If the new king of Sardinia had been genuinely liberal as a youth, he was no longer so in 1831. He made sure everyone understood that in 1833 by imprisoning a crowd of Mazzinian conspirators and having fourteen of them shot.

E. *Economic Development in Piedmont*

Economic liberalism was another matter for Charles Albert, though. The Sardinian economy was a shambles. Based on subsistence agriculture, it could not feed its own small population and had to rely upon imported grain. There were painful famines in 1817, 1827, and (over most of Europe) 1842–1847. Besides hunger, pauperism resulted.

The middle class was growing in economic power and therefore in social and political influence. Charles Albert abolished the remaining feudal customs and reformed the post office. He encouraged the arts, sciences, and works of public charity. He even extended unofficial toleration to non-Catholics. Canals were dug, marshes drained, new land brought under cultivation, mines opened (still on a small scale), roads built, the first miles of rail tracks laid, and banks (nonexistent before 1844) organized. Stone quarrying, more extensive than mining, was essential to construction, which boomed as a result of these other activities. Serious industry began in ceramics, tanning, leatherworking, and textiles (silk, wool, and cotton). Most of this industry was still of the cottage variety rather than in factories. Italy has practically no coal, severely limiting industrial possibilities;

there was, additionally, an inherent prejudice against the evils of the factory system. In 1844 about 114,000 Piedmontese worked at various industrial occupations.[28]

In Turin the city government, controlled by wealthy landowners, began to see a need for rational planning. The first zoning laws were passed in an attempt to keep industry out of the city center. Building codes, public health, the water supply, fire protection, the paving and lighting of the streets began to receive attention.[29]

F. *Political Development in the 1830s and 1840s*

Economic liberalism necessarily led to more pressure for political liberalism. Conservative men like Camillo Cavour (see chapter 45) wanted a more liberal government so that they and their economic interests could run it, but not so liberal that the masses would take control. At the radical extreme was Giuseppe Mazzini (1805–1872), who in 1831 founded Young Italy to press for one republican national state, proud of its cultural and religious heritage, free of all foreign domination. Mazzini stood for God (but not Christianity), humanity, and progress. He wrote a great deal, and he also fomented rebellion, requiring his followers to be armed and a number of times trying to stage uprisings. His pen was far more powerful than his sword, as it turned out.

Truly formidable obstacles faced Italian patriots. Italians did not think of themselves as such but as Sicilians, Neapolitans, Genoese, Florentines, etc. When Don Bosco spoke of his *patria*, he meant Castelnuovo, not Italy or even Piedmont. The Italians were of mixed ancestral stock: largely Teutonic in the north, Etruscan and Latin in the center, predominantly Greek in the south, and Arabic, Roman, Spanish, and Norman in Sicily. Each region had its own dialect, with only about 2.5 percent of the population speaking Italian. Fewer than a quarter of them could read or write. Barriers—rugged mountains, lack of roads, and tariffs—hindered commerce from one region to another and even within provinces.

The republican Mazzini was not always a practical man. But he showed a practical wisdom in 1831 by appealing to

Charles Albert as the only man who could call the people to arms and expel the Austrians, and who should then reign over a united nation as a constitutional monarch. Whether Mazzini saw this as just the first step toward a republic or not, the king wanted no part of it and, as was said, crushed Mazzini's first try at organizing a nationalist uprising. Nevertheless, most nationalists remained convinced that anti-Austrian leadership would have to come from the top. Without independent Piedmont in the lead, national unity just was not going to happen. Cesare Balbo and Massimo d'Azeglio said as much in their influential patriotic writings.

One other option was put forward by Vincenzo Gioberti in *The Moral and Civil Supremacy of the Italians*, published in 1843: a national federation under the presidency of the Pope. This idea "was adopted by a large section of the middle class and the nobility, which thought in national terms, but which dreaded any sort of revolutionary upheaval and saw the Papacy as a guarantee of the stability of political and social institutions."[30] This was not realistic in view of the Austrian position in northern and central Italy, for the Pope could not force them out.

The Popes had their own problems. In the nineteenth century, the Papal States were probably the most wretchedly governed area of Western Europe. The Papacy was an absolute monarchy; its secular government over a third of the Italian peninsula was one hundred percent clerical and generally incompetent. Lay advisors were all appointees. Finances were chaotic. Discontent was widespread, and after the Austrian intervention of 1831, the Austrians and the French occupied parts of the Papal States for several years to maintain order. Gregory XVI (reigned 1831–1846) was a well-meaning and serious man; but he was a monk and not an administrator, and he utterly distrusted liberalism. Typical of his attitude were his opposition to building railroads in the Church's territory (for with them would come trade and then subversive ideas) and his opposition to any and all revolutions (even those of Catholic Belgium and Poland against their Protestant and Orthodox masters, and to Irish emancipation).[31]

Early in his pontificate Pope Gregory made it understood that there was no compromising with the spirit of
the French Revolution. Some Catholic thinkers maintained,
nonetheless, that the Church that had baptized Greco-
Roman culture, Aristotle, and the Renaissance could also
baptize the Revolution. Chief among these was the French
priest Félicité de Lamennais (1782–1854). Finding that the
union of throne and altar was, in the long run, harmful to
the Church, they advocated popular sovereignty, separation
of Church and State, and liberty of conscience, press, association, and education—principles which had been proving
their advantages to the Church in the United States since
1789. They even urged the Pope to abandon his temporal
sovereignty and rely solely upon his spiritual authority,
which had been wondrously revivified by Pius VII's heroic
opposition to Napoleon.

Such liberal views were unacceptable to most of the
French bishops, to the Austrian government, and to the
Pope. In 1832 Gregory issued the encyclical *Mirari vos* con-
demning them as promoting rebellion and religious and
moral indifferentism.[32]

G. *Pius IX's Reforms*

Enough of the cardinals were concerned about the state of
the Church's secular domain when Pope Gregory died to
elect as his successor a relatively young moderate who took
the name Pius IX (reigned 1846–1878). The new Pope
promptly startled the world with a vigorous program of
administrative and political reform in the States of the
Church: amnesty for political prisoners and exiles, prison
inspection, freedom of the press, toleration of the Jews,
improvements in education, an agricultural institute, a railroad, a telegraph system, street lighting, and the establishment
of a civic guard and an indirectly elected consultative
assembly of laymen. In a move that appeared to be nation-
alistic, when the Austrian archbishop of Milan died, Pius
appointed an Italian.[33]

Reaction to the papal reforms varied. They were
applauded in Great Britain and the United States. Piedmon-

tese liberals saw in them the first steps toward the fulfillment of Gioberti's program. Pius's reforms were imitated in Tuscany, and they inspired increasing excitement in Lombardy and the Two Sicilies, regions oppressed by a foreign and a tyrannical government, respectively.

Metternich was confounded: "A liberal Pope is a contradiction in terms."[34] He responded in July 1847 by doubling the Austrian army in Lombardy and Venetia and ordering the Austrian garrison in papal Ferrara to occupy the entire city. That brought a strong protest from Pius, reinforcing his stature in patriot eyes. Charles Albert's stature rose too when he offered his army to the Pope. From South America the exile Giuseppe Garibaldi (1807–1882) offered his generalship. Universal condemnation compelled Metternich to withdraw the soldiers in December.

A myth developed around Pius IX, that of the liberal and nationalist Pope. He was a reformer, he was a patriot, and he was a man of genuine charity, deeply loved by ordinary people. In the uprisings of 1831 he had earned the trust of the rebels. He may have been somewhat naive, as Metternich thought. But Pius did not see himself able to go much further; specifically, he could not conceive of separating the secular government of the Church's States from their spiritual government, and therefore he could not yield genuine power to laymen. Nor could he conceive of a Pope retaining his spiritual freedom, and therefore the Church's, unless the Pope remained a temporal sovereign.[35]

In the Kingdom of Sardinia, Charles Albert had established his freedom from Austrian control early in his reign, but in the process he had alienated the other European powers. His internal concerns were economic reform, rebuilding the army that his uncle had neglected, the repression of dissent, deep personal piety, and an upright life. But popular protests in Genoa and Turin, stimulated by events in Rome, had their slow effect on Charles Albert, nicknamed "the Wavering King." By the end of 1847 the king had shuffled his cabinet in favor of moderate politicians, lifted most press censorship, and received a petition for the recognition of the civil rights of Jews and Protestants, which he granted a few months later (see chapter

48). Sardinia negotiated a customs union with Tuscany and the Papal States, which Modena and Naples were invited to join.

H. *The Revolutions of 1848–1849*

Elsewhere in Italy, progress was too slow or nonexistent. The lid blew off on January 12, 1848, not in Rome or Turin but in Palermo. Ferdinand II responded savagely, but foreign pressure and the spread of the rioting to Messina and Naples obliged him not only to back off but to grant a constitution by the end of the month. The Sicilians were not satisfied, however, and declared their independence.

Metternich asked the Pope to allow an Austrian army to cross his territory, as one had in 1821, to restore "order" in the Two Sicilies. Mindful of the recent Austrian insult at Ferrara, Pius refused.

Popular pressure, the example of Naples, and Pius's stance led in February to the promises of constitutions in Tuscany and Piedmont. At this critical juncture, Pius IX attracted notice in a motu proprio by asking God to bless Italy—a phrase he would shortly rue, for the radical nationalists seized it out of context and turned it into a blessing on the war of liberation.

On February 22 Paris rose against King Louis Philippe, and the Second Republic was established. Two weeks later the revolution struck Germany, and in another week Austria. On March 15 Metternich fled. Pius IX had to concede a constitution for the States of the Church, also on March 15. The Chartist demonstrations were shaking England. By the end of the year revolution had affected Prussia and Hungary and forced an imperial abdication in Vienna.

Charles Albert, meanwhile, promulgated a conservative constitution on March 4 (see chapters 48 and 51). Pressure for a war of liberation against Austria was incessant. Metternich's flight was the signal for Venice and Milan to declare their liberation from Austria and the establishment of republics. The uprising in Milan (March 18–22) forced Marshal Radetzky's garrison to withdraw. The rulers of Parma and Modena abandoned their duchies.

The Milanese had immediately called upon the Sardinians to join them in driving the Austrians out of Italy. This was the critical moment, and the Wavering King did not seize it in time. Charles Albert had serious problems: inexperienced generals, lack of equipment, and lack of maps. He was concerned about the attitude of Britain and the new republic in France. On the other hand, if he did not act, republican governments would be set up in Milan and Venice, and that was intolerable. On the 23rd he declared war.

More weaknesses became evident: the generals bickered with one another; the regulars did not accept the volunteers; and the king insisted on directing the war — he had personal courage in this regard, but no skill. Still, with vigor the Piedmontese might have caught the Austrians quickly and in the open. Instead, they moved their small army of twenty-three thousand men too slowly to cut off Radetzky's retreat to the safety of four major forts straddling the Lombard-Venetian frontier. Reinforcements from Tuscany were not substantial enough for the Piedmontese to risk an assault on the strong Austrian lines. The two armies sat facing each other. Token armies from Rome and Naples moved northward as if to join the great national cause, but in fact the Pope had clearly instructed his general not to cross the frontier.

Plans were laid for the formation of a Kingdom of Upper Italy, uniting Venice, Lombardy, and the duchies to Piedmont under a constitutional monarchy. Military plans received less attention, as though the Austrian defeat were taken for granted.

On April 25 the Pope's general — who just happened to be a Piedmontese — disobeyed orders and led his army into Lombardy to join his countrymen. Since public opinion already generally saw the Pope taking the Italian side, and some wanted him as the president of a federated nation, Pius took a decisive step on April 29. In an address to his cardinals, he made it clear that he was not the leader of the Risorgimento; that as a spiritual leader he could not declare war; and that he would not be president of a united Italy, but everyone should be loyal to his own prince. If his own subjects wished to volunteer as individuals, as Italians from all over were doing, they were free to do so.

As Pope he really could do little else; the Austrians, too, were his Catholic children. It was a great turning point, forever separating Pius IX from the tidal wave of nationalism. He could not liberate and then rule a united Italy. Nor could he conceive of a Pope merely reigning over his own State, much less the whole nation. Nor could he conceive of a Pope yielding his temporal sovereignty. The Papacy had become an obstacle to national unity. Pius effectively turned the leadership of the Risorgimento over to either Piedmont or Mazzini, the house of Savoy or the forces of republicanism, whichever could take the lead and keep it.[36]

On the diplomatic front, the British were pressuring the Austrians to withdraw from Italy entirely. The French republic was friendly to Italy, but that was more discomfort to Charles Albert than consolation. He was trying to keep an eye on the political situation in Turin and in Milan, lest the republicans outmaneuver him.

The Piedmontese army, its Tuscan allies, and various volunteers grew to nearly sixty thousand men. They probed the Austrian defenses and won a couple of skirmishes on April 30 and May 6; the first offered a solid opportunity to catch the defenders off guard, but the king called off the pursuit. In mid-May Ferdinand II staged a counter-revolution in Naples and recalled his army. His general and half the soldiers ignored the order and joined the Venetians defending their republic, but others felt which way the wind was blowing and drifted home. At the end of May the Piedmontese captured the major fort of Peschiera. On June 15 Emperor Ferdinand offered to cede Lombardy to Sardinia. Quite honorably but not very wisely, Charles Albert declined; he would not abandon the Venetians.

Radetzky was not inclined to yield; when he received thirty-five thousand reinforcements he engaged the renegade papal army and forced it to surrender. Then he turned on the Sardinians, still poorly supplied and poorly led, no match for a well-trained army that now outnumbered them. In a five-day battle at Custoza (July 22–27), the Austrians broke Charles Albert's army and drove it back through Milan and home to Piedmont, reduced now to twenty-five thousand men. On August 9 an armistice was agreed to. Eighty-one-year-old Radetzky's brilliant generalship saved the Hapsburg Empire by stemming the tide of revolution in Italy, which in turn had its effect throughout Europe.

But revolution was not quite finished. After Pius IX renounced the Risorgimento, tension built up in Rome. The radicals won control of the civic guard and of the streets of Rome. The liberal and capable prime minister Count Pellegrino Rossi was assassinated on November 15. The mob demanded war with Austria, the convocation of a constituent assembly, and the appointment of the most radical leaders to the government. On the night of the 24th the Pope fled to Gaeta in the Kingdom of Naples, whence he appealed to the Catholic powers for help in recovering the Church's lands (see chapters 50 and 59).

The vacuum left at Rome suited Mazzini, who moved in and helped establish a Roman Republic in February 1849. The idealistic rulers expected the rest of Italy to rally to them. Garibaldi joined them; he had been fighting a guerrilla war in the north with some volunteers up till then. But outside the Papal States there was little response.

The Piedmontese were not quite finished either. They were loath to abandon the Lombards and Tuscans who had chosen union under the flag of Savoy. The new prime minister, Vincenzo Gioberti, tried to arrange an alliance with Tuscany (which now wavered between union with republican Rome and retention of the grand duke) and with Rome (where he hoped to restore the Pope without foreign intervention). None of his stratagems worked.

The Austrians consolidated their position at home, rejected French and British diplomacy, and announced that they would not yield a foot of their territory. Popular pressure urged on Charles Albert a renewal of the war. On March 12, 1849, the armistice expired and Sardinia declared war on the 20th. Two days later Radetzky crushed the king's army of eighty thousand men at Novara and dictated harsh terms of surrender. The king accepted responsibility for the debacle, though his generals had again performed poorly. Charles Albert abdicated in favor of his son, Victor Emmanuel II (d. 1878), and left at once for Portugal, where he died in July.

The new king appointed Massimo d'Azeglio, a writer of sterling character and no political experience, as prime minister. Then he negotiated with the Austrians, who offered generous terms provided that the year-old constitution be abolished. Victor Emmanuel earned himself a nickname, "the Gallant King," by refusing absolutely:

> Marshal, sooner than subscribe to such conditions I would lose a hundred Crowns. What my father has sworn I will maintain. If you want war to the death, be it so. I will call my people once more to arms. If I fail, it shall be without shame. My house knows the road of exile but not of dishonour.[37]

Radetzky relented on the point but imposed an indemnity and partial occupation of Piedmont until peace was concluded. The war had been a complete disaster militarily and financially. But two important lessons were learned: Italian unity would need outside help, which France would supply in 1859 and Prussia in 1866 and 1870; and the States of the Church would pose a major problem for national unification. Furthermore, a courageous, conscientious, and able leader had been found in Victor Emmanuel.

The Austrians proceeded to the mop-up work of restoring their puppets in Florence, Parma, and Modena and subduing the Venetians, which was completed on August 23. Ferdinand of Naples set about reconquering Sicily.

There was a great deal of diplomatic maneuvering in response to the Pope's appeal for restoration by the Catholic powers. At first the French and British hoped for an Italian solution. The French were now a republican state, but their leader, Louis Napoleon Bonaparte (the future Napoleon III), was eager to win clerical support by restoring Pius IX, who was as adamant against any compromise with the republicans in Rome as they were against any with him.

A French army of eight or nine thousand soldiers landed near Rome on April 25 and was stunned by the heroic defense of Garibaldi's recruits. It took until July 3 for French artillery and numbers, reinforced to somewhere between twenty and thirty thousand, to overwhelm the ten thousand enthusiastic but mostly untrained republicans and open the city for the return of the Pontiff.

So Mazzini's republican way to unification had also failed. In 1859–1860 other ways would succeed. Victor Emmanuel's constitutional monarchy would provide a moderate center to which most Italians could rally. Cavour's moderate conservatism would ensure middle class support, and his careful diplomacy would win critical international support for the unification of northern Italy. And Garibaldi's bold generalship would secure the south.

Notes

1. Much of the material in the first four sections of this introduction is taken from Eugenio Ceria's Introduction to the Italian edition, pp. 1–12.

2. BM V, 577.

3. BM VIII, 256.

4. BM XII, 52.

5. Desramaut, *Les Memorie I*, pp. 117–118.

6. BM XII, 52.

7. Salesian Central Archives (ASC) *132: Autografi-Oratorio*. Microfiche *FDB Micro 57 A1–60 A2 Ms. autogr. Bosco.*

8. ASC *132: Autografi-Oratorio. FDB Micro 60 A3–63 E12 Ms. autogr. Berto corr. e add. Bosco.*

9. BM XV, 80, 99, 359.

10. Desramaut, p. 119.

11. Desramaut, pp. 116–117.

12. Stella, LW, p. xx.

13. Preface.

14. Desramaut, p. 123; cf. BM I, 86–91.

15. See chapter 5, note 4 and comment; BM I, 142–152.

16. BM XII, 52.

17. Ibid.

18. Work on a critical edition is underway at the Istituto Storico Salesiano in Rome, but it will be at least five years before it is completed (letter from Pietro Stella, March 16, 1989).

19. Address to the Rector Major and General Council of the Salesian Society, February 4, 1989, in *Atti del Consiglio Generale* LXX (1989), no. 329, pp. 24–27 at 25; cf. *Acts of the General Council*, no. 329, p. 26.

20. These are Saint Mary Domenica Mazzarello (1837–1881), cofoundress of the Daughters of Mary Help of Christians; Blessed Michael Rua (1837–1910), priest; Blessed Louis Versiglia (1873–1930), bishop and martyr; Blessed Callistus Caravario (1903–1930), priest and martyr; and the Venerables Dorothy Chopitea (1816–1891), a cooperator; Madeline Morano, FMA (1847–1908); Philip Rinaldi (1856–1931), priest; August Czartoryski (1858–1893), priest; Andrew Beltrami (1870–1897), priest; and Teresa Valsè Pantellini, FMA (1878–1907).

21. Marriott, p. 33; cf. pp. 16–36.

22. *Memoirs of Prince Metternich, 1815–1829*, III, 97; cf. Marriott, p. 41.

23. Marriott, p. 90.

24. One of those implicated in the Milan uprising was the journalist Silvio Pellico (1789–1854); he and a number of other patriots were imprisoned for up to eight years. Upon his release he published *My Prisons*, an indictment of Austrian repression and a profound Christian testimony that was very influential over the next three decades. He became secretary to Marchioness Barolo and a generous friend of Don Bosco.

25. See F. Lemmi, *Carlo Felice (1755–1831)* (Turin, 1931), p. 182.

26. When France, Spain, Austria, and Russia contemplated similar action against Spain's former colonies in America, again in the name of restoring legitimate government, Great Britain and the United States opposed them. This was the genesis of the Monroe Doctrine of December 1823.

27. In 1827 at Milan, Alessandro Manzoni (1785–1873) published his novel *The Betrothed*, which has been acclaimed as Italy's greatest literary masterpiece. Its love story is set in seventeenth-century Lombardy against a background of Spanish oppression. Readers everywhere applied it to the current situation.

28. Hearder, pp. 61–63; Woolf, p. 326.

29. Woolf, p. 285.

30. Jacques Droz, *Europe Between Revolutions, 1815–1848* (New York: Harper, 1967), p. 168. Cf. E.E.Y. Hales, *Pio Nono*, pp. 39–42.

31. See E.E.Y. Hales, *Revolution and Papacy, 1769–1846* (Notre Dame, 1966), pp. 245–279; Hearder, pp. 121, 181, 284–286; Droz, pp. 34, 193–194; Woolf, pp. 317–318; Frederick B. Artz, *Reaction and Revolution, 1814–1832* (New York: Harper, 1934), pp. 144–145, 245–246.

32. Roger Aubert, *The Church in a Secularised Society* (New York: Paulist, 1978), pp. 34–37; Alec R. Vidler, *The Church in an Age of Revolution, 1789 to the Present Day* (Baltimore: Penguin, 1971), pp. 68–72; Hales, *Revolution and Papacy*, pp. 171, 218, 259–260, 279–295; NCE, VIII, 347–348.

33. Hales, *Pio Nono*, pp. 60–66.

34. Quoted by Marriott, p. 61.

35. After two centuries of Gallicanism in France and Josephism in Austria, and after the experience of the Church in England under William Rufus, Henry II, and Henry VIII, it must have been hard for Pius IX to think otherwise, though the Western Church, at least, had managed quite well before Charlemagne, and the United States was showing the viability of what Cavour would call "a free Church in a free State."

36. Hales, *Pio Nono*, pp. 82–83.

37. Quoted by Marriott, p. 78.

MAPS

≈≈

Italy 1815

Turin–Castelnuovo Area

Castelnuovo Don Bosco–Becchi Area

Chieri

The Wandering Oratory, 1844–1846

The Pinardi Shed, 1846

*The Oratory after the first
constructions, 1852–1859*

Italy 1815

Turin–Castelnuovo Area

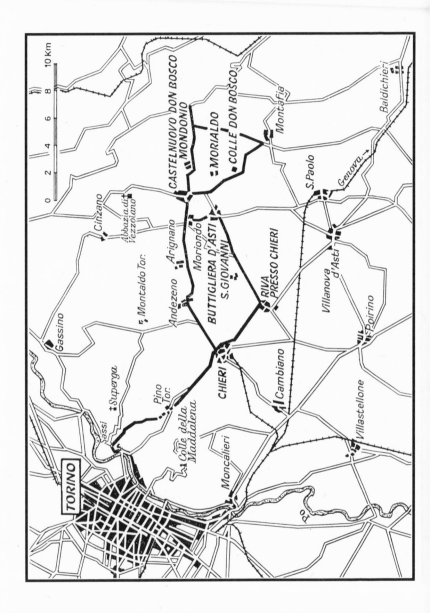

Castelnuovo Don Bosco — Becchi Area

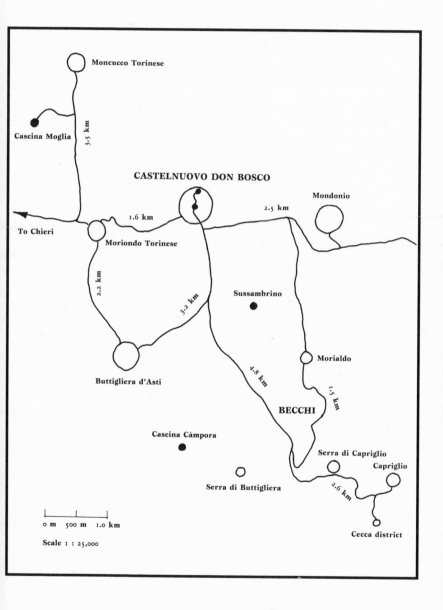

Moncucco Torinese

Cascina Moglia

3.5 km

CASTELNUOVO DON BOSCO

Mondonio

1.6 km

2.5 km

To Chieri

Moriondo Torinese

2.2 km

Sussambrino

3.2 km

Morialdo

Buttigliera d'Asti

4.8 km

1.5 km

BECCHI

Cascina Càmpora

Serra di Capriglio

Capriglio

Serra di Buttigliera

2.6 km

Cecca district

0 m   500 m   1.0 km

Scale 1 : 25,000

Chieri

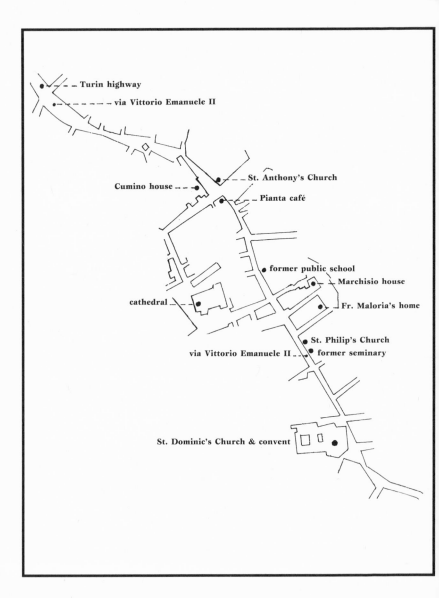

The Wandering Oratory, 1844–1846

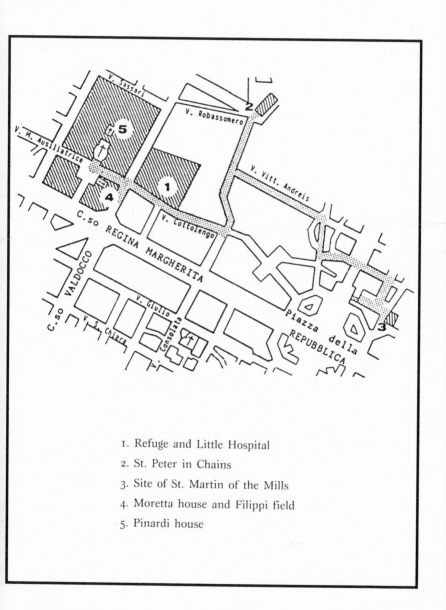

1. Refuge and Little Hospital
2. St. Peter in Chains
3. Site of St. Martin of the Mills
4. Moretta house and Filippi field
5. Pinardi house

The Pinardi Shed

First permanent site of the Oratory in Valdocco, April 1846

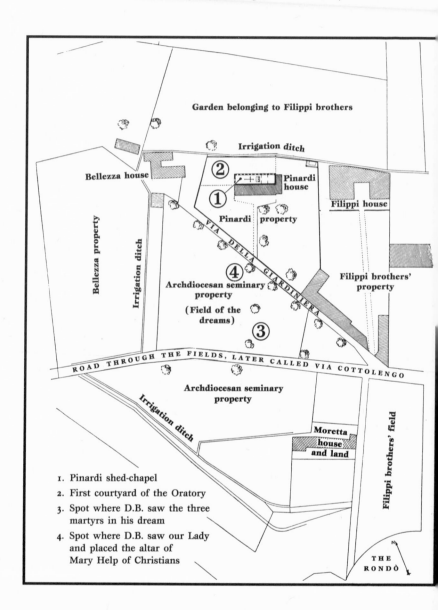

1. Pinardi shed-chapel
2. First courtyard of the Oratory
3. Spot where D.B. saw the three martyrs in his dream
4. Spot where D.B. saw our Lady and placed the altar of Mary Help of Christians

The Oratory after the first constructions, 1852–1859

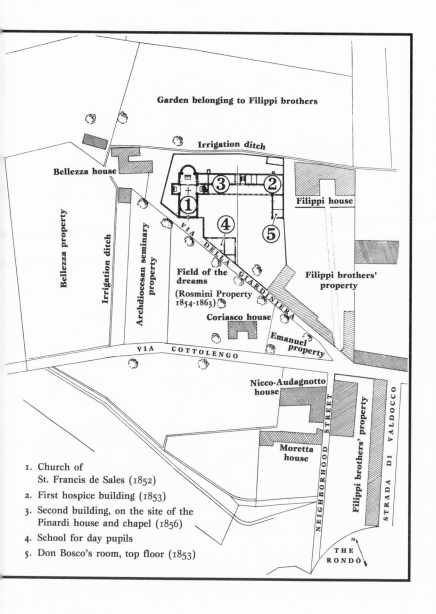

Garden belonging to Filippi brothers

Irrigation ditch

Bellezza house

Bellezza property

Irrigation ditch

Archdiocesan seminary property

Filippi house

VIA DELLA GIARDINIERA

Filippi brothers' property

Field of the dreams
(Rosmini Property 1854-1863)

Coriasco house

Emanuel property

VIA COTTOLENGO

Nicco-Audagnotto house

Moretta house

NEIGHBORHOOD STREET

Filippi brothers' property

STRADA DI VALDOCCO

N

THE RONDÒ

1. Church of St. Francis de Sales (1852)
2. First hospice building (1853)
3. Second building, on the site of the Pinardi house and chapel (1856)
4. School for day pupils
5. Don Bosco's room, top floor (1853)

Memoirs of the
Oratory of
Saint Francis de Sales

from 1815 to 1855

Preface

M any a time I have been urged to write my memoirs concerning the Oratory of Saint Francis de Sales.[1] Though I could not readily say no to the authority of the one who advised me to do this, I found it hard actually to set about the task because it meant too often speaking about myself. But now there has been added the command of a person of supreme authority, an authority that brooks no further delay.[2]

Therefore I am now putting into writing those confidential details that may somehow serve as a light or be of use to the work which Divine Providence has entrusted to the Society of Saint Francis de Sales. But I must say at the outset that I am writing these for my beloved Salesian sons; I forbid that these things be made public during my lifetime or after my death.[3]

Now, what purpose can this chronicle serve? It will be a record to help people overcome problems that may come in the future by learning from the past. It will serve to make known how God himself has always been our guide. It will give my sons some entertainment to be able to read about their father's adventures. Doubtless they will be read much more avidly when I have been called by God to render my account, when I am no longer amongst them.

Should they come upon experiences related maybe with complacency or the appearance of vainglory, let them indulge me a little. A father delights in speaking of his exploits to his dear children. It is always to be hoped that the sons will draw from these adventures, small and great, some spiritual and temporal advantage.

Portrait of Pope Pius IX from the papal portrait room at Superga

I have chosen to divide my account into ten-year periods, because each decade saw a notable development of
our work.[4]

So, my dear children, when you read these memoirs
after my death, remember that you had a loving father who
left these memoirs as a pledge of fatherly affection before
he abandoned this world. And remembering that, pray for
the happy repose of my soul.

Notes

1. Don Bosco called his work the work of the "oratory," adopt-
ing the term used by Saint Philip Neri (1515–1595). Don
Bosco meant to indicate a place and an apostolate wherein boys, adolescents, and young men could gather for the
ultimate purpose of prayer, i.e. Sunday and feast day Mass,
confession, communion, preaching, and catechism. As we
shall see, he used many means to make piety attractive to
these youngsters, including games, outings, schooling, an
employment service, and a hostel.

    On Saint Philip Neri, see NCE X, 339–341; Butler's *Lives
of the Saints*, II, 395–397; V.J. Matthews, *St Philip Neri:
Apostle of Rome and Founder of the Congregation of the Oratory*
(Rockford, Illinois: TAN, 1984); Louis Bouyer, *The Roman
Socrates: A Portrait of St. Philip Neri*, trans. Michael Day
(Westminster, Maryland: Newman, 1958).

2. The authority who first advised and then commanded was
Pope Pius IX. The saint noted his advice in 1858 but only
executed the command of 1867. See the introduction. On
Pius IX's pontificate, see the introduction and the comment
following these notes.

3. See the introduction.

4. Don Bosco, in another of his writings, also speaks of three
decades, but these only involve the history of the Oratory
itself. This fact is reported in BM V, 7. Here in the *Memoirs
of the Oratory* he makes the division using wider criteria.
The first decade takes in his life with his family as a boy
and his period as a student. The second covers the period
when he was a young seminarian and priest in the district
of his birth and in Turin. The third tells the story of what
happened to him and the Valdocco Oratory from the time
of the Pinardi shed (1846) to the first building operations
for the hospice at Valdocco.

Comment on Pius IX

Pope Pius IX (1846–1878), born Giovanni-Maria Mastai-Ferretti at Senigallia in the Marches (province of Ancona) in 1792, directed a Roman orphanage as a young priest and served as a papal diplomat in the new Republic of Chile. He became archbishop of Spoleto in 1827, bishop of Imola in 1831, and cardinal in 1840. His experience as a witness to the uprisings of 1831 and as a bishop within the Papal States convinced him that great social and administrative reforms were necessary in central Italy.

Succeeding the reactionary Pope Gregory XVI on June 16, 1846, Pius faced the nearly impossible task of balancing Italian nationalism and the interests of the Church in revolutionary times — more than complicated by the fact that the Pope ruled one-third of the Italian peninsula as his own sovereign state.

The experiences of 1848–1849 were enough to sour Pius IX on liberalism (and to finish souring the anticlerical political leaders on the Church). Only the presence of French soldiers in Rome enabled the Pope to hold the city against the tide of unification until 1870, when Napoleon III withdrew the troops on account of the Franco-Prussian War. Italy seized the papal city in 1870 and made it her capital. Pius became the "prisoner of the Vatican," as did his successors until Pope Pius XI and Mussolini resolved the "Roman Question" in 1929.

During Pius IX's exile at Gaeta in 1848–1849, the boys of the Oratory made their modest collection of thirty-three lire toward the Pope's relief (see chapter 49). Pius, familiar with the lot of orphans and the poor, was deeply touched. Thus a long and loving relationship between Pius IX and Don Bosco began.

Already thinking seriously about some form of congregation to carry on his work, Don Bosco went to Rome for the first time in 1858 to seek advice from members of the Curia and from the Pope. It was the first of many visits and cemented a close relationship that eventually led Pius to entrust very delicate missions to Don Bosco, and Don Bosco to consider Pius IX as virtually the cofounder and father of the Salesian Society.

For a brief article on the pontificate of Pius IX, see Eric John, ed., *The Popes: A Concise Biographical Dictionary* (New York: Hawthorne, 1964), II, 437–440; or NCE XI, 405–408. Longer biographies in English, both giving most of their attention to Pius's pontificate and both of high quality, are Frank Coppa's *Pope Pius IX* (259 pages) and E.E.Y. Hales's *Pio Nono* (402 pages). On Pius IX and the Salesians, see BM III-XIII, passim.

My Early Life

*First ten years • Father's death
• Family difficulties • The
widowed mother*

I was born on the day dedicated to Mary Assumed into Heaven in 1815[1] in Murialdo near Castelnuovo d'Asti.[2] My mother's name was Margaret Occhiena and she was from Capriglio;[3] my father's name was Francis.[4] They were farmers who made their living by hard work and thrifty use of what little they had. My good father, almost entirely by the sweat of his brow, supported my grandmother, in her seventies and a prey to frequent illnesses; three youngsters; and a pair of farm helpers. Of the three children, the oldest was Anthony,[5] born of his first wife; the second was Joseph;[6] and the youngest was me, John.

I was not yet two years old when the merciful Lord hit us with a sad bereavement. My dearly loved father died unexpectedly. He was strong and healthy, still young and actively interested in promoting a good Christian upbringing for his offspring. One day he came home from work covered in sweat and imprudently went down into a cold cellar. That night he developed a high temperature, the first sign of a serious illness. Every effort to cure him proved vain. Within a few days he was at death's door. Strengthened by all the comforts of religion, he recommended to my mother confidence in God, then died, aged only thirty-four, on 12 May 1817.[7]

I do not know how I reacted on that sad occasion. One thing only do I remember, and it is my earliest memory. We were all going out from the room where he had died, and I insisted on staying behind.

My grieving mother addressed me, "Come, John, come with me."

"If papa's not coming, I don't want to come," I answered.

"My poor son," my mother replied, "come with me; you no longer have a father." Having said this, she broke down and started crying as she took me by the hand and led me away. I began crying too because she was crying. At that age I could not really understand what a tragedy had fallen on us in our father's death.

This event threw the whole family into difficulty. Five people had to be supported. The crops failed that year because of a drought,[8] and that was our only source of income. The prices of foodstuffs soared. Wheat was as much as four francs a bushel, corn or maize two and a half francs.[9] Some people who lived at that time have assured me that beggars hesitated to ask for even a crust of bread to soak into their broth of chickpeas or beans for nourishment. People were found dead in the fields, their mouths stuffed with grass, with which they had tried to quell their ravenous hunger.

My mother often used to tell me that she fed the family until she exhausted all her food. She then gave money to a neighbour, Bernard Cavallo,[10] to go looking for food to buy. That friend went round to various markets but was unable to buy anything, even at exorbitant prices. After two days he came in the evening bringing back nothing but the money he had been given. We were all in a panic. We had eaten practically nothing the whole day, and the night would have been difficult to face.

My mother, not allowing herself to be discouraged, went round to the neighbours to try to borrow some food. She did not find anyone able to help. "My dying husband," she told us, "said I must have confidence in God. Let's kneel then and pray." After a brief prayer she got up and said, "Drastic circumstances demand drastic means." Then she went to the stable and, helped by Mr Cavallo, she killed a calf.[11] Part of that calf was immediately cooked and the worst of the family's hunger satisfied. In the days that followed, cereals bought at a very high price from more distant places enabled us to survive.

Anyone can imagine how much my mother worked and suffered in that disastrous year. The crisis of that year was overcome by constant hard work, by continuous thrift, by attention to the smallest details and by occasional providential help. My mother often told me of these events, and my relatives and friends confirmed them.

When that terrible scarcity was over and matters at home had improved, a convenient arrangement was proposed to my mother. However she repeated again and again, "God gave me a husband and God has taken him away. With his death the Lord put three sons under my care. I would be a cruel mother to abandon them when they needed me most."

On being told that her sons could be entrusted to a good guardian who would look after them well, she merely replied, "A guardian could only be their friend, but I am a mother to these sons of mine. All the gold in the world could never make me abandon them."[12]

Her greatest care was given to instructing her sons in their religion, making them value obedience, and keeping them busy with tasks suited to their age. When I was still very small, she herself taught me to pray. As soon as I was old enough to join my brothers, she made me kneel with them morning and evening. We would all recite our prayers together, including the rosary. I remember well how she herself prepared me for my first confession. She took me to church, made her own confession first, then presented me to the confessor. Afterwards, she helped me to make my thanksgiving. She continued to do this until I reached the age when she judged me able to use the sacrament well on my own.[13]

I had reached my ninth year.[14] My mother wanted to send me to school, but this was not easy. The distance to Castelnuovo from where we lived was more than three miles; my brother Anthony was opposed to my boarding there. A compromise was eventually agreed upon. During the winter season I would attend school at the nearby village of Capriglio. In this way I was able to learn the basic elements of reading and writing.[15] My teacher was a devout priest called Joseph Delacqua. He was very attentive to my needs, seeing to my instruction and even more to my

Christian education. During the summer months I went along with what my brother wanted by working in the fields.[16]

Notes

1. Don Bosco always believed that he had been born on August 15. His mother had been dead a number of years when the custom of celebrating his birthday at the Oratory began. Thus she could not correct the mistake about this date. Even on the document placed beside his coffin (*Salesian Bulletin*, March 1888), his successor Father Michael Rua wrote, "He was born at Castelnuovo d'Asti, August 15, 1815."

   It was only when the baptismal register was consulted after Don Bosco's death that the mistake was discovered. He had been baptized August 17 in the parish church, Saint Andrew's, by Father Joseph Festa. The register, signed by the pastor Father Joseph Sismondo, states clearly that John Melchior Bosco had been born *heri vespere natus*, i.e. on the evening of the sixteenth.

   It was a custom in Piedmont to refer to anything that happened near the fifteenth — roughly from the vigil of the solemnity through its octave — as having occurred "on the Assumption." If, when John was a child, his relatives regularly used this expression of his birthday, his later mistake is understandable.

2. Castelnuovo d'Asti, now known as Castelnuovo Don Bosco, had about 3500 inhabitants in the early nineteenth century. It is about eighteen miles from Turin.

   Morialdo, one of four districts (*frazioni*) linked with Castelnuovo, is two and a half miles south of the town. (The other three districts are Bardella, Nevissano, and Ranello.) In 1815, two or three hundred people lived in Morialdo, scattered among a number of hamlets. Don Bosco spelled it "Murialdo" in keeping with the manner in which the Piedmontese of his day pronounced the letter "o".

   For remarks on Don Bosco's birthplace, see the extended comment at the end of the notes.

3. Capriglio is a village about four miles east of Morialdo. Don Bosco's mother was born at the Cecca farm in Serra di Capriglio, a hamlet of the town of Capriglio, on April 1, 1788. She married the widower Francis Bosco on June 6, 1812. Though the Occhienas owned land, they were so poor that

The baptismal record of John Melchior Bosco is kept in the parish church of
Castelnuovo. The third entry on the page, dated August 17, 1815, reads:
"Bosco John Melchior, son of Francis Louis and Margaret Occhiena Bosco,
born yesterday evening, was solemnly baptized this evening by the Reverend
Joseph Festa. . . ." It is signed by Father Joseph Sismondo, the pastor.

their dowry for Margaret's marriage was some work that one of her brothers performed for Francis. She was twenty-four, and he was twenty-eight.

4. Francis Louis Bosco was born in Castelnuovo on January 20, 1784. He was the fourth of six children born to Philip Anthony Bosco II (1735–1802) by his second wife, Margaret Zucca (1752–1826)—the grandmother of whom Don Bosco speaks. There were also six children from Philip's first marriage. Of these twelve children, only six survived childhood. It was Philip who moved the family from Castelnuovo to the Biglione farm as tenant farmers in 1793.

   Francis married Margaret Cagliero on February 4, 1805. She bore him two children, Anthony and Teresa. Teresa, whom Don Bosco does not mention, was born on February 16, 1810, and died two days later.

5. Until recently, all Don Bosco's biographers gave February 3, 1803, as the date of Anthony's birth, on the basis of an 1885 letter from Don Bosco's nephew Francis Bosco, Joseph's son (Stella, LW, p. 10, n. 16). Anthony was in fact born on February 3, 1808. This gives us a clearer picture for interpreting the confrontation in the Bosco house between Anthony and young John (chapters 4–6): The age gap was seven years and not twelve, as formerly believed. Anthony died in 1849.

6. Joseph was born on April 8, 1813, and died in 1862.

7. Francis died on May 11 after a week's illness. He was in his thirty-fourth year, i.e. thirty-three years old. John was twenty-one months old.

8. The country around Turin is very hilly but fertile. However, the amount of precipitation and the temperature determine the quality of the annual harvest of grapes and cereals. Extremes of rain (drought one year, devastating downpours another) and of temperature are well known.

   The famine of 1817–1818 was the result of drought. There had been less snow than usual during the winter of 1816–1817, and spring frosts killed much of the early planting. Then the summer of 1817 was very dry.

9. Literally, "25 francs/16 francs an *emina*." Don Bosco consistently uses "francs" rather than "lire." Because of Piedmont's close ties—cultural, linguistic, economic, and dynastic—with France, the Piedmontese had used the word "franc" as an equivalent of the lira long before the Napoleonic occupation of Piedmont.

   The *emina* was an old Piedmontese measure of capacity. Its size varied from place to place; around Asti it was about twenty-three liters (6.3 bushels). In normal times an *emina* of maize would cost two or three lire. So the famine had, more or less, raised prices by six hundred percent.

10. The Bosco home was attached to the rear of the Cavallo home, which is the oldest structure on the little hill. In recent years, the former Cavallo home has housed the office of the rector of Don Bosco's shrine, a lobby, and a gift shop.

11. This was an act of desperation (T. Bosco, BN, pp. 15–16). The calf was the family's insurance against future disaster when money might be essential, for a fat calf would bring a good price at market. Margaret had decided that the disaster was at hand; there was no other way to feed her family.

12. What this arrangement could have been arouses our curiosity concerning both the suitor and the exact nature of the proposal. Evidently it implied some neglect of Francis Bosco's three sons, which the widow Margaret admirably refused to consider. This is the only reference that Don Bosco seems ever to have made to it, and we know nothing else about it.

13. John would have been six or seven when he first received the sacrament of penance, by which Christ acts through his priestly minister to forgive sins committed since baptism.

Pope Pius XII (1939–1958), speaking to Christian families on the feast of Saint John Bosco, January 31, 1940, referred to the little house at Becchi:

> Imagine the young widow with her three sons kneeling for morning and evening prayer. See the children, in their best clothes, going to the nearby village of Morialdo for holy Mass. See them gathered around her in the afternoon after a frugal meal in which there would only be a little bread on which she had invoked the Lord's blessing. She reminds her sons of the commandments of God and the Church, of the important lessons from the catechism, of the various means of salvation. She then goes on to speak in simple but forceful country terms of the tragic story of Cain and Abel, or of the painful death of her dear Jesus, nailed to the cross on Calvary for all of us.
>
> Who can possibly measure the lasting influence of the first lessons given by a good mother to her children? It was to such lessons that Don Bosco the priest used to attribute his loving devotion to Mary and to Jesus in the Blessed Sacrament.

14. John's ninth year was August 16, 1823–August 15, 1824, when we would say that he was eight years old. From what we have been able to find through research, he should have said, "my tenth year."

15. We should note a few points about schooling in Piedmont. Young John's particular situation also deserves some comment.

    The French occupation and the subsequent Restoration had thrown the country into a great deal of disorder. It was not until July 23, 1822, that a government education act was passed. For the first time, this law made the opening of free primary schools compulsory. However, the communes were allowed to recover their basic expenses by charging some tuition, which often amounted to something like twenty lire for the year; a hired farmhand's wages for the working season was only fifteen lire.

    The regulation envisaged instruction in the "four Rs": reading, writing, 'rithmetic, and religion. Lessons were to be given for three hours in the morning and three in the afternoon; in between, the pupils went home for dinner and perhaps for some chores.

    The law mandated that schools open on November 3, after the harvest and the double church solemnity of All Saints' and All Souls' Days; they were supposed to be open until the end of September but in practice closed on the Feast of the Annunciation (March 25), when farmhands for the coming planting, cultivation, and harvest were hired in every town square.

    Before 1822, in the ordinary rural community, the little bit of reading and writing that was taught would have been given in the home by some older member of the family. This would happen during the long Piedmontese winters when there was little farm work. Anthony almost certainly was taught this way and not in any formal schooling. John apparently had received a little such instruction from a local farmer sometime during 1823–1824.

    Because of the many practical difficulties following the French occupation, the education law was a dead letter in most country districts. Most of the teachers were priests who, for one reason or another, were not fully involved in parish work. The large number of priests in the area around Castelnuovo allowed the law to be implemented more easily there; so there were schools at both Castelnuovo and Capriglio.

16. Father Joseph Lacqua (not Delacqua, as Don Bosco writes it) was the teacher at Capriglio in 1824. He was not too happy at the idea of taking a boy from Becchi into his school, nor was he bound to take him, since Becchi belonged to the commune of Castelnuovo and not to Capriglio. Margaret had turned to him for several reasons. Anthony was totally

against John's being sent to Castelnuovo, which was farther away from Becchi. Since John had to walk to or from school four times a day, there would be more time for helping out with the farmwork if he went to Capriglio. Finally, Margaret's family lived in Capriglio.

Around this time, however, Father Lacqua needed a housekeeper. Margaret had an unmarried older sister, Joan Mary Occhiena (always called Marianne). Father Lacqua asked her to work as his housekeeper. She agreed, possibly on condition that he enroll John in the school. At any rate, the priest did take John into his school; thus John got his first schooling and also had an aunt who could provide lodging for him if the weather turned foul.

Marianne remained Father Lacqua's housekeeper until he died around 1850. She then joined Mama Margaret at the Oratory as a helper in Don Bosco's work there.

John probably attended classes at Capriglio from autumn 1824 to spring 1826, when he was nine and ten years old. He was older than the rest of the pupils, and they sometimes made fun of him. He may have attended briefly in the autumn of 1826, when a family crisis long brewing came to a boil. For more details of this period see Molineris, pp. 133–139.

Comment on Don Bosco's Birthplace

Nearly three miles south of Castelnuovo Don Bosco is Becchi, a cluster of ten farmhouses within the district of Morialdo. It takes its name from Bechis, the surname of a family once associated with the little hilltop. This name, pluralized and Italianized (from the Piedmontese dialect), became *Becchi*.

A little to the south of Becchi and farther up the hill lay the Canton Cavallo, i.e. the property and house of the Cavallos. Here the Boscos owned the farmhouse long venerated as the saint's birthplace; there he grew up, there he came for his vacations, and there (in his own new house) his older brother Joseph lived from 1839 till 1862. Becchi was John Bosco's native place.

But the research of Secondo Caselle (*Cascinali e contadini in Monferrato: I Bosco di Chieri nel secolo XVIII* [Rome: LAS, 1975]), former mayor of Chieri and devotee of Don Bosco, has proven that John was born not at this family farmstead but at the Biglione farm (*cascina Biglione*) about two hundred yards still farther up the hill, to the south. Francis Bosco was a tenant farmer contracted to Biglione, and John was born in the Biglione house.

Francis Bosco had two hired farmhands. So the Boscos, though peasants, were not destitute. Having saved his money, in February 1817 Francis was able to buy from Francis Graglia a house lower down the slope on the edge of the Becchi hamlet, with about three-quarters of an acre of land. He paid one hundred lire. The patterns of inflation and recession caused the value of the lira to fluctuate somewhat; so it is difficult to fix its true value in contemporary terms. But during the first half of the nineteenth century it was reasonably stable. Teresio Bosco (*Mem*, p. 178, n. 1; SP, p. 45) estimates that the lira was worth about four thousand 1985 lire, or US $2.60. In the 1850s and 1860s it cost Don Bosco about eighty centesimi per day to keep each boy in his community (Stella, *EcSo*, pp. 371–372).

Francis intended to renovate the house considerably and perhaps had begun to do so while fulfilling his last contract with Biglione when he caught pneumonia and died in May 1817. That tragedy did not prevent Biglione from suing Margaret Bosco to compel her to fulfill her husband's contract. Margaret moved the family to Becchi in November after the harvest, and she spent another sixty lire on renovations.

The house that Francis had bought was a decrepit affair attached to the rear of the Cavallo home. It contained very modest living quarters and a stable; overhead was a large hayloft, and the whole was roofed with tile. Margaret fixed the downstairs quarters into a decent kitchen-living room and left the stable as it was. Part of the hayloft was left over the stable, the rest of the upstairs being divided into two bedrooms that were accessible either by an outside stairs or by a trapdoor in the kitchen ceiling.

In 1886 Don Bosco dreamt that his mother took him to the top of the small hill just south of their house. Mother and son talked about the good to be done in this area as they looked down on the plain stretching around the hill. Don Bosco woke up from his sleep while still in the middle of this conversation. Afterwards, speaking of this dream, he commented that the hill did seem like a good place for a Salesian foundation since it was in the center of a number of villages too far from the churches. Details of the dream may be found in MB XIX, 382–383.

The Salesians — entirely unaware of the dream at the time — acquired the entire hilltop from its various owners in 1930. Soon after, rector major Father Peter Ricaldone and economer general Father Fidelis Giraudi chose the site for a new Salesian technical school when funds were donated for that purpose. This became the Bernardi-Semeria Salesian Institute, and it was built behind the Biglione farmhouse at the top of the hill.

The farmhouse at Becchi, which Francis Bosco bought in 1817. Here Margaret raised her three sons, and here John had his first dream-vision when he was about nine years old.

Then Fathers Ricaldone and Giraudi began to dream of building a great church in honor of the Salesians' newly canonized founder. Actual planning was not possible until the late 1950s. Ironically, the site chosen was next to the school and stretching northward; it demanded the removal of the Biglione house, which was torn down in 1958! The great Tempio di Don Bosco was constructed between 1961 and 1965. The house had stood on the site almost directly beneath the main altar of today's tempio.

The entire hilltop today is commonly known as "Colle Don Bosco" (Don Bosco's Hill).

A Dream

It was at that age that I had a dream.[1] All my life this remained deeply impressed on my mind. In this dream I seemed to be near my home in a fairly large yard. A crowd of children were playing there. Some were laughing, some were playing games, and quite a few were swearing. When I heard these evil words, I jumped immediately amongst them and tried to stop them by using my words and my fists.

At that moment a dignified man appeared, a nobly-dressed adult. He wore a white cloak, and his face shone so that I could not look directly at him. He called me by name, told me to take charge of these children, and added these words: "You will have to win these friends of yours not by blows but by gentleness and love. Start right away to teach them the ugliness of sin and the value of virtue."

Confused and frightened, I replied that I was a poor, ignorant child. I was unable to talk to those youngsters about religion. At that moment the kids stopped their laughing, shouting, and swearing; they gathered round the man who was speaking.

Hardly knowing what I was saying, I asked, "Who are you, ordering me to do the impossible?"

"Precisely because it seems impossible to you, you must make it possible through obedience and the acquisition of knowledge."

"Where, by what means, can I acquire knowledge?"

"I will give you a teacher. Under her guidance you can become wise. Without her, all wisdom is foolishness."

"But who are you that speak so?"

"I am the son of the woman whom your mother has taught you to greet three times a day."[2]

"My mother tells me not to mix with people I don't know unless I have her permission. So tell me your name."

"Ask my mother what my name is."

At that moment, I saw a lady of stately appearance standing beside him. She was wearing a mantle that sparkled all over as though covered with bright stars. Seeing from my questions and answers that I was more confused than ever, she beckoned me to approach her. She took me kindly by the hand and said, "Look." Glancing round, I realised that the youngsters had all apparently run away. A large number of goats, dogs, cats, bears, and other animals had taken their place.

"This is the field of your work. Make yourself humble, strong, and energetic. And what you will see happening to these animals in a moment is what you must do for my children."

I looked round again, and where before I had seen wild animals, I now saw gentle lambs. They were all jumping and bleating as if to welcome that man and lady.

At that point, still dreaming, I began crying. I begged the lady to speak so that I could understand her, because I did not know what all this could mean. She then placed her hand on my head and said, "In good time you will understand everything."

With that, a noise woke me up and everything disappeared. I was totally bewildered. My hands seemed to be sore from the blows I had given, and my face hurt from those I had received. The memory of the man and the lady, and the things said and heard, so occupied my mind that I could not get any more sleep that night.

I wasted no time in telling all about my dream. I spoke first to my brothers, who laughed at the whole thing, and then to my mother and grandmother. Each one gave his own interpretation.[3] My brother Joseph said, "You're going to become a keeper of goats, sheep, and other animals." My mother commented, "Who knows, but you may become a priest." Anthony merely grunted, "Perhaps you'll become a robber chief." But my grandmother, though she could not

The kitchen of the Bosco home has been refurnished with period furniture. It was probably around the breakfast table that John recounted his strange dream to the rest of the family.

read or write, knew enough theology and made the final judgement, saying, *"Pay no attention to dreams."*

I agreed with my grandmother. However, I was unable to cast that dream out of my mind. The things I shall have to say later will give some meaning to all this. I kept quiet about these things, and my relatives paid little attention to them. But when I went to Rome in 1858 to speak to the Pope about the Salesian Congregation, he asked me to tell him everything that had even the suggestion of the super-natural about it.[4] It was only then, for the first time, that I said anything about this dream which I had when I was nine or ten years old. The Pope ordered me[5] to write out

the dream in all its detail and to leave it as an encouragement to the sons of that Congregation whose formation
was the reason for that visit to Rome.[6]

Notes

1. Don Bosco is a bit vague about when this first dream occurred. He seems to mean that it was while he was going to
   school at Capriglio (see chapter 1, notes 14 and 16). As we
   shall see, many of Don Bosco's dates in these *Memoirs* are
   problematic. In chapter 31 he refers back to this dream that
   he had "when I was nine years old," which would be 1824–
   1825. Shortly before his death, he told his secretary Father
   Charles Viglietti, "I vividly revisited the scene of the dream
   I had when I was about ten years old, in which I dreamt of
   the Congregation" (MB XVIII, 340–341). He was ten in
   1825–1826. At the end of this chapter, he says that he was
   nine or ten.

   Stella (LW, p. 8) suggests that it may have been around
   the solemnity of Saints Peter and Paul, June 29, 1825; the
   imagery of the dream is consonant with one of the gospels
   of the feast (John 21:15–19). It is also possible that the question of John's schooling was broached at this time in connection with a desire that he may already have voiced, becoming
   a priest.

   On this first dream, see Desramaut, *LesMem*, pp. 250–256,
   and Stella, LW, pp. 7–10. On Don Bosco's dreams in general,
   see the extended comment at the end of the notes.

2. Throughout the Catholic world, Christian practices of piety
   were woven into different parts of the day. The Angelus in
   the morning, at noon, and in the evening was one such regular practice. This prayer celebrates the angel Gabriel's coming to the Virgin Mary and inviting her to become mother of
   the Messiah (Luke 1:26–38). Mary was to remain always
   Don Bosco's teacher and guide in his youth ministry.

3. Each member of the family showed something of his or her
   character in the interpretation offered. Joseph is the simple,
   down-to-earth farmer. Margaret speaks as a woman well
   versed in the ways of the Lord. Anthony's gruff dismissal of
   it reveals his rough character. Grandmother Bosco presents
   the voice of old age, no longer inclined to fantasies. In John
   we see the wisdom of one older than his years.

4. In asking Don Bosco about the supernatural the very first time they met, Pius IX is not specially singling him out. The Pope was peculiarly sensitive to the supernatural and looked for it whenever he suspected any hint of it (Stella, LW, p. 10, n. 15).

5. Here Don Bosco seems to combine the request of 1858 and the command of 1867. (See his preface.)

6. The purpose of Don Bosco's first visit to Rome (January 18 to April 16, 1858) was to try to secure the future of the oratories he had founded. He wanted to set a firm basis for an institution suited to the times, and for this end he carried with him a letter of recommendation from Archbishop Louis Fransoni of Turin (BM V, 561).

On this visit and the papal audiences, see Bonetti, pp. 348–358, and BM V, 523–602.

Comment on Don Bosco's Dreams

In *I Sogni di Don Bosco* (Turin: LDC, 1978), Cecilia Romero, FMA, has published a critical edition of ten of Don Bosco's dreams for which there exist manuscripts in his own hand, not including this first dream at age nine.

Giovanni Battista Lemoyne places Don Bosco's dreams in the context of his life and work (BM I, 190–191):

> *Don Bosco* and the word *dream* are correlative.... It is truly astounding how this phenomenon went on in his life for sixty years.... In both the Old and New Testaments, as well as in the lives of innumerable saints, the Lord in his fatherly love gave comfort, counsel, command, spirit of prophecy, threats and messages of hope and reward both to individuals and to entire nations through dreams.... Don Bosco's life was an intricate pattern of wondrous events in which one cannot but perceive direct divine assistance. Hence, we must reject the notion that he was a fool, or that he labored under illusions or that he was vain and deceitful. Those who lived at his side for thirty or forty years never once detected in him the least sign that he would betray a desire to win the esteem of his peers by pretending to be endowed with supernatural gifts.

Introducing MB XVII, Eugenio Ceria discusses at length the phenomenon of dreams in Don Bosco's life (pp. 7–13):

> The largest and most characteristic kind of dreams that Don Bosco had is made up of dreams that contain revelatory elements going beyond the interpretive power of his own mind. In these dreams Don Bosco

reviewed the past, viewed the present, and previewed the future. All this was generally presented to him in symbolic form. But often he was presented with realistic images. . . . (p. 8)

The manner in which Don Bosco narrated his dreams inclines one to accept their supernatural character. For the saint in his narration did his utmost to forestall that very interpretation. He did this by a simple and humble style of presentation and by avoiding everything that would lead others to suppose that he possessed special merits or enjoyed exceptional privileges. The Servant of God Father Rua, in the Processes [for canonization], rightly qualified the dreams as undoubted visions and expressed his conviction that Don Bosco felt duty-bound, for the good of souls, to relate the things that had been shown to him in dreams, and that this impulse was itself of supernatural origin. (pp. 10–11)

For a better understanding of the specific character of these dreams, we should note their logical and purposeful development. This is unusual in dreams. Dreams are usually composed of a confused sequence of images following one another without rhyme or reason. . . . In Don Bosco's dreams, on the contrary, there is always a serious and basic order to the dream sequence. And the development, whether it be simple or complicated, proceeds in an orderly fashion and without any of the wild irrationalities prevalent in common dreams. Moreover, whenever "strange" images appear, Don Bosco identifies them as such and upon inquiry receives satisfactory explanations. All this shows that the world of common dreams has been transcended. (p. 11)

In a talk with Don Bosco . . . , Father Lemoyne referred to Don Bosco's dreams as visions, and the saint said that he was correct. This led Father Lemoyne to observe in his notes: "Until about the year 1880, Don Bosco had never used this word [visions] to describe his dreams. During his last years, however, and only in confidential conversations with Father Lemoyne . . . he would not object to his using the word even though Don Bosco himself did not use it first." (p. 12)

One of the most serious students of Don Bosco's life, Alberto Caviglia, evaluates his dreams thus in *Don Bosco* (Turin: LICE, 1934, pp. 35–36):

Dreams were a recurring experience throughout sixty of Don Bosco's seventy-three years. A good number of these dreams may be regarded simply as edifying and didactic parables; they are an attempt to express symbolically the ideas, tendencies, and hopes that were part of his spiritual and educational world. But when the future of his work is revealed in a dream with uncanny accuracy, a long time before such developments could possibly have been forecast — then we are dealing with a different phenomenon.

This phenomenon, unique in the history of saints, defies explanation. For one thing, the usual scientific theories of dreams do not explain them satisfactorily. Doctor Albertotti, who was Don Bosco's physician and also a professional psychiatrist, was unable to find a satisfactory explanation in dream theory or telepathic phenomena. The believer may interpret these dreams as visions or prophecies or revelations, etc. The Church does not forbid this interpretation. . . . We may be satisfied with observing that these dreams happened and that their predictions were fulfilled.

Most recently, Morton T. Kelsey (see citation below, Brown edition) quotes from a poem of Saint Gregory Nazianzen, fourth-century father and doctor of the Church:

> And God summoned me from boyhood
> in my nocturnal dreams, and I arrived
> at the very goal of wisdom.

These lines, says Kelsey, could have been written by Don Bosco (p. x). He continues:

> It is quite clear that Don Bosco was a genius in opening himself to this dimension of reality. This ability was probably given to him by inheritance and God's special grace. The important matter is that he developed this ability, used it for God and recorded his experience. (p. xvi)

Kelsey writes that the first dream

> set the course of his entire life. . . . It told in symbolic form what was to be his life's mission. Even though he did not understand it, he couldn't forget it. When he was asked by Pope Pius IX to speak of the supernatural influences in his life, it was this dream that impressed the Pope so much that he ordered Don Bosco to write down his dreams for the encouragement of his Congregation and the rest of us. (p. xxxvi)

For more about Don Bosco's dreams, see Eugenio Ceria, *Don Bosco con Dio*, pp. 303–326 [McGlinchey translation, pp. 121–132]; Desramaut, *SpLife*, pp. 34–35; Stella, *ReCa*, pp. 507–563.

A handy collection of sixty-two of Don Bosco's dreams is the edition prepared by Eugene M. Brown, *Dreams, Visions & Prophecies of Don Bosco* (New Rochelle: Don Bosco Publications, 1986). It contains a valuable foreword by Morton T. Kelsey on dreams as a phenomenon of Christian spirituality (pp. ix–xl) and a brief introductory essay by Arthur J. Lenti, SDB, on the various types of Don Bosco's dreams and their critical evaluation (pp. xli–lii). The dreams themselves are taken from the *Biographical Memoirs*, with Lemoyne's, Amadei's, or Ceria's introductions to them or comments upon them.

PART I

The First Decade
1825 to 1835

∾ 3 ∾

The Young Acrobat

First entertainments for children • Sermons • Acrobatics • Bird nesting

Many times you have asked me at what age I began to take an interest in children. When I was ten years old, I did what was possible at my age and formed a kind of festive oratory. Take note. Though I was still pretty small, I was studying my companions' characters. When I looked closely at someone, I could usually gauge what he was thinking. This gift won me the love and esteem of the boys my own age, and I was thus in demand as judge or friend. For my own part, I tried always to help and never to hurt. So my companions were quite fond of me. I would take their side when quarrels broke out. Though I was not very big, I was strong and brave enough to stand up even to older companions. Whenever arguments, questions, or quarrels of any kind arose, I acted as arbiter, and everyone accepted my decisions with good grace.

But it was to hear my stories that they flocked round me. They loved them to the point of folly. I drew on many sources for my anecdotes — sermons, catechism lessons, and stories I had read in *The Kings of France*, in *Wretched Guerino*, and in *Bertoldo and Bertoldino.*[1]

When I appeared, my companions and even grown-ups would run to me in a crowd and clamor for a story from a fellow who scarcely understood what he had read. At times, along the road to Castelnuovo or in some field I would be surrounded by hundreds of people, anxious to hear what a poor child had to say. Apart from a good memory, I lacked any knowledge; but they seemed to think I

27

was a great scholar in their midst. "In the kingdom of the blind, the one-eyed man is king."[2]

In the wintertime, everyone wanted me in the stable[3] to tell stories. All sorts of people used to gather to spend five or even six hours of their evenings listening, motionless, to selections from *The Kings of France*. The poor speaker used to stand on a bench so that all could hear and see. These occasions were described as "listening to a sermon" since we would always begin and end the storytelling with a sign of the cross and a Hail Mary. 1826.[4]

When the weather was fine, especially on Sundays and feast days, a few strangers would come along to swell the ranks. Things were getting a bit more serious now. The entertainment now extended to tricks I had picked up from acrobats and magicians I had watched in the marketplace[5] and at fairs. I used to watch them closely to get the hang of the tricks, then go home and practise till I had mastered the skill. You can imagine all the falls and tumbles and bumps and crashes I was always having! But would you believe that by the time I was eleven I could juggle, do midair somersaults and the swallow trick,[6] and walk on my hands. I could walk, jump, and even dance on the tightrope like a professional acrobat.

From the programme of one holiday in particular you can get an idea of our general routine.

At Becchi there was a field in which grew several trees. One of them, a pear tree that is still there, was very helpful to me then. I used to sling a rope from it to another tree some distance away. I had a table with a haversack on it, and on the ground a mat for the jumps. When I had everything set up and everyone was eager to marvel at my latest feats, I would invite them to recite the rosary and sing a hymn. Then standing on the chair, I preached to them or, better, repeated as much as I could remember from the explanation of the gospel I had heard in church that morning; or sometimes I recalled episodes from something I had heard or read. After the sermon there was a short prayer, and then the show began. At that point you would have seen, just as I am telling you, the preacher transformed into a professional acrobat.

I did the swallow trick and somersaults, walked on my hands, got myself out of a tied sack, swallowed coins and then produced them from someone's nose. I multiplied balls and eggs, changed water into wine, killed and chopped up a chicken and then brought it back to life again so that it crowed better than before. These were part of my stock in trade. I walked the tightrope like an ordinary path, jumped and danced on it, and hung by one foot or one hand, sometimes by two.

This went on for several hours. At the end of it I was tired. A short prayer brought proceedings to a close, and everyone went about his business. Those who cursed or engaged in bad talk or refused to join in the prayers were not allowed to watch the show.

At this point you might ask me: Going to fairs and markets, watching magicians, getting props for my shows — all these took money; where did I get it?

I had several ways. Any money that my mother or others gave me to buy some tidbit, little tips, gifts, all this I saved for this purpose. I was also quite clever at catching birds in cages, snares, and nets and with birdlime; I was very good at finding birds' nests. Whenever I had gathered enough of these, I knew where I could get a good price for them. Mushrooms, plants used for dyes, heather[7] were all another source of money for me.

Now you might ask me, Did my mother mind my wasting my time playing magician?

I assure you that my mother loved me dearly, and I had boundless trust in her. I would not take one step without her approval. She knew everything, saw everything, and let me do it. Indeed, if I needed something, she willingly came to my help. My companions and generally all the spectators gladly gave me what was necessary to provide them with those amusements.

Notes

1. *The Kings of France* and *Wretched Guerino* refer to Carolingian epic romances put into the vernacular by Andrea da Barberino in the fifteenth century. These stories were drawn

from Tuscan or Franco-Venetian sources and were used as a wellspring for a number of popular novels.

The same is true of *Bertoldo*, a tall tale from the sixteenth-century Bolognese Giulio Cesare Croce. He portrayed a deformed but cunning peasant who wormed his way into favor with King Alboino and won his confidence. The author extended the adventures to Bertoldo's son Bertoldino.

2. Don Bosco quotes the proverb in Latin: *Monoculus rex in regno caecorum*.

3. For want of better accommodations, the stables served as community centers for the Piedmontese peasants in the winter months. Fuel was precious, and the body heat of the farm animals helped warm their masters. Sometimes the peasants even slept in the stables in the winter.

4. The text gives the date without explanation. At the beginning of the chapter, Don Bosco indicated that he was doing this already when he was ten. This would be the winter of 1825–1826. Perhaps he only meant to help his sons, reading these recollections, keep their chronological bearings.

5. At Castelnuovo, as in every town, the town square became an open marketplace one day a week. The farmers would set up booths, or just their carts, to sell their produce or livestock to one another and to the townsfolk. They would also buy necessary goods and exchange news and gossip. These weekly markets were natural targets for acrobats and other entertainers wandering from village to village. The weekly market remains customary in Castelnuovo today. In the larger cities one or more squares serve as daily markets not only for foodstuffs but also for leather goods, toys, clothing, electronic goods, etc.

6. The swallow trick consisted of grasping a pole set firmly into the ground, raising the body rigidly to a position horizontal to the ground, and then, legs apart, spinning around the pole. The opened legs were supposed to remind one of a swallow's tail.

7. Wayside herbs and flowers were long used to make household dyes. Synthetic dyes have now replaced them. Perhaps John used to collect madder (*rubia tinctorum*) for red coloring, mignonette (*reseda luteola*) or bedstraw (*galium verum*) for shades of yellow, and woad (*isadis tinctoria*) for blue. Other flora common in the Monferrato region had their own useful qualities.

The word here translated "heather" is *treppio* in Don

Bosco's text. Even Ceria is not sure of its meaning since it is not to be found in Italian dictionaries. He guesses that Don Bosco meant it for the Piedmontese *trebi* or *terbi*, which would be *erica* in Italian, a kind of heather whose bristles are useful for making rough brushes such as those used to comb down horses.

A Providential Meeting

*First communion • The mission
sermons • Fr Calosso • School in
Murialdo*

I was eleven years old when I made my first holy communion.[1] I knew my catechism well. The minimum age for first communion was twelve years. Because we lived far from the parish church,[2] the parish priest did not know us, and my mother had to do almost all the religious instruction. She did not want me to get any older before my admission to that great act of our religion, so she took upon herself the task of preparing me as best she could. She sent me to catechism class every day of Lent. I passed my examination, and the date was fixed. It was the day on which all the children were to make their Easter duty.[3]

In the big crowd, it was impossible to avoid distractions. My mother coached me for days and brought me to confession three times during that Lent.[4]

"My dear John," she would say, "God is going to give you a wonderful gift. Make sure you prepare well for it. Go to confession and don't keep anything back. Tell all your sins to the priest, be sorry for them all, and promise God to do better in the future."[5] I promised all that. God alone knows whether I have been faithful to my resolution.

At home, she saw to it that I said my prayers and read good books; and she always came up with the advice which a diligent mother knows how to give her children.

On the morning of my first communion, my mother did not permit me to speak to anyone. She accompanied me to the altar and together we made our preparation and thanksgiving. These were led by Father Sismondi, the vicar forane,[6] in a loud voice, alternating responses with everyone.

It was my mother's wish for that day that I should refrain from manual work. Instead, she kept me occupied reading and praying. Amongst the many things that my mother repeated to me many times was this: "My dear son, this is a great day for you. I am convinced that God has really taken possession of your heart. Now promise him to be good as long as you live. Go to communion frequently in the future, but beware of sacrilege. Always be frank in confession, be obedient always, go willingly to catechism and sermons. But for the love of God, avoid like the plague those who indulge in bad talk."

I treasured my mother's advice and tried to carry it out. I think that from that day on there was some improvement in my life, especially in matters of obedience and submission to others. It was not easy for me to be submissive because I liked to do things my way and follow my own childish whims rather than listen to those who gave me advice or told me what to do.

One thing that was a source of concern to me was that there was no church or chapel where I could sing and pray with my companions. To hear a sermon or attend a catechism lesson in either Castelnuovo or the nearby village of Buttigliera[7] meant a round trip of six miles. That was why they came gladly to hear the acrobat's sermons.

That year (1826) there was a solemn mission in Buttigliera.[8] It gave me a chance to hear several sermons. The preachers were well known and drew people from everywhere. I went with many others. We had an instruction and a meditation in the evening, after which we were free to return home.

On one of these April evenings, as I was making my way home amid the crowd, one of those who walked along with us was Fr Calosso of Chieri,[9] a very devout priest. Although he was old and bent, he made the long walk to hear the missioners. He was the chaplain of Murialdo.[10] He noticed a capless, curly-headed lad amidst the others but walking in complete silence. He looked me over and then began to talk with me.

"Where are you from, my son? I gather you were at the mission?"

The parish church of Castelnuovo, St. Andrew's, viewed from the side. Here John Bosco was baptized and made his first communion. It was also here that he served as a curate for five months right after his ordination.

"Yes, Father, I went to hear the missioners' sermons."

"Now, what could you understand of it? I'm sure your mother could give you a better sermon, couldn't she?"

"Yes, my mother does give me fine instructions. But I like to hear the missioners as well. And I think I understand them."

"If you can remember anything from this evening's sermons, I'll give you two pence."

"Just tell me whether you wish to hear the first sermon, or the second."

"Just as you wish," he said, "as long as you tell me anything from it. Do you remember what the first sermon was about?"

"It was about the necessity of giving oneself to God in good time and not putting off one's conversion."

"And what was in the sermon?" the venerable old man asked, somewhat surprised.

"Oh, I remember quite well. If you wish I will recite it all." Without further ado, I launched into the preamble and went on to the three points. The preacher stressed that it was risky to put off conversion because one could run out of time, or one might lack the grace or the will to make the change. There, amidst the crowd, he let me rattle on for half an hour.[11]

Then came a flurry of questions from Father Calosso: "What's your name? Who are your family? How much schooling have you had?"

"My name is John Bosco. My father died when I was very young. My mother is a widow with a family of five[12] to support. I've learned to read, and to write a little."

"You haven't studied Donato[13] or grammar, have you?"

"I don't know what they are, Father."

"Would you like to study?"

"Oh, indeed I would."

"What's stopping you?"

"My brother Anthony."

"And why doesn't Anthony want you to study?"

"Because he never liked school himself.[14] He says he doesn't want anyone else to waste time on books the way he did. But if I could only get to school, I would certainly study and not waste time."

"Why do you want to study?"

"I'd like to become a priest."

"And why do you want to become a priest?"

"I'd like to attract my companions, talk to them, and teach them our religion. They're not bad, but they become bad because they have no one to guide them."

These bold words impressed the holy priest. He never took his eyes off me while I was speaking. When our ways parted, he left me with these words: "Cheer up now. I'll keep you and your schooling in mind. Come to see me on Sunday with your mother. We'll arrange something."

The following Sunday my mother and I went along to see him. He undertook to take me for one lesson a day. To keep Anthony happy I was to spend the rest of the day helping him in the fields. He was pleased enough with the scheme because my classes would not start till the autumn, when the rush of field work would be over.

I put myself completely into Fr Calosso's hands. He had become chaplain at Murialdo only a few months before.[15] I bared my soul to him. Every word, thought, and act I revealed to him promptly. This pleased him because it made it possible for him to have an influence on both my spiritual and temporal welfare.

It was then that I came to realise what it was to have a regular spiritual director, a faithful friend of one's soul. I had not had one up till then. Amongst other things he forbade a penance I used to practise; he deemed it unsuited to my age and circumstances. He encouraged frequent confession and communion. He taught me how to make a short daily meditation, or more accurately, a spiritual reading. I spent all the time I could with him; I stayed with him on feast days. I went to serve his Mass during the week when I could. From then on I began to savour[16] the spiritual life; up to then I had acted in a purely mechanical way, not knowing the reasons.

In mid-September, I began a regular study of Italian grammar, and soon I was able to write fairly good compositions. At Christmas I went on to study Latin. By Easter I was attempting Italian-Latin and Latin-Italian translations. All this time I persevered with my usual acrobatics in the field, or in the barn during the winter. Everything my teacher said or did — his every word, I could say — provided edifying material for my audiences.

Just as I was patting myself on the back because everything was going so well, a new trial came; a heavy blow fell that shattered my hopes.

Notes

1. Until the time of Pope Pius X (1903–1914), children ordinarily did not receive first communion until they were at least twelve years old. Piedmontese pastors were strict about admission to the sacraments. This strictness was partly the result of the rigorism that had greatly affected Piedmontese morality and piety in the eighteenth century (see chapter 19, note 7 and comment, and chapter 27).

   John may have been allowed to make his first communion a little earlier than most children partly to help alleviate the family's grief over the recent death of Grandmother Margaret Zucca Bosco, February 11, 1826, when John was ten (Stella, LW, pp. 10–11).

   Holy communion is the reception of the sacrament of Christ's Body and Blood, the Holy Eucharist (see 1 Corinthians 11:23–26; Mark 14:22–25; John 6:51–58).

2. The parish church was in Castelnuovo, three miles away.

3. First communion was usually celebrated at the beginning of Holy Week or just after Easter. In 1826, Easter fell on March 26. A Catholic must receive the Eucharist at least once during the Easter season; this is his Easter duty (see chapter 40, note 7).

4. During the diocesan process for Don Bosco's canonization, Father Julius Barberis testified that Mama Margaret had told him that it was John's idea to go to confession three times during Lent, the forty-day period of penance in preparation for Easter.

5. Undoubtedly Mama Margaret instilled these principles into young John. But in reading this instruction, as well as the following one, which Don Bosco recorded almost fifty years later, we must also remember that the religious educator is speaking to his readers.

6. The pastor's name actually was Joseph Sismondo. Apparently little John scarcely knew him. He died October 3, 1826. Besides being pastor at Castelnuovo, he was also vicar forane, or rural dean, exercising jurisdiction in certain delegated matters on behalf of the archbishop (cf. Code of Canon Law, 553–55).

7. Buttigliera is about two miles northwest of Becchi.

8. The occasion of the mission was a jubilee. The Popes ordinarily proclaim a jubilee with special pilgrimages and indulgences every twenty-five years, as Paul VI did most

recently in 1975. The year 1825 was an ordinary Holy Year in Rome; the next year Pope Leo XII extended the jubilee to the whole world. In the archdiocese of Turin, Archbishop Chiaveroti fixed the time for gaining the indulgence as March 12 to September 12, 1826. Don Bosco remembered the Buttigliera mission as having been organized to help the people of the area prepare for the jubilee year indulgence, which required repentance and confession, communion, and prayer.

Sometimes the Pope announces a special jubilee, such as the one that John Paul II proclaimed for 1983, the "Holy Year of Redemption."

To celebrate his election as Pope on March 31, 1829, and to implore God's assistance, Pius VIII declared such an extraordinary jubilee. Archbishop Chiaveroti set the dates November 8–22 for gaining the indulgence. There was a preparatory triduum of sermons (i.e. a parish mission) at Buttigliera from Thursday, November 5, to Saturday, November 7.

In Don Bosco's *Memoirs* and in Lemoyne's reconstruction of events (BM I, 131–163), there are some obvious errors of fact and other difficulties. Evidently Don Bosco, writing more than forty years after the events, had forgotten about the special jubilee of Pius VIII and assumed that the occasion was the ordinary jubilee year of 1825–1826. Such an explanation, and situating the encounter with Father Calosso on November 5, 1829, rather than in April 1826, immediately clarifies these errors and difficulties.

Although Buttigliera was not in the commune of Castelnuovo, and hence not in the Boscos' and Father Calosso's parish, the renown of the preachers and the special occasion apparently attracted many people from outside the parish, as Don Bosco writes.

9. Father John Melchior Calosso was born in Chieri on January 23, 1760 (thus both Lemoyne and Stella are in error about his age); he was probably ordained in 1782 (the seminary records are incomplete, as are the records of his career). He was pastor at Bruino from at least 1791 to 1813. His brother Charles Vincent was also a priest of the archdiocese.

10. Morialdo was not a parish but only a chaplaincy or a "mission" of Castelnuovo. There had been a vacancy for some time at the Morialdo chapel before Father Calosso's assignment. Old or infirm priests often received such appointments so that they might care for the nearby families and sometimes save them a long walk to their more distant parish

churches (there were restrictions on the kinds of services permitted in such chapels). Since Father Calosso was sixty-nine years old when he was sent to Morialdo, it was a suitable duty for him. A local gentleman living in Turin had recently endowed the chapel with a stipend of eight hundred lire a year. Such arrangements were quite common in Piedmont, where, compared to our experience, there were great numbers of priests.

11. If the date that Don Bosco gave (April 1826) were correct, his feat of memory would truly be phenomenal. He was still only ten years old! As already noted, the encounter actually took place three and a half years later, when he was fourteen. Nevertheless, his recollection was extraordinary.

One might ask how John was able to remember these sermons so well. He did have a great gift in his memory, as he has already recounted and as he will recount further. In this particular case of the sermons, however, there may have been an additional factor. From his description of the encounter, it is obvious that neither his mother nor any other member of the family was with him; they were not attending the mission, probably because of their work at home. Young John may very well have been the family representative at the triduum, entrusted because of his memory as well as his piety with remembering as much as he could from the sermons and repeating them at home for the sake of the rest of the family so that they, too, would be well prepared for the jubilee indulgence. Thus John was more than ready for the challenge of unsuspecting Father Calosso — who, moreover, could easily have taken him for a younger boy since John was small of stature.

12. He must be counting Grandmother Bosco besides the three boys and their mother.

13. The term *Donato* comes from Aelius Donatus, a fourth-century exponent of classical Latin grammar. Books of Latin grammar in Don Bosco's times were referred to by this title.

John's unfamiliarity with Italian grammar, as well as Latin grammar, was normal. Not only was his previous schooling very limited, but his native tongue was Piedmontese, not Italian. Piedmontese remained his ordinary daily language until the process of Italian unification was substantially completed. In 1860, Don Bosco made the use of Italian mandatory at the Oratory; nonetheless, Piedmontese continued in use for some time (BM VI, 277).

Almost every Italian spoke a dialect. "In most of Italy,"

writes Martin Clark, "Italian, like Latin, was dead language," the exceptions being Rome and parts of Tuscany. One estimate has it that in 1870 only 2.5 percent of Italians spoke Italian. Even the upper classes — including King Victor Emmanuel II in his cabinet meetings — spoke dialect (in Piedmont the nobility often spoke French). Such linguistic variety was, of course, an obstacle to political unity, to trade, and to education, and it contributed to Italians' willingness to emigrate by the hundreds of thousands. (Martin Clark, *Modern Italy, 1871–1982* [New York: Longman, 1984], p. 35)

On Don Bosco's use of Piedmontese, see Natale Cerrato *Car ij me fieuj: miei cari figlioli* (Rome: LAS, 1982).

14. This is the only indication that Anthony had any formal schooling. He was not completely illiterate, for he could sign his name on documents. Francis Bosco had probably seen to it that Anthony learned to read and write a little, maybe from a neighbor (see chapter 1, note 15). Joseph Bosco, on the other hand, had to sign with a cross; he was only four when Francis died, and apparently no one encouraged him to acquire even minimal literacy.

15. If Father Calosso was the curate of the chapel closest to Becchi, how could John have met him only some months after his arrival? Because Father Calosso was appointed chaplain in Morialdo in September 1829 (Stella, LW, p. 17), not "only a few months before" April 1826, as Don Bosco remembered it, in conjunction with his faulty remembrance of the jubilee year; and because John was not at Becchi in September 1829; he was nearing the end of his two-and-a-half-year stay with the Moglia family (see chapter 5, comment). He returned to Becchi only after the harvest, i.e. at the beginning of November — just in time for the mission at Buttigliera, as Providence would have it.

16. The reader should not miss the strength of this word, which has slipped casually from Don Bosco's pen. To "savor" is much more than to "know" or to "practice." If John indeed "savored" the spiritual life at age fifteen, this speaks volumes about Father Calosso's direction of his soul and about John himself.

❧ 5 ❧

Hopes Dashed

School work and farmwork •
News good and bad •
Death of Fr Calosso

During the winter, when there was no pressure of farm work, Anthony was reasonable enough about the time I gave to my books. When spring[1] came, however, and work was more pressing, he began to grumble that he was left to tackle all the chores while I was wasting my time and acting the gentleman. After some lively exchanges involving Anthony, my mother, and me, it was decided in the interest of family peace that I should go to school in the morning and work in the fields in the afternoon. But how could I study? How could I manage the translations?

Take note. The walk to and from school afforded me some time to study. When I got home I would take the hoe in one hand and my grammar in the other, and along the way I would study "When *qui, quae, quod* you'd render"[2] until I reached the place of work. Then glancing longingly at the grammar, I would put it in a corner and begin hoeing, weeding, or gathering greens according to the need.

When there was a rest break, I went off on my own to study, a book in one hand, a hunk of bread in the other. I did the same thing on my way home. Written work had to be done in short periods snatched at mealtimes or in time borrowed from sleep.

Despite all my work and good will, Anthony still was not happy. One day he announced very decisively, first to my mother and then to my brother Joseph, that he could stand it no more. "I've had it up to here," he blustered. "I've had my fill of this grammar business. Look at me," he said, "I've grown big and strong without ever setting eyes on such books."

"That's nonsense!" Carried away by blind rage, I retorted in a way I should not have:[3] "Our donkey is bigger and stronger than you are, and he never went to school either. Do you want to be like him?" This so angered him that only speed saved me from a volley of blows and smacks.

My mother was heartbroken, I was in tears myself, and the chaplain was upset too. In fact when that worthy minister of God got to know how matters stood in our family, he took me aside one day and said, "Johnny, you've put your faith in me, and I won't let you down. Leave that troublesome brother of yours and come and live in the presbytery. I'll take care of you."[4]

My mother was elated when I told her of this generous offer. In April I moved into the priest's house, though I returned home to sleep.[5]

No one can imagine how supremely happy I was. I idolised Fr Calosso, loved him as if he were my father, prayed for him, and tried to help him in every way I could. My greatest pleasure was to work for him. I would have died for him. I made more progress in one day with the good priest than I would have made in a week at home. That man of God lavished affection on me, and he would often say, "Don't worry about the future. As long as I'm alive I'll see that you want for nothing. And I'll make provision for you after my death."

Things were going unbelievably well for me. I could say my cup of happiness was full. There was nothing else I could wish for. Then a fresh disaster blighted all my hopes.

One morning in April 1828,[6] Fr Calosso sent me home on an errand. I had only just made it to the house when a messenger dashed in at my heels. He said I was to get back to Fr Calosso as fast as I could. He was very ill and wanted to see me. I did not run; I flew. I found my benefactor in bed suffering from a stroke and unable to speak. He recognised me and tried to talk but no words came. He gave me the key to his money and made signs that I was not to give it to anyone. After two days of suffering, Fr Calosso gave up his soul to God. His death shattered my dreams. I have

always prayed for him, and as long as I live I shall remember my outstanding benefactor every day that dawns.

When Fr Calosso's heirs turned up, I handed over to
them the key and everything else.[7]

Notes

1. By Don Bosco's reckoning, this would be the spring of 1827.
   In fact, it was 1830. In the spring of 1827, he was staying
   with relatives at the Càmpora farm in Serra di Buttigliera
   (see note 4).

2. John used such memory aids as pieces of doggerel to imprint
   on his brain how the Latin relative pronoun agrees with its
   antecedent:

   > *Qui, quae, quod, qualora è messo*
   > *Dopo il nome antecedente,*
   > *D'accordarglisi consente*
   > *Sol nel numero e nel sesso.*

   > When *qui, quae, quod* you'd render:
   > With regard to antecedent,
   > Agree in case it really needn't—
   > Only in number and gender.

3. From Don Bosco's confession we can gauge how much he
   had to discipline his impetuous nature to make himself a
   model of meekness. It reminds us of Saint Francis de Sales,
   who was successful in a similar struggle.

   In a retreat sermon for Salesians, Don Bosco imagined
   someone envying him:

   > You may remark, "Sure, it's nice for Don Bosco to say, 'Patience,
   > patience!' But. . . . "

   > Do you think that it is easy for me to keep calm when, after
   > entrusting an important or urgent task to someone, I find that
   > task not done or badly botched? Believe me, sometimes my blood
   > boils and I am about to burst. (BM XII, 330)

4. Anthony's attitude had already caused Mama Margaret to
   send John away from home twice. The first time apparently
   was during the winter of 1826–1827, and Anthony's hostility
   was the reason. Margaret sent the boy to stay with relatives
   of her husband who were tenants at the Càmpora farm in
   Serra di Buttigliera. Serra, a district of Buttigliera, is located
   about a half mile west of Becchi and had a population then
   of about five hundred (Molineris, p. 144). Lemoyne gives this

episode passing mention (BM I, 143–144). It is unclear how long John stayed there.

The second occasion put him much farther from his step-brother. Margaret sent him to look for a job as a farmhand with the Moglia family outside Moncucco, about three miles northwest of Castelnuovo (six miles from Becchi). He stayed there from February 1827 to November 1829. See the comment following the notes for further information.

5. This was 1830, after John had been away for two and a half years, returned, and been studying with Father Calosso since the previous November. Although the division of Francis Bosco's property probably took place sometime in 1830, quite possibly with the chaplain's help, Anthony's attitude was not improving; rather the opposite.

6. Father Calosso died November 21, 1830. Thus John spent one year studying with his dear friend and spiritual guide, from November 1829 to November 1830. See Desramaut, *LesMem*, pp. 225, 231; and Molineris, pp. 152–162.

7. This simple expression implies a great deal more than it says. This "everything" included all that the key gave access to; there were 6000 lire in that box (2,400,000 lire in 1985 value, by Teresio Bosco's reckoning, or US $16,000). When one considers that the secondary school which John attended in Chieri from 1831 to 1835 charged an annual tuition of 12 lire, one sees immediately that Father Calosso had left a veritable fortune to the son of poor Mama Margaret. The simple way in which Don Bosco describes it is an impressive understatement, which probably should be connected to a dream that he had around this time: see the next chapter and the comment on the dream at the end of it.

Comment on John's Stay at the Moglia Farm

Why did Don Bosco omit such a significant episode? Ceria speculates that he was just reluctant to make family problems public, and especially to give anyone any grounds to criticize his mother. In fact, she has been severely criticized for that decision. Quite simply put, Mama Margaret was caught in a dilemma. She did the best she could. The last thing she wanted to do was to interrupt John's schooling. But Anthony's attitude — together with John's quick temper — meant that John would have been unsafe at home.

Who can say how much that separation cost John? But his love for his mother, in Ceria's opinion, prompted him to gloss over the painful experience, though apparently some details of it were known. Stella (LW, p. 16, n. 30) is much less sure why Don Bosco omitted the Moglia episode from his memoirs. Certainly it was not from any lack of fondness for those good people. In later years he faithfully returned to visit them; when he began the custom of the fall outings, he used to bring the oratory boys to visit them too.

In connection with this period of John's life, Lemoyne writes,

> John had a great mind and heart: he was obedient through virtue, not by nature. The poorest man on earth feels like a lord in his own home.... God would deal with John as he had dealt with Moses.... God likewise would prepare John through a long practice of heroic humility. He, too, would have to leave home and for about two years be forced to work elsewhere as a hired hand. How could he help not feeling keenly this humiliation? (BM I, 142)

As we have noted, Don Bosco is silent about his departure from Becchi as a youth. Various scholars, including Lemoyne, Klein and Valentini, and Desramaut, have reconstructed events thus:

Late in 1826 or early in 1827, John had to discontinue his classes at Capriglio. He lived and worked for a short while with relatives on the Bosco side of the family at the Càmpora farm in Serra di Buttigliera. He was not really needed there and was a financial burden. John probably returned home briefly, but by February 1827 the tension between Anthony and John was proving too much; Mama Margaret had to send him farther afield. He was only eleven years old. (Stella, LW, pp. 13–17; T. Bosco, SP, pp. 42–45)

John was taken into the Moglia household near Moncucco; they were acquaintances of the Occhienas. It was still winter, two months before farm laborers would normally be hired, so John's arriving on his own met with some initial difficulty, but Louis Moglia finally agreed to take him in. He eventually became a much appreciated member of the household, but of course there could be no formal schooling; he was able to get some informal lessons from the local pastor, Father Francis Cottino, and from the local schoolmaster, Father Nicholas Moglia, his host's brother.

The Moglia family still owns that farm and cherishes the memory of John's stay with them. They receive Salesian visitors most graciously, bringing out their own wine and proudly observing that Don Bosco himself once tended some of the vines that produced it.

We may reasonably conjecture the following scenario:

1. Anthony became a real obstacle to John's education in the years 1825–1827, when Anthony was between seventeen and nineteen years old.

2. Margaret, with the backing of her sister Marianne and her brother Michael, began to plan the division of Francis Bosco's estate among his three sons. This would set Anthony up on his own and free John. But she had to wait until Anthony reached his legal majority in 1829.

3. In the meantime, Margaret sent John away without telling him the plan. Uncle Michael went to Moncucco to bring him home in November 1829, when it was finally possible to confront Anthony and settle the estate with him. (See chapter 6, note 9, for further details on the division.)

In any case, around the feast of All Saints in 1829, Michael Occhiena (1795–1867) came to get John, who returned to Becchi just in time for the Holy Year triduum at Buttigliera.

For further details of this period see Molineris, pp. 143–152; T. Bosco, BN, pp. 41–45; Stella, LW, pp. 13–17.

Desramaut (p. 130) and Giraudo and Biancardi (pp. 67–68) hold that John stayed with the Moglias only a year and a half, from February 1828.

6

School at
Castelnuovo

*Fr Caffasso • Doubts • Dividing
our inheritance • School at
Castelnuovo • Music; the tailor*

That year Divine Providence brought a new benefactor into my life. He was Fr Joseph Caffasso[1] of Castelnuovo d'Asti.

It was the second Sunday of October, 1827,[2] and the people of Murialdo were celebrating their patronal feast, the Motherhood of Mary. There was a great air of activity about the place; some were preparing the church, others engaged in family chores; some were playing games, others looking on.

One person I noticed was taking no part in the festivities. He was a slightly-built, bright-eyed cleric, kindly and pure in appearance. He was leaning against the church door. Though I was only twelve years old,[3] I was struck by his appearance and felt I would like to meet him. I went over and spoke to him.

"Father," I said, "would you care to see what's going on at our feast? I'd like to act as your guide."

He kindly beckoned me closer. He asked me how old I was, what studies I had done, if I had made my first communion, how often I went to confession, where I went to catechism, and so on. I was spellbound by his manner of speaking and answered all his questions without hesitation. To show my gratitude for his friendliness, I once more offered to show him round the various entertainments and novelties.

"My dear friend," he replied, "the entertainments of a priest are church ceremonies. The more devoutly they are celebrated, the more successful they are. Our pastimes are the practices of religion. These are ever new and therefore should be diligently attended. I'm only waiting for the church to open so I can go in."

I plucked up my courage to add to the discussion. "But Father," I suggested, "though what you say is true, there's a time for everything, a time to pray and a time to play."[4]

He smiled. But I have never forgotten his parting words, which were his plan of action for his whole life: "A cleric gives himself to the Lord. Nothing in the world must be more important to him than the greater glory of God and the salvation of souls."

I was struck with admiration and longed to know the name of the cleric whose words and bearing so breathed the spirit of the Lord. I learned that he was the seminarian Joseph Caffasso, a student in his 1st year of theology. I already knew him by reputation as a model of virtue.

Fr Calosso's death was a great loss to me.[5] I wept inconsolably over my dead benefactor. I thought of him in my waking hours and dreamt of him when I was asleep. It affected me so badly that my mother feared for my health. She sent me for a while to my grandfather in Capriglio.[6]

At this time I had another dream. In it I was sorely reproached for having put my hope in men and not in our good heavenly Father.[7]

Meanwhile I thought a great deal about how to go ahead with my studies. I would see good priests working at their sacred ministry, but I could not strike up a close relationship with them. Often I would meet on the road our parish priest or his curate.[8] I would greet them at a distance and bow to them as they passed. In their distant and courteous manner, they would return my greeting and go on their way. Often, I used to cry and say to myself and even to others, "If I were a priest, I would act differently. I would approach the children, say some kind words to them, and give them good advice. How happy I would be if I could talk with my parish priest as I used to talk with Fr Calosso. Why shouldn't it be so?"

My mother, seeing how upset I was because of the obstacles in the way of my studies, and not having any hope of getting the consent of Anthony, who was now over twenty, thought about dividing our inheritance. There were serious difficulties, however, since Joseph and I were minors. Division of the property would be a complicated and costly business. Nevertheless she went ahead. My grandmother had died some years previously,[9] so our family now consisted of my mother, Joseph, who did not want to be separated from me [and me].[10]

This division took a load off my mind and left me completely free to go ahead with my studies. However, it took some months to complete all the formalities of the law. It was around Christmas before I was able to enroll at the elementary school in Castelnuovo.[11] It was 1828, and I was thirteen years old.[12]

Since I had done my studies privately and was starting a public school with a new teacher, I faced some drawbacks. Practically, I had to begin my Italian grammar all over before I could start studying Latin.

For some time, I walked from home to school every day. But that was nearly impossible during the harsh winter; I had to make four trips back and forth, covering twelve and a half miles daily. I found lodgings with an upright man, a tailor, John Roberto;[13] he had a taste for singing, especially plainchant.[14] Since I had a good voice, I took up music wholeheartedly. In a few months, I could take the stage to accompany him with fair success.

Eager to use my free time, I took up tailoring. Before long I was able to make buttonholes and hems and sew simple and double seams. Later I learned how to cut out underwear, waistcoats, trousers, and coats. I like to think I became a master tailor.[15]

In fact my landlord, seeing how I had taken to the trade, made me a good offer to get me to stay with him and carry on the business. I had other ambitions, however. I wanted to pursue my studies. While I tried my hand to keep myself busy, I never lost sight of my main objective.[16]

That year some of my companions tried to tempt me into danger; they wanted to take me gambling during schooltime. When I said I had no money, they suggested stealing it from my landlord or even my mother. One of them, pressuring me, said, "My dear chap, it's time you woke up. You must learn to live in the world. Putting your head in a sack gets you nowhere. Just get the money and you can have the same fun as the rest of us."

I well remember what my reply was: "I fail to under-stand what you're getting at. Am I to believe you're urging me to play truant and steal? But in your daily prayers, don't you say, 'The seventh commandment, You shall not steal'? Anyone who steals is a thief, and thieves come to a bad end. Besides, my mother loves me dearly, and if I need money for lawful purposes she gives it to me. I've never done anything without her permission, and I have no in-tention of starting to disobey her now. If your pals are doing that, they're evil. And if they're not doing it but rec-ommending it to others, they're scoundrels."[17]

News of this episode got to the ears of my other com-panions, and no one else proposed to me anything wrong. My teacher heard of it as well and from then on was very kind to me. Even many of the boys' relatives heard of it and urged their sons to associate with me. I was therefore in a position to choose my friends, who loved me and would listen to me like the boys of Murialdo.

Things were going well for me. But I was in for another upset. My teacher, Fr Virano,[18] was made parish priest of Mondonio[19] in the diocese of Asti. In April 1830[20] our be-loved teacher went to take up his appointment. The man who replaced him could not keep order. In fact he almost scattered to the wind all that Fr Virano had taught in the preceding months.[21]

Notes

1. Apparently Don Bosco means the year that he spent with Father Calosso, 1827–1828 according to his memory. Don Bosco always spelled Father Cafasso's name with two *f*'s.

2. In October 1827 Cafasso was sixteen, going on seventeen, and was in his second year of philosophy in the archdiocesan seminary. He began his theological studies in Novem-ber 1828 and was part of the first group of students to study at Chieri when Archbishop Chiaveroti opened the seminary there in 1829. As we have seen, Father Calosso actually died

in November 1830, by which time Cafasso was studying theology; he was ordained in 1833, at the age of twenty-two, after being dispensed from the impediment of age.

In first drafting his *Memoirs* Don Bosco did not recount his meeting with seminarian Cafasso. On revising what he had written, he added a brief marginal note. He did not write out the whole story, for it had already been written elsewhere. He obviously had before him a copy of his *Rimembranza storico-funebre dei giovani dell'Oratorio di San Francesco di Sales verso il sacerdote Caffasso Giuseppe, loro insigne benefattore* [A Eulogy of the Boys of the Oratory of Saint Francis de Sales for Their Outstanding Benefactor, Father Joseph Cafasso] (Turin: Paravia, 1860). From this book he copied the opening words of this section of the memoirs, "It was the second Sunday of October, 1827, and the people of Murialdo were celebrating," adding "etc." and then, "See the *Rimembranza di D. Caffasso*, pp. 18–20." In turn, Father Berto copied into his draft the passage indicated, ending at the words "I knew him by reputation as a model of virtue."

For a biographical sketch of Father Cafasso, see the comment at the end of the notes.

3. If Don Bosco has remembered correctly the occasion of his first meeting with his future mentor, viz. the second Sunday in October, the meeting is unlikely to have occurred before 1830, when Cafasso was, in fact, about to begin his third year of theological studies. (See Desramaut, *LesMem*, pp. 126–130.) John would have been fifteen years old; such an age better fits his behavior here. The meeting could have occurred slightly earlier, possibly June 29 or July 26, 1830 (the feasts of Saints Peter and Paul and of Saint Anne).

4. Here we have a hint of Don Bosco's future educational system. He gave another hint earlier when he told Father Calosso that many of his companions were not bad boys but were heading for trouble because they had nobody to look after them. He will add to this in a moment how he planned to relate to boys if he were to reach the priesthood.

5. Don Bosco abruptly resumes the narrative where he left it at the end of the preceding chapter.

6. His widowed maternal grandfather, Melchior Mark Occhiena (1752–1844); apparently John got his middle name from him. Stella (LW, p. 19) observes that John was in that delicate stage called adolescence; he was fifteen, and "his dreams of

future goals were shrouded in all the vaporous contours of deep emotion. . . . His adolescent idealism might well have regarded [his relationship with Father Calosso] as a sure sign of his own approach to the altar." Now those dreams had been shattered brutally, and John seemed to have no future except on the farm.

7. The reproach in this second dream suggests that Father Calosso's death had seared John's sensitive heart too much for his spiritual good.

Lemoyne identifies this dream with one related to him by Joseph Turco (BM I, 182–183). Turco was one of John's schoolmates in Castelnuovo, and his family were neighbors of the Boscos in Sussambrino (see note 9, below). In this dream, John told this countryman of his, a great Lady had come toward him leading a large flock of sheep. "Look, dear John," she said, "I entrust this entire flock to you."

Frightened, John answered, "But how can I take care of so many sheep and lambs? Where shall I find pastures for them to graze on?"

The Lady replied, "Do not worry. I will help you."

Lemoyne comments: "This episode corroborates a brief and simple statement in his memoirs: 'At the age of 16 I had another dream.'" In fact, Don Bosco's exact words were, "At this time I had another dream," without giving his age but putting it during his stay at Capriglio (November-December 1830?). The dream described by Turco contains no reproach. So it is probably not the one to which Don Bosco refers here. It resembles the one that will be described in chapter 16, note 2.

The wording and the link with John's grief suggest that this reproachful dream could have occurred between the death of Father Calosso and the day when he simply surrendered the key to the money box to the old priest's relatives. Given the probable interval between the two events and the nature of the dream, this seems more likely than during his stay at Capriglio.

For an exploration of this dream's impact on John, see the comment on it at the end of the notes.

8. The pastor of Castelnuovo was Father Bartholomew Dassano, and his assistant was Father Emmanuel Virano, whom Don Bosco will soon introduce as his teacher.

9. Molineris (pp. 164–167) suggests circumstances and dates along the following lines:

By mentioning his grandmother's death here (1830), Don

Bosco hints that the division may have been necessary because her moderating authority was gone. But, as we already noted (chapter 4, note 1), she had died on February 11, 1826, more than four years earlier. So Margaret's timing must have been based on other motives.

It seems likely that Margaret had decided by late 1829 (see chapter 5, comment) to exert her maternal authority and had enlisted the help of the new chaplain, Father Calosso, and her brother Michael. Anthony, now of legal age, remained so hostile to John's studies that a division of the inheritance of Francis Bosco appeared to be the only solution. A basic agreement with Anthony was reached so that John was able to return home from the Moglia farm, and he was to go to school in Castelnuovo right away.

The problem with Molineris's theory is that the actual division and John's Castelnuovo schooling did not occur until a year later, during which time John met Father Calosso, was tutored by him, and was still harassed by Anthony.

Perhaps Margaret made her decision while John was still living with Father Calosso. Almost certainly she had the chaplain's help and that of some relatives (Stella, LW, p. 21). After Father Calosso's death, she went ahead with it.

In late 1830, Anthony was twenty-two and preparing for his marriage to Anna Rosso of Castelnuovo, which took place on March 22, 1831. Anthony's approaching marriage offered a good occasion for settling any remaining points of contention; he seems to have been amenable to it, especially since Margaret was more than generous in his regard — she gave him her own share, and she and John went to live with Joseph.

Joseph, now eighteen, had changed his tenant's contract and moved to a new tenancy at Sussambrino, less than two miles south of Castelnuovo. For the time being, Anthony remained in the old house at Becchi, where he could look after the little bits of property that were Joseph's and John's shares.

There is some question about just when Joseph, Margaret, and John moved. The normal time for changing farm contracts was after the harvest in November. One then had four or five months to prepare for the new farm year. Thus Stella (LW, p. 22) supposes that Joseph moved in October 1831. That eliminates John's four-times-daily walk to and from Becchi (which he mentions a couple of paragraphs farther on in his narration) but creates a problem with the summer vacation that he is supposed to have spent at

Sussambrino after school closed in Castelnuovo (BM I, 177–178). And are we to suppose that Joseph went back and forth from Becchi to Sussambrino every day?

If the division of the property had been in the works for some time, Joseph would have been prepared to move as soon as the division was formalized. He might well have waited till March, after his stepbrother's wedding and around the time when he would be needed at Sussambrino. All that we can be fairly sure of is that the move occurred during the winter of 1830–1831.

This means that sometime after John began going to school at Castelnuovo, his home would have been at Sussambrino, nearer to school than was Becchi. The distance Don Bosco says he had to walk daily to and from Castelnuovo would apply, of course, only until Joseph and Margaret had moved. But John's boarding arrangement must have been worked out long before then.

For more information on the various Becchi households, see Stella, LW, p. 22, n. 42, which provides references to Molineris's studies.

10. Don Bosco left out "and me," which would conclude his thought here.

11. The school at Castelnuovo was one of those set up after King Charles Felix decreed that every commune should have an elementary school (the law of 1822).

12. The chronological error continues here. Don Bosco's original draft had "1829," and in a later copy he corrected this to "1828." Actually it was December 1830, and John was fifteen. See Desramaut, *LesMem*, p. 231. His schoolmates would have been lads of ten or eleven (Stella, LW, p. 22)—a fact that also helps us to understand John's moral ascendancy over them, though it is certainly not the only reason for it.

13. Uncle Michael Occhiena helped John with the arrangements. At first John used Roberto's house as a base for his midday meal, which he brought with him each day. On cold and stormy days, he slept over (perhaps without supper). Finally he became a full-time boarder. For a reasonable sum (payable in grain and wine, as well as in cash), Roberto provided John with meals and a place to sleep—a cubbyhole under the stairs. Mama Margaret brought John a supply of bread each week.

14. Plainchant or plainsong is the monodic and rhythmically free music of the Roman liturgy, also called Gregorian chant.

15. Don Bosco obviously uses the term jokingly, having in mind the master tailors he had in his own technical schools by the 1870s.

16. Later on John also got his mother's permission to apprentice at Evasio Savio's blacksmith shop a couple of hours a day. (This Savio was no relation to the blacksmith Charles Savio, Dominic's father.) John's quick mind left him with plenty of free time, and he needed extra money.

17. Don Bosco constantly exhorted his boys to choose good companions. His mother advised him on the same subject. Choosing good companions is a key element of the Preventive System.

18. One teacher took the three lowest classes together in one classroom (a total of perhaps thirty boys). This teacher was the curate Father Emmanuel Virano. Evidently he was a good teacher and could keep discipline.

19. Mondonio is a hamlet less than two miles east of Castelnuovo. It was later to be the home of Saint Dominic Savio, Don Bosco's most famous pupil. The Savios moved there in November 1852. One day in October 1854, Dominic walked to Becchi with his father to introduce himself to Don Bosco and to seek admission to the Oratory as a boarding student. The boy quickly became a leader among his peers, but after two years his health began to break down. He returned home at the beginning of March 1857 and died there a few days later, possibly of pleurisy (Michele Molineris, *Nuova vita di Domenico Savio* [Castelnuovo Don Bosco, 1974], pp. 268–270). After his cause of canonization was introduced, the Salesians brought his remains from Mondonio to the Basilica of Mary Help of Christians in Turin, where they are venerated today.

20. In fact, it was 1831.

21. John does not name the man who took Father Virano's place; it was Father Nicholas Moglia, who was seventy-five years old. John did not rate him highly as a teacher. Apparently Father Moglia did not think that anything good could come out of Becchi. He did not like John. When the lad handed in a well-done exercise, Father Moglia would insist that it was not John's own work. Father Nicholas was related to the Moglias of Moncucco and knew well enough who John was, but for some reason he regarded him as just a country bumpkin (see chapter 5, comment).

Comment on Saint Joseph Cafasso

Joseph Cafasso was born in Castelnuovo on January 15, 1811, of a humble family. He studied there and in Chieri, just as John Bosco would do. From his youth he was noted for his piety. Following his ordination, Father Cafasso went to Turin for further studies. He quickly became disenchanted with the Jansenistic rigorism of the seminary there (see chapter 27), and of the University of Turin, whose theology department was closely allied with the seminary.

So Father Cafasso took up his studies in the pastoral program that Father Louis Guala had organized at the Convitto Ecclesiastico (chapter 27). He distinguished himself there and, upon completing the program in 1836, joined its staff, specializing in moral theology.

Father Cafasso, a tiny and slightly deformed man, was nonetheless a a majestic figure of strong voice, serene disposition, and large heart. He soon became a renowned preacher and confessor, admired for simplicity and moderation; he was a leader in Piedmont's long fight against Jansenism.

Upon Father Guala's death in 1848, Father Cafasso succeeded him as rector of the Convitto. Whether as teacher or as superior, he showed that same care for young priests that so impressed Don Bosco. Thus Father Cafasso had a profound and long-lasting effect on a major portion of Piedmont's clergy.

More noticeable to the general public was his singular ministry in the prisons, especially for the condemned. He prepared over sixty men to die on the gallows and touched every one of them sufficiently to bring him to the sacraments.

Father Cafasso guided and assisted financially the charitable works of many good people besides Don Bosco. Much of this invaluable help Don Bosco will describe in its place.

Father Cafasso died on June 23, 1860. In November and December of that year Don Bosco published his *Eulogy* in the *Catholic Readings*, changing the title to *Biography of Father Joseph Cafasso as Recorded in Two Funeral Homilies*.

Father Cafasso was canonized in 1947. To this day he is known as "the pearl of the Piedmontese clergy." There are no biographies in English except the one in Butler's *Lives* (II, 628–631) and a translation of Don Bosco's eulogies, *The Life of St. Joseph Cafasso*, trans. Patrick O'Connell (Rockford, IL: TAN, 1983). Salesians might be interested in Eugenio Valentini's *San Giuseppe Cafasso: memorie pubblicate nel 1860 da San Giovanni Bosco* (Turin: SEI, 1960).

Saint Joseph Cafasso was the apostle of the Turin prisons. He was especially concerned for those condemned to the gallows. On the centennial of his death, the people of Turin erected this statue in his honor in the center of the Rondò, where the gallows once stood.

Comment on John's Dream in 1830

After so many frustrations, for one good year, everything had come right for John. The tense situation with Anthony was gone. His studies were finally progressing. Not only that, but there was Father Calosso's promise that the money needed for future studies would be taken care of. Most of all, for the first time John had as a guide a good and holy priest who fully understood his vocational ideal and who had years of living experience of the priesthood John longed for. Father Calosso seems to have bridged the age gap and become a friend as well as a spiritual guide and provider. One needs little imagination to feel the contrast between this atmosphere and the tension of the Becchi house. To the old chaplain John could open his heart, and in him tangibly feel the providence of God. The road to the priesthood was now open before him.

Don Bosco's young manhood and early priesthood are marked by a paradox. On the one hand there were his strength of character, the clarity of his life ideal (reinforced by dreams or visions), and the practical ability he had to attain any target he set for himself. On the other hand there was the hesitation with which he actually started his work. He repeatedly questioned his vocation, sought spiritual advice and guidance; he came close to joining the Franciscans in 1834. He overcame the hesitancy of this first period, but with the Salesians he constantly recurred to this theme: not even the smallest event in the history of the Congregation was of human making; it was all the work of the Lord through Mary.

If we accept the nature of the events as suggested here, then this early spiritual event and dream-experience was fundamental in searing this docility into the soul of one so naturally active and full of self-confident initiative. We have that deeply spiritual and peaceful "novitiate" year with Father Calosso that prepared him for this character-molding self-surrender to God, even in his spiritual goals. Just when the road ahead was all open and smooth, the Lord stepped into his path and said, "My ways are not your ways."

We do not know the exact form of the dream, only its effect. It is not in the least surprising that Don Bosco should be reticent about such an emotionally-charged experience and all it must have cost a sensitive fifteen-year-old. Tangible grace and a mystical experience would almost seem necessary in a teenager for the kind of self-effacing generosity that John showed with Father Calosso's relatives.

If, however, the dream came during that short interval between Father Calosso's death and the coming of his relatives, this problem remains: all human hope was not yet gone—John had the little box. Does the complete despair suggested by John's mood and the reprimand delivered in the dream fit better before or after he surrendered the key to his material hopes? There is some logic to locating it later.

7

School at Chieri

School in Chieri • Kindness of
teachers • The first four grades

After the loss of so much time, it was finally decided to send me to Chieri,[1] where I could continue seriously with my schooling. That was in 1830.[2] One raised in the backwoods[3] finds plenty of novelties to wonder at in even a small country village. I lodged with a woman from my own town, Lucy Matta,[4] a widow with one son. She used to stay in the city to help him and keep an eye on him.[5]

The first person I met was Fr Eustace Valimberti, of revered memory. He gave me a lot of good advice on how to keep out of trouble.[6] He invited me to serve his Mass and thus he could always advise me well. He brought me to see the headmaster in Chieri[7] and introduced me to my other teachers. Up to now, my studies had been a little of everything and amounted almost to nothing. Accordingly, I was advised to enroll in the sixth class, which today would correspond to the first year of *ginnasio*.[8]

My teacher was Dr Pugnetti,[9] also of dear memory. He was very kind to me. He helped me in school, invited me to his home, and was very sympathetic to me because of my age and my goodwill. He went out of his way to help me as much as he could.

My age and my size made me look like a pillar amongst my little companions. I was anxious to get out of that situation. After two months of the sixth class, I was at its head. I took an examination and moved up to the fifth class.[10] I went gladly to my new class because my classmates were more my size, and my teacher was the beloved Fr Valimberti.[11] After two more months, I led the class again and, by exception, was allowed to take another examination and so was promoted to the fourth class, which is equivalent to the second year of *ginnasio*.[12]

Here my teacher was Joseph Cima, a strict disciplinarian.[13] When he saw this student as big and stocky as himself coming into his class in midyear, he joked in front of the whole class, "He's either a simpleton or a genius. What do you make of him?"

Taken aback by that harsh introduction, I answered, "Something in-between. I'm just a poor young fellow who has the goodwill to do his work and get along in his studies."

He was mollified by my reply and went on with unusual kindness, "If you have goodwill, you're in good hands. I'll see that you won't be idle here. Don't worry; if you have any problems, tell me promptly and I'll sort them out for you."

I thanked him with all my heart.

After a couple of months in this class, something happened that gave rise to some comment about me. One day the teacher was explaining the life of Agesilaus in Cornelius Nepos.[14] I did not have my book with me that day, and to cover my forgetfulness, I kept my Donato open in front of me. My companions noticed, and first one and then another began to laugh. Suddenly the whole classroom was in an uproar.

"What's going on here?" shouted the teacher. "What's going on?" he shot at me, this time. Everyone was looking at me. He told me to construe the text and repeat his explanation. I got to my feet, still holding my Donato. From memory I repeated the text, construed it, and explained it. Instinctively my companions expressed their admiration and burst into applause. The teacher was angry beyond description. It was the first time, according to him, that he had failed to maintain discipline. He swung at me, but I saw it coming and ducked. Next he placed his hand on my Donato and demanded of my neighbours the reason for all the commotion.

"Bosco had his Donato in front of him all the time," my companions explained, "but he read and explained the lesson as if he had the Cornelius text." The teacher took the Donato and insisted I go on for two sentences more. Then he said to me, "In tribute to your wonderful memory,[15] I'll overlook your forgetfulness. You're blessed. Only see that your gift is put to good use."

At the end of that school year (1830–1831),[16] as a result of my high marks, I was promoted to the third class, equivalent to the third year of *ginnasio*.[17]

Notes

1. Chieri was an ancient cathedral city about nine miles southeast of Turin, separated from the great capital city by the Turinese hills, and about nine miles west-southwest of Castelnuovo. With about nine thousand inhabitants, it was easily the largest city in the area of Castelnuovo, and it was the only industrial center. The principal industry was the manufacture of cotton and silk textiles; there were some thirty factories, some of them perhaps just domestic enterprises.

   By John Bosco's time there was no longer an episcopal see at Chieri, but there were numerous convents and monasteries — of the Dominicans, Oratorians, Jesuits, Franciscans, and Poor Clares — and, since 1829, one of the archdiocesan seminaries.

   The city was also a student center, attracting to its schools several hundred boys and young men each year from the towns and villages of the area. Student life was difficult. Schooling required tuition and books. Housing was hard to find and of poor quality. To meet their rent, food, and school expenses, students had to work after school in jobs like clerking, housecleaning, tutoring younger boys, or tending horses. Chieri students dressed poorly, ate poorly, and suffered from the cold of winter. John Bosco's situation was not at all unusual except for his age. His strong peasant constitution helped him to cope with the wretched food and miserable living conditions and even to maintain his athletic prowess — as we shall see.

2. John went to Chieri on November 3, 1831.

3. "backwoods" = *boschi* in Don Bosco's text; he is punning on his name, which means "wood" in Italian.

4. Lucy Matta's (1783–1851) husband Joseph had died in 1824. The Mattas were from Morialdo. While her son John Baptist

A view of Chieri. In the 1830s, the city was known for its schools, monasteries, and convents. It was also a center of light industry. The Bosco family lived near Chieri in the seventeenth and eighteenth centuries. Don Bosco's grandfather Philip Anthony Bosco moved to Castelnuovo in 1751.

was studying at the Royal College from 1831 to 1833, Mrs. Matta rented a house in piazza San Guglielmo, off 9 via Mercanti, from James Marchisio.

Mama Margaret sent John to stay with the good lady. This meant she had to pay a steep boarding fee of twenty-one lire a month, which the family could not afford. John covered part of this sum by doing jobs for Mrs. Matta, and his mother supplied the rest in either cash or produce. The landlady soon came to realize what a treasure she had in her house in this young man, and she began to make ready use of him for her son's good. And she stopped asking rent from her tenant.

The Royal College of Chieri used these rooms — two on the ground floor and two on the second floor — for the preparatory course and the three years of grammar. John Bosco covered these four courses in two years, 1831–1833.

5. Mrs. Matta's vigilance (*assistere e vegliare*) foreshadows the Preventive System.

6. Here we have yet another intimation of Don Bosco's system. Frequently at the Oratory he would ask good boys to look after new or troublesome boys in the same way. It was part of the strategy of having good companions.

7. The headmaster or principal was appointed by the government since the school was a public one. At this time he was a Dominican, Father Pius Eusebius Sibilla.

8. In the educational system of the time, once elementary education was completed, the first stage of secondary education involved five classes (or years). The first three were sometimes known as grammar 1, 2, and 3, after which came

humanities and rhetoric. This period was followed by about two years of philosophy which, for clerical students, would be the first years of seminary studies.

The corresponding system in modern Italy consists of five years of *ginnasio* followed by three years of *liceo*. This prepares for entry to tertiary, or university, studies. There is also a "middle track" (*scuola media*) without access to *liceo*.

In Britain the corresponding system is forms 1 to 5 of compulsory education until one is sixteen or older. These are followed by optional sixth-form studies of two or three years in lower and upper sixth that can lead to entrance to university education.

The five years of the Italian *ginnasio* are approximately equivalent to the four years of college-preparatory high school in the United States or, again approximately, to the five years of Canadian high school.

By the time Don Bosco was writing his *Memoirs*, the old system had been reformed. So he gives a little explanation. In the 1830s classes were numbered in reverse order. The sixth class was the preparatory form, while the fifth, fourth, and third classes (grammar 1, 2, and 3) corresponded to forms 1, 2, and 3 of the *ginnasio*. The humanities and rhetoric years corresponded to forms 4 and 5 of secondary school. The preparatory year was equivalent to the last year of primary school (eighth grade in the American system). So its pupils were boys of twelve or thirteen, in the midst of whom was thrown this newly-arrived sixteen-year-old country lad.

The secondary and undergraduate school systems look like this:

Piedmont	Modern Italy	United States	United Kingdom
Preparatory		Grade 8	
Grammar 1	Ginnasio 1	Grade 9	Form 1
Grammar 2	Ginnasio 2	Grade 10	Form 2
Grammar 3	Ginnasio 3	Grade 11	Form 3
Humanities	Ginnasio 4	Grade 12	Form 4
Rhetoric	Ginnasio 5	Junior College	Form 5
Philosophy	Liceo	Junior College	Form 6
University	University	College/Graduate School	University

9. John's teacher in the sixth class was Father Valerian Pugnetti. "Doctor" here and elsewhere in the *Memoirs* means Doctor of Theology.

10. January 1832.

11. Father Placido Valimberti.

12. It was now about March 1832, and John had reached tenth grade (form 2).

13. Cima's first name was Vincent. He was a seminarian.

14. Cornelius Nepos (100–25 B.C.) was a Roman historian.

15. John Bosco certainly did have a phenomenal memory, which he demonstrated repeatedly. He used to say that for him to read something was to remember it. When he was already well on in years, he could still entertain his secretaries by reciting long passages from Dante. A few months before his death, he was traveling in the coach with Father Rua. The conversation came around to some point of sacred history which had inspired Metastasio (1698–1782). Don Bosco recited whole stanzas from the Italian poet; it was very unlikely that he had read any of the poetry since leaving secondary school. Various examples of his extraordinary memory are cited throughout the BM, e.g. I, 294, 315, 321–323.

16. Correct to 1831–1832.

17. In one school year John had done three years' work. No doubt his diligence and his maturity, relative to his classmates, helped him a great deal, as did his memory. Stella writes, "His marks were brilliant, at least by comparison with those of his fellow students; but his surviving notebooks reveal clearly how incomplete his training in the humanities was at that point" (LW, p. 23).

The Society for a Good Time

*My companions • The Society for a
Good Time • Christian duties*

All this time I had to use my own initiative to learn how to deal with my companions. I put them in three groups: the good, the indifferent, and the bad. As soon as I spotted the bad ones, I avoided them absolutely and always. The indifferent I associated with only when necessary, but I was always courteous with them. I made friends with the good ones, and then only when I was sure of them.[1]

As I knew few people in the town, I made it a rule to keep to myself. I sometimes had to discourage people I did not know too well. Some wanted to get me to a show, others into some gambling, and still others to go swimming.[2] And there were suggestions that I should steal fruit from the town gardens or country orchards.

One companion was so bold as to suggest that I should steal a valuable object from my landlady so that we could buy some sweets. Gradually I got to know the undesirables and firmly avoided their company. Usually I had a counter to these suggestions. I used to tell them that my mother had asked my landlady to look after me, and out of love for my mother I did not want to go anywhere nor do anything without good Lucy's consent.

This firm obedience to the good woman led to a very happy and practical conclusion. With much pleasure, Lucy asked me to take charge of her only son,* a lively youth

---

*John Baptist Matta of Castelnuovo d'Asti has been mayor of his hometown for many years and now owns a pharmacy in the same town.[3]

more interested in games than in schoolwork. She depended on me to check his homework even though he was in the class above me. I took him in hand as if he were my brother.[4] I used little prizes as bribes to get to him. I played indoor games with him and helped him to be faithful to his religious duties. Little by little he became more tractable, obedient, and studious.[5] After six months he had become so good and diligent that his teacher was satisfied and he won honors in class. His mother was so delighted that she refused to accept my monthly rent.

Since the companions who tried to coax me into their escapades were the most careless about everything, they began to come to me for help because I did them the kindness of lending them my homework or dictating it to them. The teachers frowned on this. They said that it was a false kindness that only encouraged laziness, and they strictly forbade me to do it. I then resorted to less obvious ways of helping them, such as explaining problems to them and lending a helping hand to those who needed it. Thus I made everyone happy and won the goodwill and affection of my companions. At first they came to play, then to listen to stories or to do their homework, and finally for no reason at all, just as the boys at Murialdo and Castelnuovo used to do.

That these gatherings might have a name, we called ourselves the Society for a Good Time.[6] There was a reason for the name, because everyone was obliged to look for such books, discuss such subjects, or play such games as would contribute to the happiness of the members. Whatever would induce sadness was forbidden, especially things contrary to God's law. Those who swore, used God's name in vain, or indulged in bad talk were turned away from the club at once.

So it was that I found myself the leader of a crowd of companions. Two basic rules were adopted: (1) Each member of the Society for a Good Time should avoid language and actions unbecoming a good Christian. (2) Exactness in the performance of scholastic and religious duties. All this helped my reputation, and in 1832[7] my companions respected me like the captain of a small army. I was much in demand for entertainments, for helping pupils privately, or for giving lessons or reviews at home.

Thus Divine Providence enabled me to supply my own clothes, school necessities, and other things without having to disturb my family in any way.

Notes

1. Don Bosco returns to a favorite educational theme: the importance of choosing one's companions carefully.

2. Swimming was viewed in Piedmont as a moral problem for several reasons:

    1. Drowning in the sometimes treacherous waters of the cold, swift streams was a serious risk (see chapter 11).

    2. "Skinny-dipping" clashed with the natural modesty of the people even though girls were never present.

    3. Lack of adult supervision sometimes allowed improper behavior to occur. Note young Dominic Savio's reasons for not going swimming—as Don Bosco puts those reasons into the pre-adolescent's mouth—in chapter 4 of Savio's biography (pp. 4–5 of the O'Brien edition or pp. 38–39 of the Aronica edition).

3. This note and similarly placed ones were added by Don Bosco during revision of Father Berto's copy of the manuscript.

4. John Baptist Matta, who died in 1878, was six years senior to John. Yet it seems that he was but one class ahead of John. From Don Bosco one would get the impression that John had been looking after John Baptist as though the Matta boy were his younger brother.

5. John did magic tricks, told stories, and even composed bits of poetry, as he will mention later. It is not difficult to see how much of Don Bosco's Preventive System is already at work here. And, again, we see the impact that a good companion can have on another youth.

6. The Italian, *Società dell'Allegria*, is virtually untranslatable. It has been variously rendered as the "Glee Club," "Jovial Society," "Cheerful Company," "Good Times Club," "Happy Fellows Society."

    Stella (LW, p. 31) describes the club as a "'secret' society, like the many patriotic societies then flourishing in Italy." Thus Stella reminds us that this was a revolutionary era. In

1830 there had been major, successful uprisings in Belgium and France. In 1831 lesser, unsuccessful ones occurred in the Papal States, Modena, and Parma, and there was unrest in Piedmont in spite of a rigidly controlled press. There was talk of a constitution, but King Charles Albert, who had just come to the throne, mercilessly crushed a revolutionary conspiracy. After the failures of these Italian ventures, Giuseppe Mazzini founded a new secret society, *Giovine Italia* (Young Italy) in 1831.

Don Bosco has not yet given any indication in his *Memoirs* of the great national events which were already occurring and which would eventually touch him very personally. As a country schoolboy, in a State that practiced censorship, he was probably not even aware at the time of distant events. But John must have known that there were secret societies like the Carbonari and the Freemasons and that soldiers and the police visited Chieri in 1831 and 1834 to hunt out seditious elements.

Three of John Bosco's characteristics come through in the form taken by the Society for a Good Time, a club in which he was effectively president, even if not so in name. The three qualities are a lively, enterprising apostolic zeal; a real organizing ability; and most of all, the joyful spirit that became the hallmark of all his educational work. The rest of his autobiographical narrative will show how the germ of this apostolic spirit developed.

7. We cannot be certain of the year when John and his friends organized the Society for a Good Time, but it was probably soon after John arrived in Chieri.

Life at School

Good companions • Practices of piety

Amongst the members of our Society for a Good Time I discovered some who were truly exemplary. Worthy of mention are William Garigliano from Poirino and Paul Braje[1] from Chieri. They were always ready for some good recreation, but only after they had done their homework. Both were reserved and pious, and they gave me plenty of good advice. On feast days, after the practices of piety in common at the college,[2] we used to go along to St Anthony's Church, where the Jesuits gave marvelous catechetical instructions with plenty of stories that I still recall.

During the week, the Society for a Good Time used to meet at the home of one of the members to talk about religious matters. Anyone was welcome to come to these gatherings. Garigliano and Braje were amongst the most conscientious. We entertained ourselves with some pleasant recreation, with discussions on religious topics, spiritual reading, and prayer. We exchanged good advice, and if there were any personal corrections we felt we should hand out to each other, whether these were our own personal observations or criticisms we had heard others make, we did that. Without realizing it, we were putting into practice the excellent adage, "Blessed is he who has an advisor"; and that saying of Pythagoras,[3] "If you have no friend to tell you your faults, pay an enemy to do it." Besides these friendly activities, we went to hear sermons and often went to confession and holy communion.

Here it is good to recall that in those days religion was a basic part of the educational system.[4] A teacher faced instant dismissal should he make any statement unbecoming or irreligious. If this was the way teachers were treated, you can imagine how severely pupils were dealt with for any unruly conduct or scandal.

We went to Holy Mass every morning; classes began with the devout praying of the *Actiones* and the *Ave Maria*; they ended with the *Agimus* and an *Ave Maria*.[5]

On feast days all the pupils attended the college church. Before Mass we had spiritual reading, followed by the chanting of the Little Office of Our Lady.[6] Then came Mass and the explanation of the gospel.[7]

In the evening we had a further catechetical instruction, vespers, and another sermon.[8] Everyone was expected to approach the holy sacraments; to prevent the neglect of this important obligation, once a month the students had to present a card to prove that they had gone to confession. If one fell down on this, he was barred from end-of-year examinations, no matter how good he was at studies.[9] This strict training produced marvelous results. Many years went by without any swearing or unbecoming words being heard. The pupils were as docile and respectful at school as they would have been at home. And it often happened that in very large classes everyone won promotion at the end of the year. This was the case with my own classmates in the third class, humanities, and rhetoric.

I had the great good fortune of choosing as my regular confessor Doctor Maloria, canon of the chapter in Chieri.[10] He always had a warm welcome for me. Indeed, he encouraged me to go to confession and communion more often, advice not too commonly given in those days. I do not remember that any of my teachers ever advised me along these lines. Those who went to confession and communion more than once a month were considered very virtuous; and many confessors would not permit it. Consequently, I have to thank my confessor if I was not led by companions into certain unfortunate pitfalls that inexperienced boys in large schools have to regret.[11]

During these two years,[12] I never forgot my friends at Murialdo. I kept in touch with them and sometimes went to visit them on Thursdays.[13] On autumn weekdays, as soon as they got wind of my arrival they ran to meet me and always made a big fuss over me. A branch of the Society for a Good Time was started amongst them, too. Those whose good conduct throughout the year recommended them were enrolled. Bad conduct—especially swearing or evil talk—warranted expulsion from the club.

Notes

1. Ceria says that the correct spelling is "Braia" (MO, p. 53); Stella spells it "Braja" (LW, p. 31). Presumably Ceria has Italianized the name, whereas Stella has kept the Piedmontese form.

   Garigliano, two years younger than John, was to be his companion at the seminary and at the Convitto Ecclesiastico; he died in 1902. Paul Victor Braja, three years younger than John, died on July 10, 1832. Hence the club must have been organized during the school year 1831–1832.

2. The term "college" (*collegio*) designated a state-run secondary school such as the Royal College that John attended in Chieri. Later in the nineteenth century it came to mean a private, secondary-level boarding school. It is not to be confused with an American college, i.e. the first level of higher education, leading to a bachelor's degree. See Stella, LW, pp. 124–126.

   The chapel was located on the ground floor off one of the two little courtyards where the college was situated, at what is now via Vittorio Emanuele 45.

3. Greek philospher and mathematician (ca. 580-ca. 500 B.C.).

4. The scholastic legislation of that period is to be found in an official publication, *Raccolta, per ordine di materia, dei Sovrani provvedimenti che reggono gli studi fuori dell'Università e gli stabilimenti dipendenti dal Magistrato della Riforma* [A Presentation in Topical Order of the Royal Laws for the Regulation of Studies Outside the University] (Turin: Stamperia Reale, 1834). It also contains the royal decrees promulgated in 1822 by King Charles Felix concerning religion, in a sociopolitical context of vigorous restoration. The program is wide-ranging and detailed. For instance, in the "Regulations for University Studies" there was article 123: "On days preceding the other great solemnities of Holy Church, the feasts of the Blessed Virgin, and the feasts of the patron saints of

studies, after classes the students shall be prepared to celebrate these mysteries."

Don Bosco gave similar advice for his schools and followed many of the particular practices that he evidently learned in the public schools of the 1830s.

5. All the prayers were in Latin. The *Actiones* may be translated, "Lord, may everything we do begin with your inspiration, continue with your help, and reach perfection under your guidance, through Christ our Lord" (one of the collects for Ember Saturday in Lent in the old liturgy; now the collect for the day after Ash Wednesday). The *Agimus* is the familiar "We give you thanks, Almighty God, for all your benefits: you who live and reign forever and ever." The *Ave Maria* is the Hail Mary.

Don Bosco's earliest "Regulations for the Hospice Attached to the Oratory of Saint Francis de Sales" (1852) contains this directive: "Work shall begin with the *Actiones* and *Ave Maria*, and shall end with the *Agimus* and *Ave Maria*" (BM IV, 550; cf. IV, 553). In Salesian schools periods of work and study began and ended with these prayers for many generations.

6. The Little Office of Our Lady was a simple, popular version of the Divine Office (Liturgy of the Hours) in Gregorian chant. Since this version was virtually unchanging, it was easily learned, even by nearly illiterate people (cf. chapter 40). Before Mass the schoolboys sang only lauds (morning prayer).

7. According to the general custom in nineteenth-century Piedmont, the sermon usually followed Mass.

8. Vespers (evening prayer) was sung from the Little Office. Such evening devotions were the common practice at that time.

9. Modern pedagogical practice, of course, does not tolerate such infringement on the freedom of conscience of pupils. Although Don Bosco notes the apparent good results of the practice at Chieri, he never instituted it in his own schools. Not only was he afraid that boys might be pressured into committing sacrilege, but he wanted an atmosphere of freedom. For this reason, for example, he refused to have the students go to communion row by row — a very orderly way to proceed — because it would be too obvious who did or did not approach the Lord's table; rather, at communion time the boys were to leave their places whenever they chose, if

they chose. Likewise, confessors were always available when the boys were in church, and Don Bosco himself would frequently seek out boys who he knew had not been reconciled to the Lord (see chapter 40); but no one was ever compelled to confess or to feign a confession.

10. Canon Joseph Maloria (1802–1857), who had earned a doctorate in theology from the University of Turin in 1825, was much respected for his learning. He had already been Joseph Cafasso's confessor during the latter's secondary school days, and he may have helped deepen the friendship between John and Joseph that began when they met at the Morialdo chapel (chapter 6). Father Maloria remained John's confessor from this time through his seminary years. John seems to have visited him often at his home.

As mentioned in chapter 7, note 1, Chieri had once been a cathedral city. It still had a chapter of canons attached to its *duomo*. One of them at this time was Saint Joseph Cottolengo, founder of the Little House of Divine Providence in Turin, a couple of blocks away from the place where the Oratory of Saint Francis de Sales would one day be established.

11. In this reflection, Don Bosco not only notes in passing the danger of bad companions but also cites a valuable experience that contributed to his teaching that confession and communion are the pillars of a good education. In John's youth, Jansenistic rigorism, which discouraged frequent communion, was still a powerful influence in Piedmont. We will return to this problem in chapter 19, note 7 and comment, and chapter 27.

Don Bosco always linked an adolescent's perseverance in virtue and his growth in the Christian life to the good advice, the encouragement, and the fatherly vigilance of the confessor. It should also be noted that he speaks of a "regular confessor," one who comes to know the heart of his penitent and therefore can offer sound spiritual guidance.

12. In Don Bosco's recollection, these years would probably be 1830–1832. He was in secondary school at Chieri from 1831 to 1835.

13. There was no school on Thursday afternoons, but there was on Saturday mornings.

Louis Comollo

Humanities and rhetoric •
Louis Comollo

When we had finished the first courses of *ginnasio*,[1] we had an inspection. The man who came to examine us on behalf of the School Reform Board[2] was a lawyer of outstanding merit, Prof. Fr Joseph Gazzani.[3] He was very kind to me, and I have always retained grateful memories of him; we have maintained a close, friendly relationship ever since. This good priest is still living in Upper Moltedo near Oneglia,[4] where he was born. Amongst his many charitable works, he endowed a scholarship at our college in Alassio[5] for a boy desirous of studying for the priesthood.

Though the examinations were conducted strictly, all forty-five in our class were promoted to the next class, which corresponds to our fourth year of *ginnasio*. I myself nearly failed for giving a copy of my work to others. If I was let through, I am indebted to the protection of my revered teacher Fr Giusiana, a Dominican. He set an extra paper for me, at which I did very well, and I was passed unanimously.[6]

In those days there was a praiseworthy practice by which the town awarded a prize to at least one student in each grade, remitting the twelve-franc tuition. To win this prize one had to be approved unanimously in both studies and conduct. I was lucky enough to be excused from this fee every year.[7]

That year I lost one of my dearest companions. Young Paul Braje, my dear, intimate friend, died on   in   [8] after a long illness. He was a model of piety, resignation, and living faith. He thus went to join St Aloysius,[9] whose

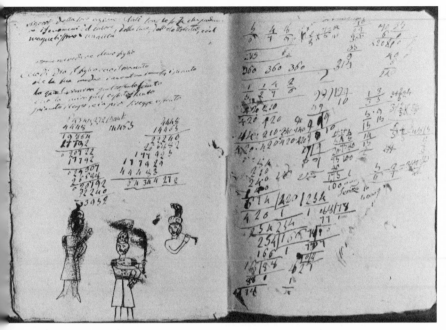

Like schoolboys everywhere, John Bosco doodled in his notebooks. This copybook of his dates from his years in Chieri.

faithful disciple he had been all his life. He was mourned by the whole college, and all the students turned out for his funeral. For a long time afterwards, during their holidays they would receive holy communion and recite the Little Office of Our Lady or the rosary for the soul of their dead friend.

To make up for this loss, however, God sent me another companion every bit as virtuous as Paul, and even more remarkable in his deeds. This was Louis Comollo, of whom I will have more to say in a moment.

At the end of my humanities year, I did very well. On the strength of my results, my teachers, especially Doctor Peter Banaudi, suggested I should ask to take the exam in philosophy;[10] and, in fact, I was promoted. But as I enjoyed my study of literature, I thought it better to continue my programme normally and take the rhetoric course, i.e. the fifth year of *ginnasio*, during 1833–34.[11] It was during that year that I met Comollo. The life of this precious friend has been told elsewhere,[12] and those who want can read it there. Here I mention only the incident that led to my noticing him amongst the humanities group.[13]

There was a rumour in the top form[14] that a saintly pupil was to join us that year. He was said to be the nephew of the provost of Cinzano,[15] an elderly priest with a reputation for sanctity. I was keen to get to know him, but I did not know his name. This is how we met: At that time it was common practice to initiate new students through a dangerous game called *cavallina*.[16] The giddy and less studious ones loved it, and generally they were the most skillful at it.

For several days they watched a reserved youngster of fifteen years[17] who had just registered at the college take his seat and settle down to read or study, heedless of the din going on round him. A boorish fellow came up to him, grabbed his arm, and insisted that he join them at *cavallina*.

"I don't know how," was the other's mortified and humble reply. "I don't know how; I've never played these games before."

"You better join us," said the aggressor, "or I'll kick and beat you till you do."

"You can treat me as you please, but I don't know what the game is, nor do I care to learn."

His crude and ill-natured fellow student grabbed his arm, shoved him, and gave him two slaps that were heard all over the room. That made my blood boil. But I held back for a moment to see if the boy under attack would give the offender what he had coming. He could easily have done so because he was older and stronger than the bully. You can imagine everyone's astonishment when the good youth, countenance red and almost livid, looked with pity at his malicious companion, and replied only, "Are you satisfied? Now go in peace; I've already forgiven you."

That heroic act made me want to know his name. It was, in fact, Louis Comollo, nephew of the provost of Cinzano, whose praises I had heard so often. From that moment on, he became my close friend, and I can say that from him I began to learn how to live as a Christian.[18] I trusted him completely and he trusted me. We needed each other: I needed spiritual help; he needed a bodyguard.

The shy and retiring Comollo never even tried to stand up to the vicious insults of our companions, whereas all of them — including those older and bigger than I — respected my mettle and my strength.[19]

That became evident one day when certain boys were bent on making fun of Comollo and another good-natured lad called Anthony Candelo. I wanted to intervene on their behalf, but the bullies gave me no heed. Another day when the harmless pair were being abused again, I shouted, "You'd better watch out. I'll deal with the next one who lays a finger on them."

A considerable number of the taller and bolder spirits ganged together to threaten me while Comollo got two smacks in the face. At that I forgot myself completely. Brute strength moved me, not reason.[20] With no chair or stick within reach, I grabbed one of my fellow students by the shoulders and swung him round like a club to beat the others. I knocked down four of them; the rest took to their heels yelling for mercy. Then what? At that moment the teacher came into the room. Seeing arms and legs flying everywhere amidst an out-of-this-world uproar, he began to shout and to strike blows left and right. The storm was about to burst upon me when he learned the cause of the disturbance. He demanded a replay of the action, or at least a show of my strength. The teacher laughed, and so did all the pupils. Everyone was so amazed that I escaped the punishment I deserved.

Comollo had a different lesson to teach me. When we could speak between ourselves, he said to me, "John my friend, I'm amazed how strong you are. But, believe me, God didn't give you strength to massacre your companions. His will is that we should love one another, forgive one another, and return good for evil."

I could only wonder at my companion's charity. I put myself entirely into his hands and let him guide me where and how he wished. By agreement with our friend Garigliano, we went together for confession, communion, meditation, spiritual reading, visits to the Blessed Sacrament, and serving Holy Mass. Comollo knew how to organise us with such gentle courtesy and sweetness that we could not refuse him.

I remember one day when we were passing a church; I was so engaged in chattering with a companion that I forgot to raise my cap. He corrected me at once, but so graciously: "John my friend," he said, "you're so lost in talking to men that you forget even the Lord's house."

Notes

1. This episode occurred at the end of the 1832–1833 school year. John had been in Chieri for two years and done the work of four years (classes 6, 5, 4, and 3).

2. The School Reform Board (*Magistrato della Riforma*) was responsible for supervising the educational reforms mandated in the Kingdom of Sardinia by the law of 1822. In 1833 the board sent an extraordinary visitor to preside at the final exams in the college at Chieri.

3. In BM I, 207, this name is spelled "Gozzani." According to the professor's grandnephew, the correct spelling is "Gazzano." Father Gazzano established the scholarship on March 1, 1872 (MB X, 317).

   In his first draft of the *Memoirs*, Don Bosco wrote, "In subsequent years he was very kind to me. In this year (1873) he is still living in Upper Moltedo near Oneglia and does many charitable works. The exams. . . . " When he reviewed the manuscript, he rewrote it, leaving the word "in" after "relationship," apparently intending to continue, "this year (1873)," but getting a little distracted by the new, complimentary subject he introduced, "This good priest. . . ."

4. More precisely, near Portomaurizio, which is a mile west of Oneglia on the Ligurian coast. The communes were united in 1923 as the city of Imperia. It is sixty miles southwest of Genoa.

5. The *collegio* became the primary Salesian apostolate from the 1860s till quite recently. Alassio is on the Mediterranean coast about fifty miles southwest of Genoa; the Salesians opened a school there in 1869.

6. The surviving records verify this. Father Hyacinth Giusiana (1774–1844) came from Cuneo, forty-five miles south of Turin. He taught grammar and was one of John's favorite teachers at Chieri.

7. No doubt there was more than luck involved in John's success. But being excused from even twelve lire's tuition was a blessing for the hard-pressed Boscos.

8. Don Bosco left the date of his friend's death blank. The family records include this note from Paul's father: "On July 10, 1832, Paul Victor Braia, aged twelve, went to his eternal rest. I can say without hesitation that this son of Philip and Catherine, nee Cafasso, must have gone straight to heaven."

   When Don Bosco begins this paragraph "In that year," the year in which he was promoted from the grammar section to the humanities year, he means the school year 1832–1833, not the calendar year 1832.

9. Saint Aloysius Gonzaga (1568–1591) was a young Jesuit of noble birth who died while caring for the sick during a plague. Noted for piety, obedience, and especially purity, he is regarded as one of the patron saints of and models for young people. He must have been particularly venerated in Chieri because his mother had been born there (her house is still standing). See NCE I, 332–333; Butler's *Lives*, II, 603–606; Maurice Meschler, *Life of St. Aloysius Gonzaga, Patron of Christian Youth* (Rockford, Illinois: TAN, 1985).

   Don Bosco held up Saint Aloysius as a model for his oratory boys and students and celebrated his feast (June 21) with great pomp. In choosing Aloysius as one of his work's patrons, Don Bosco was certainly influenced by the facts mentioned above; he may also have been influenced by Aloysius's status as a religious and a seminarian and possibly by such mundane touches as his own father's middle name and the first name of his great earthly patron, Louis Fransoni, archbishop of Turin from 1832 to 1862. Finally, there was the dearest friend of his youth, Louis Comollo, to whom Don Bosco will come in a moment. (*Luigi* is rendered as either "Aloysius" or "Louis" in English; this work uses the latter generally except for the Jesuit saint, who is almost universally known as Aloysius.)

10. Father Peter Banaudi, from Briga Marittima, taught rhetoric and humanities and was one of John's favorite teachers. He died in Turin on March 29, 1885, at the age of eighty-three. Don Bosco actually calls him *Dottor*, not *Teologo* as he does some of his other teachers (see chapter 7, note 9).

11. Actually, it was 1834–1835; when that school year ended, John was almost twenty years old.

12. Don Bosco published anonymously an eighty-two-page biography of Comollo in 1844. It was entitled *Cenni storici sulla vita di Luigi Comollo* ... [A Brief Life of Louis Comollo] (Turin: Speirani and Ferrero). See BM II, 152–156. Ten years later he printed a revised version in the *Catholic Readings* (January 10 and 25, 1854); this time he identified himself as the author. In 1884 he issued a third edition with various additions.

    Alberto Caviglia did an in-depth study of Comollo's biography in his edition of the works of Don Bosco (left incomplete at four volumes by Caviglia's death in 1943, with two more published posthumously). Caviglia made a happy discovery, becoming convinced that this biography contains a marvelous outline of the basic principles of Don Bosco's educational program. Caviglia wrote, "The spirit by which Don Bosco led to holiness the youngsters whom he educated and then memorialized in his writings is the same spirit that lives in the two young men Comollo and Bosco." He then added, "The figure, the actions, and the spirit of Comollo are an indispensable ingredient for understanding Don Bosco's youth and the development of his character. This is even more true for understanding his life before his priestly ordination."

    Caviglia's work, incidentally, is to be distinguished from the *Opere edite e inedite di San Giovanni Bosco* [Complete Works of Saint John Bosco], reprinted in thirty-eight volumes by the Center for Studies on Don Bosco at the Salesian Pontifical University (Rome: LAS, 1976–1977, 1987).

13. The humanities and rhetoric groups met in one classroom with one teacher. Comollo was a year behind John in school.

14. In the rhetoric class.

15. Louis's uncle — his great-uncle, actually — was Father Joseph Comollo (1757–1843). As provost, he exercised some authority over the other clergy of the town of Cinzano, about five miles north-northwest of Castelnuovo.

16. Don Bosco uses his Piedmontese dialect here; in Italian the game is called *cavalluccio*. It is a game a little like leapfrog, but the lads see how many can pile onto one victim's back.

17. Peter Louis Comollo was born April 7, 1817, in the hamlet of Pra in the commune of Cinzano. From his childhood he hoped to become a priest and was noted for his piety. In the fall of 1834, when John first met him, Louis was seventeen.

18. From Comollo, John learned a more perfect practice of virtue. Stella (LW, p. 32), noting Don Bosco's tendency to hyperbole, writes:

> John discovered great spiritual richness in [Comollo]. . . . Now athirst for the interior life, John was really defending the source and wellspring that he was seeking for his own soul's sake. He was defending the incarnation of the very ideal that seemed to be his own. John had already been moving toward it on his own, but his encounter with the virtuous Comollo tripped the tension wire in his heart. Seeing in him a *hero*, John wanted to be his friend.

19. It seems strange that John, at nineteen — or even seventeen, according to his memory — should have schoolmates "older and bigger" than himself. On the other hand, when he was fully grown he was only 5'4" tall (BM IV, 120). He proved his strength many times throughout his life; cf. BM IV, 492; VI, 116; VIII, 410; MB XVI, 636; XVII, 205; XVIII, 479, 490.

20. Don Bosco judges his youthful energy rather severely; but in that energy he reveals to us his natural spirit and generosity.

11

Various Events

Waiter and bartender •
A feast day • *A tragedy*

We pass on from school affairs to certain events by way of diversion. I changed lodgings during my humanities year to be nearer my teacher, Fr Banaudi, and to help John Pianta, a friend of the family, who came to Chieri that year to open a café.[1]

The lodging certainly had its dangers,[2] but as I was moving in with exemplary Catholics and was continuing my friendship with good companions, I was able to make the change without fear of moral danger.

When I finished my homework, I had a lot of spare time; I used to devote part of it to reading the Latin and Italian classics and the rest to making liquors and jams. Halfway through that year I was in a position to prepare coffee and chocolate; I knew the recipes for many kinds of sweets, drinks, ices, and various refreshments. My landlord began by giving me free lodging. Then, gauging the boost I could give to his business, he made me an attractive offer; he tried to induce me to give up my other concerns and work full time for him. But I was doing that work only for fun and relaxation; I had no intention of giving up my studies.

Professor Banaudi was a model teacher. Without having recourse to corporal punishment, he succeeded in making all his pupils respect and love him. He loved them all as if they were his own sons, and they loved him like an affectionate father.[3]

To show our appreciation, we planned a surprise for his feast day.[4] We decided to write both poetic and prose pieces for the celebration, and we had little presents which we thought he would especially like. The event was a splendid success. Our teacher was pleased beyond words, and as a token of appreciation, he took us on a picnic in the country. It was a wonderful day; both teacher and pupils were of one spirit, and each of us strove for ways to express the joy in his heart.

As we made our way back to Chieri, our teacher met someone we did not know, and he had to go off with the man; we were left by ourselves on the road for a little while. At that point some of our companions from the upper classes came up to us and invited us to go swimming with them at a place called Fontana Rossa,[5] about a mile from Chieri.[6]

I was against the idea, and so were some of my companions; but it was no use. A few came home with me while the others wanted to go swimming. It was a regrettable decision. A few hours after we got home, two of our picnic group ran in, breathless and frightened.

"Oh, if you only knew what a terrible thing's happened!" they gasped, "Philip N., who insisted so much that we go swimming, is dead."

"What!" we all exclaimed. "Philip was a good swimmer."

"Maybe he was," went on the excited messenger. "To encourage us to dive in with him, he jumped in, full of confidence, but unaware of the dangerous whirlpools in the Fontana Rossa. We waited for him to surface, but he did not appear. We raised the alarm. When help arrived, the rescuers tried everything, even at risk to themselves. It was an hour and a half later before they recovered the body."

The tragedy depressed all of us. There was no more talk of swimming that year nor the following one (1834).[7]

Some time ago I happened to meet a few of my old friends from those days. We recalled the drowning of our companion at the Fontana Rossa whirlpool with real regret.[8]

Notes

1. The two reasons Don Bosco gives for his change of lodging were really secondary. The main reason was that John Bap-

tist Matta had finished his secondary studies, and he and his mother had returned to Castelnuovo.

Joseph—not John—Pianta was not only a friend of the Boscos from Morialdo, but a distant kinsman of Margaret (Molineris, p. 185). He was Lucy Matta's brother, which means of course that she too was related to Margaret. In 1833 he went to Chieri to open a coffee shop—what is called a "bar" in Italy nowadays. Margaret asked him to board John and look after him. During the day John was to do his schoolwork, and in the evenings he was to help Pianta manage the billiard room. The billiard room also had a piano. Every week Margaret brought John some bread and other food for his main meals, while Pianta was responsible for John's soup (a substantial meal in itself).

Pianta's place was in the Vergnano house at 3 via Palazzo di Città. It is now an ice cream shop. The café measured about twenty feet by twenty. What was the billiard room, slightly larger at twenty feet by twenty-three, is now a small tailor's shop. The house is just a few yards from the Church of Saint Anthony the Abbot, which made it conve-

The place where John Pianta set up his café and billiard hall is now marked by a commemorative plaque that records John Bosco's stay there. When he had leisure time, John often met with his friends here.

nient for John to go to daily Mass. The church is at the corner of Chieri's main square, the piazza d'Armi, and via Vittorio Emanuele and is staffed by the Jesuits. Saint Anthony's was the primary meeting place of the Society for a Good Time and of the regular school assemblies for church services.

When John came to Chieri for the opening of school, however, Pianta had not finished setting up his café. So John had to seek temporary lodging with the baker Michael Cavallo — not in his house but in his stable. (Lemoyne calls him Cavalli in BM I, 216.) John earned his keep by caring for the horse and by tending Cavallo's vines a little way out of town. The youth asked only that he be free on Saturday evenings to go to confession. What was the Cavallo stable is still extant across the street from the Vergnano house. This arrangement did not last long, for some good people — just who, we do not know — noticed John's plight and urged Pianta to get on with opening his coffee shop.

2. The dangers that John perceived came from the example given by the customers who frequented Pianta's bar: gambling at billiards and other games, frivolous use of hours at a time, and offensive language.

When the aged Pianta met the Salesians John Bonetti, John Baptist Francesia, and Joachim Berto in Chieri on May 10, 1888, he told them,

> It would have been next to impossible to find a better lad than John Bosco. Every morning saw him on his way to serve several Masses in St. Anthony's Church. I had with me at home at that time my aged and sickly mother; it was really impressive to see how kindly he treated her. John would quite often spend entire nights with his books; in the morning I would still find him reading and writing by the light of his lamp. (BM I, 217)

However, good Pianta did not see fit to bring up the question of the "spacious" room he had given the young man to sleep in. Lemoyne describes it in this way:

> John's bed was a narrow strip over a small oven that was used for baking pastry. John reached it with a small ladder. But when he stretched out in these confined quarters his feet dangled beyond the thin straw-filled pallet and over the edge of the oven (BM I, 216).

This cubbyhole was in a small passageway, 11.6 feet long by 6.6 feet high by 2.6 feet wide, between the coffee room and the billiard room.

When Don Bosco was canonized in 1934, the people of

Chieri celebrated the event by placing tablets at many of the sites associated with his ten years as a resident there. One such memorial was put on Pianta's former shop, recalling young John's sacrifices. It also mentions his young friend Joseph Blanchard (1818–1893), who sometimes gave John gifts of fruits and vegetables to satisfy his hunger. The Blanchards, who were grocers, had another apartment in the Vergnano house from November 1833 till August 1834 (Molineris, p. 191).

3. Don Bosco, himself an educator with over thirty years of experience behind him at the time of writing, calls Father Banaudi a model teacher. He has singled out the fact that his teacher did not have to use punishments to make himself respected; rather, he used fatherly love for his pupils. We may suppose that Father Banaudi's methodology made a deep impression on his young student. Certainly Don Bosco describes his methodology in words that echo the Preventive System.

4. It is not hard to imagine that John was the chief organizer of the surprise party.

5. This is the local name of a stream that rushes down from the nearby hills on the northwest side of the city. It takes its name, which means "Red Fountain," from its rust-colored waters.

6. The Piedmontese mile is 2466 meters, or roughly a mile and a half in the English measure.

7. This sad event occurred in 1834, during John's humanities year of 1833–1834. Father Peter Banaudi's name day was June 29; so we may place Philip's drowning in early July, though Molineris (p. 225) suggests June 28. Molineris tried, unsuccessfully, to identify further the unfortunate boy who drowned, but he never completed his search.

The next year, the rhetoric year, John's teacher was the priest Doctor John Bosco, whose name was the same as the saint's but who was not a relative. Don Bosco mentions him in the biography of Comollo: "He had become an idol of the whole student body because of his kindness, his patience, the courteous way he dealt with all the students, and the interest he took in helping them succeed in their studies."

Divine Providence was remarkably preparing the future apostle of youth by setting before him outstanding examples of men who educated by means of loving kindness (Desramaut, *SouAut*, p. 72).

8. Don Bosco has passed over several other events of this period. On May 9, 1833, Joseph Bosco married Domenica Febbraro. The couple would have ten children. Joseph had been leasing farmland from the Mattas at Sussambrino since 1831 (see chapter 6, note 9), where his partner was Joseph Febbraro.

On August 4, 1833, John was confirmed by Archbishop John Anthony Gianotti of Sassari in Saint Blaise's Church at Buttigliera d'Asti. This was the same church to which young John had gone to hear the missionary preachers in the jubilee year of 1829. The sponsors for all seventy-two confirmands were Mayor Joseph Marsano of Buttigliera and Countess Josephine Melina. Those confirmed ranged in age from seven to twenty-nine. (BM I, 207; Molineris, pp. 198–199)

Joseph Cafasso was ordained a priest on September 21, 1833, and celebrated his first Mass at Castelnuovo soon after.

12

A Jewish Friend

Jonah

While I was still a humanities student lodging at John Pianta's café, I got to know a Jewish youngster called Jonah. He was about eighteen, was remarkably good looking, and had an exceptionally fine singing voice. He was a good billiards player too.

We met at Elijah's bookstore,[1] and he would always ask for me as soon as he came into the shop. I liked him a lot, and he was very attached to me. Every spare minute he had, he spent in my room; we sang together, played the piano, or read. He liked to hear the thousand little stories I used to tell.[2]

One day he got into a difficult quarrel which could have had sorry consequences for him. He came running to me for advice.

"Jonah, my friend," I said to him, "if you were a Christian, I would advise you to go to confession.[3] But in your case, that's not possible."

"But we Jews can go to confession, if we want to."

"Go to confession by all means, but your confessor is not obliged to secrecy. Neither can he forgive your sins or administer any sacraments."

"If you'll take me, I'll go to a priest."

"I could do that for you, but a lot of preparation is necessary."

"What sort of preparation?"

"Confession takes away sins committed after baptism. If you wish to receive any of the other sacraments, you must receive baptism first."

"What must I do to be baptized?"

"You must be instructed in the Christian religion. You must believe in Jesus Christ, true God and true man. After that you can be baptized."

"What good will baptism do me?"

"It wipes out original sin, and actual sins too.[4] It opens the way to the other sacraments. Finally, it makes you a child of God and an heir to heaven."

"We Jews cannot be saved?"

"No, my dear Jonah; since Jesus Christ came, the Jews cannot be saved unless they believe in him."[5]

"If it comes to my mother's ears that I want to become a Christian, heaven help me!"

"Don't be afraid; God is the master of all hearts. If he calls you to become a Christian, he will do it in such a way as to satisfy your mother, or provide in some way for the good of your soul."

"You are such a good friend of mine; if you were in my place, what would you do?"

"I would begin to take instruction in the Christian religion. Anyway, God will show you what to do in the future. Take this little catechism and begin to study it. Pray that God will enlighten you, and he will help you to know the truth."

From that day onward Jonah became attracted to the Christian faith. He used to come to the café and, after he played a game of billiards, he would come looking for me to discuss religion and the catechism. In a few months he had learned to make the sign of the cross, could say the *Pater*, the *Ave Maria*, and the *Credo*,[6] and knew the other principal truths of the faith. He was very happy and became better every day in his speech and his actions.

Jonah had been left fatherless as a child. His mother Rachel had heard vague reports about Jonah's intentions, but as yet she knew nothing certain. This is how the news broke: One day, while making Jonah's bed she came across his catechism, which he had inadvertently left under his mattress.

She went screaming through the house, took the catechism to the rabbi, and suspecting what was afoot, rushed to the student Bosco's lodgings. She had often heard her son speak of him. Picture to yourselves ugliness itself, and you will have an idea of Jonah's mother. She was blind in one eye and deaf in both ears; she had a big nose, hardly any teeth, and a long, pointed chin; she was thick lipped, with a twisted mouth; her voice sounded like the squeal of a foal.[7] The other Jews used to call her the "Lilith the Witch," a name they use for the ugliest thing they can imagine.[8]

I got a fright when I saw her. Before I had time to recover, she opened up on me: "I swear you've done wrong! Yes, you! You've ruined my Jonah. You've brought public disgrace on him. I don't know what will become of him. I'm afraid he'll end up a Christian, and you'll have been the cause of it."

I understood then who she was and of whom she was speaking; as calmly as I could, I explained that she ought to be happy about it and to thank me for doing him so much good.

"And what's the good of that? Is it a good thing for a person to deny his own religion?"

"Calm down, my good woman," I said to her. "Listen. I didn't go looking for your son Jonah. We met in Elijah's bookshop. We became friends without any special reason. He's very fond of me, and I like him too. As his true friend, I want him to save his soul and to get to know our religion, because outside it no one can be saved. Good mother of Jonah, please note that I only gave your son a book and told him to study it. If he becomes a Christian, he does not abandon his Jewish religion; he perfects it."

"If Jonah should have the misfortune to become a Christian, he would have to abandon our prophets, because Christians do not believe in Abraham, Isaac, and Jacob, nor in Moses and the prophets."

"We do believe in all the holy patriarchs and prophets of the Bible. Their writings, their sayings, and their prophecies are the foundation of the Christian faith."

"If our rabbi were only here, he would know how to answer you. I know neither the *Mishnah* nor the *Gemara* (the two parts of the *Talmud*).[9] But what is to become of my poor Jonah?"

So saying, she left. It would be too long to recount the many attacks that the mother, the rabbi, and various of Jonah's relatives made on me. Neither threats nor violence had any effect on that courageous young man; he withstood them all and continued to take instruction.

Since he was no longer safe amongst his family, he had to leave home and live almost as a beggar. Many people came to his aid. And that all might be done with due prudence, I recommended my pupil to a learned priest who took a fatherly interest in him. When Jonah's religious instructions were completed, he was impatient to become a Christian. A solemnity was arranged that set a good example for all the people of Chieri. Other Jews were impressed too, and later several others embraced Christianity.

Jonah's godparents were Charles and Octavia Bertinetti, who provided what the neophyte needed. After becoming a Catholic, he was able to earn an honest livelihood by his own efforts.[10] The newly-baptized's name was Aloysius.[11]

Notes

1. The Jews of Chieri lived in their own ghetto along via della Pace, as prescribed by the laws of King Charles Felix (1821–1831). They were regarded as second-class citizens, officially tolerated. Jonah's home was at the corner of via della Pace and via d'Albussano. The home and bookstore of Elijah Foa were at 12 via della Pace.

2. John and Jonah had several things in common that helped make them fast friends: they were the same age, they were both highly talented, and they were both fatherless. They used to meet in a spot in Pianta's café — probably in the billiard hall, since the piano was there — where there was room during the day to study or host a friend during John's rare moments of leisure.

   John's friendship for this Jewish youth was not an isolated event. Lemoyne (BM I, 231) cites testimony to his practical kindness. John noticed the trouble that several Jewish boys had with Saturday schoolwork. To prevent their having to violate their sabbath or else suffer the ridicule of their schoolmates for not doing their work, he would do it for them.

3. In the 1830s, to be a Christian in Italy was practically equivalent to being a Catholic. Don Bosco realized that Protestants could not receive the sacrament of penance either. The British statesman Lord Palmerston once visited the Oratory. When he saw five hundred boys working quietly in a single study hall, without a teacher monitoring them, he was astonished. He asked Don Bosco how that was possible.

"Sir," his host answered, "we possess a means unknown to you."

"How is that?"

"It's a secret revealed only to Catholics."

"And what is that secret?"

"Frequent confession and communion, and daily Mass heard with devotion."

"You're right," the visitor confessed. "We lack those powerful means of education. But can they be substituted?"

"If we don't use the means supplied by religion, we must use threats and the cane."

"Absolutely right. Religion or the cane! I'll inform my government."

This episode, taken from archival material, is recounted in the *Salesian Bulletin*, October 1922, p. 259.

4. More specifically, baptism cancels the actual, or personal, sins that one may have committed before baptism. As John told Jonah earlier, Catholics hold that sacramental penance (confession) is necessary for the forgiveness of serious sins committed after baptism. Original sin is the sin inherited by the whole human race from their first ancestors (cf. Genesis 3:1–24; Romans 5:12–21).

5. Don Bosco describes his conversation with his young friend without making any distinctions. According to the teaching of the Catholic Church:

1. There is no salvation apart from Jesus Christ, and the way to Jesus Christ is through his Church.

2. Those who know that it is God's will that they should belong to the Catholic Church are obliged in conscience to join his Church, or they will be lost.

3. One who honestly tries to please God according to the light of his own natural reason implicitly and unconsciously desires to belong to the Church and to be saved through Jesus Christ. Such a person will be saved. (See, for example, Saint Thomas Aquinas, *Summa theologiae*, III, 8, 3 ad 1; and III, 68, 2.)

Pope Pius XII excommunicated the American Jesuit

Leonard Feeney for teaching that one had to belong explicitly to the Roman Catholic Church in order to be saved (Letter of the Holy Office to the Archbishop of Boston, August 8, 1949 [DS 3866–3872], quoted in J. Neuner, SJ, and J. Dupuis, SJ, ed., *The Christian Faith in the Doctrinal Documents of the Catholic Church* [Westminster, Maryland: Christian Classics, 1975], pp. 235–37.)

John came closest to the Church's teaching when he told Jonah, "God will . . . provide in some way for the good of your soul."

For a summary of the Church's teaching on Judaism since the Second Vatican Council, see the comment at the end of the notes.

6. The Our Father, the Hail Mary, and the Apostles' Creed in Latin.

7. A foal is not yet able to give forth the full neigh of a grown horse. It is nearer to a grunt than a whinny. Don Bosco seems to have wanted to avoid the rougher but more common expression "grunt like a pig." All in all, Don Bosco's unflattering picture of Jonah's mother does no credit to his usual sensitivity to people.

8. There were various Jewish legends about Lilith, whose name comes from Isaiah 34:14 (the RSV renders it "the night hag"). Originally she was a female demon whose name comes from Akkadian. Medieval folklore turned her into the woman who deceived Adam and into a ghost that wandered around at night, devouring children.

9. *Talmud* means literally "instruction." It is the final codification of Jewish law, based on the scriptures and oral tradition, and it dates from the third and fourth centuries. It has two parts, the Mishnah and the Gemara. The first, from the second century, contains the traditional oral law; the Gemara, literally "completion," expands upon the Mishnah through the commentaries of Jewish scholars.

10. The records at Chieri verify the baptism. However, the name is not given as Jonah. Jonah may have been a middle name or a nickname. It is also possible that Don Bosco used a fictitious name to permit the man a certain anonymity. The record for 1834 reads thus:

> Bolmida. On 10 August I, Sebastian Schioppo, theologian and canon curate, by permission of the Archbishop of Turin, solemnly baptized a certain Jewish young man of Chieri named James Levi, aged 18. I gave him the name Aloysius, Hyacinth,

Lawrence, Octavian, Maria Bolmida. The godparents were Hyacinth Bolmida and Octavia Mary Bertinetti. (Stella, LW, p. 32, n. 68)

Charles Bertinetti was not the godfather, after all. He was probably there with his wife. Don Bosco's memory has slipped slightly again. See also chapter 16, note 14.

The convert lived as a faithful Christian and retained affection and gratitude toward his friend John. Lemoyne met him at the Oratory around 1880 (BM I, 243).

11. It is possible that John suggested this name himself. We have already noted his devotion to Saint Aloysius (see chapter 10, note 9). In the first five months of his priesthood (from June 10 to November 2, 1841), Don Bosco was an assistant to the provost of Castelnuovo. Lemoyne asserts that the parochial baptismal register there shows that practically all the boys that Don Bosco baptized had Aloysius for either their first or their middle name (BM II, 14). When Molineris checked the records for that period, he discovered that Don Bosco baptized only three boys, one of whom was named Luigi (pp. 264–265).

It is equally possible that John had nothing to do with the choice. Saint Aloysius was already very popular in Chieri, and the name was commonly given.

Comment on Catholicism and Judaism

Vatican II refined the teaching of the Catholic Church on the Church's role in the salvation of the human race in *Lumen gentium* and in *Nostra aetate*. The former, the Constitution on the Church, affirms that everyone is called to belong to God's people, i.e. the Church, which is necessary for salvation by the explicit will of Christ (no. 13) and subsists fully in the Roman Catholic Church; mere membership is insufficient, though, for one must "persevere in charity" (no. 14). Those who reverence the sacred scriptures, believe in the Trinity, and are consecrated in baptism are also part of the Church even if "they do not profess the faith in its entirety" and are not in communion with Peter's successor (no. 15).

> Those who have not yet received the gospel are related in various ways to the People of God. . . . Nor does divine Providence deny the help necessary for salvation to those who, without blame on their part, have not yet arrived at an explicit knowledge of God, but who strive to live a good life, thanks to His grace. (no. 16, quoted in the Abbott edition, New York, 1966)

Nostra aetate is the Council's Declaration on the Relationship of the Church to Non-Christian Religions. This landmark document's no. 4 speaks of the Jewish people and says, in particular, "The Jews still remain most dear to God because of their fathers, for He does not repent of the gifts He makes nor of the call He issues. . . . "

When Pope John Paul II made his historic visit to the synagog of Rome on April 13, 1986, he alluded to the riches of *Nostra aetate*. He then emphasized three points, quoting several times from that document's fourth paragraph:

> The first is that the Church of Christ discovers her "bond" with Judaism by "searching into her own mystery." The Jewish religion is not "extrinsic" to us, but in a certain way is "intrinsic" to our own religion. With Judaism, therefore, we have a relationship which we do not have with any other religion. You (the Jews) are our dearly beloved brothers and, in a certain way, it could be said that you are our elder brothers.

> The second point noted by the Council is that no ancestral or collective blame can be imputed to the Jews as a people for "what happened in Christ's passion" — not indiscriminately to the Jews of that time, nor to those who came afterwards. . . . So any alleged theological justification for discriminatory measures . . . is unfounded. The Lord will judge each one "according to his own works," Jews and Christians alike (cf. Romans 2:6).

> The third point . . . is a consequence of the second. Notwithstanding the Church's awareness of her own identity, it is not lawful to say that the Jews are "repudiated or cursed," as if this were taught or could be deduced from the sacred scriptures or the New Testament. Indeed, the Council had already said . . . that the Jews are beloved of God, who has called them with an irrevocable calling (cf. *Lumen gentium*, no. 16, and Romans 11:28–29).

A major Church statement on racism, issued February 10, 1989, resoundingly condemned anti-Semitism as "the most tragic form that racist ideology has assumed in our century" and reminded the world that "entertaining racist attitudes is a sin" (*New York Times*, February 11, 1989, pp. 1, 4).

Black Magic

Games • Conjuring tricks •
Self-defense

In the midst of my studies and other interests, such as singing, music, speech training, and dramatics,[1] which I undertook wholeheartedly, I also learned a variety of new games: card tricks, marbles, quoits, walking on stilts, running and jumping, all of which I enjoyed and in which I was by no means mediocre, even if I was no champion. Some of these activities I had learned at Murialdo, others at Chieri. If in the fields of Murialdo I was only a beginner, that year I developed into something of a master. At that time, not much was known about these sports because they had not been much publicised; so in the popular estimate they were a source of wonder.

What shall I say of these skills? I often gave performances both in public and in private. Since I had an exceptional memory, I knew by heart long passages from the classics, the poets particularly. I could quote at will from Dante, Petrarch, Tasso, Parini, Monti,[2] and others as if they were my own. Likewise, I could thus improvise without any trouble. In those entertainments or concerts, sometimes I sang, sometimes I played an instrument, or sometimes I composed verses which were highly praised — though in reality they were nothing more than excerpts from various authors adapted for the occasion. That is why I have never given any of my compositions to anyone. Whatever I did write down, I have burned.[3]

Conjuring was a source of wonder. People sat wide-eyed at the sight of an endless stream of balls coming out of a little box too small to hold even one, or eggs tumbling out of a little bag. But when they saw me producing balls from bystanders' noses, or heard me tell accurately how much money people had in their pockets, or when they watched me crush coins to dust between my fingers, my audiences got frightened and even lost their heads; they began to whisper that I was a sorcerer, that I had to be in league with the devil.

My landlord Thomas Cumino[4] added to the credibility of this idea. Thomas was a fervent Christian, and he loved a joke. I knew how to take advantage of his character, and I would say, his simplicity, to embarrass him thoroughly. One day, for his feast day he had very carefully prepared chicken and jelly as a treat for his lodgers.[5] But when he carried the dish to the table and uncovered it, out popped a live cock, flapping about and cackling in a thousand ways. Another time he had a pot of macaroni cooked and ready to serve, but at the last moment he found the pot full of dry bran. Sometimes when he filled the bottle with wine, he would find as he poured it out that it had turned to water. When he wanted a drink of water, he would find his glass full of wine instead. Sweets changed into pieces of bread, coins in his purse into pieces of rusty tin. A hat became a nightcap; nuts changed into pebbles right in the sack. These were everyday occurrences.

Good Thomas was nonplussed. "These things are not human," he would mutter to himself. "God does not waste time with such frivolities. It must be the work of the devil."

He did not dare mention these matters at home, so he sought advice from a nearby priest, Fr Bertinetti. Suspecting "white magic"[6] as the explanation of these tricks, he decided to refer the matter to the school superintendent, who was at that time a respected cleric, Canon Burzio, archpriest and parish priest of the cathedral.[7]

The canon was a learned man, pious and prudent, and without speaking to others asked me *ad audiendum verbum*.[8] When I arrived at his house, I found him saying his Office.[9] Smiling at me, he made a sign for me to wait. When he had finished, he asked me to follow him into his study. There he began to question me, very politely, but with a serious look.

"My friend, so far I am quite pleased with your conduct and the progress you have made in your studies. Now, however, you are the subject of much talk. They tell me you are a mind reader, that you can guess how much money people have in their pockets, that you can make black seem white, that you can tell what is happening at a distance, and similar things. That makes people talk about you. In fact, some have gone farther and suspect you of being a sorcerer or even that the devil is at work here. Tell me now, who taught you this knowledge? Or where did you pick it up? Tell me everything in complete confidence. I assure you that I will not use it except for your own good."

Keeping a straight face, I asked him for a few minutes to think over my reply. Then I asked him to tell me what time it was. He put his hand into his pocket, but his watch was not there.

"If you haven't got your watch," I suggested, "could you give me a five-soldi coin?"[10]

He checked all his pockets but could not find his purse.

"You rascal," he shouted angrily, "Either you are the devil's servant, or he's yours! You've already stolen my purse and my watch. I can't keep quiet any longer; I must denounce you. Even now I don't know what keeps me from giving you a good thrashing."

However, when he saw that I was smiling serenely, he got hold of himself and went on more calmly. "Now let's take this quietly. Explain these mysteries to me. How was it possible for my watch and my purse to vanish from my pocket unknown to me. Where are they?"

"Well, Father," I began respectfully, "I'll explain in a few words. It's all a matter of sleight of hand, information, and preparation."

"What information could you have about my watch and purse?"

"I'll explain it all quickly. Just after I came in, you gave some alms to a beggar. You left your purse on a priedieu. Then you went into another room, leaving your watch on that side table. I hid them both; you thought you had them on your person, while they were really under this lampshade." So saying, I lifted the lampshade and recovered both objects that the devil was supposed to have taken away.

The good canon had a hearty laugh. He asked me to give him a demonstration of sleight of hand, and how to make things appear and disappear. He enjoyed it all and gave me a little gift. Finally, he told me, "Go and tell your friends that wonderment is the result of ignorance."[11]

Notes

1. Part of the reason why Don Bosco became a successful educator was that he incorporated all these activities, and sports too, into his system. From the first, he seemed to know instinctively that these means would attract young-sters, to whom he could then introduce Jesus and Mary.

2. All his life Don Bosco treasured the poetry of Dante Alighieri (1265–1321) and could quote extensive passages from the *Divine Comedy* from memory. Francesco Petrarca (1304–1374), poet and diplomat, helped inspire the Renais-sance. Torquato Tasso (1544–1595) wrote epic and dramatic poetry and is best known for *Jerusalem Delivered*. Giuseppe Parini (1729–1799) is best known for his satiric epic *The Day*. Vincenzo Monti (1754–1828) was a poet, professor, and historian.

3. He forgot to burn some. We have been able to find an exer-cise book of his entitled "A Collection of Sonnets and Vari-ous Poems." He began this particular collection on May 27, 1835. Together with items by various authors and friends there are also a few of his own compositions. Among other things is a sonnet which he titled "The Constancy of Pius VII under Napoleon's Oppression." On the front page he wrote, *Quidquid agunt homines, intentio iudicat omnes* (Their intention is the measure of whatever men may do). Above that inscription is a note in Lemoyne's writing, indicating that Don Bosco left this copybook to his faithful friend before he died.

4. In 1834–1835, the last year of John's *ginnasio*, the pastor of Castelnuovo, Father Anthony Cinzano, sent him to lodge with the Cumino family. Earlier, Joseph Cafasso had also boarded with them for four years. Father Cinzano provided eight lire a month to cover John's room and board (BM I, 248).

The Cumino house is at 24 via Vittorio Emanuele, near Saint Anthony's Church. Mr. Cumino was a tailor. He offered John one of his storerooms as a bedroom. After a few months, Father Cafasso managed to get better treatment for John.

Ceria notes that John had to tend a vineyard and look after a horse belonging to Mr. Cumino (MO, p. 71); he appears to have confused this arrangement with John's earlier stay with Michael Cavallo (chapter 11, note 1).

5. Italians celebrate a person's feast day (name day) more than his birthday; it is customary for the one celebrating to give gifts or a treat rather than to receive them.

6. There had been a distinction between white magic and black magic since the Middle Ages. The latter was diabolical. White magic was understood to be natural, based on laws of physics that most people would not grasp. From the context it seems that John was accused of practicing black magic rather than the white that he records here and in the opening line of the next chapter.

7. Canon Maximus Burzio rented rooms in the Bertinettis' apartment house — which the couple would one day leave to Don Bosco (see chapter 16, note 15). From 1840 to 1863 the canon was pastor of Moncucco, where John had stayed with the Moglias from February 1827 to November 1829.

8. This was a legal term which means here, basically, "to tell him what was going on" (Desramaut, *SouAut*, p. 81).

9. The Divine Office consists of psalms, hymns, scripture readings, readings from the Fathers of the Church, and prayers. Priests, religious, and other Christians pray the Office at various times (hours) during the course of the day; hence it is also called the Liturgy of the Hours. The principal hours are readings (also called vigils, formerly called matins), morning prayer (formerly called lauds), and evening prayer (vespers). The lesser hours in Don Bosco's time were prime, terce, sext, none, and night prayer (compline); the reform of Vatican II has reduced these to two hours, midday prayer and night prayer, besides simplifying the main hours.

10. A soldo was worth five centesimi, or one-twentieth of a lira.

11. John quotes the canon's advice in Latin: *ignorantia est magistra admirationis.*

Champion Acrobat

*A race • A jump • The magic
wand • The top of the tree*

Now that I had been cleared of white magic in my amusements, I began to collect my companions round me again and to entertain them as before. Just at that time, there was a certain acrobat whom some folks praised to the skies. He had put on a public show, racing from one end of Chieri to the other in two and a half minutes, almost as fast as a speeding train.[1] Paying little attention to the consequences, one day I said that I would like to take on this braggart.[2] An imprudent companion told the acrobat, so I found myself with a challenge on my hands: *schoolboy challenges professional runner!*

The course chosen was a stretch of the Turin Highway,[3] and there was a side bet of 20 francs. I did not have that kind of money, so some of my friends in the Society for a Good Time had to come to the rescue. The event attracted a big crowd. When the the race began, my opponent got a lead on me. I soon caught up with him, however, passed him, and before we had reached the halfway mark he was so far behind that he dropped out.

"Well," he said to me, "I challenge you to a long jump, but this time I want to raise the wager to 40 francs, and more if you wish."

I took him on. He picked the place where we were to jump. The landing area was close to the parapet of a little bridge. He had first jump and he landed so close to the wall that you could not jump any further. It looked like there was no way I could win. But my skill came to the rescue. I landed in his tracks, and putting my hands on the bridge wall, I vaulted not only the parapet itself but a ditch beyond it. There was a great cheer.

"I want to challenge you, yet again," he said, "to any test of skill you want to name."

I accepted, choosing the game of the "magic wand."[4] The wager this time was 8o francs. Taking the rod, I hung a hat on one end of it while I placed the other in the palm of my hand. Then, without using the other hand, I made the rod hop from the tip of my little finger to ring finger, middle finger, index finger, and thumb; then to the knuckles, elbow, shoulder, chin, lips, nose, forehead; and then, by the same route, back to the palm of my hand.[5]

"No problem," my rival remarked. "This is my favorite event." He took the same rod and, with consummate skill, he made the rod travel up to his lips; unfortunately for him, his long nose got in the way and the rod lost its balance. He had to grab at it to save it from falling.

Seeing his money vanish again, the poor fellow blurted out in a rage, "No humiliation could be worse than being beaten by a schoolboy. I have one hundred francs left. That much I'll bet you I'll get my feet nearer the top of that tree than you will." He pointed to an elm tree beside the road.

We accepted again, though we were sorry for him and half wished him to win; we did not want to ruin him.

He climbed the elm first. He got his feet so high that had he gone any farther, [the tree][6] would have broken and thrown him to the ground. Everyone said it was impossible to climb any higher.

Now it was my turn. I climbed as high as I could without bending the tree. Then I grasped the trunk firmly in both hands, raised my body, and swung my feet up till they were about three feet above the spot that my rival had reached.

Who could ever describe the applause of the crowd, the joy of my companions, the anger of the acrobat, and my own pride at having defeated not just some fellow student but this swaggering braggart?

He was absolutely devastated; however, we tried to comfort him. Moved to pity by the poor man's sadness, we said we would return his money on one condition: that he treat

us to a dinner at Muretto's Restaurant.[7] He agreed gratefully. Twenty-two of us went, so many were my supporters.
The meal cost 25 francs, so he got back 215 francs.[8]

It had indeed been a Thursday[9] of great joy. I was covered in glory[10] for having beaten in skill a braggart. My
companions were delighted too, for they could not have
been better entertained than by a good laugh and a good
dinner. The braggart himself was pleased because he had
got back nearly all his money and enjoyed a good meal
besides. As he took leave of us, he thanked us all, saying:
"In handing back this money, you've saved me from ruin.
You have my heartfelt gratitude. I'll always remember you
gratefully, but I won't make any more bets with schoolboys."

Notes

1. In 1835, when this happened, there were no railroads in the
   Kingdom of Sardinia.

2. Don Bosco is silent about the reason for his challenge. The
   man used to give shows in the piazza d'Armi on Sundays,
   drawing many youngsters away from Saint Anthony's
   Church. John had tried to get him to suspend his activities
   during the hours of the liturgical services, but he refused.

3. This lovely old road is to the left of the present main road
   coming from Turin just before one enters Chieri. It is now
   flanked by plane trees where there used to be elms.

4. A kind of stick which in those days jugglers made common
   use of. Its name, of course, goes back to the times when
   wizards were supposed to use their wands to produce their
   magic.

5. In 1885 Lemoyne himself saw how Don Bosco could still
   handle a stick "with unbelievable dexterity" as he casually
   played around with it (BM I, 236).

6. Ceria added "the tree" to the text.

7. Perhaps he intended to say "Muletto" (Little Mule). Up to
   1915 there was a small restaurant of that name on via Castelnuovo. Caselle (*Giovanni Bosco a Chieri, 1831–1841* [Castel-
   nuovo Don Bosco, 1986], p. 35) reproduces an 1859 painting
   that shows it to have been on the piazza d'Armi facing Saint
   Anthony's Church. Molineris (p. 233) adds that Don Bosco

may have confused the name with the name of the Moretto Gate, which led toward Castelnuovo.

8. These figures are in the original manuscript. Father Berto misread the 2 in 25 as a 4 (which it resembles). On the basis of this new value of "45," he corrected the second figure to "195." But Don Bosco revised his secretary's adjusted values and restored the original. The corrections in two different forms of handwriting are clear in the manuscript. This variance explains why BM I, 236, uses the figures 45 and 195.

9. As mentioned earlier, there was no school on Thursday afternoons.

10. Don Bosco can be exceedingly humble when speaking of himself, e.g. when he says of Comollo, "From him I began to learn how to live as a Christian" (chapter 10). At other times his keen sense of humor encourages him to hyperbole regarding his accomplishments, e.g. here and when he speaks of his tailoring skills (chapter 6).

Hunger for Books

Study of the classics

Y̲ou might be asking how I could afford to give so much time to these dissipations without neglecting my studies. I will not hide the fact that I could have studied harder. But remember that by paying attention at school I was able to learn as much as was necessary. In fact, in those days,[1] I made no distinction between reading and studying, and I could easily recall material from books I had read or heard read. Moreover, my mother had trained me to get by on very little sleep, so I could read for two-thirds of the night at will, thus leaving the whole day free for activities of my own choice. I liked to devote some time to coaching and private lessons, and even though I often did this out of charity or friendship, others paid me.

At that time, there was in Chieri a Jewish bookseller called Elijah.[2] I had come to an understanding with him because of my interest in the Italian classics. For a soldo per volume I could borrow books, returning them as soon as they were read. I read a volume a day from the Popular Library series.[3]

In my fourth year of *ginnasio*, I spent much time reading the Italian authors. During the rhetoric year, I turned to the study of the Latin classics. I began to read Cornelius Nepos, Cicero, Sallust, Quintus Curtius, Livy, Tacitus, Ovid, Vergil, and Horace amongst others.[4] I read them for pleasure, and enjoyed them as if I had understood everything. Only much later did I realise that I had not. After my ordination when I took on teaching these masterpieces[5] to others, I quickly found how much concentration and preparation were necessary to penetrate their true meaning and beauty.

My studies, extensive reading, and coaching of students took most of the day and a good part of the night. Often when it was time to get up in the morning, I was still reading Livy, which I had taken up the previous evening. This practice so ruined my health that for some years I seemed to have one foot in the grave.[6] Consequently, I always advise others to do what they can and no more. The night is made for rest! Except in cases of necessity, after supper[7] no one should apply himself to scientific things. A robust person might take it for a while, but it will always prove detrimental to his health.

Notes

1. The memory weakens because of age or illness. Don Bosco has to acknowledge that even he has had to pay the penalty.

2. Apparently Don Bosco did not notice that he had already spoken of Elijah and his bookshop (chapter 12).

3. The Popular Library (*Biblioteca Popolare*) was published between 1829 and 1840 by Joseph Pomba in Turin. It was a one-hundred-volume collection of Italian classics and Greek and Latin classics in translation. Each of the 160-page, red-covered volumes was small and compact, full of neat, fine, tightly packed print. Ten thousand copies of each volume were printed (Stella, LW, p. 26, n. 52).

4. Sallust, Curtius, Livy, and Tacitus were Roman historians of the first century B.C. and first century A.D. Ovid, Vergil, and Horace were poets of the same period.

   In 1882, Cardinal Lawrence Nina complimented Don Bosco on a letter he had written to the Holy See in Latin. The cardinal asked him if he had studied the classics. Don Bosco replied that he had read many of the Latin authors and the better commentaries, and proceeded to reel off the names of the authors and titles of their books. The cardinal was happy to hear it and interrupted Don Bosco to say that he would pass the information on to the Pope. Leo XIII was a polished classical scholar; when he had read the Latin letter in question, he appreciated its style and judged that Don

Bosco, whom he thought unacquainted with the classics, could never have composed it (BM XV, 357).

5. Latin was one of the courses offered in his night school (chapters 42 and 50).

6. Lack of sleep was only one factor that worked against John's health. See chapter 16, note 7; chapter 19, note 17 and comment; chapter 22, note 4.

7. The midday heat of the Mediterranean region almost necessitates that a break from work of several hours follow the noon meal. The dependence of a preindustrial, pre-electrical society on natural daylight likewise almost necessitated that supper be eaten around dusk. Although many Italians have tried to retain these customs (very light "continental" breakfast, substantial dinner at noon or one o'clock, and light supper around eight o'clock), industry, commerce, commuting, and the international economy are changing the situation.

Vocational Decision

Choosing a state in life

So the end of the rhetoric year[1] approached, the time when students usually ponder their vocations. The dream I had had in Murialdo was deeply imprinted on my mind; in fact it had recurred several times more in ever clearer terms,[2] so that if I wanted to put faith in it I would have to choose the priesthood towards which I actually felt inclined. But I did not want to believe dreams, and my own manner of life, certain habits of my heart, and the absolute lack of the virtues necessary to that state,[3] filled me with doubts and made the decision very difficult.[4]

Oh, if only I had had a guide to care for my vocation! What a great treasure he would have been for me; but I lacked that treasure. I had a good confessor who sought to make me a good Christian, but who never chose to get involved in the question of my vocation.[5]

Thinking things over myself, after reading some books which dealt with the choice of a state in life, I decided to enter the Franciscan Order. "If I become a secular priest," I told myself, "my vocation runs a great risk of shipwreck.[6] I will embrace the priesthood, renounce the world, enter the cloister, and dedicate myself to study and meditation; thus in solitude I will be able to combat my passions, especially my pride," which had put down deep roots in my heart.[7]

So I applied to enter the Reformed Conventuals.[8] I took the examination and was accepted. All was ready for my entry into Chieri's Monastery of Peace.[9] A few days before I was due to enter, I had a very strange dream. I seemed to see a multitude of these friars, clad in threadbare habits, all dashing about helter-skelter. One of them came up to me and said: "You're looking for peace, but you won't find it here. See what goes on! God's preparing another place, another harvest for you."

I wanted to question this religious but a noise awakened me and I saw nothing more. I revealed everything to my confessor, but he did not want to hear of dreams or friars. "In this matter," he said, "everyone must follow his own inclinations and not the advice of others."

Then something cropped up which made it impossible for me to carry out my intention.[10] And since the obstacles were many and difficult, I decided to reveal it all to my friend Comollo.[11] He advised me to make a novena. Meanwhile he would write to his uncle the provost. On the last day of my novena, I went to confession and communion with this incomparable friend. I attended one Mass and served another at the altar of Our Lady of Grace in the cathedral.[12]

Then we went home and found a letter from Fr Comollo which went something like this: "Having given careful consideration to what you wrote me, I advise your friend not to enter a monastery at this time. Let him don the clerical habit.[13] As he goes on with his studies he will better understand what God wants him to do. He must not fear to lose his vocation because aloofness from the world and earnest piety will help him overcome every obstacle."

I followed this wise advice and applied myself seriously to those things which would help prepare me to take the clerical habit. I took the rhetoric examination and then I also took the entrance examination for the seminary in Chieri[14] — in the very rooms of the house which Charles Bertinetti willed us at his death,[15] in the rooms Canon Burzio rented. That year the exam was not held in Turin as was usual, because of the cholera which threatened our area.[16]

I would like to note something about the college at Chieri that certainly exemplifies the spirit of piety that flourished there. During my four years as a student in the college, I do not remember ever hearing any talk, not even a word, that could be considered impolite or irreligious.

At the end of rhetoric course, of the 25 students, 21 embraced the clerical state, three became doctors, and one became a merchant.[17]

When I got home for the holidays,[18] I gave up acrobatics. I dedicated myself to reading good books which, I am ashamed to say, I had neglected up to then. I still kept up my interest in the youngsters, entertaining them with stories, pleasant recreation, sacred music; especially, finding that many of them, even the older ones, were almost ignorant of the truths of faith, I also undertook to teach them their daily prayers and other things more important at that age. It was a kind of oratory, attended by about fifty children, who loved me and obeyed me as if I were their father.

Notes

1. John's rhetoric year was 1834–1835. Since he applied to and was accepted by the Franciscans in March–April 1834 (see note 8 below), he must be mistaken here about the year; he applied in the middle of his humanities year.

2. When John was fifteen or sixteen (see chapter 6) and again when he was about nineteen he had important dreams. He confidentially told Father Julius Barberis about the latter dream around 1870. In this dream he saw a radiant personage at the head of an immense crowd of boys. This person called out to him, "Come here! Take charge of these children and be their guide." John complained that he did not feel able to handle and instruct so many thousands of youngsters. The personage insisted with compelling authority.

   Lemoyne expands Don Bosco's phrase: "In Don Bosco's memoirs we find this entry: 'The dream I had had in Morialdo was repeated when I was nineteen and other times as well'" (BM I, 229). Desramaut offers a lengthy discussion of the number and dates of these recurrences; he is somewhat skeptical of Lemoyne's chronology (*LesMem*, pp. 250–256).

   If this dream was a factor in his decision not to enter the Franciscans, it must have occurred during the late spring or summer of 1834; John turned nineteen that August.

3. The habits to which he refers were probably his love for

games, even if they served a good purpose, and his passion for literature (see chapters 19 and 24).

One virtue he thought lacking in him was humility; elsewhere he speaks of the pride that he felt deeply rooted in himself (e.g. chapter 26). His high esteem for the priesthood is obvious. One might also recall that Saint Francis of Assisi considered himself unworthy of the priesthood and remained a deacon to the end of his life. The rigorist theology of the early nineteenth century exalted the priesthood and its responsibilities almost to a frightening degree; this ideal will recur throughout John's seminary days (cf. Stella, LW, pp. 52–54).

4. John seems to have been torn between an attraction to the religious life, a fear for his mother's old age if he entered religion, and a fear for his own vocation if he became a "priest in the world" (see note 6 below). He was quite conscious of his poverty and of the economic burden that his studies were to his mother. The Franciscans of Chieri were ready to waive the usual entrance fees for him.

5. Since John's confessor, Canon Joseph Maloria, was still a fairly young priest — he was about thirty-one — his hesitation to give such vital advice seems understandable. He may also have had some reservations about John himself, says Stella (LW, p. 27):

> Perhaps the priest was uncertain about the exact qualifications and needs of his penitent. The young man's piety was clear, but he was an acrobat and showman as well. Or perhaps the priest wished to go slowly with John, who was still taking courses in grammar and the humanities. He may not have wanted John to decide too hastily on a vocation in life. In particular, he may have been less than enthusiastic about John's entering the Franciscans as early as 1834, when the Order was facing a terrible crisis in vocations.

In a note (no. 57), Stella reports that the Franciscan Observants exceeded seventy thousand in number during the eighteenth century. The French Revolution and its aftermath were disastrous; their numbers fell to twenty-three thousand in the 1860s and continued to decline until a revitalization that began in the 1880s.

6. "This was no scruple, no empty fear," notes Teresio Bosco (*Mem*, p. 63, n. 1). At that time, he says, quoting Stella (LW, p. 39),

> Perhaps one of the main worries was professionalism for its own sake among the clergy: i.e., entering a clerical 'career' for merely

human reasons rather than from any deeper religious motive. It was one way to secure a decent future for oneself. . . . There was a feeling that a superficial religious sense and an empty interior life boded ill for the priesthood.

Bosco adds:

One sign of this danger could have been the superabundance of young men who started out on the priestly path; for the abundance of starters there was a corresponding number of unhappy quitters. Many still regarded ecclesiastical studies as a gateway, a shortcut toward a teaching position or a government job.

See also Woolf, pp. 48–49.

7. This anxiety about vocation has to be placed in context. Post-Reformation spiritual writers greatly stressed the importance of the choice of one's state of life: God had predestined every individual's vocation. Consequently, one of the principal reasons for salvation or damnation was how one responded. In the Introduction to the Salesian Constitutions, published in 1875 (about the same time that he was working on these memoirs), Don Bosco wrote:

God, most merciful and infinitely rich in graces, at the time he creates each man, establishes for him a path, by pursuing which he can very easily secure his eternal salvation. The man who enters on that path and walks along it has little difficulty in fulfilling God's will and finds peace. But if he were not to enter on that way, he would run great risk of not having the graces necessary for his salvation.

He continues at some length by quoting scripture, the Fathers, and various spiritual writers (*Constitutions of the Society of Saint Francis de Sales* [Paterson, New Jersey, 1957], pp. 4–7; cf. 1966 Constitutions [Madras, 1967], pp. 8–12]).

Stella suggests a number of books that young John might have read at this time, several of which he later used in his own spiritual writings (LW, p. 28).

In the existential language of our times, we could say that this choice had almost assumed the proportions of a radical human anxiety: "one's state in life had to be freely chosen as proof of one's fidelity to God" (Stella, LW, p. 29). Also, as the comment on his dream in chapter 6 brings out, for John Bosco, surrendering to God's will rather than doing his own had almost certainly become a fundamental principle — notwithstanding that John was very strong-willed. It is in this setting, and with consideration for the rigorist teaching on predestination quite widespread in Piedmont at that time, that we must understand his words about his personal fitness (cf. Stella, LW, pp. 50–52).

This anxiety and the subsequent spiritual and emotional intensity of life in the seminary probably had as much to do with the breakdown in John's health as his all-night reading (chapter 15), or even more. Evidently it was troubling him well before he finished high school since he applied to the Franciscans in the middle of his humanities year (March 1834) rather than at the end of the rhetoric year (June 1835).

8. The Franciscan "Register of the Postulants" verifies that John applied in March 1834 and was examined regarding his vocation, as required by canon law, on April 18 at Turin's Monastery of Saint Mary of the Angels. He was accepted on April 28. The register reports that he was found to have all the necessary qualities and was accepted unanimously (*habet requisita et vota omnia*).

As part of his application process, John went to Father Bartholomew Dassano, his pastor at Castelnuovo, for the testimonial letters required by canon law. The pastor then went to Sussambrino to talk to Margaret Bosco, urging her to talk John out of religious life: he could do much good as a diocesan priest, make a splendid career for himself, and provide for her in her old age.

Margaret promptly went to Chieri to see her son. It is surprising that he has passed over this in his memoirs, for he always remembered her advice:

> Consider carefully the step you will take. Then follow your vocation without regard to anyone. The most important thing is the salvation of your soul. The pastor urged me to make you change your mind because I might need your help in the future. But I want to tell you that in this matter I am not to be considered because God comes first. Don't worry about me. . . . I was born poor, I have lived poor, and I want to die poor. What is more, I want to make this very clear to you: if you decide to become a secular priest and should unfortunately become rich, I will never pay you a single visit! Remember that well! (BM I, 221–222)

9. The monastery and church of Our Lady of Peace are on via d'Albussano to the east of via della Pace. Today the monastery belongs to the Vincentians (Giraudo and Biancardi, pp. 83–84).

10. Whatever this was, it must have been something quite serious. Not only did it "make it impossible" for him to become a Franciscan, but he adds that "the obstacles were many and difficult." Together with the dream of the strange friars, John had two powerful influences to discourage his supposed vocation to the Franciscans. Instead, he decided to take the

examinations for admission to the rhetoric and philosophy courses, which he mentioned in chapter 10.

11. John met Comollo when Louis came to Chieri in November 1834, the beginning of John's rhetoric year (chapter 10). Perhaps he had not yet entirely ruled out the Franciscans.

12. The former cathedral is still known as the *duomo*. Its formal title is Santa Maria della Scala. During John's youth it was one of his favorite churches, and it remained important to him later. The Bosco clan was originally from Chieri; John's grandfather Philip Anthony Bosco II was baptized in the cathedral on September 18, 1735.

Don Bosco does not mention in the *Memoirs* that he taught Latin to the cathedral sacristan, Charles Palazzolo (1801?-1885), who was over thirty years old but wished to enter the seminary; he was eventually ordained. This experience, Lemoyne writes, "seems to presage the Sons of Mary Project to be established years later to promote adult vocations to the priesthood" (BM I, 219–220).

At the cathedral John also became a close friend of the bell-ringer, Dominic Pogliano, and his family (BM I, 220, 236). When Canon Burzio was about to investigate John's "black magic," Pogliano tried unsuccessfully to explain to the canon and save John the trouble (BM I, 259).

As a seminarian from 1835–1841, John Bosco continued to come to the cathedral for religious services and also to teach catechism to the young people on Sundays. Four days after his priestly ordination, he celebrated Mass at the altar of our Lady (June 9, 1841).

13. Upon entrance to the seminary, a young man began to wear the cassock and Roman collar; there was a special ceremony in which he was so vested (see chapter 17).

14. Don Bosco evidently meant the end-of-year exam in rhetoric, followed by one for admission to the seminary. In fact, it was the exams for admission to the rhetoric and philosophy courses that he took in 1834 (see note 10 above); he applied to the diocesan seminary in 1835.

15. Octavia Bertinetti was Jonah's godmother. She and her husband evidently became close friends of John Bosco. Their house was part of the mansion that had belonged to the noble Tana family, to which belonged Saint Aloysius Gonzaga's mother.

Charles Bertinetti died in 1868 and his wife in 1869. They willed all their property to Don Bosco; as a result of this inheritance the Salesians established their work in Chieri (BM XIII, 537–40). This was Saint Teresa's Oratory for girls, which was entrusted to the Daughters of Mary Help of Christians in 1878 and is still thriving. It is alleged that Saint Joseph Cottolengo once predicted that the Bertinetti home would eventually house religious (*Salesian Bulletin*, August 1878, cited in Molineris, p. 208).

16. Turin was spared during this outbreak of 1835.

17. Lemoyne, his principal biographer and his confidant for many years, writes:

> John took leave of his superiors at the school. Father Bosco [see chapter 11, note 7] and other prominent ecclesiastics told us John had won the hearts not only of his schoolmates but of the dean of studies, of the spiritual director and of all his teachers as well. They all remained very fond of him and regarded him always as their friend and confidant. As soon as he had finished the course in rhetoric, his teacher [Father Bosco], a doctor in literature and substitute professor at the University of Turin, asked him to be his friend and to be addressed informally [addressed as *tu* rather than *lei*]. This shows the great esteem in which the poor peasant boy from Becchi was regarded by his peers and superiors, not only because of his virtue, but also because a certain contrast, evident in everything he did, made him even more likeable.
>
> John was very active, full of initiative but cautious and deliberate; he had a brilliant mind and fluent speech but was not talkative, especially with superiors. This was our experience with him as a man: he was no different as a boy. (BM I, 273)

18. "Home" meant Sussambrino, where Joseph and Margaret had been living since 1831. Sometime in this period — apparently during the 1835 summer vacation — John, still unsure of what he ought to do, especially because of his poverty, went to Castelnuovo to see the pastor. Father Dassano had resigned and then been appointed pastor at Cavour. The new pastor was Father Peter Anthony Cinzano. Father Cinzano was not at home, but John chanced to meet his old friend Evasio Savio, the blacksmith (see chapter 6, note 16). Savio advised him to go to Turin and talk to their fellow townsman Father Cafasso. Though only twenty-four, Cafasso already had an outstanding reputation for holiness and wisdom. Without hesitation he advised John to enter the diocesan seminary. Savio also encouraged Father Cinzano, the mayor, and others to take an interest in John's education — i.e. to help with the expenses — which they did, and

so did Father Cafasso (BM I, 227–230; Molineris, pp. 236–241). In his memoirs Don Bosco makes no mention of these consultations.

As already recounted, John had met Cafasso in 1830 (chapter 6); but this seems to be the point at which he became John's invaluable mentor and supporter.

PART II

The Second Decade
1835 to 1845

Taking
the Cassock

Clerical investiture • Rule of life

Having made up my mind to enter the seminary, I took the prescribed examination. I prepared carefully for that most important day because I was convinced that one's eternal salvation or eternal perdition ordinarily depends on the choice of a state in life. I asked my friends to pray for me. I made a novena, and on the feast of St Michael (October 1834)[1] I approached the holy sacraments. Before the solemn high Mass Doctor Cinzano,[2] the provost and vicar forane of my region, blessed my cassock and vested me as a cleric.

He instructed me to remove my lay clothing,[3] praying: "May the Lord strip you of your old nature and its deeds." As he did so, I thought, "Oh, how much old clothing there is to cast off. *My God, destroy in me all my evil habits.*"

When he put the clerical collar round my neck, he said: "May the Lord clothe you with the new nature, created after the likeness of God in true righteousness and holiness."[4] Deeply moved, I thought to myself, "*Yes, O my God, grant that at this moment I may put on a new nature. May I henceforth lead a new life in complete conformity with your holy will. May justice and holiness be the constant objects of my thoughts, words, and actions. Amen. O Mary, be my salvation.*"

After the ceremonies in church, the provost wanted another, more worldly celebration. He brought me to the celebration of St Michael at Bardella (a district of Castelnuovo). He meant well, but I looked on it as a kindness misplaced. I felt like a newly dressed puppet on public display.

After my weeks of preparation for that long-awaited day, I now found myself sitting down to dinner amongst people of every sort, men and women, who were there to amuse themselves, to laugh and chatter, to eat and drink. These people, for the most part, spent their time in pleasure-seeking, sport, dancing, and amusements of every kind. Could such people, such society ever identify with one who that very morning had put on the robe of holiness to give himself entirely to the Lord?

The provost saw that I was ill at ease. When we got home he asked me why I was so thoughtful and reserved on a day of such public rejoicing. I replied quite frankly that the morning's ceremony at church contrasted in gender, number, and case[5] with the evening ceremony. "Moreover," I added, "seeing priests the worse for drinking and indulging in buffoonery with the guests, aroused in me almost a revulsion for my vocation. Should I ever turn out to be a priest like them, I would prefer to put this habit aside and live poorly as a layman but a good Christian."[6]

"That's the world as it is," answered the provost, "and you must take it as you find it. You must see evil if you are to recognise it and avoid it. No one becomes a battle-tried warrior without learning how to handle arms. So we too must do who are engaged in continual war against the enemy of souls."

I kept quiet then, but in my heart I said, "I will never again attend public festivals, unless obliged because of religious ceremonies."

After that day I had to pay attention to myself. The style of life I had lived up to then had to be radically reformed. My life in the past had not been wicked, but I had been proud and dissipated, given over to amusements, games, acrobatics, and other such things. These pursuits gave passing joy, but did not satisfy the heart.[7]

I drew up a fixed rule of life. To impress it more vividly on my memory, I wrote up the following resolutions:[8]

1. For the future I will never take part in public shows during fairs or at markets. Nor will I attend dances or the theatre,[9] and as far as possible I will not partake of the dinners usual on such occasions.

2. I will no longer play games of dice or do conjuring tricks, acrobatics, sleight of hand, tightrope walking. I will give up my violin-playing[10] and hunting. These things I hold totally contrary to ecclesiastical dignity and spirit.

3. I will love and practise a retiring life, temperance in eating and drinking. I will allow myself only those hours of rest strictly necessary for health.

4. In the past I have served the world by reading secular literature. Henceforth I will try to serve God by devoting myself to religious reading.

5. I will combat with all my strength everything, all reading, thoughts, conversations, words, and deeds contrary to the virtue of chastity. On the contrary, I will practise all those things, even the smallest, which contribute to preserving this virtue.

6. Besides the ordinary practices of piety, I will never neglect to make a little meditation daily and a little spiritual reading.

7. Every day I will relate some story or some maxim advantageous to the souls of others. I will do this with my companions, friends, relatives, and when I cannot do it with others, I will speak with my mother.

These are the resolutions which I drew up when I took the clerical habit. To fix them firmly on my mind, I went before an image of the Blessed Virgin and, having read them to her, I prayed and made a formal promise to my heavenly benefactress to observe them no matter what sacrifice it cost.[11]

Notes

1. Saint Michael's feast is September 29. There are two mistakes in Don Bosco's account. The day was October 25, the year 1835. The feast of Saint Raphael used to be October 24. The archdiocesan archives of Turin report October 25 as the day of John's investiture. It is quite likely that an event of such local importance as the clerical investiture of a native son would be celebrated on a Sunday, and it was customary to celebrate the feasts of important saints on the nearest Sunday. October 25, 1835, was a Sunday.

The second error concerns the feast at Bardella. If Don Bosco assumed that he was clothed in the cassock on the feast of Saint Michael, he would naturally write that the people of Bardella were celebrating Saint Michael. Bardella's patron is Saint Gabriel (Molineris, p. 234; Stella, letter, June 4, 1988), whose liturgical feast in the old calendar was March 24. Evidently, the people of Bardella were celebrating Saint Raphael's day on October 25, and Don Bosco is mistaken about its being their patronal feast. This is also the conclusion which Lemoyne reaches (BM I, 277).

Molineris also maintains (pp. 235–236) that Lemoyne created the dialog (BM I, 277–278) between John and Father Cinzano, largely because Lemoyne presupposes that Margaret and Joseph Bosco were still residing in Becchi (which was farther away than Sussambrino, where they in fact lived in 1835).

2. As mentioned in chapter 7, note 9, "doctor" refers to one's mastery of theology; in fact, Don Bosco often uses the term *teologo*, as he does here, rather than *dottore*.

The title was given not only to scholars who had earned a degree but also to those of particular learning or to holders of certain church offices; Father Cinzano was a diocesan consultor (*SouAut*, p. 94, n. 10). On vicars forane and provosts, see chapter 4, note 6, and chapter 10, note 15. Waldensian controversialists referred to Don Bosco himself as *teologo* (see chapter 60).

Lemoyne gives Father Cinzano's names as Michael Anthony (BM I, 276). Stella corrects Lemoyne and also furnishes Father Cinzano's dates, 1805–1870, on the basis of his death notice in the diocesan calendar. His name actually was Peter Anthony (*EcSo*, p. 627, and personal letter of June 4, 1988).

3. I.e., his coat and tie.

4. Don Bosco quotes the words of the clothing ceremony in Latin: *Exuat te Dominus veterem hominem cum actibus suis. Induat te Dominum novum hominem, qui secundum Deum creatus est in iusticia et sanctitate veritatis!* These words are almost a direct quotation from the Vulgate of Ephesians 4:22,24). Don Bosco's youthful prayers are underlined in his manuscript.

5. This allusion to the intricacies of Latin grammar playfully points to the complete disharmony that John found in the day's activities. We should hesitate to ascribe all of these

rather harsh sentiments to the mature Don Bosco; they reflect, instead, the prevailing moral rigorism of the 1830s.

6. These comments on the dignity of the priesthood certainly reflect Don Bosco's lifelong ideals and cannot be called Jansenistic.

7. Father Berto's copy of the manuscript uses the past tense ("did not satisfy"). Don Bosco let that stand even though his original text uses the present, "do not satisfy." The original seems to read better in that Don Bosco goes from his personal past experience, "gave passing joy," to a general principle, "do not satisfy."

8. This plan of life sealed John's preparation for his first year as a seminarian. It summarizes the insights of the recollection and prayer that went with his clothing ceremony. The learned Sisto Colombo, SDB, says that the resolutions are a program for a life "filled with God, lived in intimate conversation with him, austere, disciplined in word and thought, angelic in its purity" (*S. Giovanni Bosco, 1815–1888: Fondatore dei Salesiani e delle Figlie di Maria Ausiliatrice* [Turin: SEI, 1934], p. 49).

9. John's resolutions reflect the clerical discipline of the time, which forbade those in holy orders to attend balls, the opera, etc., or to hunt (with horses and hounds, falcons, etc.) — in short, to take part in or watch any activity that was regarded as worldly, spectacular, or potentially scandalous. In the nineteenth century this discipline was scattered through various papal and conciliar decrees; the Canon Law of 1918 codified it in cc. 138 and 140.

10. He had begun to play the violin while staying with John Roberto at Castelnuovo (chapter 6).

11. "These resolutions indicated [John's] efforts to adapt to a clerical world which was quite strict, if not rigorous" (Desramaut, *SpLife*, p. 310, n. 2). As already noted, the clergy of Piedmont were under a strong Jansenist influence. John's resolutions and his outlook go beyond canon law, influenced by this rigorism (see also chapter 16, notes 3 and 7). He seems to have struggled his whole life to balance this ideal of the priest "retired from the world" with the pastoral needs of the industrial age.

On Don Bosco's mature asceticism, see Desramaut, *SpLife*, pp. 173–196.

Mother's Farewell

Departure for the seminary

I had to be in the seminary on 30 October of that year, 1835.[1] My little wardrobe was ready.[2] My relatives were all pleased, and I even more than they. It was only my mother who was pensive. Her eyes followed me round as if she wanted to say something to me. On the evening before my departure she called me to her and spoke to me these unforgettable words:[3]

"My dear John, you have put on the priestly habit. I feel all the happiness that any mother could feel in her son's good fortune. Do remember this, however: it's not the habit that honours your state, but the practice of virtue. If you should ever begin to doubt your vocation, then — for heaven's sake! — do not dishonor this habit. Put it aside immediately. I would much rather have a poor farmer for a son, than a priest who neglects his duties.

"When you came into the world, I consecrated you to the Blessed Virgin. When you began your studies, I recommended to you devotion to this Mother of ours. Now I say to you, be completely hers; love those of your companions who have devotion to Mary; and if you become a priest, always preach and promote devotion to Mary."

My mother was deeply moved as she finished these words, and I cried. "Mother," I replied, "I thank you for all you have said and done for me. These words of yours will not prove vain; I will treasure them all my life."

The following morning I went off to Chieri, and on the

The interior courtyard of the former archdiocesan seminary at Chieri. Above the niche with the statue of our Lady is the sundial whose motto impressed John Bosco on the day of his enrollment.

evening of that same day I entered the seminary.[4] After greeting my superiors, I made my bed, and then, with my friend Garigliano,[5] strolled through the dormitories, the corridors, and finally into the courtyard. Glancing up at a sundial, I saw written, "The hours drag for the sad, fly for the happy."[6]

"That's it," I said to my friend; "that's our program. Let's always be cheerful, and the time will pass quickly."

The following day I began a three-day retreat, and I went out of my way to make it as well as I could. At the end of the retreat I approached Dr Ternavasio of Bra, the lecturer in philosophy.[7] I asked him for some rule of life by which I might fulfill my duties and win the goodwill of my superiors.

"Just one thing," replied the good priest, "the exact fulfillment of your duties."[8]

I made this advice my norm and applied myself with all my soul to the observance of the rules of the seminary. I made no distinction between the bells that called me to study, to church, to the refectory, to recreation, or to bed. This diligent observance won me the affection of my companions and the esteem of superiors. Consequently, my six years[9] at the seminary were a very happy period.

Notes

1. Don Bosco continued to write 1834 in his notebook. Ceria corrected it to 1835 in his edition. On November 5, 1835, the annual lottery for the military draft from Castelnuovo was held. John Bosco was assigned the number 41, meaning that he was very likely to be called up. Because of his entrance into the seminary a week earlier, he was exempted. (T. Bosco, SP, p. 69; Caselle, *Giovanni Bosco studente*, p. 145; cf. Stella, *EcSo*, p. 33, n. 13)

2. Father Cinzano and the people of Morialdo joined together to contribute the various items of clothing that John needed. Fathers Cinzano and Cafasso jointly prevailed upon Father Louis Guala of Turin to use his weighty influence with Archbishop Fransoni to obtain for John an exemption from the seminary boarding and tuition fees at least for the first year.

3. Just as she had when John made his first communion and when he was weighing a possible religious vocation, on this third great occasion in her son's life Margaret Bosco put her motherly love and faith into sound, disinterested advice. She selflessly balances her deep respect for the priesthood against her son's success.

4. The seminary was located in the former residence of the Congregation of the Oratory, which dated from 1658, as did the adjacent Church of Saint Philip Neri. The Napoleonic government expelled the Oratorians and confiscated their convent. They received it back under the Restoration but soon had to withdraw from Chieri for lack of members. The convent became partly a school and partly a police barracks.

Archbishop Chiaveroti bought the building in 1828; a decree of the Holy See established the seminary on May 14, 1828, but it did not open till November 1829. The church had remained open during all that time and is still open today. (Caselle, *Giovanni Bosco studente*, pp. 148, 150)

Don Bosco passes over a fundamental decision that he had to make upon enrolling in the seminary, viz. whether to live there as a boarding student or to lodge in the city and attend just the lectures and the main practices of piety at the seminary. Although bishops disliked having day students as seminarians — they thought that they were a worldly influence on the others — apparently there was little that they could do to change the practice. In the Turin archdiocese, for example, seminary enrollment in 1840 totaled 565, of whom 207 were day students. Stella concludes that John elected to shut himself in the spiritual cloister of the seminary (LW, pp. 39–40; see chapter 19, note 4 and comment).

5. William Garigliano was a friend of John's and a member of the Society for a Good Time in secondary school. During their six years in the seminary, he was one of John's inseparable companions; in the next chapter Don Bosco will mention John Baptist Giacomelli and Louis Comollo.

6. What was the seminary is now a public school. The sundial is still on the courtyard wall, and the Latin verse is still faintly legible: *Afflictis lentae, celeres gaudentibus horae.*

7. Father Francis Ternavasio (1806–1886) came from the town of Bra, about thirty miles south of Turin. He had earned a doctorate in philosophy and was a knight of the Order of Saints Maurice and Lazarus (Stella, LW, p. 42, n. 20).

8. Of this interchange Stella writes (LW, pp. 40–41):

> The bare words might well seem to come from an older Don Bosco, the experienced educator. More than once he raised the same sort of question to his own students: "You might ask me what you should do to please Don Bosco. My answer is: help him to save your soul" [BM XV, 573]. But we can see that the basic concern fits in well with Don Bosco's own temperament. He wanted to win the goodwill of others, to establish an atmosphere of mutual sympathy, harmony, and satisfaction.
>
> [Father Ternavasio's] reply is very much like the one that Don Bosco would later give to Dominic Savio. As a new seminarian, however, John Bosco probably did not associate the fulfillment of daily duties with 'holiness' in the compelling way that would be true later in the case of Savio. He probably just assumed that one

had to carry out one's duties as a seminarian properly in order to become a good priest. His later experience as an educator would prompt him to deduce certain pedagogical and spiritual principles and link them together more closely.

9. From October 30, 1835, till June 5, 1841.

Seminary Life

As there is little variety in the daily round of seminary life,[1] I shall give a brief sketch of the general background and then an account of some events in particular.

I will begin with a word about the superiors. I was greatly attached to them, and they always treated me with the greatest kindness; but my heart was not satisfied. The rector[2] and the other superiors usually saw us only when we returned after the holidays and when we were leaving for them. The students never went to talk to them, except to receive corrections. The staff members took weekly turns to assist in the refectory and to take us on walks. That was all. How often I would have liked to talk to them, ask their advice, or resolve a doubt, and could not. In fact if a superior came on the scene, the seminarians, with no particular reason, would flee left and right as if he were a monster.[3] This only served to inflame my heart to become a priest as quickly as I could so that I could associate with young people, help them, and meet their every need.

And as for my companions, I stuck to my beloved mother's advice. That is, I fraternized only with companions who had a devotion to Mary and who loved study and piety. Here I must give a word of warning to seminarians. In the seminary there are many clerics of outstanding virtue, but there are others who are dangerous.[4] Not a few young men, careless of their vocation, go to the seminary lacking either the spirit or the goodwill of a good seminarian. Indeed, I remember hearing some companions indulging in very bad language. Once a search amongst some students' personal belongings unearthed impious and obscene books of every kind. It is true that these later left the seminary, either of their own accord or because they were expelled when their true character came to light. But as long as they stayed, they were a plague to good and bad alike.

To avoid such dangerous associates, I chose some who were well known as models of virtue. These were William Garigliano, John Giacomelli of Avigliana and, later, Louis Comollo. For me, these three friends were a treasure.[5]

The practices of piety were well conducted. Each morning we had Mass, meditation, and rosary; edifying books were read during meals. In those days Bercastel's *History of the Church* was read.[6] We were expected to go to confession once a fortnight, but those who wished could go every Saturday.

We could only receive holy communion, however, on Sundays and on special feasts. We did receive communion sometimes on weekdays, but doing so meant that we had to act contrary to obedience.[7] It was necessary to slip out, usually at breakfast time, to St Philip's Church[8] next door, receive holy communion, and then join our companions as they were going into the study hall or to class. This infraction of the timetable was prohibited. But the superiors gave tacit consent to it since they knew it was going on and sometimes observed it without saying anything to the contrary. In this way, I was able to receive holy communion much more frequently, and I can rightly say it was the most efficacious support of my vocation. This defect of piety was corrected when, through an order of Archbishop Gastaldi,[9] things were arranged so as to permit daily communion, provided one is prepared.

Amusements and recreation

The game known as *Bara rotta*[10] was the most popular game we played. I used to play it in the beginning, but since this game was very similar to those acrobatics which I had absolutely renounced, I wanted to give this up too.

There was another game called tarots which was permitted on certain days, and for a while I also played this game. Even here sweetness and bitterness intermingled. I was not a great player, but I was rather lucky and nearly always won. At the end of a game my hands would be full of money, but seeing how distressed my companions were at losing it made more me miserable than they. I should add that my mind would become so fixed during a game that afterwards I could neither pray nor study; the troubling pictures of the *King of Cups*[11] and the Jack of Spades, of the 13 and the fifteen of tarots filled my imagination.[12] So I resolved to give up this game as I had given up the others. This was in 1836, mid-way through my second year of philosophy.[13]

In the longer recreation periods, the seminarians went for walks to the many delightful places round Chieri. These walks were useful for learning too. We tried to improve our academic knowledge by quizzing one another as we walked. If there was no organised walk, students could spend the recreation time walking about the seminary with friends, discussing topics of common interest, or edifying and intellectual matters.

During the long recreations, we often gathered in the refectory for what we called the "study circle." At this session, one could ask questions about things he did not know or had not grasped in our lectures or textbooks. I liked this exercise and found it very helpful for study, piety, and health. Comollo, who was a year behind me, made a name for himself with his questions. A certain Dominic Peretti, now parish priest of Buttigliera,[14] always had plenty to say and was always ready to venture an answer. Garigliano was a good listener and limited himself to an occasional interjection. I was president and judge of last appeal. Sometimes it happened in our friendly discussions that certain questions were asked or problems of knowledge raised that nobody was able to answer adequately. In these cases we divided up the problems; each one was responsible for looking up the parts assigned to him before the next meeting.

Comollo often interrupted my recreation time, leading me by the sleeve of my cassock and telling me to come along with him to the chapel; there we would make a visit to the Blessed Sacrament for the dying, saying the rosary or the Little Office of Our Lady for the souls in purgatory.

This marvelous companion was my fortune. He could, as the occasion demanded, advise me, correct me, or cheer me up, but all with such charm and charity that I even welcomed his admonitions and looked for them. I dealt familiarly with him, and I was naturally led to follow his example. Although I was a thousand miles behind him in virtue, if I was not ruined by dissipation but grew in my vocation, truly I remain in his debt above all.

In one thing alone I did not even try to emulate him, and that was in mortification. He was a young man of nineteen,[15] yet he fasted rigourously for the whole of Lent and at other times laid down by the Church. In honour of the B.V.,[16] he fasted every Saturday. Often he went without breakfast, and sometimes his dinner consisted of bread and water. He put up with insults and affronts without the least sign of annoyance. When I saw how faithful he was in even the slightest demands of study and piety, I was filled with admiration. I regarded my companion as an ideal friend, a model of virtue for any seminarian.[17]

Notes

1. At the end of the notes is an extended comment on the seminaries of Turin at this period.

2. Father Sebastian Mottura (1795–1876) of Villafranca (about twenty-five miles south-southwest of Turin), doctor of theology. Stella briefly identifies several other faculty members (LW, p. 42, n. 20). Caselle gives a fuller list (*Giovanni Bosco studente*, p. 151). John Bosco was respected by his superiors but was not close to them.

3. The accepted principle in most educational establishments of the time was that any familiarity between teacher and pupil destroyed respect. Teachers and other staff were therefore encouraged to keep apart from the students. Don Bosco makes this point in his treatise on the Preventive System. He states that this concentration on the teacher's authority means that the only close contact between teacher and student is when special punishment is needed. This climate of fear finally generates antipathy.

4. The seminarian Bosco was, to some degree, isolated from the bulk of his fellow students and their mood. These seemed to

be, and often were, too worldly when measured against his ideal of the priesthood. Don Bosco may have been referring primarily to the day seminarians, who were much more susceptible to what were considered secular, political, and other inappropriate influences. From the remarks that follow, it is obvious that these influences extended also to some of the boarders.

It is in this context that we must see Don Bosco's general reluctance to allow his pupils and his Salesians to spend much of the summer vacation at home, and to discourage other seminary superiors from letting their students vacation at home (e.g. BM XV, 288–289; Regulations of the Salesian Society [1966], no. 9).

5. John had a small circle of real friends with whom to share confidences. Garigliano was mentioned in chapters 9 and 18. John Baptist Giacomelli and Louis Comollo were a year behind him in school.

Giacomelli (1820–1901), from Avigliana (about ten miles west of Turin), always remained a friend dear to Don Bosco; eventually he became a chaplain at Saint Philomena's Hospital. He became Don Bosco's confessor after the death of Father Golzio in 1873. (See *Bollettino salesiano* XXV [1901], 295–296.)

6. The French priest Antoine Henri de Berault-Bercastel (1720–1794) wrote a twenty-four-volume *History of the Church* that went through various Italian editions. Its well-organized approach and sound principles made it useful for a long time. Don Bosco used it a great deal in his own church history textbook (Stella, LW, pp. 57–61).

7. The Jansenists (see comment below) discouraged frequent communion on the grounds that most people were unworthy of it.

8. The Church of Saint Philip Neri could be entered directly from the seminary without going out to the street. The sacristies of the seminary chapel and of the church were connected. The breakfast thus skipped consisted of a roll and a cup of milk or coffee.

9. Lawrence Gastaldi (1815–1883) was archbishop of Turin from 1871 till his death. As a young priest he was a staunch helper of the nascent Oratory, and his mother was one of the pious women who helped Mama Margaret with the cooking, washing, mending, etc. Father Gastaldi was a member of the Institute of Charity for a time and spent several years

in England. Don Bosco was influential in his appointment as bishop of Saluzzo in 1867 and in his promotion to the see of Turin.

Archbishop Gastaldi found himself constantly in conflict with Don Bosco and the Salesians; the conflict concerned the scope of the Salesian Society, its internal discipline, the formation of its members, and external control of it. The worst stages of that conflict (the suspension of Father John Bonetti and grave accusations to the Holy See against Don Bosco and the Salesians) had not begun when Don Bosco was writing the *Memoirs*; but there is no reason to suppose that he would not have complimented the archbishop for his promotion of holy communion, regardless of their conflict.

10. A game in which two sides stage a kind of mock battle. The losers are those who are reached by their opponents before they manage to reenter a refuge (*bara*).

11. Cups (*coppe*) is one of the suits of the playing cards.

12. These cards bear images of death and of the devil.

13. The academic year 1836–1837. Not only did John give up card playing, but he continued to believe that it was not a suitable pastime for clerics. He considered it a waste of time, and furthermore, associated it with gambling. "Card playing is forbidden" remained in the Salesian Regulations until 1965.

    Don Bosco's attitude toward cards did not prevent him from remaining a sharp player on occasion, e.g. when it might help him catch some boys for the Oratory.

14. Not Buttigliera d'Asti, near Castelnuovo, but Buttigliera Alta in the province of Turin. Don Bosco's friend was pastor there from 1850 to 1893.

15. Comollo, besides being two years younger than John Bosco, was very boyish in appearance.

16. Blessed Virgin (Mary).

17. We must presume that Don Bosco has idealized Comollo's general devotion and his will to act upon his beliefs. We may also presume that Don Bosco is speaking for what he thought and felt in the seminary. As Teresio Bosco points out (BN, p. 88), Comollo's unmitigated rigor led to his death; a prudent spiritual director might have reined him in. Don Bosco himself would become a prudent spiritual director for the enthusiasm of young Dominic Savio (cf. *Life of Dominic Savio*, Aronica ed., pp. 89–90; O'Brien ed., pp. 24–25).

Stella treats the relationship between John and Louis at some length (LW, pp. 70–74). Don Bosco says repeatedly that he tried to imitate Louis's virtues; Stella finds that "the communion of life between the two friends [caused] ideas and expressions [to be] taken in by osmosis. Thus they took deep root in the mind and language of Don Bosco himself" (p. 71). In Comollo's virtue Don Bosco came

> to see the essence of holiness for young people. Louis Comollo was one of Don Bosco's favorite examples, and the *Cenni* dealing with his life was one of the texts used for spiritual reading at the Oratory. But the influence of Comollo may also have had something to do with Don Bosco's somewhat excessive turn to asceticism, rigidity, and diffidence in the seminary (p. 74).

Comment on the Turin Seminaries

Don Bosco's seminary life at Chieri must be put into context. Archbishop Columban Chiaveroti had opened the seminary at Chieri in 1829, only six years before John entered. Its capacity was about one hundred seminarians, a fairly large number for the time. There were other archdiocesan seminaries at Bra and Giaveno and attached to the University of Turin. Total seminary enrollment in 1834 was 180, of whom 70 were studying in Turin. By 1840 enrollment in the four seminaries had tripled to 565. As Don Bosco indicates in his description, the seminarians appear to have been a mixed bunch.

The post-Napoleonic era in Piedmont was marked by political and religious controversy. In the Church, the clash centered around two currents in moral theology. One took a very strict view of sin and the way moral norms were to be interpreted. This "rigorist" current and its strict requirements for salvation are usually associated with Jansenism — though it could more accurately be called probabiliorism (see chapter 27, note 8). The other, more "benign" attitude allowed probable opinions to be used more easily, after the teaching of Alphonsus Liguori (died 1787, canonized 1839). The first group accused the second of being laxists. The rigorists were, at least implicitly, proponents of the ideas of the French Revolution.

The rigorists dominated the University of Turin, with which the archdiocesan seminary was associated. The principal proponents of the benign current were the Jesuits, the Oblates of the Virgin Mary (founded by Father Pius Bruno Lanteri), and the faculty of the Convitto Ecclesiastico, and they were associated with the *ancien régime*. Not only moral theology but also per-sonalities were involved in the controversy, which eventually led to street demonstrations and faculty dismissals. Given the alliance of throne and altar in Restoration Italy, overtones of secular poli-tics colored the controversy, and King Charles Felix felt compelled to intervene on at least one occasion. The bad climate that all this created and the disturbing effect it had on the seminarians in Turin convinced Archbishop Chiaveroti of the need to open a seminary away from some of the capital's turmoil. Himself a monk, he also felt the need to train a more spiritually minded clergy (cf. chapter 16, note 6). The new seminary at Chieri was the result (Stella, LW, pp. 35–40).

By post-Vatican II standards both the rigorist and the benign currents would probably appear fairly strict. They were domi-nated by a heavy preoccupation with salvation and damnation, and all this in a strong atmosphere of predestination (cf. chapter 16). All their emotional and moral effort was to rouse the sinner and stir up deep anxiety so that he could seriously get to work at saving his soul. Stella (LW, pp. 45–70) speculates that this period of John Bosco's life was probably a very introspective one and, to some degree, at odds with his natural character and attitude to-ward living his faith.

Given the climate of the times and the need to remind the seminarians of their priestly commitment, there was a good deal of regimentation. There was a strong stress on salvation and more strongly on damnation as far as the priest was concerned. (In this context the death of Comollo and the circumstances surrounding it are worth remembering; see chapter 22.) A typical book of that time, Giambattista Compaing's *Della santità e dei doveri de' sacer-doti* [The Holiness and the Duties of Priests] (Bergamo, 1824), has as one of its meditations: "Very few priests will be saved."

The effect of a climate of this kind on John Bosco, when he was on the first step of a life consecrated to his ideal of the priesthood and all its responsibilities, can easily be guessed. Also, after the very active years of his youth, for the first time he was not dashing between study and work; he actually had time on his hands to reflect and worry. As we have already observed in treat-ing of his vocation, he had a soul that was very sensitive to searching out the will of God and to reining back his own strong character. He now saw some of his very human and friendly re-lationships and the ways of his youth as worldly and dangerous. Some of his resolutions of this period show a scrupulous strict-ness and a need to chain human nature in a way that is a little out of tune with the more mature later spirit that he learned from

Saint Francis de Sales. (This saint himself went through a period of deep anxiety when he was a student and before he reached the strong, gentle calm of his later life).

In this period John seems to have been below normal, even physically, at least for a time. His seminary friend Father Giacomelli gave the following testimony concerning his first encounter with John (November 1837): "I saw a seminarian in front of me [in class] who . . . was pale and thin and looked unwell. In my opinion, he would hardly last till the end of the school year." (BM I, 300)

John's seminary years were a mixed experience. Don Bosco was later to show a certain anxiety about sending his own clerics to study in the diocesan seminary at Turin.

20

Summer Activities

Vacations

Holidays were dangerous times for clerical students. In those days our summer break ran to four and a half months.[1] I spent a lot of time reading and writing; but not knowing how to organise myself properly, I got little out of it. I tried different kinds of handicrafts as well. On the lathe I turned spindles, pegs, spinning tops, and wooden balls. I made clothes and shoes and I worked wood and iron. To this very day there are in my house at Murialdo a writing desk, a dinner table, and some chairs, masterpieces to remind me of my summer holiday activities.[2] I worked in the fields, too, harvesting hay and wheat. I trimmed the vines, harvested the grapes, and made the wine, and so on.

I also found time for my youngsters, as I used to, but this was possible only on feast days. It was a great consolation for me to catechise many of my companions who were sixteen or seventeen years old but were deprived of the truths of the faith. I also taught some of them quite successfully to read and write. They were so anxious to learn that many youngsters of a variety of ages surrounded me. I charged no tuition, but I insisted on *diligence, concentration*, and *monthly confession*. At first some were not inclined to accept these conditions. They went their own way, but their departure served to inspire and spur on those who stayed.

I also began to preach and to lecture with the permission of my parish priest, and with his help. In Alfiano I preached on the Holy Rosary in the holidays after my year of physics.[3] In Castelnuovo d'Asti, at the end of my first year of theology, I spoke on St Bartholomew the Apostle.[4] In Capriglio I preached about the nativity of Mary.[5] But I do not know how much fruit this bore. Everywhere I got high praise. In fact vainglory somewhat carried me away, till I was brought down to earth as follows:

One day, after my sermon on the birth of Mary, I asked someone who seemed to be one of the more intelligent what he thought of it. He was full of praise for it but spoiled it by saying, "Your sermon was on the souls in purgatory." And I had preached on the glories of Mary! The parish priest of Alfiano, Joseph Peleto, was a learned and holy man. I also asked for his opinion of my sermon there.

"Your sermon," he said, "was very good. It was well put together, well delivered, and embellished with scriptural quotations. Go on like that and you will be a success as a preacher."

"Did the people understand it?" I asked him.

"Hardly," he replied. "Only my brother priest and I, and perhaps a few others, knew what it was about."

"How is it," I wanted to know, "that such simple concepts were not understood?"

"To you they are simple," he explained, "but to ordinary people they appear difficult. Allusions to the Bible,[6] philosophizing on one or another aspect of church history, are things the people do not understand."

"What do you suggest I do?"

"Give up your high-sounding language and stick to dialect where possible, and when you use Italian, speak the language of the people, the people, the people. Instead of speculations, use examples, analogies, and simple, practical illustrations. Bear in mind always that the common people understand hardly anything you have to say because the truths of the faith are never sufficiently explained to them."[7]

This fatherly advice has served as a guiding principle for the rest of my life. I still have copies of those early sermons in which, to my shame, I can now see nothing but affectation and vanity.[8] But God, in his goodness, saw to it that I should have that kind of correction. It was a lesson for me which henceforth bore fruit in my sermons, catechism classes, instructions, and in the writing in which I began to engage.[9]

Notes

1. The summer holidays lasted from the feast of Saint John the Baptist (June 24) to All Saints' Day (November 1).

2. Don Bosco is, of course, joking when he calls these samples of his carpentry "masterpieces." Since they were kept at the family home in Becchi (which Don Bosco always called "my house"), his Salesian readers would have seen them many times. They are kept as relics in the house that belonged to his brother Joseph, built across the courtyard from the house where they lived as children.

3. During John's second year of philosophy (1836–1837), metaphysics was one of the main courses. We do not know why he calls it "physics."

   The feast of the Holy Rosary, commemorating the Christian victory over the Turks at Lepanto in 1571, is celebrated on October 7. Since at that time big feasts were kept on the nearest Sunday, these sermons of which Don Bosco speaks would have been delivered on Sundays.

   In the early years of the Oratory hospice, the feast of the Rosary became the focal point for the yearly outings for the best boys. Don Bosco set up in Joseph's house a small chapel in honor of the Holy Rosary; there he would solemnize the feast with his boys and the people of the neighborhood. See the comment on the fall outings following chapter 48.

4. The summer of 1838. The feast of Saint Bartholomew falls on August 24.

5. The nativity of our Lady is celebrated on September 8.

6. It is not biblical preaching as such that is discouraged here, but casual references to persons and events that uneducated people would not understand. Much preaching, even at Mass, was moral or dogmatic rather than biblical.

7. The Salesian archives possess two of Don Bosco's sermons written in Piedmontese, one on Mary's assumption into heaven, the other on her birth. Until the end of the last century it was still common enough for even bishops to preach in dialect. (See also chapter 4, note 13.)

Don Bosco's Italian is constantly flavored by "Piedmontisms." Several traces of dialect color his agricultural vocabulary at the beginning of this chapter, for example; for repeated instances, the reader may consult Ceria's notes in the Italian edition.

As regards preaching, Don Bosco was, of course, writing for the edification of his sons. The principles of effective preaching were a constant theme with him (e.g. BM II, 179–181, 265–266; III, 45–53; IX, 14–16). The same lessons that Don Bosco began to learn during these vacations were reinforced by Father Cafasso at the Convitto Ecclesiastico (BM II, 65–67).

8. The archives also preserve two of his sermons in rather sophisticated Italian, one on the rosary and the second on the birth of Mary. These may be the ones he speaks of. The language is polished with rather long, well-structured sentences. There is good continuity and the style is not overly rhetorical. They show a literary style not found in his later work because he consciously changed it (see the dialog with the Waldensians in chapter 60).

9. Probably an allusion to writings which John used to read in the seminary study circles at recreation time (see the previous chapter). He and a dozen or so seminary friends also used to get together during vacations for the same purpose. One's prose and poetry were read out and then subjected to comment. These meetings were started by a seminarian named James Bosco (BM I, 331; VII, 13), but John was their soul and spirit. He was so exact in his comments that he became known as the "grand master of grammar" among his friends.

Caviglia evaluates Don Bosco's style as a writer:

His writing is simple, clear, and well ordered, with a slow, measured style. He is objective and uses concrete imagery. . . . He cultivated a style intended to communicate easily with the young and the ordinary people. Words and style had to be as easy to understand as possible, in the simplest kind of language that the young and unschooled working people used. He sought to be in tune with the character and spirit of the "ordinary person," in the best and complete sense of this phrase. (*Don Bosco: profilo storico* [Turin: SEI, 1920], pp. 97, 99)

21

Days in the Country

A feast day in the country • *The violin* • *Hunting*

When I said that holidays in the country were a time of danger, I was speaking for myself. A poor cleric will often find himself in grave danger without realising it. I learned this through experience.

One year I was invited to celebrate a feast day at the home of some relatives of mine. I did not want to go, but discovering that there was no cleric to serve in church, I yielded to the insistent invitations of one of my uncles and went.

When the sacred ceremonies, at which I served and sang, were over, we went to dinner. All went well till the wine began to go to the heads of some of the party. Then they began to use language which should not be tolerated by a cleric. I tried to protest but could not get the words out. Not knowing what to do, I decided to leave. I got up from the table, got my hat, and was ready to go; my uncle stopped me. At that moment, there was an outburst of even more objectionable language as someone began to insult all the others at table. In a flash, all was pandemonium. There were angry shouts and threats, backed up by horrible racket of glasses, bottles, plates, spoons, forks, and then knives. In this extremity, I beat a hasty retreat. When I got home, from the bottom of my heart I renewed the resolution so often made before to remain withdrawn if I wanted to avoid falling into sin.

A different kind of experience, none the less unpleasant, befell me at Crovaglia, a district of Buttigliera. It was the feast of St Bartholomew. I was invited by another uncle to assist at the church services, to sing, and even to play the violin, which I had given up, though it was my favorite instrument.[1]

The church services went very well. My uncle was in charge of the celebrations, and the dinner was at his house. So far, so good. Dinner over, the guests asked me to play something of a light nature for them. I refused.[2]

"At least," one of the musicians said, "play along with me. I'll take the lead, and you play the accompaniment."

I felt awful! I did not know how to get out of it. Taking up the violin, I played for a while. Then I heard the murmur of voices and the sound of a lot of dancing feet. I went to the window, and out in the courtyard was a crowd dancing happily to the sound of my violin. Words could not describe the anger that welled up in me at that moment.[3] Turning on the dinner guests, I addressed them vehemently: "How is it, after I have so often spoken against public shows, that I should have become their promoter? It will never happen again."[4] I smashed the violin into a thousand pieces. I never wanted to use it again, though opportunities for doing so were not lacking at sacred ceremonies.[5]

Another incident happened to me while I was hunting. During the summer, I used to go bird-nesting; in the autumn, I'd catch the birds with birdlime, use traps,[6] or even shoot them.

One morning, I found myself running after a hare. From field to field, from vineyard to vineyard, up hill and down dale, I chased my quarry for several hours. Eventually I got near enough to take a shot at him. The poor animal, its ribs broken by the shot, rolled over, leaving me deeply upset at the sight of the poor creature in its death throes.

The gunshot brought some of my companions on the scene. While they were admiring the dead hare, I took a long look at myself. There I was in my shirt-sleeves, my cassock discarded, wearing an old straw hat that made me look like a smuggler. I realised I was more than two miles[7] from home. I was quite mortified. I apologised to my companions for the bad example I had given them by throwing off my cassock. I went straight home, once more making a resolution to be done with every kind of hunting. This time, with the Lord's help I was able to live up to my word. May God forgive me for that scandal.[8]

These three incidents taught me a terrible lesson. Henceforward I resolved to be more reserved. I was convinced that he who would give himself entirely to the Lord's service must cut himself off from worldly amusements. It is true that often they are not sinful; but it is certain that on account of conversation, of the manner of dressing, of speaking, and of acting, there is always some risk to virtue, especially to the most delicate virtue of chastity.

Louis Comollo's friendship

As long as God preserved the life of this incomparable companion, we were always very close to each other. During the holidays, we often corresponded[9] and visited back and forth. In him I saw a holy youth, and I loved him for his rare virtue. He loved me for the help I gave him with his studies. When I was with him, I modeled myself on his conduct.

Once during the holidays, he came to spend a day with me.[10] Just then, my relatives were in the fields for harvest. He asked me to check over a sermon he was to preach on the feast of the Assumption.[11] Afterwards, he practised his delivery, accompanied by gestures. We talked with delight for hours. Suddenly we realised it was nearly dinner time. There was nobody in the house but us. What were we to do? "Just a minute," said Comollo, "I'll light the fire. You get a pot ready and we'll cook something."

"Right you are," I replied, "but first let's catch a chicken in the yard. It'll provide us with soup and dinner. That's what mother would like us to do."

In no time we had our chicken. But which of us felt up to killing it? Neither of us. So as to come to the conclusion that we wanted, we decided that Comollo was to hold the bird down on a block, and I was to cut off its head with a sickle. The blow was struck, and the head dropped from the body. The two of us got squeamish and took off screaming.

"We're just childish," Comollo said after a while. "The Lord gave us the beasts of the earth for our use. Why should we be so squeamish?" Without further difficulty we picked up the chicken, plucked it, cooked it, and had our dinner.

I would have gone to Cinzano to hear Comollo's Assumption sermon, but I myself had to preach on the same theme at another venue.[12] When I went the next day, I heard praise of his sermon from all sides. That day (16 August) was the feast of St Roch.[13] It was popularly known as "the Feast of the Kitchen" because relatives and friends took occasion to invite their loved ones to enjoy some public entertainment.

Here something happened which showed the extent of my audacity. They waited for the preacher for that solemn occasion right up till the moment when he was to go to the pulpit, and he had not turned up. In an effort to help the provost of Cinzano out of his embarrassment, I did the rounds of the many priests present, begging and insisting that someone say a few words to the numerous people assembled in the church. There were no takers. Some even got annoyed by my repeated pleading and turned harshly on me: "You're a fool, you know! It's no joke to preach off the cuff on St Roch. Instead of pestering others, why don't you do it yourself?"

Those words brought applause from everyone. I was humiliated, my pride wounded. "I certainly wasn't looking for this," I said, "but as everyone else has refused, I accept."

The people in church sang a hymn to give me time to collect my thoughts. I had read the life of the saint. I recalled his story as I mounted the pulpit. I have always been told that the sermon I preached that day was the best I have ever given.

It was on this vacation and on this same occasion (1838)[14] that my friend and I went walking together to the top of a hill,[15] where we had a wonderful view of the meadows, fields, and vineyards below.

"Look, Louis," I began to say to him, "what a lean harvest there will be this year! The poor farmers! So much work for such poor returns."

"The hand of the Lord weighs heavily upon us," he replied. "Believe me, our sins have brought this on us."

"I hope the Lord will give us better crops next year."

"So do I. I hope there will be good times for those who are here to enjoy them."

"Come on, away with such gloomy thoughts. Let's be patient for this year. Next year we'll have a bumper grape harvest and we'll make better wine."

"You'll drink it."

"Perhaps you mean to keep drinking water as usual."

"I'm looking forward to a much better wine."

"What do you mean by that?"

"Never mind, never mind. The Lord knows what he's doing."

"That's not what I asked. I want to know what you mean by *I'm looking forward to better wine*. Do you mean you'll be in paradise?"

"Though I have no guarantee of going to heaven when I die, yet I have a well-grounded hope of it. For some time I've had such a burning desire to taste the happiness of the blessed that it seems impossible for my life to last much longer."

As Comollo spoke these words, his face glowed with cheer. He was bubbling with good health and looking forward to returning to the seminary.

Notes

1. Molineris identifies the district as Crivelle and the uncle as Matthew Bosco (p. 242).

2. According to Lemoyne's account of the incident (BM I, 312), one of his excuses was that he did not have his violin with him. But someone offered to lend him one.

3. We have already seen several instances of John's anger (chapters 5 and 10).

4. We have already alluded to the natural modesty of the Piedmontese. Even up to the middle of this century, in southern Europe the moral attitude toward dancing was generally much stricter than in the Anglo-Saxon countries. Attendance of men and women at public dances was often condemned

from the pulpit as a danger to chastity. Certainly in Don Bosco's time, the idea of a cleric playing the violin at a dance would have been scandalous. In Britain, Ireland, and the United States, a strong moral strain (often called puritanical) likewise discouraged dancing. For example, see Joseph E. Marks III, *The Mathers on Dancing* (Brooklyn: Dance Horizons, 1975), which includes a thirteen-page bibliography of English-language books on the morality of dancing published between 1685 and 1963.

5. It would have been his own violin that he smashed after getting home, not the borrowed one he held in his hand at that moment. Lemoyne puts the following words in Don Bosco's mouth:

> I then got up and went home. Then I took my violin, trampled on it, and smashed it into a thousand pieces. Never again did I play such an instrument, not even at church services. I had made a solemn promise and I kept it. Later I taught others how to play it, but without ever handling it. (BM I, 312)

It is more than likely that Lemoyne filled out what is missing in Don Bosco's *Memoirs* with details that he heard in his frequent chats with the saint.

6. The traps were such as to take the birds unharmed, like lobster pots.

7. More than three miles in the English measure.

8. This is another example of the exalted ideal of the priestly state. We also recall that he had forsworn hunting when he donned the clerical habit.

9. Don Bosco quotes three of these letters in Comollo's biography.

10. After John's first year of theology (1838).

11. In his biography of Comollo Don Bosco writes: "I have this sermon with me. Even though he uses well-known authors, the form and expression is obviously his own, and his strong love for the Mother of God comes through clearly."

12. This was the sermon at Alfiano that he mentioned in the previous chapter.

13. Saint Roch (ca. 1350-ca. 1378) came from Montpellier, France, and was especially known for his care of the sick. As San Rocco he is widely venerated in Italy because the plague has spared cities through his intercession.

14. According to his biography of Comollo, the following anecdote actually occurred just before the beginning of the school

year, i.e. in late October. Apparently Don Bosco hurried through his writing of this part and did not check it against the earlier work, as he usually did.

15. From these words, the rest of the chapter is copied in Father Berto's hand straight from Comollo's biography (pp. 61–63). Don Bosco's first draft contains his instructions to do so.

22

Louis Comollo's Death

The memorable events surrounding the edifying death of this dear friend have already been described in another place. Whoever wishes can read them at his pleasure. But here I would like to mention something that caused a lot of talk, something hardly touched upon in the memoirs already published.[1] Given our friendship and the unlimited trust between Comollo and me, we often spoke about the separation that death could possibly bring upon us at any time.

One day, after we had read a long passage from the lives of the saints, we talked, half in jest and half in earnest, of what a consolation it would be if the one of us who died first were to return with news about his condition. We talked of this so often that we drew up this contract: "Whichever of us is the first to die will, if God permits it, bring back word of his salvation to his surviving companion."

I did not realise the gravity of such an undertaking; and frankly, I treated it lightly enough. I would never advise others to do the like. We did it, however, and ratified it repeatedly, especially during Comollo's last illness. In fact, his last words and his last look at me sealed his promise. Many of our companions knew what had been arranged between us.

Comollo died on 2 April 1839. Next evening he was solemnly buried in Saint Philip's Church.[2] Those who knew about our bargain waited anxiously to see what would happen. I was even more anxious because I hoped for a great comfort to lighten my desolation. That night, after I went to bed in the big dormitory which I shared with some twenty other seminarians, I was restless. I was convinced that this was to be the night when our promise would be fulfilled.

About 11:30 a deep rumble was heard in the corridor. It sounded as if a heavy wagon drawn by many horses were coming up to the dormitory door. It got louder and louder, like thunder, and the whole dormitory shook. The clerics tumbled out of bed in terror and huddled together for comfort. Then, above the violent and thundering noise, the voice of Comollo was heard clearly. Three times he repeated very distinctly: "Bosco, I am saved."[3]

All heard the noise; some recognised the voice without understanding the meaning; others understood it as well as I did, as is proved by the length of time the event was talked about in the seminary. It was the first time in my life I remember being afraid. The fear and terror were so bad that I fell ill and was at death's door.[4]

I would never recommend anyone to enter into such a contract. God is omnipotent; God is merciful. As a rule he does not take heed of such pacts. Sometimes, however, in his infinite mercy he does allow things to come to fulfillment as he did in the case I have just described.[5]

Notes

1. In the first editions (1844 and 1854) of his biography of Comollo, Don Bosco wrote:

   > It seems good to note here why Comollo's death affected me so deeply. What caused this were two apparitions of his after he died. One of these was witnessed by a dormitory full of people. ... Even though the details remain sharply etched in my memory, I believe that, at least for the present, it is better to omit them.

   The first apparition is described in BM I, 350–351. In the 1884 edition of Comollo's biography, Don Bosco included the details of the second apparition, calling it "an event that caused something of a sensation both inside and outside the seminary."

2. Comollo had a frail constitution, which he wracked with severe penances and the somewhat gloomy theology of salva-

tion that prevailed in the seminary (Stella, LW, pp. 45–74; cf. Molineris, pp. 216–217; BM I, 298–300). His last days are described in BM I, 340–348.

In Comollo's biography Don Bosco wrote,

> The rector of the seminary was deeply impressed by the unusual circumstances of his death. Unhappy at the idea of the body being buried in the public cemetery, that very morning he hurried to Turin to see the civil and church authorities. He obtained permission from them to bury Comollo in the Church of St. Philip attached to the seminary.

Caselle located the grave under the sanctuary floor on the right-hand side (archdiocesan paper of Turin, November 30, 1986; Caselle, *Giovanni Bosco studente*, pp. 154–155, 198).

3. In the former seminary, a plaque on a corridor wall marks where the dormitory was and briefly mentions these events.

In the 1884 edition, Don Bosco gives a fuller description which varies in a few details (pp. 106–107):

> On the stroke of midnight, a deep rumble was heard at the end of the corridor. The rumble became deeper and louder as it drew nearer. It was like the sound of a large cart, or a railway train, or even artillery fire. I do not know how to describe the sound adequately except to say that it was such a mixture of throbbing and rather violent sounds as to leave the hearer utterly terrified and too frightened for words.

> As the rumble drew nearer it made the ceiling, walls, and floor of the hallway vibrate like sheets of metal struck by the hand of some mighty giant. Yet the sound approached so that it was very difficult to pinpoint how close it was, the way one is uncertain where a locomotive is on the track just from the jet of steam.

> All the seminarians in the dormitory woke up, but no one spoke. I was frozen with fear. The noise came nearer and nearer and grew more frightening. It reached the dormitory; of itself the door slammed open. The roar grew louder, but there was nothing to see except a ghostly multicolored light that seemed to control the sound. Suddenly there was silence, the light intensified, and Comollo's voice was distinctly heard. It called out his companion's name ["Bosco"] three straight times and then said, "I am saved."

> At that moment the dormitory grew even brighter. The noise erupted again, much longer and louder than before. It was like thunder, so violent that the house seemed about to collapse; then suddenly it stopped and the light vanished. My companions leapt from their beds and ran in all directions. Some huddled in one corner of the room while others gathered round the prefect of the dormitory, Father Joseph Fiorito from Rivoli. Everyone passed that night waiting anxiously for daylight. All this deeply

affected me; I was so scared that I would have preferred to die.

Don Bosco went on to note that, though many years had passed, some witnesses were still alive. Father Fiorito, the priest mentioned in this account, described the apparition several times to the superiors at the Oratory (BM I, 351–352). His sister Genevieve and Father Michael Chiantore, one of the seminarian-witnesses, both testified to the event in writing (Salesian Central Archives, S123 Comollo; cf. Desramaut, *LesMem*, p. 74, n. 21).

4. Stella writes,

> Conscious of the holiness that was specifically demanded of one approaching the altar, John Bosco was driven to detach himself from habits and attitudes that seemed to him to be incompatible with the priestly state. All of this took place in a general atmosphere of ascetic tension, of ongoing control and inhibition. His was an ongoing ascetic effort that drove him to fasts and abstinences, and to fits of anger with himself when he found himself indulging his old worldly abilities such as feats of agility or violin-playing. This ascetic tension helped to drive his friend Comollo to his death, and John Bosco himself to the very limits of his strength. (LW, p. 66)

This grave illness apparently lasted from April 1839 until early 1840; he had to have recovered by the time he was approved for minor orders, which he received in March 1840. The sickness seems to have been a combination of depression and nervous breakdown. It was induced by a number of factors: an extremely exalted ideal of the priesthood that magnified his sense of inadequacy; the permanent commitment entailed in ordination to the subdiaconate (see chapter 25); his asceticism; the shock of his friend's death and the frightening encounter with the supernatural.

As John grew sicker, food nauseated him and he could not sleep. Finally a doctor ordered complete rest; Mama Margaret brought John some good wine and millet bread. These two prescriptions somehow had the right effect. (BM I, 357)

5. After the account of the apparition in the biography of his friend, Don Bosco continues: "When it is a case of establishing a link between the natural and the supernatural, a poor human being can suffer serious effects. This is more particularly the case when it is a question of things not necessary for our eternal salvation."

Could there have been another reason for the terrifying circumstances that accompanied the apparition? Perhaps some consciences needed a sharp shock. Comollo two days before his death had said of his fellow seminarians, "Some of them are bad" (biography, p. 86.) Don Bosco said the same thing in chapter 19. The events did, in fact, produce some good. In the first editions of Comollo's life, Don Bosco wrote: "The rector of the seminary spoke to me only a short while ago. He assured me that the good effect produced in the seminarians by Comollo's death persists to this day."

Father
John Borel

A prize • The sacristy •
Dr John Borrelli[1]

In the seminary I was quite fortunate in that I always enjoyed the affection of my companions and of all my superiors. At the mid-year examinations it was customary to give a 60-franc prize, for each of the different years, to the person who obtained top marks for study and conduct. God truly blessed me; for the six years I spent at the seminary, I won this prize. In the second year of theology[2] I was made sacristan. It was not a post that carried much weight, but it showed one was appreciated by the superiors and it did carry with it another sixty francs. All this meant that I could provide for half my fees, while good Fr Caffasso provided the rest.[3] The sacristan has the job of seeing to the cleanliness of the church, the sacristy, and the altar; he also has to look after the lamps, candles, and all the other objects needed for divine services.

This was the year in which I had the good fortune of making the acquaintance of a man who was really zealous in the sacred ministry. He had come to preach our seminary retreat. He appeared in the sacristy with a smiling face and a joking manner of speaking, but always seasoned with moral thoughts. When I saw the way he celebrated Mass, his bearing, his preparation, and his thanksgiving, I realized at once that here was a worthy priest. He turned out to be Dr John Borrelli of Turin.[4] When he began to preach, I noted the simplicity, liveliness, clarity, and fire of charity that filled all his words; we were unanimous in rating him a man of real holiness.

In fact we all raced to go to confession to him in order to speak of our vocations and receive some advice. I too wanted to discuss the affairs of my soul with him. When, at the end, I asked him for some advice on how best to preserve the spirit of my vocation[5] during the year and particularly during the holidays, he left these memorable words with me: "A vocation is perfected and preserved, and a real priestly spirit is formed, by a climate of recollection and by frequent communion."

The retreat preached by Dr Borrelli was a landmark in the life of the seminary. Even after many years had passed, the holy points he had made in his preaching, or given in personal advice, were remembered and repeated to others.

Notes

1. Don Bosco always spells the name this way. He seems to have considered "Borel" as a kind of dialect abbreviation of the more Italian-sounding "Borrelli."

2. This was 1838–1839.

3. We saw in chapter 18, note 2, that Father Guala had arranged for John to be excused from tuition and fees for his first year at the seminary (1835–1836). Presumably Father Cafasso covered these expenses in 1836–1838, less John's academic prize money.

4. Father Borel (1801–1873) was a Salesian before the Salesians existed. As we shall see, he played an indispensable role in the founding of the Oratory. Only Father Cafasso and Father Borel stuck with Don Bosco during the critical phase of 1845–1846. It was Father Borel who kept the Oratory running during Don Bosco's near-fatal illness in the summer and fall of 1846. Giraudi wrote of him (p. 65):

   > This man, small in stature, worked in the Refuge [see chapter 30], the state prisons, and in many other parts of the city. This large-hearted, generous priest still found time to come and work in the Oratory. He stole hours from his normal sleep to come and hear confessions. Though tired from many activities, he denied his body rest it needed so that he could give the evening sermon to the youngsters on feast days and so relieve Don Bosco of this burden at least. [See chapter 53.]

   > Recalling his merits in the *Biographical Memoirs*, Lemoyne exclaims, "Eternal praise to that incomparable priest!"

Father John Borel, Don Bosco's stalwart friend and invaluable helper in the first days of the Oratory. Don Bosco respected his priestly zeal and holiness of life.

A bronze plaque set along the portico of the Oratory outside the so-called Pinardi chapel testifies perpetually to his zeal.

Father Borel's character and activity are amply described in BM I–X.

5. Note that John wanted to preserve "the spirit" of his vocation, not just the vocation. To be a priest was not enough; he had to be a worthy one, as he described Father Borel, as his seminary textbooks constantly repeated, as Margaret Bosco would very pointedly tell him after his ordination (chapter 25, note 18). Stella's observation that many sought ordination only to make comfortable careers for themselves (LW, p. 39) comes again to mind.

24

Studies

I had some mistaken notions about my studies that could have had sad consequences had I not been saved by a truly providential event. Accustomed to reading the classics all during my school days, I had grown so familiar with the outstanding characters of mythology and pagan fables that I found little satisfaction in anything ascetical.[1] I had reached the point where I could convince myself that fine language and eloquence could not be reconciled with religion.[2] The very works of the holy Fathers[3] appeared to me as the products of limited intellects, excepting always the principles of religion which they expounded with force and clarity.

At the beginning of my second year of philosophy, I paid a visit to the Blessed Sacrament one day. I had no prayer book with me, so I began to read *The Imitation of Christ*.[4] I went through some chapters dealing with the Blessed Sacrament. I was so struck by the profound thoughts expressed, and the clear and orderly way these great truths were clothed in fine language that I began to say to myself: "The author of this book was a learned man." Again and again, I went back to that golden little work. It was gradually borne in on me that even one verse from it contained so much doctrine and morality as I had found in whole volumes of the ancient classics. To this book I owe my decision to lay aside profane literature.

Subsequently, I went on to read Calmet's *History of the Old and New Testaments*.[5] Next I tackled the *Jewish Antiquities* and *The Jewish War* of Flavius Josephus;[6] Bishop

Marchetti's *Discussions on Religion*[7] followed; then Frayssinous,[8] Balmes,[9] Zucconi,[10] and many other religious writers. I even enjoyed Fleury's *Church History*, unaware that it was a book to avoid.[11] With yet more profit I read the works of Cavalca,[12] Passavanti,[13] and Segneri,[14] and all of Henrion's *History of the Church*.[15]

Perhaps you will say that with so much time given to extraneous reading I must not have been studying the treatises. This was not the case. My memory continued to be a blessing to me. Paying attention at lectures and just reading the treatises were sufficient for me to perform my duties. Thus I was able to spend the hours of study reading different books. The superiors knew all about this and left me free to do it.

One subject close to my heart was Greek. In my secondary classical studies I had already mastered its basic elements. With the help of a dictionary, I had worked my way through the first translations after I had studied the grammar. A good opportunity soon arose for me to deepen my knowledge of it.

When cholera threatened Turin in 1836, the Jesuits had to send the boarders from Our Lady of Mount Carmel College away to Montaldo.[16] This move meant that they had to double their teaching staff because they had to cover the classes for the day students who continued to come to school. Fr Caffasso, who was consulted, proposed me for a Greek class. This spurred me to get down to the serious study of the language to make myself capable of teaching it. Besides that, I was lucky enough to meet a priest of the Society, named Bini, who had a profound knowledge of Greek. I learned a lot from him. In only four months he pushed me to translate almost the whole New Testament, the first two books of Homer, and a selection of the odes of Pindar and Anacreon.[17] That worthy priest, admiring my goodwill, continued to help me.[18] For four years, each week he corrected a Greek composition or translation which I sent him, and he returned it promptly with suitable comments. By this means I managed to be able to translate Greek almost as well as I could Latin.

At this time, too, I studied French and the principles of Hebrew.[19] These three languages, Hebrew, Greek, and French, always remained my favourites after Latin and Italian.

Notes

1. His error reflected the inclinations of the period, even in church circles. Classical studies were the core of all education.

2. John's attitude was not unlike young Augustine's: *Confessions*, III, v, 9.

3. The Fathers of the Church are writers of the first centuries of Christianity esteemed for their sound doctrine and holy lives, e.g. Saint Justin Martyr, Origen, Saint Cyprian, and Saint Augustine.

4. John began his second year of philosophical studies in November 1836. The *Imitation* always remained one of his favorite books. When he did not find time for spiritual reading during the day, he would kneel before going to bed and read or reflect on a few verses from this book (BM IV, 318). He would sometimes pull it from his pocket, open it at random, then ask the person to whom he presented it to read the top lines (BM III, 432; VIII, 323). He recommended it to youngsters in the life of Dominic Savio (Aronica ed., pp. 111–112; O'Brien ed., pp. 34–35; cf. *Il Giovane provveduto* [Turin, 1885], p. 18) and to adults in *The Key to Heaven* (*La Chiave del Paradiso* [Turin, 1857], p. 38).

5. Augustin Calmet (1672–1757), a French Benedictine, published *A Literal Commentary on the Old and New Testaments* (*Commentaire littéral sur tous les livres de l'Ancien et du Nouveau Testament*, 26 vols., 1707–1716). An Italian translation came out in Turin in 1830–1831. "Calmet was one of the best Catholic exegetes of the 18th century" (NCE II, 1084).

Evidently John Bosco read most, if not all, of these works in Italian translations. A number of them were being published in Turin in the Select Economical Library of Religious Works during the 1830s (Stella, LW, p. 56, n. 55). Stella has thoroughly dissected their influence, as well as others', on Don Bosco's spirituality and theology in *ReCa*. He touches more briefly on these authors in LW, pp. 54–65. BM I, 284, mentions that John also read works by Antonio Cesari and Danielo Bartoli in the seminary.

6. Flavius Josephus (ca. 37–ca. 101) is virtually our only source

for Jewish history between the end of the biblical period and the end the first century, though not always a reliable one. After taking part in the rebellion against Rome (66–70), he turned coat and thus lived to tell the story in *The Jewish War*. He followed that work with the *Antiquities*, which tell the history of the Jews from creation up to the revolt; to it he appended an apologetic autobiography. Though he finally settled in Rome and enjoyed imperial patronage, he wrote in Greek.

7. Giovanni Marchetti (1753–1829), titular archbishop of Ancyra (Ankara), was a theologian of the Apostolic Datary of the Roman Curia. He wrote *Family Tracts on the History of Religion* (*Trattenimenti di famiglia sulla storia della religione*, 2 vols., Turin: Bianco, 1823), which may be the work that Don Bosco had in mind. By the title *Discussions on Religion* there was a work by Father Alfonso Nicolai (*Ragionamenti sopra la religione*, 8 vols., Venice and Genoa, 1770).

8. Bishop Denis Antoine Luc de Frayssinous (1765–1841) was a celebrated French preacher, member of the French Academy, and court official. A moderate Gallican and a firm royalist, he "was the outstanding Catholic apologist during the early Restoration period" (NCE VI, 82). Don Bosco must have read some of his apologetics.

   Gallicanism is an ecclesiological theory which holds that the Church in each nation should be administratively independent of the Holy See. It tends toward doctrinal independence as well, as France's long Jansenist controversy shows; and even more does it invite the interference of the civil government.

9. Jaime Luciano Balmes (1810–1848) was a Spanish apologist and philosopher. After ordination Don Bosco would have read his *Protestantism, Catholicism, and European Culture* (*El Protestantismo comparado con el Catolicismo en sus relaciones con la civilización europea*, 4 vols., Barcelona, 1842–1844) in translation (Carmagnola, 1852). In the nineteenth century it was regarded as classic. Pope Leo XIII, who had known Balmes, described him as "the foremost political talent of the 19th century and one of the greatest in the history of political writers" (cited in NCE II, 32).

   The only one of his works to appear in Italian while Don Bosco was in the seminary was a treatise on matrimony (1839), which does not fit this context. Don Bosco has slipped here, either citing the wrong author or confusing the time at which he read him. See Stella, LW, p. 55, n. 54.

10. Ferdinando Zucconi (1647–1732), a Jesuit, authored *Theological Lectures on Sacred Scripture* (*Lezioni sacre sopra la divina Scrittura*, 5 vols., Rome, 1729).

11. Claude Fleury (1640–1723), a protegé of Bossuet, was a member of the French Academy, a renowned educator, and confessor to King Louis XV. His *Histoire ecclesiastique* (20 vols., 1691–1720) covered the period up to 1414. Its Gallicanism led to its condemnation by the Index, which is undoubtedly why Don Bosco disapproved of it. Implied here is a criticism of the seminary superiors, who did not give suitable guidance to their students. John probably enjoyed the literary qualities of Fleury's work, and its otherwise edifying character. One may wonder how he could have read it without becoming aware of its Gallican leaning.

12. Domenico Cavalca (1270–1342) was a Dominican from Tuscany, the author of many ascetical tracts and reflections. One of the earliest Italian writers, he used a clear and direct style. His best known works were *The Pattern of the Cross* and *Lives of the Holy Fathers*; the former is his most original and mystical work. (Angelo Mercati and Augusto Pelzer, *Dizionario Ecclesiastico*, I [Turin: Unione Tipografico, 1953], 556)

13. Jacopo Passavanti (1302?–1357) was a Florentine Dominican, famous as a preacher, teacher, and ascetical writer. His major work, *The Pattern of True Repentance* (*Specchio di vera penitenza*, Turin, 1831), is a series of Lenten sermons and some additional material. He is frank and energetic in fighting every form of vice and has an attractive Italian style. (*Dizionario Ecclesiastico*, III [Turin, 1958], 96)

14. Paolo Segneri (1624–1694) was a Jesuit preacher, ascetical writer, and theologian of the Curia's Sacred Penitentiary. Don Bosco certainly read his *Lenten Sermons* (*Quaresimale*, Florence, 1679, often reprinted), *The Well-trained Christian*, and perhaps *Food for the Soul*. He "manifests a tremendous command of figures and imagery, indomitable vigor and zeal, and a multiplicity of converging proofs and arguments. . . . His style was in the best classical tradition . . . " (NCE XIII, 48–49).

15. Mathieu Richard Auguste Henrion (1805–1862) was a lawyer and church historian of Gallican tendency. His *Histoire générale de l'église* (12 vols., 1835–1836) was published in Italian translation in 1839.

16. Our Lady of Mount Carmel College was a Turin boarding

school for the nobility. It took its name from a former Carmelite convent and Our Lady of Mount Carmel Church on via del Carmine. Though well regarded, it was suppressed and confiscated in the anti-Jesuit fever of 1848. The college owned a magnificent country residence at Montaldo, a village about four miles north-northeast of Chieri. The cleric Bosco taught Greek there and looked after a dormitory from July 1 to October 17; we learn this from a certificate given him by the college rector, Father P. Dassi, which is preserved in the seminary record. The rector expresses his personal satisfaction because of his *honestate morum, pietate in Deum et Sacramentorum frequentia* [sound morals, piety, and frequent reception of the sacraments].

17. Pindar (522?-443 B.C.) and Anacreon (572?-?488 B.C.) were lyric poets.

18. Once more the exalted ideal of the "worthy priest" appears— this time in connection with helping an inexperienced youth.

19. Don Bosco's working knowledge of French served him well during his life, first enabling him to minister to French troops in Turin during the war of 1859, and especially assisting him on his many trips to France to establish the Salesians there and to beg for funds for his works and the building of the Church of the Sacred Heart in Rome.

    While in Rome in 1884, Don Bosco was speaking to Monsignor Menghini, a learned professor of Hebrew. The discussion came around to a controversial passage in the book of Proverbs (30:18–19). Don Bosco cited it in Hebrew and the professor did the same. Lemoyne, who was present, recorded the passage in Latin, mistakenly attributing it to Ecclesiasticus (MB XVII, 122).

25

Priestly Ordination

Sacred ordinations • Priesthood

The year Comollo died (1839) I received the tonsure and the four minor orders,[1] the third year of theology. When the school year ended, I got the idea of attempting something almost impossible—to cover the course of a year's theology during my holidays. With this in mind and without telling anyone, I presented myself to Archbishop Fransoni[2] to ask permission to study the fourth-year texts[3] during the holidays. In the following school year (1840–1) I would complete the quinquennium. I quoted my advanced age—I was 24—as the reason for my request.[4]

That holy bishop made me very welcome and, after verifying the results of the exams I had taken till then in the seminary, granted the favour I was asking on condition that I take all the treatises in the course I wanted to take. My vicar forane, Dr Cinzano, was charged with carrying out the wishes of our superior. After two months of study, I finished the prescribed treatises, and for the autumn ordinations[5] I was admitted to the subdiaconate.

When I think now of the virtues required for that most important step, I am convinced that I was not sufficiently prepared for it.[6] But since I had no one to care directly for my vocation, I turned to Fr Caffasso. He advised me to go forward and trust in his advice.

I made a ten-day retreat at the House of the Mission in Turin.[7] During it I made a general confession so that my confessor would have a clear picture of my conscience and would be able to give me suitable advice. Though I wanted to complete my studies, I quaked at the thought of binding myself for life. Before I took the final step I wanted to receive the full approbation of my confessor.[8]

Henceforward I took the greatest care to practice Doctor Borrelli's advice: a vocation is preserved and perfected by recollection and frequent communion.

On my return to the seminary I was put into the fifth year and made a prefect. This is the highest responsibility open to a seminarian.[9]

Sitientes day[10] of 1841 saw my ordination as deacon; in the summer I would be ordained a priest. I found the day I had to leave the seminary for the last time very difficult. My superiors loved me and showed continual marks of benevolence. My companions were very affectionate towards me. You could say that I lived for them and they lived for me.[11]

If anyone wanted a shave or his tonsure renewed, he ran to Bosco; if he wanted someone to make a biretta for him, to sew or patch his clothes, Bosco was the man he turned to. So you can imagine how sad was the parting from that place where I had lived for six years, where I received education, knowledge, an ecclesiastical spirit, and all the tokens of kindness and affection one could desire.

My ordination day was the vigil of the feast of the Blessed Trinity.[12] I said my first Mass in the church of St Francis of Assisi,[13] where Fr Caffasso was dean of the conferences.[14] Though a priest had not said his first Mass in my home place for many a day, and my neighbours were anxiously waiting for me to say mine there, I preferred to say it without fuss in Turin. That day was the most wonderful day of my life.

At the *Memento* in that unforgettable Mass I remembered devoutly all my teachers, my benefactors spiritual and temporal, and especially the ever-lamented Fr Calosso, whom I have always remembered as my greatest benefactor.

On Monday I said Mass in the Church of Our Lady of Consolation[15] to thank the great Virgin Mary for the innumerable graces she had obtained for me from her divine Son Jesus.

On Tuesday I went to say Mass in St Dominic's Church in Chieri, where my old professor Fr Giusiana was still living.[16] With fatherly affection he assisted me. I spent the whole day with him, one I can call a day in paradise.

Thursday was the solemnity of Corpus Christi. I went home and sang Mass in the local church and took part in the procession of the Blessed Sacrament.[17] The parish priest invited to dinner my relatives, the clergy, and the people of standing in the vicinity. They were all happy to be a part of it because my compatriots loved me very much and they were all glad everything had turned out well for me. I went home that evening to be with my family.[18] As I drew near the house and saw the place of the dream[19] I had when I was about nine, I could not hold back the tears. I said: "How wonderful are the ways of Divine Providence! God has truly raised a poor child from the earth to place him amongst the princes of his people."[20]

Notes

1. Comollo died in April 1839. Caselle (*Giovanni Bosco studente*) has found documentation for these ordinations and John's diaconal and presbyteral ones (pp. 203, 207). According to this, John received the tonsure and minor orders on Saturday, March 28, 1840, the day before the fifth Sunday of Lent.

   The rite and the subsequent ordinations took place in the Church of the Immaculate Conception, the private chapel of the archbishops of Turin (corner of via Arsenale and via Lascaris).

   Tonsure was the cutting or shaving of a patch of hair from the crown of the head; it marked one's canonical entrance to the clerical state before both Church and State. The four minor orders were acolyte, reader, exorcist, and doorkeeper. In the 1973 reforms of the Latin liturgy, these rites were suppressed and replaced by admission to candidacy for ordination (for diocesan seminarians) and installation to the ministries of acolyte and reader (no longer exclusively clerical).

2. This is Don Bosco's first mention of his great patron Louis Fransoni (1789–1862), archbishop of Turin from 1832. On his promotion to the see of Turin from Fossano, he actively encouraged the work of Father Guala and the Convitto Ecclesiastico in clerical formation. In the political and social storms of the 1840s and '50s, he was one of the "intransigents" who feared that any concession to popular government or the separation of Church and State would lead to the downfall of religion and the monarchy. After the govern-

ment exiled him in 1850, he governed the archdiocese from Lyons and became for the conservative elements of Piedmontese society a symbolic martyr to the cause of the rights of the Church. See Stella, *EcSo*, various references to Fransoni; Denis Mack Smith, *Cavour* (NY: Knopf, 1985), pp. 26, 49; William Roscoe Thayer, *The Life and Times of Cavour* (Boston: Houghton Mifflin, 1911), I, 124, 288–293. See also chapter 55, note 7.

Don Bosco enjoyed excellent relations with Archbishop Fransoni. As we shall see, the archbishop actively encouraged his work, defended it against public opposition, and appointed him head of all the oratories in the city. He also approved the beginning stages of the Salesian Society. See BM II–VI.

3. The texts were Alasia's *De poenitentia* [Penance] and Gazzaniga's *De Eucharistia* [The Eucharist]. On these authors, see Stella, LW, pp. 49–50.

4. The quinquennium was the five-year period of theological study prior to ordination. John turned 25 in August 1840.

5. Customary times for ordinations were near the ember days, special days of fast and abstinence. They were observed on the Wednesday, Friday, and Saturday preceding the first Sunday of Lent and following Pentecost, the feast of the Holy Cross (September 14), and the feast of Saint Lucy (December 13). In Turin the spring ordinations were usually on the day before the fifth Sunday in Lent (Caselle, *Giovanni Bosco studente*, pp. 203, 207).

6. The subdiaconate was the definitive step by which one permanently committed himself to the clerical life, to celibacy, to praying the breviary, etc. Teresio Bosco says of the solemn vow of chastity, "From this vow the Church dispensed no one for any reason" (BN, p. 99). Even apart from the exalted priestly ideal that John fostered, it is natural to hesitate before taking such an irrevocable step, as anyone who has been ordained or married knows.

The subdiaconate was suppressed in the 1973 liturgical reforms. The ordinand now makes his definitive commitment in conjunction with the diaconate.

John was ordained subdeacon on Saturday, September 19, 1840. In those days admission to the subdiaconate required that one have an ecclesiastical patrimony of five thousand lire. Since John's share of the inheritance from his father was insufficient, Joseph made up the difference by giving him another field, which consequently became known as the field of Don Bosco's patrimony.

A cleric was expected to able to maintain himself in a suitable manner. He should not have to depend on his bishop for his livelihood or be forced to undertake some worldly profession; still less should he be reduced to begging. The property required as such assurance was his ecclesiastical patrimony. The salaries and stipends of most priests were not nearly adequate to support them. Nowadays most diocesan priests are salaried either by their dioceses or, in some countries, by the government. Religious priests are provided for by their communities, of course, as they always were. See *The Catholic Encyclopedia* (NY: Appleton, 1907), I, 312.

7. Archbishop Chiaveroti had especially entrusted to Saint Vincent de Paul's Congregation of the Mission the formation of the clergy of Turin. For this purpose they ran a retreat house in Turin at what is now 23 via XX Settembre. The church is called the Church of the Visitation because Saint Jane Frances de Chantal founded a convent of the Visitation there; it and their church were confiscated during the Napoleonic regime. It passed first to the diocesan clergy and then to the Vincentians, led by Father Mark Anthony Durando (1801–1880). Thus the Vincentians brought to Turin the beneficent spirituality of Bérulle and Saint Francis de Sales. All the preordination retreats were made here. See Molineris, pp. 248–249; Giraudo and Biancardi, pp. 123–124.

8. When Don Bosco insisted on frequent confession as a key to a sound education and to a solid religious life, the forgiveness of sin was only one aspect. The other was prudent spiritual direction, especially when it was a matter of deciding on one's state of life. In chapter 16, he lamented the lack of such guidance in his own case.

9. As prefect he exercised authority over his fellow students and was responsible for their conduct (BM I, 374).

10. Saturday of the fourth week of Lent, March 27 in 1841. The name comes from the opening word of the introit of the day's Latin Mass. At his preordination examination on February 17, one of the examiners was Father Lawrence Gastaldi, who gave him a grade of only *fere optime* (A−).

Roman Catholic deacons assist bishops or presbyters during the sacred liturgy. In particular, they proclaim the gospel and distribute communion; they may also preach, baptize, and witness marriages.

11. His peers also were sad to see him go. Lemoyne gathers some of their testimony in BM I, 383–384. The curial records of Turin contain a list of the seminarians of 1840–1841. John Bosco is described therein as "zealous and promising." At his final exam on May 15, he obtained the grade *plus-quam optime* (A+).

12. Archbishop Fransoni ordained John and his fifteen classmates presbyters on Saturday, June 5. They made their preordination retreat from May 26 to June 4. At the end of the retreat John made nine resolutions, which he wrote in an exercise book. See the comment following the notes.

    With his ordination as a presbyter (a "priest," in common usage), John was empowered to celebrate the Holy Eucharist, hear confessions (for which further authorization was required), and anoint the sick. He also took the title "Don" (from the Latin *dominus*) by which Italian priests are commonly called and by which he has been known ever since.

13. At this first Mass he was assisted by his benefactor and spiritual director Father Cafasso. Newly ordained priests had to be assisted for some time through the complicated rubrics of the Mass. Don Bosco used the altar of the Guardian Angel (the side altar closest to the main altar, on the left). The Church of Saint Francis of Assisi, at the corner of via S. Francesco d'Assisi and via Barbaroux, belonged to the Franciscans until 1801, when Napoleon suppressed religious orders and turned the monastery into a barracks. Father Guala became rector of the church in 1808, and in 1818 he set up the Convitto Ecclesiastico in the former monastery.

14. Father Cafasso was in charge of the faculties of moral theology and preaching at the Convitto, where instruction was given in two daily lectures. Father Cafasso's were renowned (see chapter 6, comment, and chapter 27).

15. Our Lady of Consolation (*La Consolata*) is the principal patroness of Turin; her church is a favorite of the faithful. It is located on via della Consolata, a block south of corso Regina Margherita. The church is actually two baroque churches joined, built by Guarini (1679) and decorated by Juvara (1714). The campanile may date from the tenth century. Saint Joseph Cafasso's body is preserved there.

16. The Church of Saint Dominic dates from the fourteenth century and is entrusted to the Dominicans, Father Giusiana's

order. The miraculous cincture of Saint Thomas Aquinas is kept as a relic there. Don Bosco celebrated Mass at the altar of Our Lady of the Rosary, about midway down the right side of the church.

17. We know from other sources that on the Wednesday Don Bosco celebrated Mass in the Chieri cathedral at the altar of Our Lady of Grace, where he had often prayed as a youth.

    His Mass "at home" was at Saint Andrew's in Castelnuovo, where Father Cinzano was still the pastor. Corpus Christi is still a holy day of obligation in Italy, and it was also a public holiday then. The procession was a major part of the religious festivities.

18. In 1839 Joseph had built himself a house a few yards away from the old family home, and he, his family, and Margaret moved back to Becchi. Don Bosco spoke frequently and emotionally of that evening with his mother. Lemoyne has recorded what she told him:

    > You are now a priest, and you celebrate Mass. You are, therefore, closer to Jesus Christ. But remember that to begin to say Mass is to begin to suffer. You will not become aware of this immediately, but little by little you will realize that your mother was right. I am sure that you will pray for me every day, whether I be still living or dead, and that is enough for me. From now on you must think only of saving souls; never worry about me. (BM I, 388)

    We see, then, that Mama Margaret had special advice for the four most solemn moments of her son's life: first communion, choice of vocation, clothing ceremony, and priesthood.

19. The "place of the dream" is the field where he saw himself in the landmark dream at age nine. Today a monument marks the place near his home.

20. An allusion to Psalm 113:7–8.

Comment on Don Bosco's Ordination Resolutions

In his notebook John wrote:

> Souvenir of the spiritual retreat prior to the celebration of my first Mass. The priest does not go to heaven or to hell alone. If he does God's work he will go to heaven with the souls he has saved by his good example. If he has been a cause of scandal, he will go to perdition

along with the souls that were damned through his scandal. Therefore I pledge myself to keep the following resolutions:

1. Never to go for a stroll unless for grave reasons like visiting the sick, etc.

2. To be very rigorous in the use of my time.

3. To suffer, work, humble myself in all things whenever it is a question of saving souls.

4. The charity and gentleness of Saint Francis de Sales are to be my guide.

5. I will always be satisfied with whatever food is presented to me, if not harmful to my health.

6. I shall drink my wine mixed with water, and then only to the extent that it will benefit my health.

7. Work is a powerful weapon against the enemies of the soul. Hence I shall not take more than five or six hours of sleep. I shall take no rest during the day, particularly after lunch. Only in case of illness shall I make an exception to this rule.

8. I shall set aside some time every day for meditation and spiritual reading. During the day I shall pay a brief visit to the Blessed Sacrament, or at least raise my heart in prayer. I shall spend at least a quarter of an hour in preparation for Mass and another quarter of an hour in thanksgiving.

9. I shall never indulge in conversations with women, except to hear their confession or when it is necessary for their spiritual welfare. (BM I, 385)

The fourth resolution is Don Bosco's first definite reference to Saint Francis de Sales. An incident at the seminary gives an earlier hint. According to Father Giacomelli's testimony,

John was called *Bosco of Castelnuovo* to distinguish him from another seminarian by the same surname. . . . In this connection I remember a little incident which, though unimportant, impressed me. The two Boscos were joking about their names and wondering whether they should use some nickname for clarity's sake.

The other Bosco said: "Bosco means wood. I like *nespolo* wood [medlar, hard and knotty], so call me *Nespolo*."

"I, instead, like *sales* [willow, in Piedmontese] wood which is soft and flexible, so call me *Sales*."

Was he perhaps already thinking about the future Society of Saint Francis de Sales while he tried to imitate the benignity of this saint? Sensitive as he was even in minor things, he would easily have been carried away by anger if he had been less virtuous. No other seminarian (and there were many) was so prone to flare up. It was evident, nevertheless, that John fought earnestly and steadily to keep his temper under control. (BM I, 302)

Authentic portrait of Saint Francis de Sales, painted in 1618. It is preserved at the Visitation monastery at Moncalieri (Turin).

Several of these ordination pledges would eventually turn up in the Salesian rule in one form or another; perhaps the third is the most noteworthy. In the first draft of the Constitutions it becomes: "Let everyone be ready to suffer, if necessary, heat, cold, thirst, hunger, hardships, and contempt whenever these may contribute to the greater glory of God, the welfare of souls, and the salvation of one's own soul" (BM V, 644, no. 12). This article remained exactly the same until 1972 (cf. article 42), when it was slightly modified. In the 1984 Constitutions, the last paragraph of article 18 reads: "[The Salesian] does not look for unusual penances but accepts the daily demands and renunciations of the apostolic life. He is ready to suffer cold and heat, hunger and thirst, weariness and disdain whenever God's glory and the salvation of souls require it."

The best studies of Saint Francis de Sales available in English are two translations from French: Maurice Henry-Coüannier, *Saint Francis de Sales and His Friends*, trans. Veronica Morrow (Staten Island, N.Y.: Alba House, 1973), and André Ravier, S.J., *Francis de Sales: Sage and Saint* (San Francisco: Ignatius, 1988).

26

First Priestly Ministry

*Priestly work begins • Sermon at
Lavriano • John Brina*

In that year (1841) my parish priest was looking for a
curate. I helped him out for five months.[1] I found the work
a great pleasure. I preached every Sunday. I visited the sick
and administered the holy sacraments to them, except penance since I had not yet taken the exam.[2] I buried the dead,
kept the parish records, wrote out certificates of poverty,[3]
and so on. My delight was to make contact with the children and teach them catechism. They used to come from
Murialdo to see me, and on my visits home they crowded
round me. Whenever I left the presbytery there was a
group of boys, and everywhere I went my little friends
gave me a warm welcome.

As I had a certain facility in expounding the word of
God, I was in much demand as a preacher, to give festal
homilies in the nearby villages. At the end of October that
year I was invited to preach on St Benignus at Lavriano.[4]
I was happy to accept because that was the birthplace of
my friend Fr John Grassino, now parish priest in
Scalenghe.[5] I was anxious to do justice to the occasion and
so prepared and wrote out my address carefully, trying to
make it popular and at the same time polished. I studied it
well, determined to win glory from it.

But God wanted to teach a terrible lesson to my pride.
It was a feast day, and I had to say holy Mass for the
people before setting off. To get there in time for the sermon I had to go on horseback.[6] Sometimes trotting, sometimes galloping, I was about halfway along and had reached
the valley of Casalborgone between Cinzano and Bersano.

As I passed a millet field, a flock of sparrows took sudden flight. The noise of their flight frightened the horse, and he bolted down the road and across the fields and meadows. Somehow I managed to stay in the saddle, but then I realised that it was slipping under the horse's belly. I tried an equestrian maneuver, but the saddle was out of place and forced me upwards, and I fell head first onto a heap of broken stones. From a hill close by, a man could see this regrettable accident; he ran to my assistance with one of his workers and, finding me unconscious, carried me to his house and laid me on his best bed. They gave me the most loving care, and after an hour I came to and realised that I was in a strange house.

"Don't let that worry you," my host said, "and don't be upset that you're in a strange house. Here you'll want for nothing. I've sent for the doctor, and someone has gone to catch your horse. I'm a farmer, but I have everything I need. Do you feel any pain?"

"God reward you for your charity, my good friend," I said. "I don't think I've done much damage. A broken collar bone, maybe. I can't move it. Where am I?"

"You're on Bersano Hill in the house of John Calosso, better known as *Brina*.[7] I'm at your service. I, too, have got round a bit and know what it is to need help. Many a spill I've had going to fairs and markets!"

"While we're waiting for the doctor, tell me some of your stories."

"Oh," he said, "I have lots of things I could tell you. Like this one. One autumn a few years ago, I was going to Asti on my donkey to collect winter provisions. On my way home, when I got to the valley of Murialdo, my poor beast, quite overloaded, fell in a mud hole and lay there in the middle of the road unable to move. Every effort to get her up again proved useless. It was midnight, dark and wet. Not knowing what else to do, I shouted for help. In a few minutes someone answered from a little house nearby. They came, a seminarian and his brother, and two other men with a lamp to light their way. They got her out of the muck, having first unloaded her. They took me and all my baggage to their house. I was half dead and covered with mud. They cleaned me up and put new life into me with a magnificent supper. Then they gave me a nice, soft bed. In the morning before I left I wanted to pay them for all they had done for me, but the seminarian turned everything down flat, saying, "Who knows? Someday we may need your help."

I was moved to tears by his words. When he saw my reaction, he asked me if I were ill.

"No," I replied, "your story gives me great pleasure, and that's what moves me."

"How happy I would be," he went on, "if I knew what I could do for that good family! What fine people!"

"What was their name?"

"Bosco," he said, "popularly known as Boschetti.[8] But why are you so moved? You know them, maybe? How is that seminarian?"

"That seminarian, my good friend, is this priest whom you have repaid a thousand times for what he did for you. The very one whom you've carried to your home and put into this bed. Divine Providence wants to teach us through this incident that one good turn deserves another."

You can imagine the wonder, the pleasure, that good Christian and I both felt, that in my hour of need God had let me fall into the hands of such a friend. His wife, his sister, his other relatives, and his friends were delighted to know that the one who had so many times featured in their conversation was actually in their house.

The doctor arrived a short time later. He found no bones broken. After a few days I could head home on the recaptured horse. John Brina came the whole way home with me. For as long as he lived we remained fast friends.

After this warning, I firmly resolved that in the future I would prepare my sermons for the greater glory of God, and not to appear learned and erudite.[9]

Notes

1. From June 10 to November 2. These five months were an internship of sorts, his first ministerial experience except for teaching catechism and the few sermons he preached as

a seminarian. Nowadays seminarians gain a great deal of experience during the time of their studies, including a mandatory year of internship between ordinations to the diaconate and to the presbyterate. In the next chapter Don Bosco will speak of the decision which he had to make during the summer concerning his future.

2. Before a priest is permitted to hear confessions, he must demonstrate competence and be granted canonical faculties by his bishop or his religious superior to do so. Don Bosco was granted temporary faculties on November 30, 1842, and permanent ones on June 10, 1843.

3. Entitling a person or family to public assistance.

4. He was to preach there on the last Sunday in October. The feast of Saint Benignus is November 1; he was martyred at Dijon, France, late in the second century. Lavriano (or Lauriano) is a village about ten miles north of Castelnuovo.

5. Father Grassino (1820–1902) entered the seminary in the fall of 1840 (Stella, *EcSo*, pp. 412–413). He helped Don Bosco in his early work as director of the oratory in Borgo Vanchiglia (Turin) and vice director at Valdocco; later he was rector of the Giaveno minor seminary while it was under Don Bosco's direction (Molineris, p. 269; BM VI). He never became a Salesian, and in fact he and Don Bosco had a falling out in 1861 over control of the Giaveno seminary.

6. John learned to ride in the summer of 1832. During the previous school year he had shot through three classes at Chieri. Feeling the need for some review, he took some summer lessons with the assistant pastor at Castelnuovo. He spent the day at the rectory. As a bit of compensation, Father Dassano, the pastor at that time, asked John to look after his horse. While exercising the horse, John not only learned to ride it, but even played the acrobat by learning to stand on its back while it was at a gallop. (BM I, 204–205) Such feats and his gifted memory did not guarantee that he would remember all that goes into mastering a horse, including such fundamentals as properly cinching the saddle.

7. Molineris (p. 270) gives the man's name as Cafasso, not Calosso. He also reports that the nickname "Brina" came from the farmstead.

In 1875 Don Bosco had a dream in the course of which two of the stalwarts from the early days of the Oratory, Gastini and Buzzetti, tried to get him to mount a horse. Don Bosco objected that he had done that once before and fallen off. Eventually he yielded, and the dream proceeded. (BM XI, 240)

8. "Little Boscos," a nickname probably given them because, like Don Bosco, most of the family were of small stature.

9. John several times made resolutions and had difficulty keeping them, e.g. in giving up his "worldly" ways like hunting and violin-playing (chapters 17 and 21) and in preaching for the good of God's people (chapter 20 and here). Saints do not drop straight down from heaven but have to work at overcoming their faults like everyone else.

27

Learning to Be a Priest

The Convitto Ecclesiastico

At the end of the holidays, I had three situations to choose from. I could have taken a post as tutor in the house of a Genoese gentleman with a salary of a thousand francs a year.[1] The good people of Murialdo were so anxious to have me as their chaplain that they were prepared to double the salary paid to chaplains up to then. Last, I could have become a curate in my native parish.[2]

Before I made a final choice, I sought out Fr Caffasso in Turin to ask his advice. For several years now he had been my guide in matters both spiritual and temporal. That holy priest listened to everything, the good money offers, the pressures from relatives and friends, my own goodwill to work.

Without a moment's hesitation, this is what he said: "You need to study moral theology and homiletics. For the present, forget all these offers and come to the Convitto."[3]

I willingly followed his wise advice; on 3 November 1841, I enrolled at the Convitto.[4]

The Convitto Ecclesiastico completed, you might say, the study of theology. In the seminary we studied only dogma, and that speculative; and in moral theology only controversial issues. Here one learnt to be a priest. Meditation, spiritual reading, two conferences a day, lessons in preaching, a secluded life, every convenience for study, reading good authors — these were the areas of learning to which we had to apply ourselves.[5]

At that time, two prominent men were in charge of this most useful institution: Doctor Louis Guala and Fr Joseph Caffasso. Doctor Guala was the work's founder.[6] An unselfish man, rich in knowledge, prudent, and fearless, he was everyone's friend in the days of the regime of Napoleon I. He founded that extraordinary seedbed where young priests fresh from their seminary courses could learn the practical aspects of their sacred ministry. This proved very valuable to the Church, especially as a means of eradicating the vestiges of Jansenism that still persisted in our midst.[7]

Amongst other topics the most controversial was the question of Probabilism and Probabiliorism.[8] Chief amongst the former's advocates were Alasia and Antoine,[9] along with other rigorist authors. The practice of this doctrine can lead to Jansenism. The Probabilists followed the teaching of St Alphonsus, who has now been proclaimed a Doctor of the Church.[10] His authority can be called the theology of the Pope since the Church has proclaimed that his works can be taught, preached, and practised, as they contain nothing worthy of censure.

Dr Guala took a strong stance between the two parties; starting from the principle that the charity of O.L.J.C.[11] should be the inspiration of all systems, he was able to bring the two extremes together. Things came together so well that, thanks to Doctor Guala, St Alphonsus become our theological patron. This was a salutary step, long desired, and now we are reaping its benefit. Fr Caffasso was Guala's right-hand man. His virtue, which withstood all tests, his amazing calm, his shrewd insight, and his prudence enabled him to overcome the acrimony that was still alive in some probabiliorists against the Liguorians.[12]

Dr Felix Golzio, a hidden gold mine amongst the Turinese clergy, was also at the Convitto.[13] In his modest life-style he was hardly noticeable. But he was a tireless worker, humble and knowledgeable; he was a real support, or better, Guala and Caffasso's right-hand man.

The prisons, hospitals, pulpits, charitable institutes,[14] the sick in their homes, the cities, the villages, and we might add, the mansions of the rich and the hovels of the poor felt the salutary effects of the zeal of these three luminaries of the Turinese clergy. These were the three models placed in my path by Divine Providence. It was just up to me to follow their example, their teaching, their virtues.

Fr Caffasso, who for six years had been my guide, was especially my spiritual director. If I have been able to do any good, I owe it to this worthy priest in whose hands I placed every decision I made, all my study, and every activity of my life.[15] It was he who first took me into the prisons, where I soon learned how great was the malice and misery of mankind. I saw large numbers of young lads aged from 12 to 18, fine healthy youngsters, alert of mind, but seeing them idle there, infested with lice, lacking food for body and soul, horrified me. Public disgrace, family dishonour, and personal shame were personified in those unfortunates. What shocked me most was to see that many of them were released full of good resolutions to go straight, and yet in a short time they landed back in prison, within a few days of their release.

On such occasions I found out how quite a few were brought back to that place; it was because they were abandoned to their own resources. "Who knows?" I thought to myself, "if these youngsters had a friend outside who would take care of them, help them, teach them religion on feast days ... Who knows but they could be steered away from ruin, or at least the number of those who return to prison could be lessened?"

I talked this idea over with Fr Caffasso. With his encouragement and inspiration I began to work out in my mind how to put the idea into practice, leaving to the Lord's grace what the outcome would be. Without God's grace, all human effort is vain.[16]

Notes

1. This was a substantial sum of money. John's room, board, and tuition at the seminary had been 240 lire per year. As late as 1858, elementary school teachers in Piedmont were making only 300 lire per year (Mack Smith, p. 132).

2. Two of the offers emphasized salary. Margaret, instead, took this attitude: "My son in the house of a rich gentleman? What would these 1,000 lire profit him, or me, or his brother Joseph, if John were to lose his soul?" (BM II, 30). See also her advice on his vocation (chapter 16, note 8).

3. Seminary training in Chieri was primarily intellectual, emphasizing dogma. But there is more than a little likelihood that Father Cafasso understood his younger friend's spiritual intensity and saw a need to temper it not only with pastoral practice under guidance ("field training") but also with a more moderate spirituality and moral theology. On the Convitto, theology in Piedmont, and Don Bosco's maturation, see Stella, LW, pp. 78–100. On Saint Joseph Cafasso's spirituality, see his *The Priest, the Man of God: His Dignity and His Duties*, trans. Patrick O'Connell (Rockford, Illinois: TAN, 1971).

   We may also wonder whether Father Cafasso, knowing John's commitment to young people and the crying need for someone to begin to care for the hordes of youngsters in the great city, did not see an opportunity to bring the two together: Don Bosco and poor, abandoned youth.

4. The term *convitto* means a residence hall. Room and board at the Convitto amounted to 30 lire a month. Don Bosco was excused from a total of 341 lire during his three school years there. No doubt he was able to pay some of the fees from his own priestly stipends. His register of Mass intentions from those years is in the Salesian archives (AS 132 Quaderni, 7; Stella, *EcSo*, pp. 414–416). How he paid the rest is unknown, but we may guess that Fathers Guala and Cafasso had a hand in it, as before.

5. The program normally lasted two years; sometimes an exceptional priest might take another year. The daily schedule is given in Giraudo and Biancardi, pp. 131–132. There were at least forty students in residence while Don Bosco was there.

6. To say that Father Guala (1775–1848) was the founder of the Convitto is only partly correct. The man really responsible was the Servant of God Father Pius Bruno Lanteri, founder of the Oblates of the Virgin Mary and of Saint Ignatius Retreat House at Lanzo. Imbued with the spirituality of Saint Ignatius Loyola and of Saint Alphonsus Liguori, he was intent on fostering a more benign outlook in the Turinese clergy. See NCE VIII, 379; Leon Cristiani, *A Cross for Napoleon: The Life of Father Bruno Lanteri (1759–1830)*, trans. Keith Mayes and Madeleine Soudée (Boston: St. Paul Editions, 1981).

   Father Guala had been trained in Genoa, where society was under Italian rather than French influences, the clergy more Alphonsian than Jansenist. In Turin he became Father Lanteri's most outstanding disciple, earning credit for financing and directing the Convitto for the renewal of the clergy. It was he who established the institute at Saint Francis of Assisi Church (1818). See Stella, *EcSo*, pp. 43–54; Bonetti, p. 6. Archbishop Fransoni, a native Genoan, had likewise been trained in a moderate moral and pastoral theological approach. He opposed the theologians of the University of Turin, very actively supported the Convitto, and promoted priests who had been trained there.

7. Jansenism was a complex of very rigid doctrines dealing with grace and free will, as well as the conditions needed for receiving the sacraments. It was based on the *Augustinus*, a posthumous work of Cornelius Jansen (1585–1638), bishop of Ypres in Flanders, which expounded the theology of Saint Augustine. The Popes condemned the book's doctrine of grace repeatedly, most solemnly in the bull *Unigenitus* (1713).

   A century and a half of turmoil over Jansenism disturbed both Church and State in France. Gallicanism, the influence of the Jesuits, royal authority, and other points were at issue. See NCE VII, 820–826; more briefly, *Encyclopedia of Theology: The Concise Sacramentum Mundi*, ed. Karl Rahner (New York: Crossroad, 1986), pp. 727–730.

   Since Piedmont was so closely linked to French culture, it was affected by these currents. When Don Bosco speaks of the "vestiges" of Jansenism, it is something of an understatement. See Stella, LW, pp. 78–91; Cristiani, pp. 11–16.

8. Probabilism, a system in moral theology, taught that an action may be presumed lawful if it is backed by a solidly probable opinion, i.e. if it is based on reasons sufficient to win a prudent assent. See NCE XI, 814–815. It was much favored by the Jesuits, mortal enemies of the Jansenists; Saint Alphonsus promoted a similar system, called equiprobabilism.

   Probabiliorism was another moral theory. It held that it is never lawful to hold a probable opinion if there is another opinion which is more probable. Those with a Jansenist outlook held to this theory. These rigorists maintained that the recently canonized Saint Alphonsus was responsible for lamentable laxity among the clergy. See NCE XI, 814.

9. He means, "the latter's," i.e. the probabiliorists. Giuseppe Antonio Alasia (1731–1812) was strict in practical matters; but that he had Jansenist tendencies is anything but clear. In

fact both Fathers Guala and Cafasso used his *Penance* as a text at the Convitto (Stella, LW, pp. 49–50).

Paul Gabriel Antoine (1678–1743) was a French Jesuit. His *General Moral Theology* (1726) was widely acclaimed, though Saint Alphonsus thought it too severe. (NCE I, 641)

10. Saint Alphonsus Liguori (1696–1787), founder of the Redemptorists and prolific writer in moral theology, had been canonized only in 1839. He was proclaimed a Doctor of the Church by Pope Pius IX in 1871, shortly before the composition of the *Memoirs*. Don Bosco took his thoughts on the importance of following one's vocation from Saint Alphonsus: see Introduction to the *Constitutions of the Society of Saint Francis de Sales* (Paterson, New Jersey, 1957), pp. 4–16; 1966 Constitutions (Madras, 1967), pp. 8–22. On Saint Alphonsus, see NCE I, 336–341; Butler's *Lives*, III, 242–249; D.F. Miller and L.X. Aubin, *Saint Alphonsus Liguori* (Rockford, Illinois: TAN, 1987).

11. Our Lord Jesus Christ.

12. The conferences and lessons at the Convitto, says Stella, did not teach a particular theological system or theory of the apostolate. Instead, they posed practical cases and the art of caring for souls. "Situations from everyday life were presented, and then put to the test in such priestly activities as preaching, giving catechism lessons, and so forth" (LW, p. 98). Among Stella's resources for studying the Convitto is at least one notebook made by a student from Father Cafasso's lectures (conversation, June 6, 1986).

13. After Father Cafasso died in 1860, Don Bosco chose Father Golzio (1808?–1873) as his confessor and spiritual director. Like Father Cafasso, Father Golzio was convinced that God was leading his penitent by extraordinary means. He presided over the Convitto from 1867 until his death.

14. At a time of tremendous social upheaval (see chapter 28, note 1 and comment), Turin was remarkable for its public and private associations and institutions to care for the poor, the sick, and the ignorant. This extensive network of charity, as well as the broad mingling of social classes through housing patterns in the city center, receives much credit for sparing Turin, alone among major Italian cities, an uprising in 1848 (Woolf, pp. 291–292, 326).

15. Don Bosco means what he says quite literally, as will be evident in chapter 30. As his confessor and director of soul,

Father Cafasso guided his spiritual development and every major decision (cf. Stella, LW, pp. 97–98). This docile attitude goes back, at least in part, to that searing adolescent experience of Father Calosso's death and the dream that followed (chapter 6).

16. Is it accidental that the chapter dealing with Jansenism should end on a note of grace? At the least, here is a reminder to Salesians and all apostles that all their genius, all their hard work, all their initiative cannot guarantee a healthy spiritual response; God's grace still must touch the human heart, and the apostle is only a medium which may facilitate that. Moreover, the apostle must be a person of prayer, not just a doer of deeds, because only prayer gives access to divine grace.

Bartholomew Garelli

*The feast of the Immaculate
Conception
and the beginning of the festive
oratory*

Hardly had I registered at the Convitto of St Francis,
when I met at once a crowd of boys[1] who followed me in
the streets and the squares and even into the sacristy of the
church attached to the institute. But I could not take direct
care of them since I had no premises. A humourous incident[2] opened the way to put into action my project[3] for the
boys who roamed the streets of the city, especially those
released from prison.

On the solemnity of the Immaculate Conception of Mary
(8 December 1841), I was vesting to celebrate holy Mass at
the appointed time. Joseph Comotti, the sacristan, seeing a
boy in a corner, asked him to come and serve my Mass.

"I don't know how," he answered, completely embarrassed.

"Come on," repeated the sacristan, "I want you to serve
Mass."

"I don't know how," the boy repeated. "I've never served
Mass."

"You little brat," said the sacristan, quite furious, "if you
don't know how to serve Mass, what are you doing in the
sacristy?" With that he grabbed a feather duster and hit the
poor boy about the head and shoulders.

As the boy beat a hasty retreat, I cried loudly, "What are
you doing? Why are you beating him like that? What's he
done?"

"Why is he hanging round the sacristy if he doesn't
know how to serve Mass?"

"But you've done wrong."

"What does it matter to you?"

"It matters plenty. He's a friend of mine. Call him back at once. I need to speak with him."

"*Tuder! Tuder!*"[4] he began to shout, as he ran after him. Promising him better treatment, he brought the lad back to me. He came over trembling and tearful because of the blows he had received.[5]

"Have you attended Mass yet?" I asked him with as much loving kindness[6] as I could.

"No," he answered.

"Well, come to Mass now. Afterwards I'd like to talk to you about something that will please you."

He promised to do as I said. I wanted to calm down the poor fellow's spirit and not leave him with that sad impression towards the people in charge of that sacristy. Once I had celebrated my Mass and made due thanksgiving,[7] I took my candidate into a side chapel. Trying to allay any fear he might have of another beating, I started questioning him cheerfully:

"My good friend, what's your name?"

"My name's Bartholomew Garelli."

"Where are you from?"

"Asti."

"Is your father alive?"

"No, my father's dead."

"And your mother?"

"My mother's dead too."

"How old are you?

"I'm sixteen."

"Can you read and write?"[8]

"I don't know anything."[9]

"Have you made your first communion?"

"Not yet."[10]

"Have you ever been to confession?"

"Yes, when I was small."

"Are you going to catechism classes now?"

"I don't dare."

"Why?"

"Because the other boys are smaller than I am, and they know their catechism. As big as I am, I don't know anything, so I'm ashamed to go."

The sacristy of the Church of Saint Francis of Assisi. Here Don Bosco met
Bartholomew Garelli on December 8, 1841, while preparing to celebrate
Mass, and thus began the Salesian work.

"If I were to teach you catechism on your own, would you come?"

"I'd come very willingly."

"Would you come willingly to this little room?"

"I'd come willingly enough, provided they don't beat me."

"Relax. No one will harm you. On the contrary, you'll be my friend and you'll be dealing with me and no one else. When would you like us to begin our catechism?"

"Whenever you wish."

"This evening?"

"Okay."

"Are you willing right now?"

"Yes, right now, with great pleasure."

I stood up and made the sign of the cross to begin; but my pupil made no response because he did not know how to do it. In that first catechism lesson I taught him to make the sign of the cross. I also taught him to know God the Creator and why he created us. Though Bartholomew's memory was poor, with attentive diligence in a few feast days[11] he learned enough to make a good confession and, soon after, his holy communion.

To this first pupil some others were added.[12] During that winter, I concentrated my efforts in helping grown-ups who needed special catechism, above all those who were just out of prison. I was beginning to learn from experience that if young lads just released from their place of punishment could find someone to befriend them, to look after them, to assist them on feast days, to help them get work with good employers, to visit them occasionally during the week, these young men soon forgot the past and began to mend their ways. They became good Christians and honest citizens.[13] This was the beginning of our Oratory.[14] It was to be blessed by the Lord with growth beyond my imagining at that time.

Notes

1. Seasonal migration from country to city had been a regular part of European life for ages, dependent on the cycles of weather, economic prosperity, family size, and other factors (Woolf, p. 281). After Charles Albert came to the throne in 1831, the capital became the locus of economic development as government, the army, public works, and public transport expanded, and factories and housing went up. In 1839 the king approved construction of a rail line from Turin to Genoa.

   The employment opportunities in construction, machine operation, and common labor contrasted more sharply with the realities of rural life, where there were repeated poor harvests. A typical field worker earned about one hundred lire a year, plus some produce, against a cost of living three times as much. Many migrants, therefore, chose to stay in the city.

   At the same time, the Austrian masters of Venetia and

Lombardy became increasingly repressive, causing additional migration of labor and capital to (and additional political unrest in) independent Piedmont. Advances in medicine and hygiene contributed to a sudden and dramatic increase in the population of northern Italy, as was happening over most of western Europe.

For a longer discussion Turin's urbanization and industrialization, see the comment at the end of the notes.

2. Not as funny as it was providential.

3. In the last chapter he mentioned that he had already begun to discuss some ideas with Father Cafasso. The manuscript shows that Don Bosco struggled with his phrasing, making two attempts before finally settling on "put into action my project," quite possibly aiming at simplicity of style.

4. A Piedmontese term used in jest or scorn for a German; cf. "Kraut."

5. After his first reception in the sacristy, why did the boy come back at all? Perhaps Don Bosco had shouted loudly enough at Comotti that the boy overheard even as he fled; perhaps once or twice he had been among the "crowd of boys" that followed Don Bosco through the streets and "even into the sacristy." He must have had an inkling of Don Bosco's sympathy.

6. *Amorevolezza*, one of the three key words of the Preventive System (together with "reason" and "religion").

7. Cf. his ordination resolution number 8. No doubt a "due thanksgiving" in this case was not one that would have kept the boy waiting for fifteen minutes.

8. According to the 1848 census of the Kingdom of Sardinia, half the population of Piedmont, a third of Liguria's, and a tenth of Sardinia's were literate — this all within a State where an education reform law in 1822 had mandated free primary schools in every commune (chapter 1, note 15). Piedmont was the most literate region in the Italian peninsula (Clark, p. 36). The whole of united Italy was but 26% literate in 1861. Ten years later only 33% of the persons marrying could sign the parish register themselves; in contrast, 77% in England and Wales could do so (Clark, p. 35).

The Turinese were the most literate of the Piedmontese. The 1848 census revealed that 59.7% of them could read and write. The majority of those who could not were women: 33,119 of them (49.3% of the female populace, 60% of the illiterates). Only 31.5% (22,856) of men and boys were illiterate. Of all those unable to read or write, 29,364 were under the age of twenty — well over half the illiterates. Of course, many of these were not yet of school age. The under-twenty group of illiterates divides almost evenly between boys (47.7%) and girls (52.3%). That near-equality partly reflects the inclusion of the preschoolers; in 1840–1841 there were 519 girls attending nine elementary schools for the poor, compared to 927 boys in ten schools (T. Bosco, BN, p. 109).

9. At this point Lemoyne inserts two further questions, which he must have heard from Don Bosco. These questions shed light on Don Bosco's psychological and pedagogical approach to the young:

> "Can you sing?"
> Wiping his eyes, the boy stared in surprise at Don Bosco and answered: "No."
> "Can you whistle?"
> The boy's face broke into a smile, which was what Don Bosco wanted, because it showed that the boy felt at ease. (BM II, 58)

The first thing was to win the boy's confidence, both in himself and in his would-be teacher.

10. This was not unusual (cf. chapter 4, note 1).

11. When Don Bosco speaks of "feast days" and calls his work the "festive" Oratory, he means any day on which Mass was an obligation, the numerous holy days and Sundays alike; these days were also public holidays, meaning that young workers without families were left idle. The Siccardi Laws of 1850 reduced the holy days to six per year as regards civil observance.

12. Garelli continued to come to catechism for a time and brought some friends with him. Then he disappeared. All we know about him is that he visited the Oratory even after 1855 (BM II, 59).

13. Don Bosco's classic definition of the objectives of the Salesian work.

14. Don Bosco always dated not only his work but even the founding of the Salesian Society from this historic catechism lesson. When he was seeking letters of recommendation from various bishops in order to seek the Holy See's approval of the Salesian Society, he introduced its history thus: "This Society's origins are found in the simple catechetical instructions conducted by Father John Bosco in a hall adjacent to

St. Francis of Assisi Church . . . " (BM IX, 35). Echoing this, the Salesian Constitutions today announce: "This Society had its beginning in a simple catechism lesson" (article 34). This is Don Bosco's first use of the word "Oratory" since the second sentence of chapter 3.

In this account, Don Bosco omitted one detail of great interest. After the sign of the cross, "he recited a Hail Mary, asking our Lady to give him the grace to save that boy's soul" (BM II, 59). He recalled this in 1885 during a conference for the Salesians: "All the blessings and graces showered upon us by heaven are the fruit of that first Hail Mary said with fervor and a right intention, together with young Bartholomew Garelli there in the Church of Saint Francis of Assisi" (MB XVII, 510).

Comment on Turin in the 1840s

The period 1830–1860 was a critical one in Turin's development into a great industrial center, surpassed in Italy only by Milan. The city, founded as a Roman colony, is well situated on the fertile plain where the Dora River joins the Po. The Alps form mighty ramparts on three sides of this plain.

By the late Middle Ages Turin had become the seat of the House of Savoy, one of Europe's oldest dynasties. The dukes not only played their powerful French and Austrian neighbors off against each other but managed generally to prosper in the process. As part of the Treaty of Utrecht (1713), Victor Amadeus II assumed the title of king, which made Turin a royal capital. After the acquisition of Sardinia in 1720, the State was known as the Kingdom of Sardinia.

Census figures reveal the capital city's growth:

	1838	*1848*	*Growth*
Inhabitants	117,072	136,849	+16.9%
Families	26,351	33,040	+25.4%
Individuals per family	4.44	4.14	
Dwellings	2,615	3,289	+25.8%
Families per dwelling	10.08	10.05	

These figures represent only the stable population. The 1838 census also counted 1521 soldiers and 4787 students. Besides these there were uncounted migrant workers, convicts, and people, especially youngsters, living in the streets.

The figures for persons per family, of course, do not tell the story of the numbers of single individuals, especially young males, living and working (or looking for work) in the city; nor the size of actual families. Nor do the figures for families per dwelling reveal that there was a great disproportion between center-city mansions, which often took in tenants for their upper stories, and working-zone tenements.

The northern industrial areas of the city soon turned into slums, of which Borgo Dora was the worst. Its 1838 population of 11,579 grew to 20,000 by 1851; already in 1838 its average of 19.8 families per dwelling was far higher than the 15.3 of the whole northern zone. (See Woolf, p. 291.) All the characteristics of the urban slum were present here: crowding; unemployment and underemployment; hordes of youngsters; lack of hygiene, schooling, recreational opportunity, and city services; and virtually no pastoral care. (Cf. the description of Vanchiglia in chapter 50, note 20.)

The urban population continued to burgeon as Piedmont took the lead in Italian national affairs and liberal statesmen like Cavour pushed education and economic expansion. By 1858 Turin's population had grown another 31.4% to 179,835, and only three years later, when the first census of new Kingdom of Italy was taken, it was 204,715. This was roughly equal to the population of Leeds, Edinburgh, and Baltimore. It surpassed Sheffield's, Belfast's, and Boston's. London (over 3,000,000), Birmingham, Dublin, Glasgow, New York (814,000), Brooklyn, and Philadelphia were larger.

Of the other cities in the Italian peninsula, only Milan was growing comparably: a 27% increase in population from 1847 to 1861, to 240,000. Rome's population was slowly climbing; it reached 184,000 in 1860 (up 22.7% in twenty-five years). Italy's largest city since early modern times was Naples, whose population was holding steady around 450,000. Genoa's likewise was steady (less than 120,000 in 1861). Two other great cities were in demographic decline: Venice, down 10.9% to 122,000 between 1797 and 1845; and Palermo, down 7.6% to 194,000 between 1815 and 1861. (Woolf, pp. 283–284)

The transfer of the national capital to Florence in 1865 drastically slowed Turin's economic and demographic growth; a slow recovery during the 1870s was followed by a dynamic expansion in the 1880s, the last decade of Don Bosco's life.

The city's industrial expansion was concentrated in the northern sectors, where a system of canals connecting to the Dora River offered the necessary water power. These sectors, from west to east, were Martinetto, Valdocco, Borgo Dora, Pallone (or Balón), and Vanchiglia. Between 1830 and 1850 zoning laws required all industrial operations to relocate to these areas; they had been scattered throughout the city, including the residential city center.

The manufacture of heavy machinery, boilers, and similar products was concentrated in Borgo Dora. Martinetto specialized in textiles (cotton and silk), tanning and leatherwork, brickmaking, and tile kilns. Textiles and leather goods were also prominent in the Pallone district, where the public flour mills were located as well. Valdocco, on the other hand, remained mostly open fields, with a few taverns and brothels that gave it an unsavory reputation coexisting with two establishments that helped Turin earn fame as a center of religious and social charity, viz. the Cottolengo Institute and the works of Marchioness Barolo.

Women and children were a high percentage of the factory workers. Factory conditions, like those in Britain and the United States in the 1840s, were miserable. A worker earned a pittance of a wage (which was, nonetheless, more than a farm laborer earned) for fourteen-hour days (seventeen in peak silk season), five and a half or six days a week. In Turin in 1845, cotton spinners and weavers earned 188 lire per year, dyers 322, and bricklayers 500. White-collar workers took in anywhere from 500 to 2400 lire per year in 1850. (T. Bosco, SP, p. 76; Hearder, p. 63)

Further information on the socio-economic background in which Don Bosco began his labors may be gathered from Stella, *EcSo*; Stella, LW, pp. 101–107; Woolf, *History of Italy, 1700–1860*; Dicastero per la Formazione, *Sussidi 1 per lo studio di Don Bosco e della sua opera: Il tempo di Don Bosco*; Giuseppe Melano, *La popolazione di Torino e del Piemonte nel secolo XIX* (Turin, 1961); T. Bosco, BN, pp. 104–109.

The First Days
of the Oratory

The Oratory in 1842

All my efforts that winter[1] were concentrated on getting the little Oratory established. My aim was to bring together only those children who were in greatest danger, ex-prisoners by preference. Nevertheless, as a foundation on which to build discipline and morality, I invited some other boys of good character who had already been taught.[2] These helped me maintain order, and they read and sang hymns. From the very beginning I realised that without songbooks and suitable reading matter, these festive gatherings would have been like a body without a soul.[3] In those days, the feast of the Purification (2 February)[4] was still a holy day of obligation. On that day in 1842, I already had about twenty children with whom we were able to sing for the first time "Sing Praises to Mary, O Tongues of the Faithful."[5]

By the feast of the Annunciation to the Virgin,[6] our numbers had risen to thirty. On that day we had a small celebration. In the morning, the pupils[7] went to the holy sacraments. In the evening we sang a hymn, and after catechism we had a story by way of a sermon. Because the side chapel we had been meeting in could no longer contain our numbers, we moved into the sacristy chapel, which was nearby.

Our Oratory programme ran along these lines. On every feast day, the boys were given a chance to receive the holy sacraments of confession[8] and communion. But one Saturday and Sunday each month was set aside for fulfilling this religious duty. We came together in the evening at a fixed time, sang a hymn, had a catechism lesson followed by a story, and then the distribution of something, sometimes to all, sometimes by lot.

Amongst the boys who came to the Oratory in its earliest days I would like to single out Joseph Buzzetti, who came regularly and gave good example. He had such an affection for Don Bosco and that feast day gathering that he refused to go home to his family (at Caronno Ghiringhello), which the others, his brothers and friends, used to do.[9] His three brothers, Charles,[10] Angelo, and Joshua, were also outstanding. John Gariboldi and his brother were then only lads, and now they are master bricklayers.

As a rule the Oratory boys included stonecutters, bricklayers, stuccoers, road pavers, plasterers, and others who came from distant villages.[11] They were not church-goers, and had few friends; so they were exposed to the dangers of perversion, especially on feast days.

Good Doctor Guala and Fr Caffasso enjoyed these assemblies of the children. They gladly supplied me with holy pictures, leaflets, pamphlets, medals, small crucifixes to give as gifts. At times they provided me with the means to clothe some of those in greater need, and to feed others for weeks at a time until they were able to support themselves by their work. Moreover, as the boys' numbers grew they sometimes gave me permission to gather my little army in the adjoining courtyard for recreation. If space had allowed, we would have been a hundred; but we had to restrict ourselves to about eighty.[12]

When the boys were preparing for the holy sacraments, Dr Guala or Fr Caffasso would always come along for a visit and tell some edifying story. Dr Guala wanted to make a special feast in honour of St Anne,[13] the feast of the bricklayers; after the morning ceremonies he invited all of them to breakfast with him. Almost a hundred gathered in the big conference hall. There all were provided with ample provisions of coffee, milk, chocolate, pastries, cakes, semolina, and other sweet dainties much loved by children. The noisy excitement of that feast can be imagined, and the numbers that could have come if we had had the room!

On feast days, I gave all my time to my youngsters. During the week I would go to visit them at their work in factories or workshops.[14] Not only the youngsters were happy to see a friend taking care of them; their employers were pleased, gladly retaining youngsters who were helped during the week, and even more on feast days, when they are in greater danger.

On Saturdays, my pockets stuffed sometimes with tobacco, sometimes with fruit, sometimes with rolls, I used to go to the prisons. My object always was to meet the youngsters who had the misfortune to find themselves behind bars, help them, make friends with them, and thus encourage them to come to the Oratory when they had the good fortune of leaving that place of punishment.

Notes

1. The winter of 1841–1842.

2. Don Bosco realized from the first the value of peer ministry. "Those who had been taught" could catechize small groups of boys, especially younger ones, or at least read to them from the catechism. We should not imagine Don Bosco lecturing to eighty or a hundred boys, ranging in age from seven to twenty and having various degrees of previous instruction.

3. "An oratory without music is a body without a soul" became one of Don Bosco's favorite aphorisms (cf. BM XV, 41).

4. Today called the feast of the Presentation of the Lord.

5. The hymn *Lodate Maria, O lingue fedeli* was a favorite among the Salesians. It figures in Don Bosco's dream of the raft (BM VIII, 143–150, at 146–147).

6. March 25, also a holy day at that time.

7. Don Bosco calls them *allievi*, a word that he will use repeatedly and apparently casually. It reminds Salesians that their past pupils include youths from their clubs and parishes as well as from their schools.

8. Don Bosco himself did not yet have faculties to hear confessions. He would have relied upon others, including Fathers Guala and Cafasso, for this ministry.

9. Buzzetti (1832–1891) became a distinguished member of the Salesian Society as a coadjutor brother. He had taken the

cassock, intending to become a priest, but he lost a finger in an accident and had to lay aside that hope (see chapter 55, note 24). He stayed with Don Bosco anyway, serving as a much valued administrative aide. Almost every volume of the BM mentions him. A brief biography is presented in the *Dizionario Biografico dei Salesiani*, ed. Eugenio Valentini et al. (Turin: Ufficio Stampa Salesiano, 1969), p. 61, and a longer one in Eugenio Ceria, *Profili di 33 coadiutori salesiani* (Colle Don Bosco: LDC, 1952); in English, see Enzo Bianco, *Don Bosco's Lay Religious*, trans. Peter Swain (New Rochelle: Don Bosco Publications, 1984), I, 48–51 (Indian ed., *Religious for Modern Times*, pp. 50–53). For longer biographies, see Stella, *EcSo*, p. 159, n. 4.

Construction work was seasonal, usually from April to December. During the winter layoffs, most apprentices and migrant workers returned to their families. Caronno Ghiringhello, now called Caronno Varesino, is a town in the province of Varese in Lombardy, about thirty miles north-northwest of Milan.

If Don Bosco's memory is accurate, Joseph came to Turin to work with his brothers (there were seven in all) when he was ten.

10. Charles Buzzetti (1829–1891) eventually became a contractor and built a number of buildings for Don Bosco at the Oratory, including the Basilica of Mary Help of Christians. His death was noted in the *Bollettino salesiano* XV (1891), 112, as Joshua's (1841–1902) was later: XXVI (1902), 22.

11. Don Bosco emphasizes those who worked in the booming construction trades of the expanding city. Data on occupations for the the 1840s are lacking, but in 1861 there were in Turin 1481 bricklayers, 81 plasterers and whitewashers, 61 pavers, 38 roofers, and 23 building painters (Stella, LW, p. 102, n. 5). It is unlikely that these figures include all the apprentices.

Regardless of their work, those who came from out of town, then as now, were naturally those most at risk in the city: uncomfortable with strange customs and dialect, most likely to be preyed upon by unscrupulous bosses, by landlords, or by gangs, least likely to have friends or family close by or to feel comfortable in church or catechism class. (Cf. John's feelings on first arriving in Chieri, chapter 7.)

On the kinds of boys who frequented the Oratory, see the comment below.

12. The courtyard is so small that one wonders how Don Bosco could have gotten half that many boys into it, at least for recreation.

13. July 26.

14. Don Bosco pioneered the apostolate of going to workers in their shops and factories rather than waiting for them to come to the church or approach the clergy.

Comment on the Oratory Boys of the 1840s

The boys and young men whom Don Bosco drew to himself in the first ten years of the Oratory can be divided into three classes:

1. Those who came from the country, even from other regions (the Val d'Aosta, Lombardy, Liguria, and as far away as Venetia and Savoy), to find seasonal work and opportunity in the city. After 1850 these became fewer in number; as the city grew, permanent residents made them unnecessary.

2. Those who lived in the tenements of the industrial zones where there were no schools and few parishes; they were often dirty, smelly, ill, and unsupervised. Even if they lived with responsible parents, these might be working ninety hours a week during peak times.

3. Those who attended the Catholic elementary schools for the poor, run by the Christian Brothers. In attendance they were the most consistent element of the Oratory, the best instructed, and generally the most easily guided.

The youngsters in the first two categories were those "poor and abandoned youths" who were Don Bosco's first concern. When they could not find jobs or were idle on Sundays and holy days, they tended to form gangs ("bad companions") and get into trouble: legal, moral, or both. Their attendance at the Oratory fluctuated a great deal, depending on the season, work, and other factors. The boys in the third group were to "leaven" the mass; of course, since most of them lived in the same neighborhoods as the others, Don Bosco was also using prevention in their case.

The 1861 census counted 885 poor males (all ages) without a profession, 13,603 other males without a profession, 1222 day laborers without a specific trade, and 10,098 male students (Stella, LW, p. 102, n. 4). These figures add up to almost 25% of Turin's stable male population.

The youths who frequented the Oratory were generally not

young boys but adolescents and young men. About three-quarters were between eleven and fifteen; many were in their late teens, and a few in their early twenties. After the establishment of the Oratory hospice in the 1850s, the average age came down. See Stella, *EcSo*, pp. 159–162.

Move
to Valdocco[1]

*The sacred ministry • Taking a post
at the Refuge (Sept. 1844)*

At that time I began to preach publicly in some of the churches in Turin, in the Hospital of Charity, in the Hospice of Virtue,[2] in the prisons,[3] and in the College of St Francis of Paola. I preached triduums,[4] novenas, and retreats. After two years of moral theology I did my examination for faculties to hear confessions.[5] This put me in a better position to cultivate discipline, morality, and the good of the souls of my youngsters in the prisons, at the Oratory, or at work.

It was consoling for me to see forty or fifty youngsters outside my confessional during the week and especially on feast days, waiting hours and hours for their turns for confession. This is how things normally ran at the Oratory for nearly three years, up to the end of October 1844.[6]

Meanwhile, new things, changes, and even tribulations were being prepared by Divine Providence.[7]

When I had completed three years of moral theology,[8] I had to undertake some specific sacred ministry. Comollo's uncle Fr Joseph Comollo, parish priest of Cinzano, was now advanced in years and sick. He was advised by the archbishop to ask me to help him administer his parish, which he was too old and infirm to handle any longer.[9] Dr Guala himself dictated my letter of thanks to Archbishop Fransoni; he was preparing me for something else.[10]

One day, Father Caffasso took me aside and said, "Now that you've finished your studies, you must get to work. These days the harvest is abundant enough.[11] What is your particular bent?"

"Whatever you would like to point me towards."

"There are three posts open: curate at Buttigliera d'Asti, tutor in moral theology here at the Convitto, and director[12] at the little hospital beside the Refuge.[13] Which would you choose?"

"Whatever you judge best."

"Don't you feel any preference for one thing rather than for another?"

"My inclination is to work for young people.[14] So do with me whatever you want:[15] I shall know the Lord's will in whatever you advise."

"At the moment what's the wish nearest your heart? What's on your mind?"

"At this moment I see myself in the midst of a multitude of boys appealing to me for help."

"Then go away for a few weeks' holiday. When you come back I'll tell you your destination."

I came back from the holiday,[16] but for several weeks Fr Caffasso never said a word. And I asked him nothing.

One day he said to me, "Why don't you ask me about your destination?"

"Because I want to see the will of God in your choice, and I don't want my desires in it at all."[17]

"Pack your bag and go with Dr Borrelli. You'll be director at the Little Hospital of St Philomena, and you'll also work in the Refuge.[18] Meanwhile God will show you what you have to do for the young."

At first this advice seemed to cut across my inclinations. With a hospital to take care of, preaching and confessions in an institute for more than four hundred girls, there would be no time for anything else. Nevertheless this was the will of heaven, as I was soon assured.

From the first moment that I met Dr Borrelli, I always judged him to be a holy priest, a model worthy of admiration and imitation. Every time I was able to be with him, he always gave me lessons in priestly zeal, always good advice, encouraging me in doing good. During my three years at the Convitto, he often invited me to help at the sacred ceremonies, hear confessions, or preach for him. Thus I already knew and was somewhat familiar with my field of work. We often had long discussions about procedures to be followed in order to help each other in visiting the prisons, fulfilling the duties entrusted to us, and at the same time helping the youngsters whose moral condition and neglect made increasing demands on priests. But what could I do? Where could I bring these youngsters together?

Dr Borrelli said, "For the time being you can bring the boys who are coming to St Francis of Assisi to the room set aside for you.[19] When we move to the building provided for the priests beside the little hospital, we can scout around for a better place."

Notes

1. The Valdocco district is located between the remains of the ancient city wall and the Dora River, northwest of the piazza della Republica (the huge public square formerly called piazza Emanuele Filiberto, popularly known as Porta Palazzo). It may take its name (Latin, *vallis* + *occisorum*)

The charitable works of Marchioness Barolo stretch for a block along via Cottolengo. Don Bosco served as a chaplain to the girls at the Refuge from November 1844 to July 1846, and the Oratory gathered at the Little Hospital of Saint Philomena from October 1844 to May 1845.

from the tradition that three Roman soldiers of the Theban legion (Saints Octavius, Solutor, and Adventor) were slain there for their Christian faith, ca. 300 A.D. (see chapter 31, note 9). There was no parish church in Valdocco; it was part of Saints Simon and Jude parish in Borgo Dora.

2. This hospice sheltered about a hundred youngsters.

3. There were four prisons in Turin: in the towers near Porta Palazzo, in via San Domenico, near the Church of the Holy Martyrs, and in the cellars under the Senate (Palazzo Madama).

4. Three-day programs of sermons or other devotions.

5. Archbishop Fransoni had already instructed Fathers Guala and Cafasso to examine Don Bosco's suitability for hearing confessions so that he might be granted provisional faculties (letter of November 30, 1842; BM II, 100). The final examination was given when the young priest completed the two-year program in pastoral and moral theology. The document granting Don Bosco permanent faculties is dated June 10, 1843.

On Don Bosco's qualities as a confessor, see Stella, LW, pp. 90–91; BM II, 67–68, 116–117, 119–122; BM III, 329–333.

6. That is, until just before the new school year began at the Convitto and he moved to the Refuge, as he will recount.

7. In this chapter, especially in his relationship with Father Cafasso, we see how completely Don Bosco wishes to subordinate himself to God's will. The lesson of his dream after Father Calosso's death (chapter 6) has been learned well.

8. The Convitto program lasted two years, but the students most outstanding for academics and piety could do a third year. Father Guala granted such a third year to Don Bosco. He was given a post as a special tutor, and some students who found the courses rather heavy going were put into his special care.

9. Father Comollo died February 1, 1843, aged eighty-six. At this point in his draft, Don Bosco left a note for Father Berto: "Cf. the letter." This is the above-mentioned letter of November 30, 1842, in which the archbishop asks Don Bosco to go to Cinzano and instructs him to see Father Guala about faculties for confession, which he would need in that ministry.

10. Fathers Guala and Cafasso had something else in mind for

Juliet Frances Colbert de Maulévrier, marchioness of Barolo, one of the great philanthropists of nineteenth-century Piedmont, a truly pious woman and a benefactress of the Oratory

Don Bosco and wanted to prevent the archbishop from moving him permanently away from the city.

11. An allusion to Matthew 9:37.

12. That is, chaplain.

13. Marchioness Barolo had founded two institutions in Valdocco along via Cottolengo near the Little House of Divine
Providence (the Cottolengo Institute). The first of these was
a halfway house for prostitutes trying to reform. From its
patroness, Mary Refuge of Sinners, it was known as the Refuge. The Little Magdalen House was for abandoned and
runaway girls less than fourteen years old; Father Mark Anthony Durando was its religious superior for thirty-three
years. In 1844 the marchioness began construction on a third
charitable enterprise, a small hospital for girls, dedicated to
Saint Philomena. Father Borel was the chaplain of these
works, and he asked for an assistant. He and Don Bosco had
rooms in the Refuge. The Oratory met in the priests' quarters of the unfinished hospital in 1844–1845.

Juliet Frances Colbert de Maulévrier (1785–1864), the
childless widow of Marquis Charles Tancred Falletti of
Barolo (1782–1838), was a highly cultured and wealthy
woman, much esteemed at court. A polished writer and a
connaisseuse of art, she kept a salon whose guests included
Balbo, Balzac, Cavour, d'Azeglio, Lamartine, Maistre, Pellico,
Sclopis, and others.

She was a truly pious person whose spiritual guides
included Fathers Lanteri and Cafasso. Fathers Borel and
Cafasso both warned Don Bosco that she tended to be dom-
ineering, but she was truly struggling to overcome that fault.
In addition to her regular devotions, she did penance, visited
the women's prison, nursed the sick, sponsored numerous
schools and other works of charity, founded two congregations of sisters, and planned to found a congregation of
priests under the patronage of Saint Francis de Sales. Her
religious and educational ministry in the women's prison
induced her to found works to keep girls from getting into
trouble and to help young women who wished to reform,
and so her works in Valdocco were born. (BM II, 182–185;
T. Bosco, BN, pp. 125–126)

14. This is one of the rare instances when Don Bosco uses the
generic *gioventù* rather than a strictly masculine form. It is
fair to say that he saw the need for an apostolate among
girls and young women. In fact, he spent nearly two years

(November 1844 to July 1846) working directly with girls in the Barolo institutions. But he concluded that his own direct calling—in a culture that strictly separated boys and girls in social settings—was to work with boys and young men.

15. An echo of Luke 1:38.

16. During his "vacation" Don Bosco preached a ten-day retreat at the town of Canelli, about forty miles southwest of Turin, about midway between Alba and Acqui. He followed this by preaching the novena for the feast of the Rosary at Castelnuovo, during which he visited his mother and brother at Becchi. (BM II, 178–179)

17. There almost seems to be a game of cat and mouse in this dialog between the two saints, which must have exasperated Father Cafasso. Knowing the thoughts, feelings, and inclinations of one's client is an essential part of giving spiritual direction, as Don Bosco did not seem to realize fully at this point. He realized it when he wrote the Introduction to the Salesian Constitutions (see ed. 1957, pp. 45–50; ed. 1967, pp. 52–58).

18. Father Borel introduced Don Bosco to the marchioness, who was at once impressed by his attitude of recollection and simplicity; to her these marked him as a holy person (BM II, 360). She was so eager to secure his services for her institutions that she not only assigned him a stipend of six hundred lire per year but also granted him permission to continue his work with boys and young men. Don Bosco, in turn, "detected a great humility under her majestic demeanor, and sensed that her reserve and noble bearing were blended with the affability and kindness of a mother ... " (BM II, 185).

The Refuge is located at 26 via Cottolengo; the Little Hospital is next door at no. 24.

19. At the Refuge, as a temporary expedient until new quarters adjacent to the hospital were completed. In fact, Don Bosco never moved into the hospital, but the Oratory did meet there, as mentioned in note 13, above.

Another Dream

On the second Sunday in October 1844, I had to tell my boys that the Oratory would be moving to Valdocco. But the uncertainty of place, means, and personnel had me really worried. The previous evening I had gone to bed with an uneasy heart. That night I had another dream,[1] which seems to be an appendix to the one I had at Becchi when I was nine years old. I think it advisable to relate it literally.

I dreamt that I was standing in the middle of a multitude of wolves, goats and kids, lambs, ewes, rams, dogs, even birds. All together they made a din, a racket, or better, a bedlam to frighten the stoutest heart. I wanted to run away, when a lady dressed as a shepherdess signaled me to follow her and accompany that strange flock while she went ahead. We wandered from place to place, making three stations or stops. Each time we stopped, many of the animals were turned into lambs, and their number continually grew. After we had walked a long way, I found myself in a field where all the animals grazed and gamboled together and none made attacks on the others.

Worn out, I wanted to sit down beside a nearby road, but the shepherdess invited me to continue the trip. After another short journey, I found myself in a large courtyard with porticoes all round. At one end was a church.[2] I then saw that four-fifths of the animals had been changed into lambs and their number greatly increased. Just then, several shepherds came along to take care of the flock; but they stayed only a very short time and promptly went away.[3]

Then something wonderful happened. Many of the lambs were transformed into shepherds, who as they grew took care of the others. As the number of shepherds became great, they split up and went to other places to gather other strange animals and guide them into other folds.[4]

I wanted to be off because it seemed to me time to celebrate Mass; but the shepherdess invited me to look to the south. I looked and saw a field sown with maize, potatoes, cabbages, beetroot, lettuce, and many other vegetables.

"Look again," she said to me.

I looked again and saw a wondrously big church.[5] An orchestra and music, both instrumental and vocal, were inviting me to sing Mass. Inside the church hung a white banner on which was written in huge letters, *Hic domus mea, inde gloria mea.*[6]

As my dream continued, I wanted to ask the shepherdess where I was. And I wanted to know the meaning of that journey with its halts, the house,[7] the church, then the other church.

"You will understand everything when you see in fact with your bodily eyes what you are looking at now with the eyes of your mind."

Thinking that I was awake, I said, "I see clearly, and I see with my bodily eyes. I know where I'm going and what I'm doing." But at that moment the bell of the Church of St Francis sounded the *Ave Maria,*[8] and I woke up.

This dream lasted most of the night. I saw it all in great detail. But at the time I understood little of its meaning since I put little faith in it. But I understood little by little as the dream began to come true. Later, together with another dream,[9] it served as a blueprint for my decisions.[10]

Notes

1. On Don Bosco's dreams, see chapter 2, comment.

   Lemoyne and Ceria reconstruct that Don Bosco had six dreams between 1830 and 1845 that gradually clarified the one which he experienced at the age of nine or ten. Each succeeding dream explained the previous one and added something to it. Two have been mentioned already: when he

Don Bosco began to dream of a great church in Valdocco in 1844. The dream was realized by the Church of Mary Help of Christians, built between 1863 and 1868. In the background to the right of the church may be seen the vine-covered windows of Don Bosco's rooms in the hospice annex that was built in stages between 1853 and 1876. The Salesian alumni erected a bronze statue of Don Bosco in the piazza of Mary Help of Christians in 1920.

was about fifteen, he was reproached for not sufficiently trusting in God (chapter 6), and when he was nineteen, he was instructed to take care of young people (chapter 16, note 2).

He does not mention two other dreams in the *Memoirs*. From one that came when he was twenty-one he learned what type of boys he should work with (BM I, 285). The next year he learned that he was to work in Turin (BM I, 315–316).

The fifth and sixth dreams — the one narrated here and the one recounted in note 9, below — tell of the rise of a great work in the fields of Valdocco and of his helpers' origins. They announce the Salesian Oratory of Turin, the founding of the Salesian Society, and its spread.

There are considerable problems with this six-dream reconstruction, including Lemoyne's identification of the 1830 dream with the one described to him by Joseph Turco. See Desramaut, *LesMem*, pp. 250–257.

2. The courtyard and porticoes are the Oratory of Saint Francis de Sales; the church is the Church of Saint Francis de Sales, built in 1852 (chapter 55).

3. A number of priests and seminarians helped Don Bosco for a while, then left him. Father Borel alone stayed through thick and thin. (See chapters 38, 52, and 53.)

4. With the exception of Father Victor Alasonatti (1812–1865), the seventeen men who joined Don Bosco in formally establishing the Salesian Society in December 1859 had all been youngsters at the Oratory.

5. The Basilica of Mary Help of Christians, constructed between 1863 and 1868. The field where it was to be built became known as "the field of the dreams" on account of this and the next dream (note 9).

6. Latin: "This is my house; from it my glory will go forth."

7. The building with the porticoes, i.e. the Pinardi house and its annex.

8. The morning Angelus bell at Saint Francis of Assisi Church; Don Bosco had not yet moved from the Convitto. The Angelus includes three Hail Mary's.

9. On February 2, 1875, Don Bosco related this dream to Fathers Barberis and Lemoyne (BM II, 232–233):

> I seemed to be in a vast meadow with a huge crowd of boys who were fighting, swearing, stealing, and doing other blamable things. The air was thick with flying stones, hurled by youngsters who were fighting. They were all abandoned boys, devoid

of moral principles. I was about to turn away when I saw a Lady beside me. "Go among those boys," she said, "and work."

I approached them, but what could I do? I had no place to gather them, but I wanted to help them. I kept turning to some people who were watching from a distance, and who could have come to my aid, but no one paid attention or gave me any assistance. I then turned to the Lady. "Here is a place," she said, and pointed to a meadow.

"That's only a meadow," I said.

She replied: "My Son and His Apostles did not even have a place to lay their heads" [Cf. Matt. 8:20]. I began to work in that meadow, counseling, preaching, hearing confessions, but I saw that almost all my efforts were in vain. I had to have some building where I could gather and house those abandoned by their parents and those despised and rejected by society. Then the Lady led me a little further to the north and said: "Look!"

I did so and saw a small church with a low roof, a small courtyard, and a great number of boys. I resumed my work, but since the church was becoming too small, I again appealed to the Lady and she pointed out another church, much larger, and a house adjacent to it. Then she took me closer, to a field that was tilled and that lay almost opposite the facade of this new church. "In this place," she added, "where the glorious martyrs of Turin, Adventor and Octavius, suffered martyrdom, on these clods soaked and sanctified by their blood, I wish that God be honored in a very special manner." So saying, she put out her foot and pointed to the exact spot where the martyrs had fallen. I wanted to leave a marker there so as to find the place again when I returned, but I could not see a single stick or stone. Nevertheless, I kept the place clearly in mind. It coincides exactly with . . . the front left corner as one faces the main altar of the Church of Mary Help of Christians.

In the meantime, I found myself being surrounded by a very vast and ever increasing number of boys, but, as I kept looking to the Lady, the premises and the means were also growing accordingly. I saw then a very grand church on the very spot she had pointed out as the place where the soldiers of the Theban legion had been martyred. There were a great many buildings all around, and in the center stood a beautiful monument.

While these things were taking place and I was still dreaming, I saw that priests and clerics were helping me, but after a while, they left. I tried everything to get others to stay, but after a while they too left me alone. Then I turned once more to the Lady for help. "Do you want to know what to do to keep them?" she asked. "Take this ribbon and bind their foreheads with it." Reverently I took the white ribbon from her hand and noticed the word *Obedience* written on it. I immediately gave it a try and began to bind the foreheads of these volunteers. The ribbon worked wonders, as I went ahead with the mission entrusted to me. All my helpers gave up the idea of leaving me, and stayed on. Thus was our Congregation born.

The ribbon symbolizes religious profession, whose key in the Salesian tradition is the vow of obedience.

The first church mentioned in this dream is the chapel in the Pinardi shed (chapter 39); the second, the Church of Saint Francis de Sales, next to the Pinardi house (chapter 55); and the last, large one, the basilica. The spot indicated by our Lady is at the entrance of the Chapel of the Relics in the basement, marked by a golden tile.

Since this dream explains the one narrated in the *Memoirs*, it must have occurred subsequently. The meadow appears to be the field belonging to the Filippi brothers (chapters 36 and 39); so the dream must have occurred between the Oratory's move from the Refuge (August 1845: chapter 33) and the end of its stay at the Moretta house (February 1846: chapter 36). The eight-month period of the "wandering Oratory" (August 1845 to April 1846) was one of the greatest strain and anxiety for Don Bosco; the dream evidently was to strengthen and encourage him. (An excellent chronology of the Oratory's wanderings, consolidation, and expansion from 1841 to 1851 is presented in Giraudo and Biancardi, pp. 118–119.)

When Don Bosco was building the basilica, he asked his learned friend Canon Lawrence Gastaldi (the future archbishop) to research where the martyrs had shed their blood. The canon concluded that they had died outside the city walls near the Dora Gate in the general area where the Oratory was located. He published his findings in the January 1866 issue of *Catholic Readings* under the title *Biography of Saints Solutor, Adventor, and Octavius*. In the dream, our Lady mentioned only the last two since the first escaped from Turin and was captured and executed at Ivrea, some twenty-seven miles north-northwest of Turin.

10. In his transcription of the dream (BM II, 190–191), Lemoyne misread Father Berto's manuscript as amended by Don Bosco. Lemoyne added "at the Refuge" after "for my decisions"; but "at the Refuge" is actually part of the title of the next chapter. See illustrations on p. xxv.

∞ 32 ∞

The Oratory at the Refuge

O_n the second Sunday of October,[1] feast of the maternity of Mary, I broke the news to my youngsters that the Oratory would be moving to the Refuge. At first they were somewhat upset; but when I told them of the spacious grounds waiting just for us to sing, run, jump and enjoy ourselves, they were pleased. They eagerly looked forward to the next Sunday, to see the new situation which seized their imaginations.

The third Sunday of October was dedicated to the purity of the Virgin Mary. A little after noon a mob of youngsters of all ages and conditions descended on Valdocco looking for the new Oratory. "Where's the Oratory? Where's Don Bosco?" they shouted to all and sundry.

No one knew what they were talking about. No one in that neighbourhood had heard of either Don Bosco or the Oratory. The questioners, believing that they were being teased, raised their voices more insistently. The locals, believing that they were being insulted, shouted indignant threats. Matters were getting serious when Dr Borrelli and I heard the commotion and came out of the house. At sight of us, the noise died down and calm was restored. The boys crowded round us asking where the Oratory was.

We had to tell them that the real Oratory was not ready yet, but meantime they could come to my room. It was quite big and would serve us well enough. In fact things went quite well that Sunday. But on the following Sunday, so many pupils from the locality came in addition to the old ones that I no longer knew where to gather them.

My room, the corridor, the stairs were all thronged with children.

On the feast of All Saints, Dr Borrelli and I prepared to hear confessions. But everybody wanted to go; what could we do? There were more than two hundred children but only two confessors. One boy was trying to light the fire; another decided to put it out. The one brought wood, the other water. Buckets, tongs, shovel, jug, basin, chairs, shoes, books — everything was turned topsy-turvy while they were trying to tidy things up!

"We can't go on like this," said the dear Doctor. "We really must find a more suitable place."

Yet we spent six feast days in that restricted space, which was the room above the main entrance hall of the Refuge. Meantime, we went to speak to Archbishop Fransoni. He understood how important our project was.

"Go," he told us, "and do what you think best for souls. I give you all the faculties you may need. Speak with Marchioness Barolo. She may be able to provide better accommodations for you. But tell me, couldn't these boys be taken care of in their own parishes?"

"For the most part," [I replied,] "these youngsters are foreigners[2] who spend only a part of the year in Turin. They don't have any idea what parishes they belong to. Many of them are badly off, speaking dialects hard to understand, so that they understand little and are little understood by others. Some are already grown up and don't like associating in classes with little boys."

"That means," continued the archbishop, "they need a place of their own, adapted to their own needs. Go ahead, therefore. I bless you and your project. If I can be of service to you, come by all means, and I will always help in any way I can."

I went in fact to speak with Marchioness Barolo. As the little hospital was not to be opened till August of the following year, that charitable lady was happy to put at our disposal for use as a chapel two large rooms intended for the recreation of the priests of the Refuge when they should transfer their residence there. Access to the new Oratory, therefore, was through where the door of the hos-

pital is now, along an alley running between the Cottolengo Institute and the aforementioned building, to what is
now the priests' residence, and inside up to the 3rd floor.[3]

That was the site Divine Providence chose for the first
Oratory church.[4] We began to call it after St Francis de
Sales for two reasons: 1st, because Marchioness Barolo had
in mind to found a congregation of priests under his patronage, and with this intention she had a painting of this
saint done, which can still be seen at the entrance to this
area;[5] 2nd, because we had put our own ministry, which
called for great calm and meekness, under the protection of
this saint in the hope that he might obtain for us from God
the grace of being able to imitate him in his extraordinary
meekness and in winning souls.[6]

We had a further reason for placing ourselves under the
protection of this saint: that from heaven he might help us
to imitate him in combating errors against religion, especially Protestantism, which was beginning to gain ground
in our provinces, and more especially in the city of Turin.[7]

On 8 December 1844, a day dedicated to the Immaculate
Conception of Mary, the long-awaited chapel was blessed,
with the archbishop's permission.[8] It was a bitterly cold
day. There was deep snow, and it was still snowing heavily. Holy Mass was celebrated, and many youngsters went
to confession and communion. I finished that sacred liturgy
with a few tears, tears of joy, because in a certain way I
saw that the work of the Oratory was now established,
with the object of entertaining the more abandoned and
endangered youths after they had fulfilled their religious
duties in church.

Notes

1. October 13, 1844.

2. Don Bosco's use of "foreigners" rather than "visitors" or
"migrants" added weight to his point. Turin counted fourteen
parishes within the old city and just two in the swarming
industrial zones. The pastors and their curates were no more
prepared to cope with an exploding immigrant population
than were their American counterparts at the end of the
nineteenth century.

In a similar situation at Milan, the local clergy had long since organized festive oratories to meet the needs of the displaced young. Some of Turin's young priests were available and interested in tackling the problem. There certainly were enough priests around: 851 of them in Turin in 1838, i.e. one for every 137 permanent residents. In 1840 Father John Cocchi (1813–1895) established the first oratory for poor and abandoned boys in Annunciation parish in the filthiest section of Turin, called *Moschino* (Gnat). He named it the Guardian Angel Oratory. The next year he moved it to Vanchiglia. (Stella, LW, pp. 106–107; cf. pp. 86–87)

3. In American terms, the fourth floor. The alley is the viale delle Maddalenine, which opens into 22 via Cottolengo.

4. What Don Bosco calls a "church" is more properly called a "chapel." While the Oratory was associated with Saint Francis of Assisi Church, it had no particular patron. At an unspecified time Don Bosco began to think of this lack; he and Father Cafasso independently arrived at the choice of Saint Francis de Sales (BM II, 196), but apparently the name was adopted only after the move to Saint Philomena's Hospital.

   Stella has published a essay on the relationship between Don Bosco and Saint Francis: "Don Bosco e S. Francesco di Sales: Incontro fortuito o identità spirituale?" in Picca and Struś, *San Francesco di Sales*, pp. 139–159 (a rough translation of this article is available in photocopy from Don Bosco Publications). For further investigation, see Pedrini, *St. Francis de Sales, Don Bosco's Patron*, and the whole of Picca and Struś.

5. Time and weather have since obliterated the mural.

6. In defining the scope of the festive oratories in their Regulations (published around 1852), Don Bosco wrote:

   > This oratory is placed under the patronage of Saint Francis de Sales, because those who intend to dedicate themselves to this kind of work should adopt this saint as a model of charity and affability. These sources will produce the fruits that we expect from the oratories. (BM III, 68)

   This tallies with the fourth resolution he made at his ordination.

7. The nineteenth century was not an ecumenical age, and Don Bosco's relations with Protestants, generally, were anything but friendly.

   Protestantism, technically, was illegal in the Kingdom of Sardinia. But for centuries isolated communities of Waldensians (see chapter 48) had dwelt in the Val d'Aosta. In the great migrations to the cities, they and their ministers came too. Pressures for legal toleration grew (to be granted in 1848), and they began to proselytize, especially in the pastorally neglected areas of town. Missionary societies, particularly in Great Britain, eagerly subsidized their works.

8. This chapel was the first of the three stopping places shown to Don Bosco in his dreams. The second would be at the Dora Mills, and the third, at Father Moretta's house.

The Oratory
out of the
Refuge

The Oratory at St Martin of the Mills
• *Difficulties* • *The hand of*
the Lord

Our chapel beside St Philomena's Hospital was coming along nicely. On feast days, youngsters came in big numbers to make their confessions and go to communion. After Mass there was a short explanation of the gospel. In the afternoon we had catechism lessons, hymn singing, a short instruction, the litany of our Lady, and benediction.[1] Various intervals were filled with games and amusements, which took place in the alley which still runs between the convent of the Little Magdalens and the public road. We spent seven months there. We thought that we had found heaven on earth; then we had to leave our beloved asylum and go look for another.

Marchioness Barolo, though she cast a kindly eye on every charitable work, still, as the opening of her little hospital approached (it opened 10 August 1845), wanted our Oratory far away before then. It is true that the area we had been using had no internal communication with what was to be the chapel, the school, or the recreation center. Even the shutters were fixed in place and turned upwards.[2] None the less we had to obey.

We positively pestered the municipal government of Turin.[3] Through the kind offices of Archbishop Fransoni, we were allowed to move our oratory to the church of St Martin of the Mills, or rather, to the public mills.[4]

Imagine us then, on a July Sunday[5] in 1845, making our way laden with benches, kneelers, candlesticks, some chairs, crucifixes, and pictures large and small. Everyone carried some object suited to his strength. We must have looked like emigrants on the move; with laughter and din and misgivings we marched out to establish our headquarters in the place just indicated.

Dr Borrelli gave an appropriate talk before we set out and another when we arrived at our new church. That worthy minister of the sanctuary, who enjoyed a popularity more unique than rare, spoke these thoughts:

"My dear boys, cabbages never form a big, beautiful head unless they are transplanted. The same is true of our Oratory. So far it has been moved from one place to another many times,[6] but in the different places where it has stopped it has always grown bigger, with no little advantage to the boys involved. We started at St Francis of Assisi with catechism and a little singing. That was as much as we could do there. At the Refuge we made just a whistle stop, as train travelers say, so that our boys might receive spiritual help by way of confession, catechism classes, sermons, and games during the months we were there.

"There, beside the little hospital a real Oratory began, and we thought we had found true peace, a place suitable for us. But Divine Providence ordained that we had to move again and come here to St Martin's. How long will we stay here? We don't know. We hope we'll be here a long time; but however long our stay, we believe that like transplanted cabbages, our Oratory will grow in the number of boys who love virtue, will increase their desire for music, singing, evening classes, and even day courses.

"Will we be here long, then? We mustn't let this thought worry us. Let's throw all our worries into the Lord's hands; he'll take care of us. It's certain that he blesses us, helps us, and provides for us. He'll show us a good place for contributing to his glory and the good of our souls.

"Now the Lord's graces form a kind of chain with each link locked into the next; so if we turn to good account the graces he gives us, we are sure that God will grant us bigger graces. And if we fall in with the aims of the Oratory, we will progress from virtue to virtue, till we reach that blessed homeland where the infinite mercy of O.L.J.C. will reward each of us as his good works deserve."[7]

An immense crowd of youngsters attended that solemn ceremony, and a *Te Deum*[8] of thanksgiving was sung with the greatest emotion.

We carried out our religious devotions as we had at the Refuge, though we could not celebrate Mass or give benediction in the evening.[9] This meant that the boys could not receive communion, which is the fundamental element to our institution.[10] Even our recreations were often disturbed, broken up because the lads were forced to play in the street and in the little square in front of the church where a constant stream of people on foot, carts, horses, and carriages passed by. Since we had nothing better, we thanked heaven for what we had been given and hoped for some better spot.

But fresh problems fell upon us. The millers, their apprentices, and other employees could not put up with[11] the jumping, the singing, and the occasional shouting of our pupils. They grew alarmed and agreed to lodge a complaint with the municipal government. It was then that people began to say that such meetings of youngsters were dangerous, that at any moment they could erupt in riots and revolution.[12] This fear was founded on the prompt obedience with which the boys responded to every little order of the superior. Without any foundation, it was added that the kids were doing untold damage in the church, outside the church, on the pavement. It seemed that if we continued meeting there Turin must be ruined.

Our troubles came to a head when a secretary at the mills wrote a letter to the mayor of Turin. In it he included all the vague rumours and amplified the imagined damages.* He said that the families connected with those businesses could not go about their duties in peace. He added, finally, that the Oratory was a hotbed of immorality.[14]

Though the mayor was convinced that these charges were unfounded, he wrote a stiff letter ordering us to take

---

*The mayor sent an inspector, who found the walls, the outside pavement, the floor, everything about the church in good order. The only damage consisted of a little scratch on one wall, which a lad might have made with the end of a nail.[13]

The public flour mills near the Dora River in Borgo Dora. To a chapel dedicated to Saint Martin, Don Bosco brought the Oratory from July to December 1845. The millers' complaints about the boys compelled them to seek another site.

our Oratory elsewhere at once.[15] General disappointment, useless sighing! We had to go.

It is worth noting, however, that the secretary, whose name is   (never to be published),[16] author of that famous letter, never wrote anything else. He was suddenly stricken by an uncontrollable shake in his right hand. Within three years he was dead. God permitted his son to be abandoned, thrown out into the street and obliged to seek food and lodging at the hospice which was open at that time in Valdocco.[17]

Notes

1. Benediction of the Blessed Sacrament is a service of worship before the Holy Eucharist exposed on the altar; at its conclusion the priest blesses the worshipers with the Sacrament.

2. Their slats turned upwards.

3. Father Cafasso asked Countess Bosco of Ruffino, wife of one of the city council, to use her influence when Don Bosco's application was submitted. The application was rejected. But Don Bosco obtained a permit from city hall when he brought a recommendation from the archbishop, along with a petition from Father Borel. The permit was required because the site which he had in mind was municipal property.

4. The public mills stood at the northeastern corner of Porta Palazzo (piazza Emanuele Filiberto), where a canal provided the water power for grinding grain, pressing olives, and retting hemp. The site is now piazza Don Albera. A chapel dedicated to Saint Martin served the millers and their families and in Piedmontese gave its name to the general site: *San Martino dei Molassi* (Saint Martin of the Mills). In Italian the mills took their name, the Dora Mills, from the nearby river.

5. It was July 13.

6. The phrasing does not seem to suit the Oratory's situation if it has moved but twice, from Saint Francis Church to the Refuge to the mills. In fact, it was the third move, for events that will be described in the next chapter preceded the move to Saint Martin's.

7. Despite Don Bosco's categorical statement, omitted in his draft but added with the complete narration in Father Berto's copy, some have tried to attribute this sermon on the cabbages to Don Bosco himself rather than to Father Borel. Giraudi clarified the matter (p. 44 n.):

   In the part of the *History of the Oratory* which appeared in the May 1879 *Salesian Bulletin*, Father Bonetti quoted word for word from Don Bosco's memoirs. But in *St. John Bosco's Early Apostolate* [p. 22], which was published a few months after his death on June 5, 1891, he attributed this pep talk to Don Bosco instead of Father Borel. Ten years later Lemoyne repeated what *Early Apostolate* said [BM II, 239]. But Don Bosco's clarity, precision, and repetition leave no doubt.

   Don Bosco viewed the galley proofs of the *History of the Oratory* and saw no need to alter what he had written about this detail of the move to the Dora Mills. The Salesian Central Archives, moreover, possess a copy of the sermon in Father Borel's hand (see reproduction in Ceria, MO, facing p. 148).

8. A liturgical hymn of praise traditionally used on major occasions of public thanksgiving; it ordinarily concludes the Office of Readings on Sundays and feast days as well.

9. Saint Martin's chaplain reserved these privileges to himself. Since the faithful who assisted at his Mass filled the chapel, Don Bosco had to take his boys to some other church in Turin for Mass and the sacraments.

10. The "institution" may be taken to be the Oratory, or perhaps the whole Salesian Family with its aims and its works.

Up to this time, no one in Piedmont had promoted frequent communion as Don Bosco did. It was and remains "the fundamental element" of his institutions, without which, he said, it is impossible to help a boy improve. See "Treatise on the Preventive System" (*Constitutions of the Society of Saint Francis de Sales*, ed. 1957, regulation 94; ed. 1985, p. 249 and article 36).

As our references to theological rigorism have indicated, not everyone approved of this. In the late 1850s a prominent Turinese priest reproved Don Bosco for encouraging his boys to approach the sacraments so often. He said it would be enough to go on the big feasts. Don Bosco tried to convince him of the good effects deriving from frequent reception of the sacraments; when he did not succeed, he advised the priest to speak with Father Cafasso. It does not seem that he did so. Don Bosco later told the story to seminarian John Baptist Anfossi, who eventually became a canon of the cathedral and repeated it to Lemoyne in a letter (July 9, 1903; BM VI, 184–186).

11. Starting at "could not put up with," the rest of this chapter and the next one in the original manuscript are in Father Berto's hand. So is a marginal note at the beginning of the preceding paragraph. Later we shall come across a second passage in his script. Don Bosco's handwriting indicates that he made some modifications in them, so he obviously saw the two passages in the original and in the copy. Don Bosco probably instructed that a copy be made from something which he had already written, or possibly he dictated the text at these points.

12. Revolution was a touchy subject and not just rhetoric. Much of Europe had experienced revolution in 1820–1821 and again in 1830–1831. The military garrison at Alessandria had revolted in 1821, and King Victor Emmanuel I had felt obliged to abdicate before order was fully restored. Republicans like Mazzini were a constant source of worry to the absolutist Sardinian government. As if revolution by the masses were not enough of a concern, the Austrian army in Lombardy was ready to intervene if the Piedmontese should get any ideas about popular government or Italian nationalism. Under the surface of society were running the currents that would carry Europe, including Piedmont, to the epic events of 1848.

No doubt many of the complainants were also well aware of what kinds of boys gathered around Don Bosco: a few young schoolboys and a lot of delinquents, runaways, unemployed — potential troublemakers.

13. The footnote, too, is in Father Berto's handwriting.

14. The complaint may mean immorality in the broad sense, encompassing such activities as vandalism, theft, gambling — Don Bosco cast as *Oliver Twist*'s Fagin! It may also be narrowly construed as a complaint that some of the kids were urinating into the canal (T. Bosco, SP, p. 115).

15. "At once" in the sense of "without appeal." The city council's letter is dated November 18, 1845. It canceled Don Bosco's permit for Saint Martin's as of January 1, 1846.

In an unpublished foreword (entitled "A Brief History of the Oratory of Saint Francis de Sales from 1841 to 1854") to an early manuscript of the Regulations of the Oratory, Don Bosco wrote:

> We spent two tranquil months there, even though the place had many drawbacks. We could not celebrate Mass, give benediction of the Blessed Sacrament, or recreate freely. This calm heralded a storm to come. It was to strain the Oratory severely. The rumor went around that such boys' gatherings were dangerous, that in one moment they could pass from recreation to rebellion. A fine rebellion ignorant boys could stage without money or arms, lads who came together only to learn catechism, and who would have been frightened by a single crow flapping its wings. . . . I tried my best to show that the rumors were baseless, all in vain. The clear-cut order was issued commanding us to leave at once the area that we had enjoyed.

This archival document is in Don Bosco's own hand.

On the following Sundays, the Oratory used the church

courtyard only as an assembly point and then went else-where (see chapter 35).

In September 1845, Don Bosco met Mickey Rua (1837–1910), who lived near the Dora Mills. His father had died in August, and Mickey and his brothers needed a new father. Thus the loving designs of Providence brought together Don Bosco and the boy who would become his right-hand man and first successor. (Cf. BM II, 248) Pope Paul VI beatified Michael Rua in 1972.

16. Don Bosco wrote the unfortunate secretary's name, but his wishes that it never be published have been respected. This is an example of the saint's delicate charity.

17. The hospice, of course, was at the Oratory of Saint Francis de Sales.

One Day at Saint Peter in Chains

The chaplain's housekeeper •
A letter • A sad event

Since the mayor and the city council in general were persuaded that the charges brought against us had no foundation, it was an easy matter for us, especially since we had the backing of the archbishop, to get permission to hold our meetings in the church and courtyard of the Cemetery of Christ Crucified, popularly known as St Peter in Chains.[1] So, after a two-month stay at St Martin's, we had to move to a new place.[2] Though we felt a bitter sadness about moving, the new place was more convenient for us. The long portico, the spacious yard, and the church for our sacred functions all so aroused the youngsters' enthusiasm that they were overcome with joy.

But in that place we came up against a formidable and unsuspected rival. This was not the ghost of one of the great numbers of the dead who slept peacefully in the nearby tombs. This was a living person, the chaplain's housekeeper. No sooner had she heard the pupils singing and talking, and, let us admit, their shouting too, than she rushed out of the house. In a furious rage, with her bonnet askew and her arms akimbo, she launched into tongue-lashing the crowd of merrymakers. Joining in her assault upon us were a small girl, a dog, a cat, all the hens, so that it seemed that a European war was about to break out. I tried to approach her to calm her down, pointing out to her that the kids meant no harm, that they were just playing innocently. Then she turned and gave it to me.

At that point I decided to end the recreation. I gave a

The interior courtyard of the cemetery chapel of Saint Peter in Chains. The Oratory met here on May 25, 1845, but were chased off by the chaplain and his housekeeper.

short catechism lesson, and after we recited the rosary in church, we broke up hoping to come back the next Sunday to a better reception. Quite the contrary! When the chaplain came home that evening, the good housekeeper denounced Don Bosco and his sons as revolutionaries and desecrators of holy places. An undisciplined rabble, she said. She prevailed upon the good priest to write a letter to the civil authorities. He wrote while the servant dictated, but with so much venom that a warrant was issued immediately for the arrest of any of us who should return there.[3]

Sad to say, that was the last letter written by Fr Tesio, the chaplain. He wrote it on Monday, and within a few hours he suffered a stroke from which he died very soon afterwards.[4] Two days later a similar fate befell the house-keeper.[5] News of these events spread like wildfire and deeply impressed the souls of the boys and of everyone who heard it. Everyone had a mad desire to come and hear about these sorry cases.[6]

But since we were forbidden to meet at St Peter in Chains, and the time was so short to make alternative arrangements, no one, not even I, had any idea where our next meeting would take place.[7]

Notes

1. This was a shrine which the Valdocco vegetable sellers had built in 1746. It was a solid structure, with a porch, a spacious yard, and porticoes all around, located a block north of the Cottolengo Institute on via San Pietro in Vincoli. Beside it was a cemetery no longer used for burials. The proper name of the place was the Cemetery of Christ Crucified. The chapel was demolished in 1934, but a mausoleum remains.

    The Italian *San Pietro in Vincoli* was caricatured in Piedmontese: *San Pe' d'ij Coj,* "Saint Peter of the Cabbages," probably because of the vegetable growers who built it. When we realize that the Oratory's brief relationship with this site preceded the move to the Dora Mills, we see where Father Borel picked up the idea for his famous sermon on the cabbages.

2. The events narrated in this chapter happened *before* the stay at the Dora Mills. Salesian historian Francesco Motto has researched the episode, correcting not only Don Bosco's memory but also Lemoyne's findings ("L'Oratorio di don Bosco presso il cimitero di S. Pietro in Vincoli," in *Ricerche storiche salesiane,* July-December 1986, pp. 199–219).

    Another group had been holding catechism at Saint Peter's. But a city council decree of May 23, 1845, forbade catechetical assemblies at the chapel, presumably judging these not to be duly respectful of the dead. Apparently Father Joseph Tesio, the chaplain, was not informed of the ordinance. Lemoyne may be correct in supposing that he had no idea what kind of an invasion of street urchins was to descend upon his cemetery on Sunday, May 25, as a result of his having granted Don Bosco permission to bring his troops to Saint Peter's. The chaplain himself was away, and he may have been delighted that Don Bosco would hear confessions and celebrate Mass for whoever usually came, as well as for his boys.

3. By the following Sunday, June 1, a copy of the ordinance was posted on the church door.

4. According to the death certificate, Father Tesio died on Wednesday, May 28, at 12:30 a.m., at the age of sixty-eight. This was two months before the sojourn at the Dora Mills, which began on July 13. From June 1 to July 6, Don Bosco assembled the boys at the Refuge each Sunday and feast day and then took them to various churches outside the city.

5. The death of the housekeeper, Margaret Sussolino, cannot be confirmed. She remained at the chaplain's quarters for a few days after his death and then disappeared from the history of Turin, probably returning to her native town.

6. One circumstance not mentioned here rendered these unexpected deaths still more impressive. Father Michael Rua testified to it during the gathering of information in view of Don Bosco's beatification (*Summarium*, p. 312):

> A certain boy named Melanotte, who came from Lanzo, witnessed the scene with the irate housekeeper. He told me many years later that Don Bosco showed neither anger nor annoyance at the insults hurled at him. Turning to his boys, he said with a sigh: "Poor thing! She tells us not to set foot here again! If only she knew that next Sunday she will be in her grave!"

Melanotte also heard Don Bosco make a similar remark to Father Tesio. The chaplain came home before Don Bosco and the last few boys left, and after hearing the housekeeper's story, he angrily forbade Don Bosco ever to return (BM II, 225–226).

Saint Peter in Chains is not reckoned as one of the recognized Oratory sites of Don Bosco's dreams (see chapter 31) because it was only a one-day stopover.

7. After Father Tesio's death Father Cafasso took steps to have the city council appoint Don Bosco the new chaplain of Saint Peter's. The city council had this power in view of the cemetery's status as a national monument (Molineris, p. 279). Another's application, however, was accepted on June 18. A subsequent petition for reconsideration of the prohibition to use Saint Peter's was denied (July 3). It was at that point that permission to use Saint Martin's was granted. (BM II, 227–229)

More Problems

The Oratory at the Moretta house[1]

O n the Sunday following that prohibition, a large number of youngsters went to St Peter in Chains because it had not been possible to send them word of the ban. When they found everything locked up, they came in a body to my room beside the little hospital. What was I to do? I had a pile of equipment for church and for recreation; a mob of children trailing me wherever I went; but not an inch of ground on which to assemble them.

Trying to conceal my dismay, I put on a cheerful face for everyone and tried to keep their hopes up by telling them a thousand wonderful things about the future Oratory, which at that moment existed only in my own mind and in the decrees of the Lord.[2]

To entertain them on feast days, I took them sometimes to Sassi,[3] sometimes to Our Lady of the Pillar,[4] to Our Lady of the Fields,[5] to the Mount of the Capuchins,[6] and even as far as Superga.[7] In these churches I arranged to celebrate Mass for them in the morning and explain the gospel. In the afternoon we had a little catechism, hymn-singing, and some stories. Then we toured or hiked till it was time to head for home. It seemed that this critical state of things would have to bring any thought of an Oratory to nothing, but instead the number of boys coming increased extraordinarily.

In the meantime, we had moved into November (1845), not a very practical season for outings or walks to places outside the city. In agreement with Dr Borrelli, we rented three rooms in the house belonging to Fr Moretta,[8] which is the one near, almost in front of, the Church of Mary Help [of Christians] today. Now the house is practically a new one because of renovations.[9] We spent four months there, anxious about the location, yet happy at least to be able to collect our pupils in those rooms and give them instructions and especially an opportunity to go to confession. That same winter we began night classes.[10] It was the first time that this kind of school was spoken of in our area.[11] Consequently it was much discussed: some favored it; others were against it.[12]

At that time, also, some strange rumours began to get round. Some called Don Bosco a revolutionary; others called him a madman, or even a heretic.[13] This was their reasoning: "This Oratory alienates youngsters from their parishes. As a result, the parish priests will find their churches empty and will no longer know the children, for whom they must render an account before the tribunal of the Lord. Therefore Don Bosco should send the children to their own parishes and stop gathering them in other places." This is what two respectable parish priests of this city told me when they called on me, also on behalf of their colleagues.

"The young men whom I gather," I told them, "are not regular members of parishes. For the most part they know neither parish nor pastor."

"Why?"

"Because almost all of them are visitors who have been abandoned by their relatives in this city; or they have come here looking for work and failed to get it. Boys from Savoy, Switzerland, the Val d'Aosta, Biella, Novara, Lombardy are the ones who most frequently come to my activities."

"Couldn't you send these youngsters to their various parishes?"

"They don't know where their parishes are."

"Why not teach them?"

"It isn't possible. They're far from home, they speak diverse dialects, they have no fixed places to stay, and they don't know the city. These considerations make it difficult,[14] if not impossible, for them to belong to any parishes. Besides, many of them are grown men already: 18, 20, even

25 years old. And they are completely ignorant in matters of religion. Who could ever expect them to mix with kids of 8 or 10 who are much better instructed?"

"Couldn't you go with them yourself and teach them catechism in their parish churches?"

"At most I could go to one parish, but not to all. It could be done if every parish priest would come himself, or send someone to fetch these children and accompany them to their respective parishes. Even that would be difficult because many of these boys are dissipated, even dissolute. These, attracted by the games and outings which we organise,[15] decide to attend the catechism classes and the other practices of piety too. Therefore it would be necessary for every parish to establish a fixed place where these youngsters could be assembled and entertained in pleasant recreation."

"Those things are impossible. There aren't any places, nor do we have priests free on feast days for these activities."

"What then?" I asked.

"Then do as you think best. In the meantime, we'll decide amongst ourselves what it's best to do."

The problem then became a talking point amongst the parish priests of Turin. Should the oratories be promoted or opposed? Some were for, some against. The parish priest of Borgo Dora, Fr Augustine Gattino,[16] and Dr Ponzati, parish priest of St Augustine,[17] brought me their decision: "The parish priests of Turin, meeting in their regular conference, discussed the advisability of the oratories.[18] After weighing the fears and the hopes, the pros and the cons, they concluded that each parish priest could not provide an oratory in his own parish and that they would encourage the priest Bosco to continue until some other decision should be reached."[19]

While these things were going on, the spring of 1846 arrived. The tenants at the Moretta house were upset by the shouting and the din of the constant coming and going of the youngsters. They complained to the landlord, all threatening to withhold their rent if these noisy meetings did not stop. So the good priest Moretta had to tell us to look immediately for another place to gather our young men if we wished to keep our Oratory going.[20]

Notes

1. At this point the original manuscript is again in Don Bosco's hand.

2. After the Oratory had been expelled successively from the Refuge, Saint Peter's, and the Dora Mills in about six months' time, Don Bosco's frustration was understandable. He was confident that God would provide a solution; fortunately, he was not aware of the difficulties that still lay between him and the solution.

3. What was then the village of Sassi is now part of Turin. It is about three miles from Valdocco, on the other side of the Po, opposite its junction with the Dora; the mount of Superga rises behind Sassi.

4. Our Lady of the Pillar (*Madonna del Pilone*) is a shrine dedicated to the Annunciation. It is across the Po, between Sassi and the Regina Margherita Bridge. The seventeenth-century church at 195 corso Casale replaced a simpler shrine, a pillar on which was an image of the Virgin (hence the name). The boys had to ferry across the river (see BM II, 106, 305).

5. A Capuchin monastery about a mile and a half north-north-east of Valdocco down the road toward Lanzo (north of the Dora). The church, built in the fourteenth century, is at 98 via Massaia. Don Bosco brought the boys there on a pilgrimage after the Filippi brothers told him that they were canceling his lease to their field (chapter 39).

6. A wooded hill about 165 feet high on the right bank of the Po, a strategically important site in earlier centuries. Its location between the church of the Great Mother of God and the Umberto I Bridge, directly opposite the heart of the city, presents an excellent panorama. The church and Capuchin monastery at the top date from 1583. The friars always gave Don Bosco's urchins a warm welcome.

7. Superga is a 2200-foot mountain northeast of Turin, crowned by a majestic baroque basilica, about two miles from Sassi. Designed by the renowned Filippo Juvara (1685–1735), the church was built between 1717 and 1731 to fulfill a vow which King Victor Amadeus II made in 1706, praying that Turin might withstand a French siege. The dome towers 245 feet; the crypt contains the tombs of the House of Savoy from the time of the church's construction until the transfer of the national capital in 1865. One room in the attached monastery contains portraits of all the Popes, from Saint Peter to John Paul II. The mountaintop offers a spectacular

view of the entire city below (nowadays often obstructed by smog) and of the Alps beyond.

8. From the Dora Mills in the crowded Borgo Dora slum, Don Bosco and Father Borel turned again to the still-rural Valdocco district. They found a two-story house a block west of the Barolo institutions, between what is now via Maria Ausiliatrice and corso Regina Margherita. Its owner, Father John Baptist Anthony Moretta (1777–1847), rented out some of the rooms. The ground floor had a cellar, a stable, and nine rooms; the top floor had nine more rooms fronted by a long balcony, accessible by two wooden staircases. Apparently Don Bosco and Father Borel decided to set up there in November, even though they technically had a permit for Saint Martin's through December.

9. Part of the Moretta house stood where the church of the Salesian Sisters' oratory for girls was built in 1889 (now the parish church of Mary Help of Christians). Another part of the house survived until 1934, when it was demolished to make room for the courtyard of the Salesian publishing house Società Editrice Internazionale.

10. Don Bosco began to offer evening classes at the Refuge late in 1845. Many boys came to his and Father Borel's rooms every evening except Saturday and the vigils of holy days of obligation. Their rooms became classrooms, and the two priests taught reading, writing, and arithmetic. One can imagine how tiring this work was in view of the lateness of the hour and the number and quality of the pupils.

In the Moretta house, where there was more room, Don Bosco improved the facilities somewhat. Two hundred boys came every evening — still making for very crowded rooms. Don Bosco was assisted by at least three of his fellow priests (see his footnote to chapter 44).

Uneducated workers of all ages were eager for basic schooling; demand far outstripped the opportunity. For example, in 1846 Charles Ignatius Giullio had 150 places in his school, but 700 adults applied. The following year classrooms were added to accommodate 800; 1500 tried to register. (Stella, LW, p. 104)

11. Don Bosco will repeat in chapter 42 that his night courses were the first to be set up. In 1934 the Christian Brothers contested his claim. The question is discussed in MB XVII, 850–852, where the conclusion is:

If one is speaking of night schools in the strict sense, the

Brothers were ahead of Don Bosco by a matter of months. Having technical teachers at their disposal, they opened their school in January 1846 with a full program. If, however, one is speaking of evening courses plain and simple, that is, classes given in the evening to workers who had labored all day in shop, yard, or field, Don Bosco led the way, though only by a few months (November 1845).

12. Advocates of popular education, who were promoting night courses at this time, aroused suspicion among the important leaders of Church, State, and society. Conservatives saw in education a threat to the foundations of the regime, imputing liberal political motives to anyone who wanted to teach the masses. (The *Communist Manifesto* would be published within three years.) Archbishop Fransoni was one those who was concerned. See BM II, 165–175; Woolf, pp. 326–328.

   Don Bosco argued that the question was whether the works were good in themselves and worthy of promotion rather than what inspired them or who helped them. Worthy projects ought to be given Christian direction, forestalling any irreligious spirit that might misdirect them. With this purpose, he set to work (BM II, 199, 272).

   Because they were too close to the events, it is easy to understand how even devout people might look on Don Bosco's activities with a disapproving eye. Reputable authors hold that if the ideas of Don Bosco and others had been acted upon, perhaps a lot of evils would have been avoided. Many institutions which arose at this period would have had less irreligious leanings, and it would have been less trouble later trying to put things right. See Tommaso Chiuso, *La Chiesa in Piemonte dal 1797 ai giorni nostri* (Turin: Speirani, 1888), III, 197.

13. Many of these suspicions were brought to Father Cafasso, who was recognized as an intimate of Don Bosco. Since Father Cafasso was most highly regarded, he was able to temper some of the objections just by saying, "Leave him alone." (BM II, 274–275)

14. With the words "make it difficult," Father Berto's script again takes over the first draft, up to the end of chapter 37. The spelling is Don Bosco's; for example, we find words like *paroco, parochia, and parochiale* with only one *r*, which is how they would have been pronounced in Piedmontese.

15. Undoubtedly, Don Bosco's interest in them and his kindness toward them were as attractive as the recreational opportunities that he offered them.

16. Father Gattino was the pastor of Saints Simon and Jude parish, whose territorial boundaries included Valdocco. On his dealings with the Oratory over the years, consult MB XX.

17. Father Vincent Ponzati (1800–1874) was one of the priests who not long after tried to pack Don Bosco off to the insane asylum (BM II, 323–325). He continued to have a testy relationship with the Oratory (cf. BM III, 132–133). Stella spells his name "Ponsati" (*EcSo*, pp. 581, 639). His parish church was a block east of Our Lady of Consolation Church, on via San Agostino, just off the southwest corner of Porta Palazzo.

18. Presumably, Father Cocchi's Guardian Angel Oratory also came into the discussion.

19. Undoubtedly it is the duty of the pastor to impart religious instruction to his flock. The pastors of Turin, seeing that such instruction was given at the Oratory, solved the question in a wise and praiseworthy manner, rather than put up unreasonable opposition.

20. Don Bosco received notice to quit on March 2, 1846. He had already paid the month's rent of fifteen lire.

   Although he does not mention it, Don Bosco's health had begun to fail noticeably during this winter, which was particularly bitter. Overwork and endless worry had run him down, and quite possibly his constitution had not fully recovered from the rigors of his seminary days. Several people, including Father Borel, tried to get him to ease up.

The Oratory Outdoors

The Oratory in a field • *An outing to Superga*

With deep regret and no little inconvenience to our assemblies in March of 1846, we had to leave the Moretta house and rent a field from the Filippi brothers.[1] Today an iron foundry or smelting works occupies this ground.[2] There I was, under the open sky, in the middle of the field bounded by a broken-down hedge, which gave free admission to all and sundry. The youngsters, between three and four hundred of them, looked upon their Oratory as heaven on earth, even though its ceiling and walls were the sky.

But in a place like this, how could one hold religious services? Doing the best we could, we held catechism classes, sang hymns, sang vespers.[3] Then Dr Borrelli or I would stand on a hillock or on a chair and give a short sermon to the youths, who came up close to hear it.

For confessions, this is how we managed: I would be in the field early on feast day mornings, where many would already be waiting for me. I would sit on a hillock hearing one's confession while others were preparing or making their thanksgiving. Afterwards many went back to their games.

At a fixed time of the morning, all the boys assembled in answer to a bugle call. A second blast on the bugle brought them to silence, giving me a chance to speak and tell them where we were going for Mass and holy communion.

Sometimes, as I said, we went to Our Lady of the Fields, to the Church of Our Lady of Consolation, to Stupinigi,[4] or to the places mentioned earlier. Since we often trudged to centres a good distance away, I will describe one hike we did to Superga, which was typical of the others.

The royal basilica of Superga, northeast of Turin, was constructed by the architect Filippo Juvara between 1717 and 1731, complete with monastery, library, royal apartments, and crypt for the royal tombs. Don Bosco brought the boys here on memorable all-day hikes.

When the boys had collected in the field, we let them play bocce, piastrelle,[5] stilt-walking, etc., for a while. A drum was sounded, then a bugle call, to call them together and signal that we were ready to move out. We usually arranged that all of them should have heard Mass beforehand. Soon after 9:00 we set out for Superga. Some carried baskets of bread, some cheese, salami, fruit, or other provisions for the day. They kept quiet till we were outside the populated parts of the city, but from then on they began yelling, singing, and shouting, though they kept ranks.[6]

On reaching the foot of the hill, where the path climbs

to the basilica, I found a lovely little pony, already saddled up, which Fr [Joseph] Anselmetti, pastor of the church, had put at my disposal. There was also a note from Dr Borrelli, who had gone on ahead. It read: "Come along with our dear boys, and don't worry. The soup, the dinner, and the wine are ready."

I mounted the horse and read the letter aloud. They all crowded round the horse, and after hearing the message, broke into applause and cheers, shouting and singing. Some pulled the horse by his ears, others by the muzzle or the tail, bumping sometimes into the poor beast, sometimes into his rider. The gentle animal took it all with more patience than his rider would have shown. Amid that uproar the music struck up, provided by a tambourine, a bugle, and a guitar. It was absolute discord, but it served as a backing for the noisy voices of the boys. The result was wonderfully harmonious.

Worn out with all the laughing, joking, singing, and I would say, the yelling, we reached our destination. The perspiring youngsters gathered in the courtyard of the shrine and were soon given food enough to satisfy their voracious appetites. When they had a while to rest, I called them all round me and told them all the details of the wonderful history of the basilica, with its royal tombs in the crypt, and the Ecclesiastical Academy which Charles Albert had established there and the bishops of the Kingdom of Sardinia supported.[7]

Dr William Audisio,[8] the president, generously provided the soup and main course for all the guests. The parish priest donated the wine and the fruit. We took a couple of hours for a tour of the area and later assembled in the church, where many people had already taken their places. At 3:00 p.m. I gave a short discourse from the pulpit, after which some of the best choir boys sang a *Tantum ergo*.[9] Their clear voices and the novelty of it won everyone's admiration.

At six we sent up some balloons to signal our departure. With renewed and lively thanks to our benefactors we struck out again for Turin, singing, laughing, running, and sometimes praying on our way.

When we got to the city, the boys dropped out of our procession a few at a time at points along the route closest to their homes and returned to their families. When I got back to the Refuge, I still had with me 7 or 8 of the strongest lads, who had carried the equipment used during the day.

Notes

1. The field was across the lane on the east end of Father Moretta's property. An old shed on it provided a place for storage of the Oratory's recreation equipment. The Filippi brothers were John, Anthony, and Charles (Giraudo and Biancardi, p. 156).

2. This foundry was at the corner of via Cottolengo and via Cigna across from the SEI publishing house. Today a huge building occupies the property, including a gasoline station on corso Regina Margherita.

3. Evening prayer was commonly sung by the people as a Sunday evening devotion.

4. Stupinigi, six miles southwest of Turin, was the royal hunting lodge (another of Juvarra's architectural gems); a large park surrounds it.

5. *Bocce* is similar to lawn bowls, played on a dirt court. *Piastrelle* is a throwing game played with flat, puck-like pebbles.

6. Father Ascanio Savio (see chapter 50) testified that he had seen the youngsters going in groups or in procession singing hymns.

7. The Academy, founded by royal decree in 1833, provided advanced religious and academic formation for select clerics of Piedmont. To qualify for admission, they had to have degrees in theology and canon law. The four-year program specialized in canon law, homiletics, and moral theology. When they returned to their dioceses, the graduates were often given important appointments. The Academy was suppressed in 1855. In fact there had not been any students there since 1848, when Father Audisio was dismissed for political reasons.

8. Father William Audisio (1802–1882), a native of Bra, wrote on canon law, Church history, and homiletics. He spent the last years of his life in Rome, where he was widely consulted as an expert canonist.

9. The final two stanzas of the hymn *Pange lingua*, composed by Saint Thomas Aquinas. The *Tantum ergo* was always sung at benediction of the Blessed Sacrament, often to elaborate music (which is what Don Bosco implies here).

.

Vicar Cavour's Opposition

Threats from Marquis Cavour •
The Oratory in trouble again

Words cannot describe the enthusiasm these expeditions aroused in the youngsters. They thoroughly enjoyed the mixture of devotions, games, and outings, and they became so attached to me that they not only obeyed my every command, but they were eager that I should give them some task to do. One day, a carabiniere[1] saw me bring four hundred chattering and playful boys to silence in the field by raising my hand; he exclaimed, "If this priest were an army general, he could take on the most powerful army in the world." Really, the obedience and affection of my pupils bordered on foolishness.[2]

This very thing gave renewed credence of the rumour that Don Bosco and his sons could start a revolution at a moment's notice. It was a ridiculous claim, but local authorities swallowed it again, especially Marquis Cavour, father of the famous Camillo and Gustavo.[3] At that time he was vicar of the city, which means he was in charge of the civil power.[4] He therefore summoned me to city hall and reasoned with me at length about the silly stories about me which were then doing the rounds. He ended up by saying, "My good priest, take my advice: let these scoundrels[5] go their own way. They will bring only trouble on you and the public authorities. I have been assured that these meetings are dangerous, and therefore I cannot permit them."

I replied, "Lord Marquis, I have no other aim but the betterment of these poor sons of the people.[6] I do not ask for financial assistance but only for a place where I can bring them together. In this way I hope to reduce the number of loafers and those headed for prison."

"You're fooling yourself, my good priest. You're labouring in vain. Because I regard such meetings as dangerous, I cannot give you any place for such assemblies. And where will you get the money you need to pay rent and to meet the expenses that care of these vagabonds entails? Let me say again: I cannot allow you to hold these meetings."

"My Lord Marquis, the results so far convince me that I am not working in vain. Many totally abandoned youngsters have been gathered, freed from dangers, apprenticed to some trade, and are no longer dwelling in the prisons. So far, material support has not been lacking to me. This matter is in God's hands, who sometimes uses worthless instruments to accomplish his sublime designs."

"Have patience, and do as I say. I cannot allow such meetings."

"My Lord Marquis, don't grant this concession for my sake, but for the good of so many abandoned youngsters who would, most likely, come to a sad end."

"Quiet! I'm not here to argue. This is a disorder, and I wish to and must put a stop to it. Don't you know that every meeting is banned, unless held with lawful permission?"

"My meetings have no political scope.[7] I teach catechism to poor boys, and I do so with the archbishop's permission."

"Does the archbishop know what is going on?"

"He is fully informed. I have never taken a step without his consent."

"But I cannot allow these gatherings."

"I cannot believe, Lord Marquis, that you want to forbid me to teach catechism when my archbishop permits it."

"And supposing the archbishop were to tell you to drop this ridiculous undertaking of yours, would you put difficulties in the way?"

"None whatsoever. I undertook this work on the advice of my ecclesiastical superior, and I have continued with it. At the least sign from him I would be ready to do his bidding."

"Go. I shall speak with the archbishop. But don't be obstinate in accepting his orders,[8] or I shall be forced to take severe measures which I would prefer not to use."[9]

At this stage of the proceedings, I believed that we would be left in peace for at least a while. Imagine my disappointment, therefore, when I arrived home to find a letter from the Filippi brothers, ordering me out of the place leased to me!

"Your boys," they told me, "with their continuous trampling in our field have killed the grass down to the very roots. We are prepared to forgo the rent owing if you are out of the field in two weeks. There can be no extension beyond that."[10]

When my friends got wind of these latest difficulties, many came to advise me to quit. Others, noting my preoccupation and seeing me always surrounded by boys, began to say I had gone mad.

One day, in the presence of Fr Sebastian Pacchiotti[11] and others, Doctor Borrelli suggested to me: "Let's cut our losses now and salvage what we can. Let's send away all the youngsters except for about twenty of the youngest. While we continue to teach catechism to them, God will open the way and opportunity of doing more."[12]

"There's no need to wait for further opportunity," I told them. "The site's ready: a spacious courtyard, a house with many children, a portico, a church, priests, clerics, all at our disposal."

"But where are these things?" Dr Borrelli broke in.

"I don't know where they are, but they do exist, and they are ours."

At this Dr Borrelli burst into tears. "Poor Don Bosco!" he exclaimed. "He's losing his mind."

He took me by the hand, embraced me, and went off with Fr Pacchiotti, leaving me alone in my room.

Notes

1. A member of the most elite military corps; today, the Italian national police force.

2. Don Bosco is not really exaggerating, as will be evident when he falls ill (chapter 43).

3. Camillo Cavour was the great statesman who united Italy; on him and his brother, see chapter 45. Their father, Michele Benso (1781–1850), marquis of Cavour, was an important figure in Turin. After collaborating with the French to some extent during the Napoleonic occupation, Cavour

fell from favor during the Restoration. He tied his fortunes
to Charles Albert while that prince was likewise persona non
grata (1821–1831), and when Charles Albert became king,
the Cavour fortunes rose. In the intervening years both king
and marquis had become thorough conservatives. The marquis became vicar of police for Turin in 1835, and in that
capacity he was concerned about Don Bosco's little army of
potential revolutionaries.

The first time that Cavour encountered Don Bosco may
have been the Sunday when he and a friend were walking
near the Citadel, at the southwest edge of the city. They
came upon a priest and a horde of boys playing in the
meadows. On learning the priest's identity, the vicar is supposed to have remarked to his companion, "He's either a
lunatic or a candidate for the Senate," the latter being one of
the city jails. (BM II, 313) As we shall see, more than one
person drew the former conclusion.

4. Piedmont was an absolute monarchy till 1848. As vicar of
police, Cavour exercised authority in the king's name over
both criminal and civil matters in Turin.

5. While the vicar was probably sincerely afraid of some kind
of an uprising, and at the least had citizen pressure on him,
his fundamental attitude is indicated by his terminology.

6. Don Bosco politely and compassionately tries to correct
Cavour's attitude, as he will also correct Marchioness Barolo
(next chapter).

7. It was a fundamental principle of operation with Don Bosco
to steer clear of all politics so that no one could fault the
good done for society. He was fond of saying, "My politics
is the politics of the Our Father." As events showed repeatedly, especially in 1848–1849 and the early 1860s, being
entirely apolitical, perceived as such, and allowed to be such
was easier said than done. See also chapter 51.

8. Don Bosco always obeyed religious and civil authorities
wholeheartedly, even in indifferent matters. More than once
he had to swallow his pride to do so. But when it came to
protecting his boys or, later, the Salesian Society, he was
uncompromising. Some would have called him obstinate.

9. Cavour did not stop at words. He was sending policemen to
keep an eye on the Oratory's doings (cf. the carabiniere, and
chapter 41).

10. These events are hard to date precisely. Don Bosco seems to
have rented the Filippi field around March 1 (the first Sun-

day in Lent), and apparently the brothers canceled the lease in mid-month. Don Bosco first tried to get the owners to change their minds, and then he appealed to their mother. Those tactics having failed, he searched for another field to rent. All in vain. (Giraudo and Biancardi, pp. 154–155; cf. T. Bosco, SP, pp. 125–126).

11. Father Pacchiotti (1806–1884) was another of the chaplains at the Refuge and a regular helper at the Oratory catechism lessons. He later became a canon at Giaveno.

12. Even Father Borel has gotten discouraged enough to doubt Don Bosco's charism!

An Ultimatum
from the
Marchioness

*Good-bye to the Refuge • Fresh
imputations of insanity*

Marchioness Barolo became alarmed by all that was being said about Don Bosco, especially because the city council of Turin were opposed to my projects. One day she came to my room to speak to me. She began, "I am very pleased with the care you take of my institutions. Thank you for all you have done to introduce in them hymn-singing, plainchant, music, arithmetic, and even the metric system."[1]

"No thanks necessary. These are duties which priests must perform. God will repay everything. No need to mention it further."

"I wanted to say that I regret very much how your multiple occupations have undermined your health. You cannot possibly continue to direct my works and that of your abandoned boys, especially now when their number has increased beyond counting. I propose to you that from now on you concentrate just on your obligations, that is, the direction of my little hospital. You should stop visiting the prisons and the Cottolengo[2] and give up all your care for the youngsters. What do you say to that?"

"My Lady Marchioness, God has helped me up to now and will not fail me in the future. Don't worry about what should be done. Fr Pacchiotti, Dr Borrelli, and I will do everything."

"But I cannot allow you to kill yourself. Whether you like it or not, so many diverse activities are detrimental to

Don Bosco amid his boys in 1861 by the photographer Francesco Serra.
Soldà has identified the picture as a photomontage.

your health and my institutions. And then there are the gossip about your mental health and the opposition of the local authorities, which oblige me to advise you . . . "

"Advise me to do what, My Lady Marchioness?"

"Give up either the work for boys or the work at the Refuge. Think about it and let me know."

"I can tell you right now. You have money and will have no trouble in finding as many priests as you want for your institutes. It's not the same with the poor youngsters. If I turn my back on them at his time, all I've been doing for them now will go up in smoke. Therefore, while I will continue to do what I can for the Refuge, I will resign from any regular responsibility and devote myself seriously to the care of abandoned youngsters."

"But how will you be able to live?"

"God has always helped me, and he'll help me also in the future."

"But your health is ruined; you're no longer thinking straight. You'll be engulfed in debt. You'll come to me, and I tell you here and now that I'll never give you a soldo for your boys.[3] Now take my motherly advice. I'll continue to pay your salary, and I'll increase it if you wish. Go away and rest somewhere for a year, three years, five years. When you're back to health, come back to the Refuge and you'll be most welcome. Otherwise you put me in the unpleasant position of having to dismiss you from my institutes. Think it over seriously."

"I've thought it over already, My Lady Marchioness. My life is consecrated to the good of young people. I thank you for the offers you're making me, but I can't turn back from the path which Divine Providence has traced out for me."

"So you prefer your vagabonds[4] to my institutes? In that case, you are dismissed from this moment. This very day I shall arrange for somebody to take your place."

I pointed out to her that such a sudden dismissal would give rise to conjectures that would do neither of us credit. It would be better to act calmly and preserve between us that charity about which we should both have to answer before the Lord's tribunal.

"In that case," she concluded, "I give you three months'

notice. After that you will leave the direction of my little hospital to others."

I accepted my dismissal, abandoning myself to whatever God's plan for me might be.[5]

Meanwhile, the reports that Don Bosco had gone mad were gaining strength. My friends were grieved; others were amused. But they all kept far away from me. The archbishop did not interfere. Fr Caffasso advised me to bide my time;[6] Dr Borrelli kept quiet.[7] Thus all my helpers left me alone in the midst of about four hundred boys.[8]

At that time some respectable persons wanted to take care of my health. "This Don Bosco," they said amongst themselves, "has some fixations which will inevitably end up in madness. Perhaps he would benefit by treatment. Let's take him to the asylum[9] and leave it to them to do whatever they think best."

Two of them were appointed to come with a carriage to pick me up and escort me to the asylum. The two emissaries[10] greeted me politely and then inquired about my health, the Oratory, the future building and church; they sighed deeply and exclaimed aloud, "It's true."

After that they invited me to go for a drive with them. "A little air will do you good. We have a carriage at hand. We'll go together and have time to converse."

At this point I understood their game, and without letting on that I had them figured out, I walked with them to the carriage, insisting that they get in first and take their places. But instead of getting in there myself, I slammed the door shut and called out to the coachman, "Straight to the asylum with all speed. They're expecting these two priests there."

Notes

1. See chapter 42, notes 25–26.
2. The Little House of Divine Providence, better known as the Cottolengo Institute, is a massive complex of hospitals, homes, and other care units for the most abandoned members of society: the deaf, dumb, blind, crippled, insane, aged,

and others. It takes up several city blocks to the east of the Basilica of Mary Help of Christians and the Barolo Institutes and shelters some five thousand persons at any given time.

Saint Joseph Benedict Cottolengo (1786–1842), a native of Bra and canon of the ancient cathedral of Chieri, was a wealthy priest moved by the plight of the sick poor. After founding his work in Turin in 1827, he was compelled to relocate outside the city center during the cholera epidemic of 1831; so he set up in Valdocco. Eventually he founded several religious congregations to provide various services for the Little House, such as nursing, training for those who care for the inmates, and contemplative prayer. He absolutely refused any kind of endowment for his institution, and to this day the Little House depends entirely on voluntary alms. Cottolengo was canonized in 1934 (the same year as Don Bosco); his feast day is April 30. See Butler's *Lives*, II, 191–192.

3. Not only did she not carry out her threat, but she remained a benefactress of Don Bosco's work (BM II, 424, 430). The full dialog reveals both her headstrong nature and her great generosity.

4. The marchioness used expressions similar to Cavour's. Don Bosco's priestly heart preferred to call them "poor children" or "poor and abandoned youth."

5. This short sentence summarizes a whole tragedy. The one who was devoting himself totally to the most abandoned was now totally abandoned (recall the pathetic ending of the preceding chapter).

The marchioness wrote to Father Borel about Don Bosco's health on May 18 (BM II, 360–361). Her confrontation with Don Bosco probably came at the end of that month; his service at Saint Philomena's Hospital terminated at the end of August (BM II, 364; Giraudo and Biancardi, p. 164), three months after she served him notice of dismissal.

6. In a moment of weakness Father Cafasso, too, was proposing a suspension of operations. This would surely have gravely damaged the Oratory.

7. Father Borel had already suggested reducing the number of boys (preceding chapter), which Don Bosco could never consider. Fearing for Don Bosco's sanity, perhaps, Father Borel thought it better not to say anything.

8. It was a tragic situation. Marquis Filippo Crispolti summed

up Don Bosco's position magnificently in a commemorative lecture (*Questioni vitali* [Rome: Pustet, 1908], p. 343):

> The weakness of human judgment, in Don Bosco's case, was not confined to adversaries or shortsighted people. Even upright people and experts were afflicted.... Those who should have been able to read the depths of his soul and discern there his steady ascent toward God and God's reaching down toward him — such people were not lacking among simple folks — should have rejoiced from the start at the great things that would arise from his efforts, for their seeds were already evident.

9. The asylum was along corso San Massimo (now corso Regina Margherita) one block south of the Refuge, between the Rondò and the Church of Our Lady of Consolation.

10. The two were Father Vincent Ponzati, pastor of Saint Augustine parish, and Father Louis Nasi of Corpus Domini parish. Both were learned men inspired by charity. Father Nasi (1821–1896) was always on the best of terms with Don Bosco and continued to help him with catechism lessons, preaching, and music. He later became a canon of the cathedral.

Palm Sunday
1846

Transfer to the present Oratory of
St Francis de Sales at Valdocco

While all this was going on,[1] we came to the last Sunday on which I was allowed to keep the Oratory in the field (5 April 1846).[2] I said nothing at all, but everybody knew how troubled and worried I was. On that evening as I ran my eyes over the crowd of children playing, I thought of the rich harvest awaiting my priestly ministry. With no one to help me, my energy gone, my health undermined, with no idea where I could gather my boys in the future, I was very disturbed.

I withdrew to one side, and as I walked alone I began to cry, perhaps for the first time. As I walked I looked up to heaven and cried out, "My God, why don't you show me where you want me to gather these children? Oh, let me know! Oh, show me what I must do!"

When I had finished saying this, a man called Pancrazio Soave came up. He stammered as he asked me, "Is it true that you're looking for a site for a laboratory?"

"Not a laboratory, but an oratory."

"I don't know the difference between an oratory and a laboratory, but there's a site available. Come and have a look at it. Mr Joseph Pinardi,[3] the owner, is an honest man. Come and you'll get a real bargain."

At that very moment my faithful colleague from the seminary, Fr Peter Merla, showed up. He was the founder of a pious work named the *Family of St Peter*.[4] Filled with zeal for his sacred ministry, he had begun his institute because so many single girls and disgraced women, after suffering imprisonment, found themselves sadly abandoned.

For the most part, honest society abhorred them, and they could find neither bread nor employment. When he had a little free time, that worthy priest hastened eagerly to help his friend. Usually he found me alone amongst a mob of boys.

"What's wrong?" he asked as soon as he saw me. "I've never seen you so down. Has something bad happened?"

"Misfortune, no. But I'm in a real predicament. Today is the last day on which I'm allowed to use this field. It's evening already, two [hours] to nightfall.[5] I have to tell my sons where to assemble next Sunday, and I don't know where. This friend here says he knows of a place that might do. Can you keep an eye on the recreation for a while? I'll go take a look, and I'll be back before long."

When I reached the place indicated, I saw a shabby little two-storey house with a worm-eaten wooden stairway and balcony. All round were gardens, pastures, and fields.[6] I was about to climb the stairs, but Pinardi and Pancrazio stopped me.

"No," they told me. "The place we have in mind for you is here in back."

There was a long shed; one side of its roof leaned against the wall of the house, and the other ended about three feet above the ground.[7] If it were necessary, it could be used as a woodshed, but not much else. To get into it I had to bend my head so as not to bump against the ceiling.

"I can't use it," I said. "It's too low."

"I'll fix it to suit your needs," Pinardi graciously suggested. "I'll dig it out, I'll make steps, I'll put in a new floor. I really would like you to establish your laboratory here."

"Not a laboratory, but an oratory, a little church where I can bring together some youngsters."

"Better still. I'll gladly help with the work myself. Let's draw up a contract. I can sing too, so I'll come along and give a hand. I'll bring two chairs, one for me and one for my wife. And I have a lamp at home, too; I'll bring that as well."

The good man seemed to be beside himself with joy at having a church in his house.

"Thank you, my good friend," I said, "for your kindness and goodwill. I accept these generous offers. If you can lower the floor at least a foot (20 in.),[8] I'll take it. But what's your price?"

"Three hundred francs. I have better offers but I prefer yours because you're going to use the place for the public good and religious purposes."

"I'll give you three hundred and twenty if you'll throw in the strip of ground round the house as a playground for the boys,[9] and if I can bring my kids here as soon as next Sunday."

"I understand. It's a deal.[10] Come, by all means. Everything will be ready."

I made no more demands. I ran right back to my boys. I gathered them round me and began to shout in a loud voice, "Great news, my sons! We've got a place for our Oratory, a more reliable one than we've had till now. We'll have a church, a sacristy, classrooms, and a place to play. Sunday, next Sunday, we'll go to our new Oratory, which is over there in Pinardi's house." And I pointed the place out to them.[11]

Wild enthusiasm greeted this announcement. Some ran around shouting and jumping for joy; some stood stock still; some raised their voices, I would say, to yelling and screaming. They were moved like people who feel so intensely happy that they cannot express their feelings. Overcome with deep gratitude, we thanked the holy Virgin for hearing and answering the prayers which we had made to her that very morning at Our Lady of the Fields.[12] Now we knelt for the last time in that field and said the holy rosary. After that, everyone went home. Thus we said good-bye to that place which each of us had loved out of necessity, but which each of us, hoping for something better, left behind without regret.

On the following Sunday, 12 April, which was Easter Sunday, all the church furniture and the equipment for recreation were brought there, and we went to take possession of our new place.

258 • *Memoirs of the Oratory*

Notes

1. On May 10, 1864, Don Bosco gave a conference to the Salesians. John Bonetti, who was then a deacon, made a summary of it immediately after, which is in the Salesian archives. Don Bosco narrated some of the events concerning the founding of the Oratory. In a dream he was shown a house not far from the Refuge, where he still lived; the house was destined for him and his young men. The next morning he told Father Borel right away, "Now we have a house!" Don Bosco went to look for it and discovered that it was a brothel! He exclaimed, "These are illusions from the devil," and blushed at his own credulity. He said nothing about it and continued with the wandering Oratory.

   However, Don Bosco recalled, the very same house was shown to him in a dream a second time. The next day he returned to the neighborhood and wept. How could he accept that he was supposed to go into such a place? He told himself, "It's time to ask the Lord for enlightenment, for delivery from these troubles."

   Yet a third time he saw the same house in a dream. This time he heard a voice saying, "Have no fear of going to this place. Don't you know that God can enrich his people with the spoils of the Egyptians?" [cf. Exodus 3:21–22; 12:35–36]

   This set his mind at rest. He was trying to find a way to buy the house when the Oratory was expelled by the Filippi brothers and the Pinardi offer came. The house in question was owned by Mrs. Teresa Bellezza. See chapters 40 and 54; BM II, 421–423.

2. Don Bosco wrote "March 15." In Father Berto's copy, Father Bonetti's easily recognized handwriting has changed it to "April 5." Further on in this account, as well as in his brief history of the Oratory up to 1854, Don Bosco asserts that the following Sunday was Easter Sunday, April 12.

   Giraudi discovered and published the Pinardi contract (p. 68), which is dated April 1. It is possible that the deed was drawn up shortly after April 5 and dated retroactively to the beginning of the month. It is more likely that Don Bosco has telescoped the events of several weeks and his personal distress: he received notice from the Filippis on March 8 (T. Bosco, SP, pp. 125–126) or March 15 (Giraudo and Biancardi, pp. 154–155); he met Soave and Pinardi on March 15 and reached an oral agreement about the shed; the lease was signed April 1, but the chapel was not ready till the 12th.

There is quite a discrepancy between Don Bosco's description of the barren shed and the contract's ample description of the spaces to be leased, which indicates either that Don Bosco's memory has romanticized a bit, or that a lot of work was done before occupancy. Perhaps the Oratory used the grounds about the house to play in on April 5 (and one or two earlier Sundays?), but the boys had to attend Mass elsewhere as they had done since August 1845; perhaps they used these Sundays (March 22 and 29, April 5) for hikes.

3. Pinardi's first name was Francis. He came from Arcisate in the province of Varese in Lombardy. Soave had come to Turin from Verolengo (a nearby town); he was trying to start a starch factory (T. Bosco, SP, p. 126).

4. Father Merla (1815–1855) was a teacher from Rivara Torinese. During the summer of 1850, Don Bosco arranged for him to teach Latin to three of his most promising boys, one of whom was Michael Rua (BM IV, 97–98). Father Merla's charitable work still survives; under the direction of the Vincentian Sisters of the Cottolengo Institute, it cares for men in need, as well as women. Ever since Don Bosco's day the Salesians have rendered spiritual assistance to Father Merla's work out of gratitude to Don Bosco's good friend.

5. The word "hours" was omitted, in error, from a long addition to Father Berto's copy of the manuscript.

6. Pinardi bought the house and land (one acre) for fourteen thousand lire in July 1845 from the Filippi brothers. The whole property was enclosed by a wall. The house, which ran lengthwise from west to east, had six rooms on the ground floor and five on the second. There were a stable and a woodshed at the east end. In November Pinardi rented the house to Pancrazio Soave.

A new shed was under construction along the north, or back, wall of the house and was not included in the lease to Soave. Pinardi rented it separately, first to a hatmaker — the irrigation ditch which ran along the northern edge of the property made it a convenient site for any artisan who needed a little water — and then to some washerwomen, who also used a small laundry shed standing in the northeast corner of the yard.

Fields, crisscrossed by irrigation ditches, lay all around the house. Pinardi's property fronted on via della Giardiniera.

PER virtù della presente Scrittura, ossia Capitolazione d'affittamento, 'l signor *franceso fu Gioanni Pinardi nato in Arusate Regno Lombardo veneto, ed in questa citta domiciliata*

per *Le* e suoi eredi, conced *e* a titolo d'affittamento alle seguenti condizioni, ed a quelle risultanti dagli articoli 1725, 1726 e seguenti del Codice Civile del 20 di giugno 1837, al signor *Teologo Gioanni Borel del fu Gius Antonio nato e residente in questa citta*

qui present *e* stipulant *e* ed accettant *e* per *Le e suoi* eredi e successori, li seguenti membri situati nella Casa propria. del signor *franceso Pinardi* nella Parrocchia di *Borgo dora* sezione *Borgo dora* contrada *Giardiniera* isola Porta N.º cioè *tre membri di cui un grande Camerone oblourgo cortile davanti, ed a lato dei medi*

Il detto affittamento principierà il *Primo* di *Aprile* mille ottocento quarant *a sei* , continuerà sino a *ottanta* di *Aprile* mille ottocento *quarantanoae*, e durerà anni *tre consecutivi* mediante l'annua somma di *lire trecento 300—* che l dett *e* signor *Teologo Borel* promett *e* e s'obbliga ——di pagare in buona moneta al signor *franceso Pinardi* od a chi ne sarà legittimamente autorizzato, di sei in sei mesi, la metà anticipatamente, cioè alla metà d'ogni semestre, secondo lo stile di questa Città.

The first page of the contract between Francis Pinardi and Father John Borel for the rental of a three-room shed from April 1846 to April 1849 at three hundred lire per year

7. Documents which Giraudi found in the building department of the Turin municipal archives show that "about three feet" exaggerates its lowness. The outside wall of the shed was more than three feet high, but some earth piled against the wall made it appear lower than it was.

   During the reconstruction done between Don Bosco's oral agreement with Pinardi and the Oratory's transfer to its new home, the wall did have to be raised, presumably leveling off the roof. The contract specifies that the shed-turned-chapel had nine windows and three small doors (Giraudi, p. 68). Nevertheless, the ceiling was still quite low, as will appear in chapter 45.

   The shed ran the length of the house (not counting the woodshed), about sixty-six feet, and was twenty feet wide (Giraudi, p. 70).

8. As already mentioned, measurements in Piedmont varied; the Turinese foot was about fourteen inches. For some reason Don Bosco specifies parenthetically that he wanted at least twenty inches dug out.

9. The plot of ground in question was the backyard, between the house and the ditch, and the west yard, between the house and the wall along the Bellezza land. The backyard, measuring about 230 feet by 26 feet, became the Oratory's first courtyard. The west yard, which faced the main entrance to the new chapel, was about 102 feet by 66 feet; it became the main playground.

10. The contract ran from April 1, 1846, to April 30, 1849. Although Don Bosco says that they agreed upon an annual rent of 320 lire (francs), the contract spelled out "three hundred ten," and the "ten" was crossed out, perhaps as a further act of kindness on Pinardi's part. The contract was actually made between Father Borel and Pinardi, either because Pinardi knew him but not Don Bosco (Ceria, MO, p. 168), or because Father Borel had money and Don Bosco did not.

11. Via della Giardiniera ran diagonally to the northwest from via Cottolengo, starting at the northern end of the Filippi field. Pinardi's property was some six hundred feet up the road.

12. This pilgrimage to attend Mass and ask our Lady's help in finding a place for the Oratory was the occasion of a strange happening. Along the way the boys prayed the rosary, chanted the Litany of Our Lady, and sang hymns.

As they left the road and started up the lane to the monastery, the church bells began to peal a welcome for them. They noticed that immediately, for they had never heard the bells before, though they had been there a number of times. It was rumored that the bells had rung of their own accord; in any case, neither the Capuchin superior nor anyone else ever learned who had rung them.

The friars treated the boys to breakfast, and then the boys returned to town for their last day of using the Filippi field, still unsure of their future. (BM II, 327–328)

PART III

The Third Decade
1846 to 1856*

*[Sic.]

A Typical
Sunday

The new church

Even though this new church was really a hovel,[1] still, since we held our lease by a formal contract, we were freed from the anxiety and the grievous inconvenience of having to move so often from one place to another. To me it seemed then truly to be the place of which I had dreamed and seen written: *Haec est domus mea, inde gloria mea.*[2] Heaven, however, had other plans.

The house close beside us caused no little difficulty: it was a house of ill fame; and there were difficulties from the Gardener's Inn, now called the Bellezza house,[3] where all the good-time Charlies of the city congregated, especially on feast days. Nevertheless, we were able to overcome all the problems and began to hold our meetings regularly.

When our work was done,[4] the archbishop on   April granted the faculty of blessing and consecrating that humble building for divine worship. That was done on Sunday,   April 1846.[5] To show his satisfaction the archbishop renewed the faculty already granted while we were at the Refuge to have sung Masses; to offer triduums, novenas, and retreats; to admit to confirmation and to holy communion;[6] and to certify that *all those who regularly attended our programme had fulfilled their Easter duty.*[7]

A regular meeting place, the signs of the archbishop's approval, our solemn ceremonies, the music, the noise from our play garden[8] attracted children from all directions. Several priests began to drift back.[9] Amongst those who helped in our work should be noted Dr Joseph Trivero,[10]

A sketch of the Pinardi house and property as they appeared in 1846. The shed with seven windows became the Oratory chapel after the windows were enlarged and two doors added for the sacristy and a storeroom. The shed to the left of the chapel served as a woodshed and a stall.

Dr Hyacinth Carpano,[11] Dr John Vola,[12] Dr Robert Murialdo,[13] and the intrepid Dr Borrelli.

This is how we arranged our functions. The church was opened early in the morning on holy days, and we heard confessions until it was time for Mass, which was scheduled for eight o'clock. Often, because there were so many for confession, Mass had to be put off till nine or even later. One of the priests, when they were present, assisted, and the prayers were recited in alternating choirs. Those who were prepared went to holy communion during Mass.

When Mass was over and the vestments put away, I stood up on a low rostrum to explain the gospel. Then this was changed in order to begin a regular presentation of Bible history. These narratives were presented in simple and popular language, vividly portraying the customs of the times, the places, the geographical names and locations.

This pleased very much the youngest, the adults,[14] and even the priests who were present. After the instruction, there were classes till noon.[15]

At one o'clock in the p.m. recreation began, with bocce, stilts, rifles, wooden swords,[16] and our first gymnastics equipment. At two-thirty we started catechism. On the whole, ignorance abounded. Many times I began to sing the *Ave Maria*, but not one of the approximately four hundred youngsters present could continue if I stopped.

After catechism was over, since we were not yet able to sing vespers, we recited the rosary. Later we began to sing *Ave Maris Stella*, then the Magnificat, then *Dixit*, and on to the other psalms, and finally an antiphon.[17] In the space of a year, we had become capable of singing the whole vespers of our Lady. These practices were followed by a short sermon, usually a story in which some virtue or vice was personified. It all concluded with the singing of the litanies[18] and with benediction of the Blessed Sacrament.

When we came out of church, there was a period of free time for each to do as he pleased. Some continued their catechism class, some practised their singing, some worked at their reading. Most of them, however, jumped about, ran, and enjoyed themselves in various games and pastimes. All those exploits of jumping, running, juggling, tightrope walking, stick balancing that I had learned long before from acrobats, were practised under my instruction. In this way I could control that crowd, which, in the main, could be described thus: "Like a horse or a mule, without understanding."[19]

I must say, however, that despite their great ignorance I always admired the great respect they had for everything in church and for the sacred ministers, and their eagerness to learn more about their religion.[20]

I made use of that unorganized recreation period to introduce my pupils quietly to thoughts of religion and use of the holy sacraments. To one I might whisper[21] a recommendation to be more obedient, to be more prompt in attending to his duty; to another I would suggest regular attendance at catechism, or at confession, or so on. In this way these play periods provided me with an opportune means of making personal contact with a crowd of youngsters who, on Saturday evening or Sunday morning, would willingly come for confession.

Sometimes I would even call them away from their games to lead them to confession when I had seen some resistance to that important obligation. I will mention one case out of many.

One youngster had been constantly reminded about his Easter duty. Every Sunday he promised to do it, but then he never kept his word. One feast day when our devotions were over, he was in the thick of the games, running and jumping everywhere and bathed in perspiration, his face flushed; he no longer knew whether he was in this world or in the other. I stopped him in his tracks and asked him to help me with something in the sacristy. He wanted to come just as he was, in shirt sleeves.

"No," I told him, "put on your jacket and come."

When we got to the sacristy, I led him to the apse[22] and said, "Kneel on this prie-dieu."

He did, but he wanted to move the kneeler.

"No," I replied. "Leave everything as it is."

"Then what do you want me to do?"

"Make your confession."[23]

"I'm not ready."

"I know."

"What then?"

"Then get ready, and I'll hear your confession."

"Fine, that's fine," he exclaimed. "I really need it. You did well to catch me like this; otherwise I wouldn't have come, out of fear of my companions."[24]

While he prepared, I read part of my breviary. Then he made a good confession and a devout thanksgiving. From that time on, he was always amongst the most diligent boys in fulfilling his religious duties. He used to tell the story to his companions, concluding thus: "Don Bosco used a clever stratagem to cage the blackbird."

As night fell, we all returned to church when the bell rang. There we said a few prayers or recited the rosary and the Angelus, and everything ended with the singing of the "Praised for ever be."[25]

As they left the church, I went in their midst and accompanied them while they sang and shouted. When we reached the Rondò,[26] we would sing a verse from some hymn. Then I would invite them back for the following Sunday, and with a loud chorus of "good nights" all round, each went his way.

Quite unusual was the scene of the departure from the Oratory.[27] As they came out of church, each would wish the others good night a thousand times without making any move to leave his companions.

"Off home with you," I would urge them repeatedly. "It's getting late. Your people are waiting for you." To no avail. I had to let them gather round. Six of the strongest made a kind of seat by linking hands, and on this improvised throne I had to sit. Then they organised a procession, carrying Don Bosco over the heads of the tallest boys on that platform of arms, and wended their way with laughter, song, and yelling to the roundabout commonly called the Rondò. There they sang some more hymns and ended with a solemn rendition of "Praised for ever be."

When they finally settled into a deep silence, I was able to wish them all a good night and a happy week. They all answered as loud as they could, "Good night!" And then I was let down from my throne.[28] Each headed for his own family, while some of the oldest accompanied me as far as my home;[29] I would be half dead with fatigue.

Notes

1. The Pinardi chapel has been called the Bethlehem of the Salesian Family because of its poverty and because of what began in that miserable location. The Chapel of the Resurrection, usually called the Pinardi chapel, now stands on the site. It remains the center, both geometrically and spiritually, of the Salesian motherhouse.

2. The phrase is quoted slightly differently here than earlier. Don Bosco seems to have seen this slogan in three different places, at three different times, and in slightly different forms.

   The first time was in the dream narrated in chapter 31. The second occasion is this one, connected with the Pinardi chapel, which seems to have led him, at this point, to believe that it must be the place he had seen earlier. More than thirty years later, after the Basilica of Mary Help of Christians had been built, he was reading over a draft of the *Memoirs*, and he wrote in the margin, "Heaven, however, had other plans."

The third time, he read the inscription in a dream on the front of a house capable of accommodating two hundred boys. This house later replaced the Pinardi house next to the Church of Saint Francis de Sales. On this third occasion, the wording ran, *Hic nomen meum, hinc inde exibit gloria mea* ["Here is my name; from this side and that my glory will go forth"]. *Hinc . . . inde*—from this side and that side of what? From either side of via della Giardiniera, which ran through the property that eventually belonged to the Oratory and which was wiped out in 1865 in connection with the building of the Basilica of Mary Help of Christians. On one side of via della Giardiniera was the new-born Oratory, and on the other was "the field of the dream" where the basilica would later rise (BM III, 323).

3. See chapter 39, note 1. The widow Teresa Bellezza owned the land and house on the west side of the Pinardi property. She rented the rooms to several tenants, one of whom ran the tavern called the Gardener's Inn (*Albergo della Giardiniera*); this took its name from the street on which it was located (or, possibly, vice versa). It is not clear whether the tavern was directly involved in the prostitution or whether that was the business of one or more of the other tenants. See also chapter 54.

4. The contract reveals the extent of the shed's transformation as it was turned into a chapel (Giraudi, p. 68). The amount of work involved is most unlikely to have been completed in just a week—Holy Week, at that. If Don Bosco and Pinardi made an oral agreement in mid-March, we have a reasonable amount of time. See chapter 39, note 2, on the dating of these events; Giraudo and Biancardi are sure that the work began at the end of March (p. 156).

According to Father John Baptist Francesia (*Vita breve e popolare del venerabile Giovanni Bosco* [Turin: SEI, 1925], p. 118), who began to frequent the Oratory in 1850 and knew some of the young men involved, much of the renovation work was done by Don Bosco and the boys themselves; many of them were construction workers, after all.

The long shed was divided into three rooms. The main one was the chapel, about fifty feet in length. Behind it (moving eastward) were a little sacristy, which could be entered through either the chapel or an external door, and a storage room (for the recreation equipment) with access only from the courtyard. The north wall of the chapel contained seven tiny windows; each of the two small rooms had one window.

5. Don Bosco leaves both dates blank. He must have expected Father Berto to find the archbishop's rescript so that he could supply the dates. The chancery document is dated April 10, Good Friday. A comment after the notes discusses the problem of the actual date of blessing.

6. "To admit [the boys] to confirmation and to [first] holy communion" meant that Don Bosco was entitled to certify to the pastors of the parishes wherein they resided that these youngsters had been properly catechized and could be admitted to these rites along with the other young people of the parish.

7. The obligation of every Catholic who is of age to receive the Eucharist at least once during the Easter season was one of the gravest in Church law. This was generally to be done in one's own parish church. Prior to the codification of canon law in 1917, the period for fulfilling this law varied from place to place; generally it ran from Palm Sunday to the Sunday after Easter, but in some places it was extended, e.g. to begin on Ash Wednesday or to end on Ascension Thursday. The penalty for failure to receive was severe: in effect, the person was not to be regarded as a Catholic. (*Catholic Encyclopedia* [New York, 1911], XI, 517) Most of this strictness is gone today, but the obligation remains (canon 920).

   Consequently Don Bosco emphasized this faculty as most significant. When he later approached the Holy See to seek approval for the Salesian Society, he cited the granting of this privilege as the first official recognition of his emergent congregation.

8. This "garden" was just a bare field on the north side of the chapel; if it had grass when the Oratory arrived, it surely did not have it for long. When he spoke to certain audiences or wrote to civil authorities, Don Bosco almost never used the word "courtyard" to designate the playground. The term "play garden" evoked certain children's schools in fashion at the time, including Froebel's kindergartens.

9. When it was commonly believed that Don Bosco was insane, or at best, on the verge of a nervous breakdown, all his helpers withdrew except the "intrepid" Father Borel.

10. Father Trivero (1816?–1894) came from the Biella area, some forty miles north-northeast of Turin in the Alpine foothills. His family served the royal household, and he became guardian of the chapel of the Holy Shroud (which belonged to the royal family) in the cathedral of Turin. (Stella, LW, p. 87)

11. Father Carpano (1821–1894) was a kind and brilliant priest, ordained in 1844, after which he studied at the Convitto. Father Cafasso directed him to Don Bosco, to whom he was a great help because of his abilities as a preacher, a catechist, and an academic teacher. He zealously visited the jails and took into his own home newly released delinquents while they hunted for jobs. He seems to have become discouraged and disappeared during the most trying days of the wandering Oratory, March 1846 (BM II, 334). But when Don Bosco fell ill in July, he was at Father Borel's side to hold the fort, and he was steadfast thereafter with both time and money. (See references in BM II–IV.)

12. There were three learned priests named Vola in Turin at this time: John Baptist, John Ignatius, and Joseph. According to Ceria (MO, p. 174, n. 29), it was the last who worked with Don Bosco; it was, instead, John Ignatius Vola (1798–1858), whose biography by Canon Lawrence Gastaldi was published in the March–April 1865 issue of the *Catholic Readings*.

13. Father Robert Murialdo (1815–1883) was the cousin of Saint Leonard Murialdo (1828–1900), founder of the Pious Congregation of Saint Joseph. They were of noble blood. Both were good friends and helpers of Don Bosco. Robert, in particular, became heavily involved in Don Bosco's projects for some years. He was also director of Father Merla's Family of Saint Peter. On Saint Leonard Murialdo, see NCE X, 83.

14. A reference either to the wide age-range of Don Bosco's "boys," i.e. from about seven to over twenty-one years old, or to the laymen who helped him (see chapter 42).

15. The classes were mainly for the three Rs. At noon the boys went home for a bite to eat, and Don Bosco and his helpers got a bit of rest.

16. The rifles, too, were wooden. In the last years of the 1840s, relations between the Kingdom of Sardinia and the Austrian Empire were increasingly strained. More and more Italians from all over the peninsula looked to King Charles Albert for national leadership, for some concrete steps toward throwing

Austria out of Venetia, Lombardy, Tuscany, Parma, Modena, and Emilia-Romagna (see introduction and chapter 48). War was in the air, especially in the capital. Naturally the boys loved to play soldiers, the "Italians" challenging the "Austrians." Reluctantly, Don Bosco put up with this game that the boys so loved.

These games continued until they reached their height during the First War of Independence (1848–1849). The most famous battle in the history of the Oratory saw the boys, in their thoughtless excitement, sweep to a victory over the lettuce, beans, and herbs of Mama Margaret's garden, an extensive space in front of the house. The poor woman was so distressed that she was ready to pack for Becchi; fortunately her son was able to convince her to accept the loss and start her garden over again. But not long after, the garden was eliminated in favor of more playground space. (BM III, 310–311)

17. Don Bosco was teaching the boys to sing evening prayer from the Little Office of the Blessed Virgin in plainchant.

    The *Ave Maris Stella* is a Marian hymn of seven stanzas. The Magnificat is Mary's hymn of praise (Luke 1:46–55), which is sung or said every evening as part of vespers.

    Five psalms formed the core of morning and evening prayer. The first psalm of evening prayer was Psalm 110, whose first words in Latin are *Dixit Dominus*. The others were Psalms 113, 122, 127, and 147:12–20.

    The psalms and the Magnificat are each introduced by an antiphon, a scriptural or patristic verse which is repeated at the end.

18. He probably means the Litany of Loreto (the Litany of the Blessed Virgin), a series of invocations beseeching Mary and the saints to pray for the suppliants.

19. Psalm 32:9, which Don Bosco quotes in Latin: *Sicut equus et mulus, quibus non est intellectus.*

20. Don Bosco's ability to inspire these unlettered boys and young men with such sentiments was unusual at that time and place.

21. Literally, *con una parola nell'orecchio*, a favorite little device of Don Bosco to catch a boy at ease and give him an encouraging word, or a conscience-stirring one, as the situation required.

22. The area of the church behind the main altar.

23. Don Bosco, of course, had surmised that the reason why he

did not make his Easter communion was that some grave sin was on his conscience. The boy at least had the respect not to receive the Sacrament sacrilegiously.

24. Out of fear for what they would think or say of him. On human respect, see also chapter 49.

25. This is a short quatrain which they sang in Italian:

> Praised forever be
> the names of Jesus and Mary.
> Praised forever be
> the name of Jesus, the Word Incarnate.

26. An open circular space, where the corso Regina Margherita is met by corso Valdocco, corso Principe Eugenio, and via Cigna. It gained notoriety because public hangings were carried out in this prominent spot. The city has erected there a statue of Saint Joseph Cafasso with a condemned man as a moving tribute to his charismatic priestly ministry.

27. With a touch of repetition, Don Bosco now proceeds to give more details of the weekly departure rites. Ceria (MO, pp. 177–178) offers no explanation for the repetition. One may suppose that Don Bosco added it to the Berto manuscript during revision.

28. A scene of this nature was reproduced on a great banner near the main entrance to Saint Peter's Basilica during Don Bosco's beatification ceremonies (June 2, 1929). It showed Don Bosco being carried triumphantly in an armchair by a jubilant group of his pupils. The background depicted the Piedmontese countryside. A Latin couplet read:

> *Sustollunt humeris festo clamore Joannem*
> *Laetantes juvenes, quos alit unus amor.*
>
> Inspired by a single love, cheering youths
> Bear John upon their shoulders with festive shouts.

29. Until he fell ill in July (chapter 43), Don Bosco still lived at the Refuge, which was a block north of the Rondò. The oratory routine resumed after he returned in the fall, and possibly this leave-taking ritual did too; then the walk home would have been three blocks.

Comment on the Blessing of the Pinardi Chapel

The day of the new chapel's blessing was a memorable one in Don Bosco's life and the progress of his work. So the exact date is of interest to Salesians. At the end of the preceding chapter, he said that the Oratory moved into the Pinardi chapel on Easter Sunday, April 12. Now he seems to imply that the transformed shed was blessed on that day. Around 1854, in the already mentioned "Brief History of the Oratory," he recalled, first, that "on Easter Sunday the new chapel was opened," and a bit further on, that "in 1846 on a Sunday in April the church was blessed." Ceria therefore concludes that both opening and blessing took place on the same day, Easter Sunday (MO, pp. 172–173).

Ceria's interpretation fails to explain why Don Bosco would have left the date of consecration blank here, having given the date of opening just a few lines above. It also ignores the vagueness of the second reference in the "Brief History."

Bonetti's *History of the Oratory*, published in serial form under Don Bosco's editorial eye, gives us another record of these events in the *Salesian Bulletin* (October 1879). After describing the Oratory's move to its new chapel on April 12, Bonetti continued: "Don Bosco that same morning blessed and dedicated to divine worship the modest building and celebrated holy Mass, assisted by us and the neighbors." By "us" Bonetti meant the old-time Oratory boys, on whose recollections he based the whole narrative. Bonetti himself did not come to the Oratory until 1855. Lemoyne follows Bonetti, adding some details from another source (BM II, 334).

A discrepancy on the date of the blessing remains. Archbishop Fransoni had delegated Father Borel to perform the ceremony. On the back of the archbishop's decree, Father Borel wrote, "The undersigned came to bless the Oratory on April 13, the second day of Easter." Lemoyne was aware of this; he left a note on a printed copy of Bonetti's account in which he proposed to investigate further. Evidently he never got to it.

We have two irreconcilable statements. Other sources of information are lacking. In view of the immediate necessity, Don Bosco may have been authorized to bless the church privately on Easter Sunday, while Father Borel performed the solemn public ritual the following day. This solution respects Don Bosco's assertions. But a semipublic oratory, like this chapel, need not be blessed for it to be used for divine worship. It is only required that the local bishop declare it a place suitable for divine worship (1917 canons 1192, 2, and 1193).

Or Don Bosco may have simply given the premises the customary Easter blessing for houses.

Or again, Don Bosco may be mistaken regarding the date of the blessing. In view of his repeated problems with dates and Father Borel's clear statement, this is the most likely solution.

The King Saves the Oratory

Cavour, again • The city council • The police

In spite of the order, discipline, and tranquility that reigned in the Oratory, Marquis Cavour, vicar of the city,[1] maintained that our assemblies had dangerous aims. Knowing that I had always proceeded with the consent of the archbishop, he called a city council meeting at the archbishop's residence because that prelate was rather ill just then.

The city council was a select group of municipal department heads. In their hands rested the whole power of the civil administration. The council's head, called the council president, the first councilor, or also the vicar of the city, was more powerful than the mayor.

Said the archbishop: "When I saw all those dignitaries assembled in that hall, I thought I was at the last judgement."

There was much discussion for and against, but in the end they decided that these meetings absolutely should be blocked and dispersed because they threatened public order.

One member of the council was Count Joseph Provana of Collegno, our outstanding benefactor.[2] At that time he was comptroller general, or minister of finance, in King Charles Albert's government. Many times he had sent me donations both on his own behalf and on behalf of our sovereign. This prince was very pleased to hear all about the Oratory. When we had a celebration of any kind he would gladly read the account which I would send him in writing, or which Count Collegno would give him orally. Many a time he informed me how much he esteemed this kind of the priestly ministry, comparing it to work in the foreign missions. He expressed a sincere wish that every city and province in his kingdom should establish similar

King Charles Albert protected the Oratory when the city government felt threatened by such large gatherings of boys and young men. This lithograph by Goldini portrays the king at the battlefront in 1848. The original belongs to the Royal Library of Turin.

institutions. At New Year's, he always used to send me a subsidy of 300 lire with this greeting: "For Don Bosco's little rascals."[3]

When he found out that the council was threatening to ban our meetings, he charged Count Collegno to communicate his will in these words: "It is my wish that these assemblies be promoted and protected. If there is danger of disorders, ways should be studied to forestall them and prevent them."

The count had listened in silence to the whole lively debate. When he observed that they were resolved on the banning order and final break-up, he got to his feet and requested the floor. He conveyed the sovereign's wishes and let them know that the king meant to protect that microscopic work.

These words silenced the vicar and silenced the city council. Without delay the vicar ordered me to appear again, continued his menacing tone, and told me I was obstinate.[4] He concluded with these well-meant words: "I have no wish to harm anybody. You work with good intentions, but what you're doing is fraught with danger. Since I have a duty to safeguard public order, I'm going to send men to watch you and your meetings. Should the slightest thing compromise you, I'll immediately scatter your rascals;[5] and you'll give me an account of what's coming up in the future."

Perhaps it was pressure he was subject to, perhaps it was some illness he was battling. In fact, that was the last time that Vicar Cavour went to city hall. He was stricken with very painful gout, and within a few months he was dead.[6]

But for the six months that he lived,[7] every Sunday he sent some agents or policemen to spend the whole day with us, watching all that was said or done in church or outside it.

"Well," Marquis Cavour said to one of these guards, "what did you see and hear in the midst of that rabble?"

"Lord Marquis, we saw a huge crowd of boys enjoying themselves in a thousand ways. In church we heard some hair-raising sermons. They said so many things about hell and devils that it made me want to go to confession."[8]

"And what about politics?"

"Politics weren't even mentioned. Those boys wouldn't understand anything about politics. Now if you were to start a discussion about bread and butter, that is a subject each of them would be qualified to speak about."

When Cavour died, no one else at city hall bothered us. In fact, whenever there has been an occasion the Turin authorities were always favourable to us until 1877.[9]

Notes

1. Vicar of the king as regards the maintenance of civil order: chief of the secret police. According to Thayer (I, 42), the vicar met daily with the king to inform him of anything of interest, including gossip and suspicions, that his agents had reported to him. Cavour "accepted unpopularity as a part of his trade, conscious that, in hunting down political plotters, he was serving his king and country, and feeling well repaid by Charles Albert's confidence."

2. Count Collegno (1785–1854) and his family are dear to Salesians. They were always friends of Don Bosco and supporters of his work. They still treasure as a precious relic a copy of the 1852 edition of *The Companion of Youth*, which Don Bosco gave to the count's young son as a first communion souvenir in 1860. The counts are mentioned often in BM II–XII.

3. While Don Bosco always held the royal family in very high regard, he had a special affection for Charles Albert (1798–1849). On at least one occasion he attributed to the royal family a major role in the founding of the Salesian Congregation (BM XV, 341). This chapter offers ample testimony of the king's gracious and even necessary assistance.

4. In the circumstances, one may wonder who was being obstinate. But we should not be too hard on the marquis. He must have had secret accusations from people who were either annoyed that so many young boys were enticed away from their influence, or who got fainthearted when they saw Don Bosco's "army" practicing with their wooden rifles and swords and obeying his commands so readily. Certainly Cavour betrayed their sentiments in the ensuing conversation.

5. Don Bosco puts in Cavour's mouth a less uncomplimentary term than he did in the earlier conversation (when the boys were "scoundrels"). Cavour later referred to them as "those ragamuffins whom Don Bosco loves to call himself the chief of."

6. Don Bosco's memory is at fault here. Cavour died on June 15, 1850, three years after his retirement.

7. Just when these meetings took place is not clear. The "six months" refers, broadly, to Cavour's remaining time as vicar,

until illness and the changing political atmosphere compelled him to leave public life. He served as vicar from June 27, 1835, to June 17, 1847. When he retired, the guards were called off.

During the marquis's last illness, through the intercession of a mutual friend, Don Bosco was able to visit him and soothe his ruffled feathers. When he was ready to leave, the marquis handed him two hundred lire, quite a big chunk of money. He paid several more visits to the ailing man. We assume that it was during these visits to the family mansion that Don Bosco became acquainted with Gustavo and Camillo Cavour.

8. Father Julius Barberis (1847–1927), the Salesians' first master of novices (1874–1900), was a confidant of Don Bosco. Happily, he also kept a daily chronicle of significant events and conversations at the Oratory up till the transfer of the novitiate from Valdocco in 1879. On December 27, 1877, he recorded a conversation he had with Don Bosco about the early days of the Oratory. Among other things, Don Bosco said:

> I'd especially like to have a painting showing . . . several hundred lads docilely hanging on my words, with six uniformed policemen, two by two, standing stiffly at attention in different spots of the church, arms folded, listening to my sermon. They were a great help in supervising the boys, although they were there to spy on me. The painting might be even more interesting if it showed the policemen wiping away a furtive tear with the backs of their hands or muffling their faces in their handkerchiefs to hide their emotions. Or they could be shown kneeling among the boys who thronged by my confessional, waiting their turn. My sermons, you see, were directed more to them than to the boys, because I spoke about the four last things: sin, death, judgment and hell. (BM XIII, 314).

9. Until 1877, the city granted the Oratory an annual subsidy of three hundred lire. Starting in 1878, the municipal authorities neither granted a subsidy nor showed their previous favor. Don Bosco added "until 1877" in Father Berto's copy of the text.

The ending of the subsidy to the Oratory may have been linked with the transition of national political power from the liberals of the Right, who supported Cavour's policy of a free Church in a free State, to the more radical liberals of the Left, who were quite decidedly anticlerical. This shift occurred in 1876. See Clark, *Modern Italy*, pp. 81–88.

∾ 42 ∾

Beginning the Night School

Sunday school • Night school

At St Francis of Assisi, I was already conscious of the need for some kind of school. Some children who are already advanced in years are still completely ignorant of the truths of the faith. For these, verbal instruction would prove long and mostly tedious. They quickly would stop coming. We did try to give them some lessons, but we were beaten by lack of space and of teachers ready to help us. At the Refuge and later at the Moretta house, we started a regular Sunday school,[1] and when we came to Valdocco[2] we also started a regular night school.

As we wanted to get some good result, we took just one subject at a time. For example, one or two Sundays were devoted to going over and over the alphabet and the structure of syllables. Then we started right off on the small catechism and, syllable by syllable, pupils were taught to read one or two of the first catechism questions. That served as a lesson for the week.

The following Sunday that work was reviewed and a few more questions and answers were added. In this way in about eight weeks I could succeed in getting some to read and study on their own a whole page of catechism. This was a great time-saver. With the other method, the older boys would have had to come to catechism for some years before they could be properly prepared just for confession.

The Sunday school project was a boon to many. But that was not enough: not a few of the slower pupils forgot what they had learned the previous Sunday. It was then that we introduced night courses. We had begun them at the

Refuge, put them on a more regular basis at the Moretta house, and better yet as soon as we had our established place at Valdocco.

The night courses brought two good results. They inspired the youngsters to come to learn to read, which they realised was very important.[3] At the same time, these classes gave us an excellent opportunity to instruct them in religion, which was the object of our concern.

But where could I find so many teachers, when almost every day brought the need of adding new classes? To meet this need, I myself began to give lessons to some youngsters from the city. I taught Italian, Latin, French, and arithmetic without a fee. In return they were obliged to help me teach catechism and run the Sunday and night schools. These young teachers of mine, at first numbering eight or ten, continued to increase. This is how our academic programme started.[4]

When I was still at the Convitto of St Francis of Assisi, amongst my students was John Coriasco, who is now a master carpenter. Felix Vergnano is now a dealer in ribbons and braids. Paul Delfino is now a technical instructor. At the Refuge was Anthony Melanotte, who now has a spice shop. John Melanotte[5] is a confectioner. Felix Ferrero is a broker. Peter Ferrero is a compositor. John Piola has his own carpentry shop. There were others too: Louis Genta, Victor Mogna, and others who came only once in a while. I had to spend a lot of time and money, and as a general rule the bulk of them let me down when I needed them.[6]

To these I can add other pious gentlemen from Turin. Mr Joseph Gagliardi, a dealer in knick-knacks; Joseph Fino, in the same business; Victor Ritner, a jeweler; and others were dependable. Priests used to help me especially by celebrating holy Mass, preaching, and teaching catechism to the more mature young men.

Books presented a major problem because when we had worked through the short catechism we had no other textbooks. I took a look at all the little *Bible Histories* which were used in the schools. None of them suited my need. Lack of a popular style, unsuitable stories, and long or outdated questions were common defects. Many events were presented in a fashion dangerous to the morality of the youngsters.[7] All of them failed to focus on points that should serve as the foundation for the truths of our faith. The same could be said of facts referring to external worship, purgatory, confession, the Eucharist, and the like.

With a view to providing for this area in education what the times absolutely demanded, I set about compiling a *Bible History*.[8] I aimed for a simple and popular style, free of the defects already mentioned. That was my reason for writing and publishing the text called *Bible History for Schools*.[9] I could not guarantee an elegant production, but I worked entirely with the good intention of helping young people.[10]

After a few months of school, we gave a public exhibition of our feast day teaching. The pupils were questioned on all of Bible history, on the geography of the Bible, and all the related questions. Present as spectators were the dis-

Don Bosco was a prolific writer of school texts, devotional books, and popular works of a religious nature. Pictured here are his Bible History, *various editions of* The Companion of Youth, History of Italy, Key to Heaven, The Catholic's Companion, The Catholic in the World, *a French edition of* Church History, *and other works.*

tinguished Fr Aporti,[11] Boncompagni,[12] Dr Peter Baricco,[13] Prof. Joseph Rayneri;[14] all applauded the experiment.

The success of the Sunday and night courses encouraged us to introduce arithmetic and art to our classes in reading and writing. These schools were the first of their kind in these parts.[15] Everybody talked of them as a great innovation. We often had visits from professors and other persons of distinction. Even the city sent a deputation under the direction of Comm. Joseph Duprè[16] to see for themselves if the results of our night school were as good as they were reported to be. They themselves examined the boys in pronunciation, arithmetic, and recitation. They found it hard to explain [how young men] who were illiterate until they were 18 and even 20 years of age had progressed so well in manners and instruction in a few [months].[17] After seeing such a great number of young adults gathering at night to go to school instead of roaming the streets, those gentlemen left full of enthusiasm. When they reported back to the full city council, an annual prize of three hundred francs was assigned to the Oratory. This prize was given every year up to 1878[18] when, for some reason that could never be learned, it was withheld and given to another institute.[19]

At that time, Chev. Gonella,[20] whose zeal and charity are leaving a glorious and imperishable memory in Turin, was director of the work called the Schools for the Poor.[21] He often came to visit us, and a year later (1847) he introduced the same kind of schools and the same methods in the work entrusted to him. And when he reported everything to the administrators of that work, in full session they voted an award of a thousand francs for our schools.[22] The city government followed his example, and within a few years night schools were established in all the principal cities of Piedmont.

Another need showed up: a prayer book suitable for the times. There is no shortage of prayer books which have been put together by excellent people and are available to everyone. But, on the whole, these books were written for educated people, for adults, and most of them could be used by Catholics, Jews, or Protestants. Seeing how insidious heresy was spreading quietly every day,[23] I undertook to compile a book suitable for the young, adapted to their religious ideas, based on the Bible, and setting out the foundations of the Catholic religion clearly and concisely. This was *The Companion of Youth.*[24]

I had to do the same thing to teach arithmetic and the metric system. True, the metric system did not become obligatory until 1850, but it was introduced in the schools in 1846.[25] Though it was introduced by law in the schools, there were in fact no textbooks. I supplied this need with a booklet entitled *The Metric System Simplified.*[26]

Notes

1. Besides catechism, the boys who wanted it were taught to read, write, and work with numbers (see chapter 35).

2. To the Pinardi house; the Moretta house and the Refuge were also in Valdocco.

3. Piedmont had already made great strides in combating illiteracy by 1846, relative to the previous situation and to the situation in the rest of Italy. See chapter 28, note 8.

4. When Don Bosco began his hospice, his boarders were divided into two groups, the students (referred to here), and the "artisans," boys working at various trades. This set-up, in turn, became the model for the Salesian schools: academic, trade or technical, and later, agricultural.

5. One of the Melanotte brothers is the same boy who overheard Don Bosco's remarks to the housekeeper and Father Tesio at Saint Peter in Chains (chapter 34, note 6).

6. As in his earlier mention of Joseph Buzzetti, we presume that Don Bosco has singled out these past pupils because they proved reliable and because many of his Salesian readers would recognize their names.

7. Don Bosco believed that education should offer positive examples to the young; certain biblical episodes narrated without due reserve or explanation would make a bad impression. In the nineteenth century there was almost a prohibition against reading some parts of the Old Testament for this reason. Don Bosco believed this even more of secular history and literature.

   Many parts of the Bible, especially of the Old Testament, require commentaries in order to be understood. In recent years an emphasis on the study of the scriptures, the abundance of good translations and commentaries, ecumenism, the liturgical reform, and a return to biblical preaching have opened up the riches of the whole Bible to Catholics (as well as other Christians) in a new way.

8. A striking feature of Don Bosco's *Bible History for Schools* was that, in narrating episodes from both the Old and the New Testament, he took every opportunity to show how the truths of the Catholic Faith and liturgical practice are solidly founded on the Bible. One of his purposes, already hinted at when he chose Saint Francis de Sales as his patron, was to refute the Protestant teaching that the Catholic Church had invented certain dogmas and imposed excesses in external worship. His purpose was neither polemic nor subterfuge; he simply wanted to take advantage of an opportunity to touch on such questions.

9. *Storia sacra ad uso delle scuole* was published in 1847, revised in 1853, and reprinted twenty-four times by 1900 (BM II, 312). Long after Don Bosco died, it was still considered one of the best Bible histories for school use. Modern biblical and historical studies now render much of it outdated.

10. Don Bosco uses here *gioventù*, youth of both sexes.

11. Father Ferrante Aporti (1791–1858), from the province of Mantua, was a controversial educator; over the objections of the archbishop, King Charles Albert appointed him a professor at the University of Turin and required his courses for teacher certification. He was rector of the university from 1855 to 1858, and Victor Emmanuel II named him a senator in 1849. Aporti deserves the credit for establishing kindergartens in Italy, though there was a kindergarten already in Turin, established by Marquis Barolo in 1825. While not agreeing with Father Aporti on a number of pedagogical issues, Don Bosco won his confidence and helped him a great deal. See various references to him in BM II–VI, especially II, 148–149 and 165–172; *Catholic Encyclopedia* (New York, 1907), I, 624.

12. Count Charles Boncompagni (1804–1880) was a lawyer and statesman from Turin. In 1848 he sponsored an education reform law which was the first step toward establishing State control of schooling; it was fiercely opposed by the clergy (Stella, *EcSo*, p. 231). This law prepared the way for the more sweeping reforms of the 1859 Casati Law. The

count played a major role in the Piedmontese annexation of Tuscany and Modena in 1859–1860.

13. Father Peter Baricco (1819–1887), doctor of theology, was deputy mayor of Turin for many years.

14. Father Joseph Rayneri (1809–1867) was a professor of pedagogy and of philosophical anthropology at the Royal University of Turin. He used to advise his students, "If you want to see pedagogy in action, go to the Oratory of St. Francis de Sales and watch Don Bosco" (BM III, 21). He was a close friend of the Salesians and taught several of them in the university. Lemoyne sometimes calls him "Raineri"; Stella gives his name as John Anthony, rather than Joseph (*EcSo*, p. 640).

15. This refers to night courses conducted for young workers; see chapter 35, note 11.

16. Chevalier Joseph Louis Duprè (d. 1884) was a prominent Turinese banker and philanthropist and a city councilor (Stella, *EcSo*, pp. 80–81, 87–88). He served on Don Bosco's lottery committee in 1851–1852 (chapter 55) and helped the Oratory in many other ways. "Comm." is the abbreviation for *Commendatore*, one of the ranks of knighthood.

17. Ceria supplied the bracketed words, which were apparently omitted in a note hastily added to the copy.

18. As in the earlier case (chapter 41), Don Bosco wrote "up to 1878" and the rest in the copy. The original sentence had ended with " . . . every year up to the present."

19. This "other institute" was the School for Artisans [*Collegio degli Artegianelli*], founded in Valdocco in 1863. This was one of the projects of the Charitable Society for Orphaned and Abandoned Youngsters, started by Fathers John Cocchi and Robert Murialdo and two other priests in 1850. Unlike the Oratory, the School of Artisans had the royal license call the *exequatur*. The school's first director was Father Joseph Berizzi (1824–1873). (Stella, *EcSo*, pp. 119–120, n. 82) He was followed by Saint Leonard Murialdo, who left Don Bosco's Saint Aloysius Oratory (see chapter 47) for a sabbatical in 1865 and succeeded Father Berizzi in 1866.

20. Chevalier Mark Gonella (1822–1886), a banker, was one of Don Bosco's outstanding benefactors. See MB XX for various references to him.

21. The Schools for the Poor (*La Regia Opera della Mendicità Istruita*, usually shortened to *La Mendicità Istruita*), was a

movement aimed at educating the masses in religion, trades, and academic subjects. It was founded in 1743 by the abbot of Garessio (a village near Mondovì, south of Turin near the border with Liguria) and by Brother Fontana, an Oratorian. When Victor Amadeus III legally recognized the work in 1776, it added "Royal" to its name. King Charles Felix invited the Christian Brothers (De La Salle Brothers) to Turin in 1824 to take over its schools for boys; a congregation of sisters ran the schools for girls. There was so much hunger for basic schooling that these schools could never take in all the applicants to them. (P. Carrera, *Cenni sulla Regia Opera della Mendicità Istruita* [Turin: Bono, 1878]; Stella, *EcSo*, pp. 61–65)

22. The funds were granted in 1850 when Don Bosco applied for them (MB XVII, 853).

23. Don Bosco faults these prayer books with being too general and virtually ignoring doctrine. One of his concerns was always that Catholic doctrine should be clearly presented.

    Italy was a Catholic nation, and Catholicism was the only legal religion in the peninsula until Charles Albert granted a constitution to his subjects in 1848. While he was ever cordial with individuals of any faith or of no faith, in that pre-ecumenical age Don Bosco never compromised in condemning and combating Protestantism.

24. We notice almost the same purpose as with the *Bible History*. *Il Giovane Provveduto per la pratica dei suoi doveri negli esercizi di cristiana pietà* [The Companion of Youth], 352 pages, appeared from the Paravia Press of Turin in 1847 and was warmly received. It included quite a bit of material from pamphlets which Don Bosco had published earlier, such as devotions to the Seven Sorrows of Mary, to Saint Aloysius, and to the Guardian Angels (see chapter 43, note 1).

    The Companion of Youth was reprinted twice that year, selling twenty thousand copies. During Don Bosco's lifetime the manual ran through 122 printings of about fifty thousand copies each in at least three editions (cf. Aubry, p. 73, n. 1, as cited below). The 1863 edition had grown to 430 pages, and the 1885 had 520 pages.

    In 1934 Sisto Colombo (*S. Giovanni Bosco, 1815–1888* [Turin: SEI], p. 110) wrote:

    > Anyone proposing to write the history of religious devotion and worship in Italy in the last century must consider this book. There is in it no trace of Jansenistic rigorism or of superstition. It appeals to the heart, recalls the pure sources of Christian life,

and fosters frequent reception of the sacraments. Some might classify this as a new approach, but really it is a prudent return to the classic teaching of old.

In LW, Stella evaluated it as a book that at first seems to be just "simply a manual of prayers and practical devotions"; but in fact

> Don Bosco intended it to serve as a method and way of life. This aim applies to its various parts: the devotional part; the earlier part explaining the religious way to understand one's own existence, creation, growth from adolescence on, and the daily manifestations of life; and the *Fundamentals of the Catholic Religion*, a piece of apologetics published as *Warnings to Catholics* in 1850 and inserted into the *Companion of Youth* the following year. (p. 267)

References to *Il Giovane Provveduto* are, of course, numerous in Stella's *ReCa*; there are scattered references in Desramaut's *SpLife*; and Aubry includes excerpts, with a short introduction, in *The Spiritual Writings of Saint John Bosco* (New Rochelle: Don Bosco Publications, 1984), pp. 73–80.

25. Trade within the Kingdom of Sardinia — not to mention the rest of Italy, or Italian trade with the rest of the world — was seriously hampered by the lack of a uniform system of weights and measures.

Napoleon introduced the metric system to all of the French Empire, but the Restoration also restored the earlier economic chaos. Gradually the benefits of uniformity became evident. In September 1845 King Charles Albert by royal decree abolished all the ancient local Piedmontese systems and adopted the metric system. It was to be introduced over a four-year period and come into full operation on January 1, 1850; in the meantime, the people had to be educated in the new system.

26. Marchioness Barolo appreciated Don Bosco's work in teaching the metric system at the Refuge (chapter 38). His textbook, *Il sistema metrico decimale ridotto a semplicità* (Turin: Paravia, 1846), was successful enough to go through eight printings, including an expanded edition. (BM II, 374–379)

Don Bosco went further. In 1849 he wrote and produced a three-act comedy, *The Metric System*. Father Aporti and various other celebrities came to see it performed. They said that he could not have conceived a more effective means of popularizing the metric system, because humor would help it catch on. The entire sketch may be found in MB III, 623–652.

A Serious Illness

*Sickness and recovery • Planning to
stay at Valdocco*

My many commitments in the prisons, the Cottolengo
Hospital, the Refuge, the Oratory, and the schools meant
I had to work at night to compile the booklets that I absolutely needed.[1] On account of that, my already frail
health[2] deteriorated to such a degree that the doctors advised
me to stop all my activities. Doctor Borrelli, who loved me
dearly, for my own good sent me to spend some time with
the parish priest of Sassi.[3] I rested during the week and
went back to work at the Oratory on Sunday. But that was
not enough. The youngsters came in crowds to see me; the
boys from the village came too.[4] So I was busier than in
Turin, while I was causing a great deal of inconvenience to
my little friends.

Not only those who attended the Oratory hastened, one
could say, every day, to Sassi, but also the pupils of the
Brothers of the Christian Schools.[5] This episode is one of
many. A retreat was being preached to the students in the
St Barbara Schools,[6] which were under the care of these
same religious. As I was confessor to a great number of the
boys, they came in a body to the Oratory looking for me at
the end of the retreat. Not finding me there, they set out
at once for Sassi, two and a half miles from Turin.[7] It was
raining. The boys were not sure of the way and went wandering about the fields, meadows, and vineyards looking for
Don Bosco. Eventually about four hundred of them, all
worn out by their hike and by hunger, bathed in perspiration and covered with dirt, and mud too, showed up and
asked to go to confession.

"We've made the retreat," they said. "We want to be

good. We all want to make a general confession. So we got our teachers' permission to come here."

They were told to return at once to their college in order to keep their teachers and families from worrying, but they insisted that they wanted to go to confession. The local school master, the parish priest, his assistant, and I heard as many as we could, but we would have needed at least fifteen confessors.

But how to restore, or rather to appease, the appetite of that multitude? That good parish priest (it was Dr Abbondioli) gave those pilgrims all the food he had: bread, polenta,[8] beans, rice, potatoes, cheese, fruit — everything was provided for them.

Imagine the consternation when the preachers, teachers, and some prominent persons invited for the closing of the retreat arrived for Mass and the general communion and found not one pupil in the college! It was a real mess. Measures were taken to ensure that it would never happen again.

Back home again, I was exhausted and took to my bed.[9] I had bronchitis, combined with coughing and violent inflammation.[10] A week later, I was judged to be at death's door. I had received holy Viaticum and the anointing of the sick. I think that just then I was ready to die. I was sorry to abandon my youngsters, but I was happy that before I departed I had given a solid foundation to the Oratory.[11]

When the news spread that my illness was grave, the show of widespread, serious regret could not have been greater. Constant streams of tearful youngsters came knocking at the door to inquire about my health. The more they were told, the more they wanted to know. I heard the conversations between them and the housekeeper,[12] and I was deeply moved by them. I heard later what their affection for me had moved them to do. Without prompting they prayed, fasted, went to Masses, and received holy communions. In turns they prayed all night and day for me before the image of Our Lady of Consolation.[13] In the morning they lit special candles for me, and until the late evening large numbers were always praying and imploring the august Mother of God to preserve their poor Don Bosco.

Some made vows to recite the whole rosary for a month, others for a year, some for their whole lives. There were some who promised to fast on bread and water for months, years, and even their whole lives. I know that some brick-layer apprentices fasted on bread and water for entire weeks, without lessening from morning to evening their heavy work. In fact, when they had any bit of free time they rushed to spend it before the Most Blessed Sacrament.

God heard their prayers. It was a Saturday evening, and it was believed that it would be the last night of my life. So said the doctors who came to see me, and so was I

The Church of Our Lady of Consolation is dedicated to the patroness of Turin. It was a favorite church of Don Bosco's; when Mama Margaret died in 1856, it was here that he came to pray. When Don Bosco was gravely ill in 1846, the Oratory boys came here to pray for his recovery.

convinced myself. I had no strength left because of a continuous loss of blood. Late in the night I grew drowsy and slept. When I woke I was out of danger. Next morning when Doctor Botta and Doctor Caffasso examined me, they told me go thank Our Lady of Consolation for the grace received.[14]

My boys could not believe it if they did not see me. They saw me in fact soon after, when I went with my walking stick to the Oratory. The emotion can be imagined but not easily described. A *Te Deum* was sung. There were a thousand acclamations and indescribable enthusiasm.

One of the first things to be done was to change into something manageable all the vows and promises which many had made without due thought when my life was in danger.

This illness overtook me at the beginning of July 1846, just at the time I was due to leave the Refuge and move elsewhere.[15]

I went home to Murialdo to spend some months of convalescence with my family.[16] I would have stayed longer there in my home town, but the youngsters began to turn up in crowds to see me, indicating that it was no longer possible to enjoy either rest or tranquillity.

Everyone advised me to get away from Turin for a few years and go to some unknown place to recover my former health. Fr Caffasso and the archbishop were of this opinion. But that seemed too drastic to me; it was agreed that I could return to the Oratory provided that for a couple of years I would refrain from hearing confessions and preaching. I disobeyed.[17]

When I got back to the Oratory, I continued to work as before, and for 27 years I had no need of either doctors or medicine.[18] This leads me to believe that work does no damage to bodily health.

Notes

1. Indirectly Don Bosco has documented his prodigious work load. He was a very busy writer during this period 1844–1847. Besides the three works treated in the preceding chap-

ter and the biography of Comollo (chapter 10, note 12), he published seven other textbooks, prayer books, and even agricultural advice:

Corona dei sette dolori di Maria [The Seven Sorrows of Mary] (Speirani and Ferrero, 1844), 42 pages (BM II, 157–158)

Cenni istruttivi di perfezione [Brief Advice on Christian Perfection] (1844), 82 pages

Storia ecclesiastica, ad uso delle scuole, utile ad ogni stato di persone [Church History for Schools] (Speirani and Ferrero, 1845), 398 pages (BM II, 257–261; III, 215–220)

Il divoto dell'Angelo custode [Devotion to the Guardian Angel] (Turin: Paravia, 1845), 72 pages (BM II, 207–211)

Le sei Domeniche e la novena in onore di S. Luigi Gonzaga, con un cenno della vita del medesimo Santo [Six Sundays and a Novena in Honor of Saint Aloysius, with a Brief Biography] (Speirani and Ferrero, 1846), 46 pages (BM II, 281–285)

L'Enologo italiano [Italian Wine-making] (1846), 150 pages (BM II, 367–368)

Esercizio della devozione alla misericordia di Dio [The Practice of Devotion to God's Mercy] (Turin: Botta, 1846), 112 pages (BM II, 427–429)

Finally, when he established the Company of Saint Aloysius in 1847 (see chapter 45), he drew up and published its regulations: *Regolamento della Compagnia di S. Luigi* (BM III, 148–149, 459).

2. As we have already seen, Don Bosco's once-strong constitution was broken by his rigorous asceticism and, probably, emotional pressure in the seminary (chapter 22).

3. Father Peter Abbondioli (1812–1893) was a friend and supporter of Don Bosco for many years (cf. BM V, 29).

4. This is another testimony that Don Bosco inadvertently let slip. He really was a magnet where boys were concerned.

5. The De La Salle Christian Brothers were prominent in the schools of Turin, directing the Schools for the Poor and other institutions.

6. These were schools run by the city.

7. From the city center, that is.

8. Polenta is a staple of the Piedmontese diet. It is a mush composed mostly of cornmeal.

9. Don Bosco was still living at the Refuge and ministering at the Barolo institutions.

10. He began coughing up blood some weeks before; that, and

the symptoms which he names, indicate that he probably had pleurisy (T. Bosco, BN, pp. 153–154). For extended discussion of Don Bosco's health, see Molineris, *Don Bosco inedito*, pp. 312–337, 365–371; Molineris, *Vita episodica di Don Bosco* (Castelnuovo Don Bosco, 1974), pp. 421–445.

11. A solid foundation? The Oratory had moved into Pinardi's shed but three months before. Even if the shed was now a chapel, it was still "really a hovel," as he put it in the first line of chapter 40. Of Don Bosco's certainty that this latest move firmly established the Oratory, Giraudi remarks, "What courage, what faith on Don Bosco's part! Having led his youngsters to that poor shelter, he knew that he had reached his goal and said he had put the Oratory on 'a solid foundation'" (p. 75). See BM II, 387.

12. The marchioness provided a man-servant for her chaplains. Francesia confirms these visits and adds that Mama Margaret came to be with her son (*Vita breve e popolare*, pp. 123–124).

13. The boys kept their vigil at the Church of Our Lady of Consolation, the title by which the Virgin Mary is specially revered in Turin.

14. Don Bosco omits much of the drama of the case (cf. BM II, 384–385). It is unlikely that Doctor Ca[f]fasso was related to Father Cafasso.

15. It was probably on the first Sunday of the month (July 5) that he collapsed, after a long, hot day's work. He was due to leave the Refuge at the end of August (BM II, 364; Giraudo and Biancardi, pp. 118, 164).

16. From August to November. While he was away, his collaborators looked after the Oratory under the direction of Father Borel. Meanwhile, the marchioness had Don Bosco's room at the Refuge cleared out, and Father Borel fitted up a modest room for him in Pinardi's house; in June Don Bosco (with Father Cafasso's financial backing) had begun to rent the rooms of the top floor from Soave as the tenants' leases expired one by one (see chapter 44, note 2).

17. The earlier attitude of complete detachment from his own will and abandonment to his spiritual director's advice has been mitigated (cf. chapter 30).

18. He fell seriously ill in 1871–1872 (BM X, 122–156).

Mama Margaret Moves to Valdocco

Permanent residence at the Valdocco Oratory

After convalescing for several months at home, I felt I could return to my beloved sons. Every day many of them were coming to see me or were writing to me, urging me to come back to them soon. But where could I find lodging? I had been sent away from the Refuge. What means did I have to keep my work going, work that was daily becoming more demanding and expensive? How was I to support myself and the persons who were indispensable to me?[1]

At that time, two rooms fell vacant in the Pinardi house,[2] and these were rented as a dwelling for me and my mother.

"Mother," I said to her one day, "I should take up residence in Valdocco, but considering the people who live in that house, I can't take anyone with me but you."[3]

She knew what I was hinting at and replied straightaway, "If you think such a move is God's will, I'm ready to go right now."

My mother made a great sacrifice. At home, even though we were not well off, she was in charge of everything, everyone loved her, and to young and old she was a queen.[4]

We sent ahead some of the more necessary items, and together with my things from the Refuge, these were delivered at our new lodgings. My mother filled a hamper with linen and other things we would need. I took my breviary, a missal, and some of the more important [books][5] and copybooks. This was our entire fortune. On foot, we set out from Becchi towards Turin.[6] We made a short stop at Chieri, and on the evening of 3 November 1846, we arrived at Valdocco.

When my mother laid eyes on those barren rooms, she said jokingly, "At home I had so many worries about administration and direction. Here I'll be much more at ease: I have nothing to manage, nobody to command."

But how were we to live? What were we to eat? How could we pay the rent and supply the needs of the many children who constantly asked for bread, shoes, clothes, or shirts, which they needed to go to work? From home we had brought some wine, millet, beans, grain, and so forth. To meet initial expenses, I had sold part of a field and a vineyard. My mother sent for her wedding trousseau, which up to then she had jealously preserved intact. From some of her dresses we made chasubles; from the linen we made amices, purificators, surplices, albs, and towels.[7] Everything passed through the hands of Mrs. Margaret Gastaldi,[8] who since then has helped look after the needs of the Oratory.

My mother also had a little gold necklace and some rings; they were quickly sold to buy braid and trimmings for the sacred vestments. My mother was always in good humour. One evening, she laughingly sang to me:

> *Woe to the world if it should learn*
> *We're just penniless strangers!*

When our domestic affairs were somewhat organised, I rented another room, which was intended for a sacristy. As we lacked classrooms, for the time being we had to use the kitchen or my room.

But the students — prime little rascals — either destroyed everything or put everything topsy-turvy. When we started, some classes met in the sacristy, in the apse, or in other parts of the church. But the noise, the singing, the coming and going of one group disturbed whatever the other groups were trying to do. After a few months, we were able to rent two other rooms and so organise our night classes better.[9] As was said above,[10] during the winter of

In November 1846, after Don Bosco had recovered from illness, he and Mama Margaret came to live at the Pinardi house. The original is one of six paintings by Crida decorating the sacristy of the Basilica of Mary Help of Christians.

1846–7 we got excellent scholastic results.* Every evening we had an average of three hundred pupils. In addition to the academic side, the classes were animated by plainchant and vocal music, which we have always cultivated.

Notes

1. By the end of August 1846, just the rent for chapel, play yards, and rooms totaled six hundred lire per year. Besides that, Don Bosco's expenses included equipment, supplies, fuel, and furnishings for the Oratory; food, clothing, and other assistance for needy boys; and his personal needs. Father Borel was the treasurer, and his notebooks give us a great deal of information about expenses and benefactors. Father Cafasso gave huge sums of money openly; Marchioness Barolo did so anonymously, despite her earlier promise. See BM II, 364, 389–390; Stella, *EcSo*; Giraudo and Biancardi, p. 166.

2. As leases expired, Don Bosco bought them up from Pancrazio Soave at double the previous rate—not only because he wanted more space but also because most of the tenants were of an unsavory sort (some of them apparently were prostitutes [see chapters 50 and 54]). As early as June 5 he had already leased the three easternmost rooms on the second floor of the house at five lire per room per month; the lease ran from July 1, 1846, to January 1, 1849. Before he left for Becchi at the beginning of August, he secured a fourth room on the same floor, subleasing from one of Soave's tenants, Peter Clapiè (BM II, 364–365, 388; Giraudo and Biancardi, pp. 163, 166).

   Don Bosco implies at first that he had no thought of living in these rooms. He told Soave he would not use them until he had the whole house. Further down he reveals that he dared not live there as long as disreputable persons oc-

---

*Let it be remembered that the first night school set up in Turin was the one opened at the Moretta house in November 1845. We could take only two hundred students into three rooms, or classes.[11] The good results from the school prompted us to reopen it the following year as soon as we had fixed quarters in Valdocco.

Amongst those who helped in the night school and taught the young men speech through the use of skits and little plays, Prof. Dr Chiaves, Father Musso,[12] and Dr Hyacinth Carpano must be remembered.

cupied the rest of the building, lest he cause scandal and harm to his good name.

3. An almost Franciscan simplicity marks both the events and the style of this chapter: the son's invitation and his mother's acceptance; the silent, detached departure and journey on foot; the entry into the empty house; Mama Margaret's calm and generous surrender of her wedding trousseau; her light-hearted singing — all these make a chapter of rare beauty.

   Don Bosco did his sons and daughters a service in preserving these moments for us, as did the artist who portrayed in the sacristy of the Basilica of Mary Help of Christians the two pilgrims arriving at Valdocco.

4. Margaret was living with Joseph and his family in Becchi. Anthony and his family now lived in a little house next to Joseph's, on the site occupied since 1915 by the chapel of Mary Help of Christians. And, of course, Margaret was fifty-eight years old and knew nothing of the great city.

5. Ceria supplies the apparently missing word.

6. They had to walk some eighteen miles. Chieri was about halfway.

7. These are some of the various vestments and linens used in the Catholic liturgy, especially the Mass.

   The chasuble is a large, flowing outer garment worn at Mass by a priest or bishop. It may be of white, green, violet, red, or gold, depending on the liturgical color of the day. Prior to Vatican II (1962–1965), black was also used, and the chasuble was usually much smaller and boxish in shape.

   The amice is a white linen rectangle with two strings which the priest or other minister wears over his shoulders and around his neck beneath the alb. Its main purpose is to protect the more valuable outer garments from stains. It is less commonly used today than formerly.

   Purificators are linen pieces used to wipe the chalice clean before and after use.

   The alb is a sleeved white linen vestment which covers the entire body, worn over the minister's ordinary garments (and the amice) and beneath the outer ritual vestments. It is modeled on the Roman tunic.

   Surplices are knee-length, loose-fitting, sleeved white linen vestments, worn by ministers or choir members over a cassock or choir robe. A shorter (waist-length) form of this vestment, technically called a cotta, is commonly used.

White linen towels are used after ritual washings, e.g. of the celebrant's hands at Mass.

8. Don Bosco calls Mrs. Gastaldi by the more distinguished *madama* rather than *signora*; she was the mother of the future archbishop, Canon Lawrence Gastaldi. Not only did she care for the church linens, but she and other pious ladies also washed and mended the boys' clothes (BM III, 178–179). The canon was a close friend of Don Bosco in these years.

9. On December 1, 1846, Don Bosco obtained use of the whole house and grounds from Soave for 710 lire per year, with a 59-lire bonus thrown in. In addition Soave could continue to operate his starch-making business on the ground floor until March 1, 1847. The lease was to expire at the same time as that of the upper-floor rooms (at the end of 1848). (BM II, 418–419) This time Don Bosco signed the contract himself, which indicates a certain amount of financial security.

Lemoyne, who got his information from well-informed sources, describes how Don Bosco conducted these classes:

> It was a wonderful sight, every night, to see the rooms in the Pinardi house all lit up and full of boys and young men.... In one room they could be seen standing before large charts on the wall, or else with books in hand. In other rooms they sat at desks practicing writing, while others knelt or sat on the floor before plain benches used as desks, and scribbled large letters in their exercise books.

> From time to time Don Bosco, to see that order was maintained, would appear on the balcony, glance over the classes, and then go down to the ground floor.... The Christian Brothers enjoyed coming to Valdocco in the evening to observe him and study his method of teaching so many boys at one and the same time. (BM II, 436)

10. Chapter 42.

11. A regulation from the ministry of education allowed a maximum of seventy pupils per class (T. Bosco, *Mem*, p. 162, n. 2).

12. Two priests named Musso were collaborating with Don Bosco at this time: Canon Musso, an elementary teacher, and Father John Baptist Musso (d. 1887), a secondary teacher. Don Bosco seems to be referring to the latter (Stella, *EcSo*, pp. 172, 636).

Father Chiaves, besides being a secondary school teacher, was a doctor of theology; hence his double title. In 1848 he and Father Carpano helped Don Bosco with a journalistic experiment, *L'Amico della gioventù* [The Friend of Youth]

(Stella, *EcSo*, pp. 172, 344). Don Bosco engaged him to tutor Buzzetti, Gastini, Bellia, and Reviglio (his four most promising students) in Italian in 1849, and in 1850 to prep them for their examination for admission to the clerical habit (BM III, 385–386; IV, 97). A man of practical talents as well, Father Chiaves prepared the fireworks display for the celebration of the dedication of the new Church of Saint Francis de Sales in 1852 (BM IV, 307). Much loved by the boys, he was still helping out at least until 1853 (BM IV, 380).

The Company
of Saint Aloysius

Regulations for the oratories •
Company and feast of St Aloysius •
Visit of Archbishop Fransoni

When we got firmly settled at Valdocco, I gave my full attention to promoting the things that could work to preserve our unity of spirit, discipline, and administration. In the first place, I drew up a set of regulations in which I simply set down what was being done at the Oratory, and the standard way in which things ought to be done. Since this has been printed elsewhere, anyone can read it as he wishes.[1]

This little Rule brought this notable advantage: Everybody knew what was expected of him, and since I used to let each one be responsible for his own charge, each took care to know and to perform his appointed duties.

Many bishops and parish priests asked for copies, studied them, and adopted them when they introduced the work of the oratories to the cities and villages of their respective dioceses.

When the framework for the smooth running and administration of the Oratory had been set up, it was necessary to encourage piety by means of a set of standard practices. We did this by starting the *Company of St Aloysius*. The Regulations were drawn up in a style that I believed suitable for young people.[2] I sent them to the archbishop. Having read them, he passed them on to others who studied them and then reported back to him. He praised and approved them, and he granted special indulgences on the date .[3] These Regulations can be read elsewhere.[4]

The Company of St Aloysius caused great enthusiasm amongst our youngsters: they all wanted to enroll in it.

Two conditions were demanded for membership: good example in and out of church; and avoidance of bad talk and frequent reception of the holy sacraments. A very notable improvement in morality[5] was soon evident.

To encourage all the boys to celebrate the six Sundays in honour of St Aloysius,[6] we bought a statue of the saint and had a banner made. The boys were given the opportunity of going to confession at any time of day, evening, or night. Because hardly any of them had yet been confirmed, they were prepared to receive that sacrament[7] on the feast of St Aloysius.

What a crowd! With the help of various priests and gentlemen, however, they were prepared and all was in readiness for the saint's feast day.* It was the first [time][14] that celebrations of this kind were held at the Oratory, and it was also the first time the archbishop came to visit us.

In front of our little church was erected a kind of pavilion under which we received the archbishop. I read something appropriate for the occasion. Then some of the boys put on a little comedy entitled *Napoleon's Corporal*.[15] It was just a caricature of a corporal who, to express his surprise at that solemnity, came out with a thousand pleasantries. That made the prelate laugh a great deal and he really enjoyed it; he said that he had never laughed so much in his life. He responded very kindly to all, expressing the great consolation which our institution gave him. He praised us and encouraged us to persevere and thanked us for the cordial welcome which we had given him.

He celebrated holy Mass[16] and gave holy communion to more than three hundred youngsters; then he administered the sacrament of confirmation.[17] It was on that occasion that the archbishop, just as the mitre was being put on his head, forgot that he was not in the cathedral; he raised his head too quickly and banged into the church ceiling. That amused him and all those present. He often used to relate

---

*Amongst those who were happy to enroll in the Company of St Aloysius are to be noted Fr Antonio Rosmini,[8] Canon Archpriest Peter De Gaudenzi (now bishop of Vigevano),[9] Camillo and Gustavo Cavour,[10] Card. Antonucci (abp of Ancona),[11] His Holiness Pius IX,[12] Card. Antonelli,[13] and many others.

Archbishop Louis Fransoni of Turin ordained Don Bosco in 1841, encouraged him in his work for abandoned boys, and guided his first steps toward founding a religious congregation. He was exiled in 1850 because of his opposition to the secularizing laws of the Sardinian parliament.

this incident with pleasure, thus recalling our meetings.[18] Father Rosmini said that it reminded him of similar happenings in the countries and churches of the foreign missions.[19]

I must add that two canons from the cathedral and many other churchmen came to assist the archbishop at these sacred ceremonies. When the ceremony ended, we wrote a record of the event, noting who had administered the sacrament and the name of the sponsor,[20] and the place and day. Then the certificates were collected, sorted according to the various parishes, and passed on to the diocesan chancery to be sent to the parish priests concerned.[21]

Notes

1. The complete text is published in BM III, 441–453. One may note in it the intention, prudently veiled, of laying the groundwork for the formation of a religious congregation. For example, the titles given to the priest-superiors of the Oratory correspond to those later assigned to the superiors of Salesian houses. Even the spirit which should animate such a society may be discerned.

   These Regulations, drafted in 1847 and touched up repeatedly in succeeding years, were printed in 1852 and again revised in 1854–1855. Important in regard to their compilation is what Don Bosco wrote in the October 1877 issue (vol. I, no. 2) of *Bibliofilo Cattolico* [The Catholic Booklover] (the title was changed to *Bollettino salesiano* [Salesian Bulletin] soon after):

   > Let it be remembered that the Regulations for these oratories are nothing more than a collection of observations, precepts, and maxims that many years of study and experience (1841–1855) have suggested. Journeys were undertaken; schools, institutes, penitentiaries, orphanages, and workhouses visited and their constitutions studied; the most reliable educators were consulted. Whatever could help our purpose was gleaned and arranged in order, resulting in our brief Regulations.

   Among these studies and consultations, Don Bosco spent eighteen days in Milan toward the end of 1850 studying Father Seraphim Allievi's flourishing Saint Aloysius Oratory (BM IV, 119–126). It was a jubilee year, and Don Bosco had been invited to preach to the boys to prepare them for the special papal indulgences (cf. chapter 4, note 8).

The festive oratories had been firmly established in Milan for a century; there were fifteen of them in the city in 1850. Among the oratories that Don Bosco studied were those of Saints Philip Neri and Charles Borromeo; among the rules, the *Regulations of the Saint Aloysius Oratory Established in Milan in 1842* (Father Allievi's) and the *Regulations for the Children of the Holy Family Oratory.* (Stella, LW, p. 105, n. 15; Giraudo and Biancardi, p. 170)

Father Allievi, whom Lemoyne describes as "a learned, zealous priest and a true apostle of youth," returned the visit in January 1862, partly to ask Don Bosco's advice about founding a religious congregation to carry on his work (BM VII, 36).

We have a souvenir of Don Bosco's 1850 trip, viz. the passport which he needed to pass from the Kingdom of Sardinia into the Austrian Empire (pictured in MO opposite p. 196). This document, precious to the Salesians who knew Don Bosco, is doubly precious now, for it gives us a description of him in his thirty-sixth year: height, 5′4″; hair and brows, dark brown; forehead, medium; eyes, brown; face, oval; complexion, olive. It adds that his profession is "elementary school teacher"! (BM IV, 120).

2. Don Bosco's use of *gioventù* indicates that this encouragement to piety is equally applicable to young women.

3. Don Bosco omitted the date. The document is dated April 12, 1847.

4. The Regulations of the Company of Saint Aloysius were published in 1847. They are reprinted in BM II, 148–149, 459.

5. "Morality" in the sense of general conduct. For these boys that would include not only language and courtesy, but also such virtues as diligence and honesty at their jobs and their school lessons, obedience at home, truthfulness, patience with one another, etc.

6. The year before (1846), Don Bosco had published a pamphlet of reflections and prayers entitled *Six Sundays and a Novena in Honor of Saint Aloysius.* These devotions served to prepare the boys (and others of the faithful) to celebrate well the feast of this secondary patron of the Oratory, which occurs on June 21; they also encouraged regular devotion to and imitation of this model for young people. The pamphlet was reprinted in June 1854 as part of the *Catholic Readings.*

7. Confirmation is one of the three sacraments by which a per-

son is initiated into full membership in the Body of Christ, the Church. (The others are baptism and the Eucharist.) By this sacrament one publicly confesses his faith and is confirmed in it by the laying on of hands and anointing with sacred chrism. The usual minister of the sacrament is the bishop.

8. Benefactors and prominent persons were enrolled as honorary members. Don Bosco had a genius for finding ways to promote his work among the upper classes and to help the boys find virtue attractive and heroic.

On Father Rosmini, see chapter 53 and chapter 54, note 9.

9. Peter Joseph De Gaudenzi (1820–1891) was the archpriest and a canon of the cathedral of Vercelli, an ancient episcopal see about forty miles northeast of Turin, near the Lombard border. (An archpriest represents the bishop and heads a college of priests. The title is rarely used nowadays.) Canon De Gaudenzi highly esteemed Don Bosco and was very generous with him. He helped promote the *Catholic Readings* and in 1851 donated 230 lire toward the building of the Church of Saint Francis de Sales (Stella, *EcSo*, pp. 360, 418). Vigevano, a small city in the Lombard province of Pavia, is about fifteen miles east of Vercelli. His name recurs often in the BM. See also chapter 53.

10. Don Bosco has already alluded to the sons of Michele Benso, marquis of Cavour. Unlike their father, the brothers admired Don Bosco and his work exceedingly, often visited it, supported it, and enjoyed seeing so many boys enjoying themselves in a wholesome manner. Some think that their kindness toward Don Bosco was rooted in their distant relationship with Saint Francis de Sales; their paternal grandmother was descended from the saint's brother. Camillo had great affection for Saint Francis, and on his feast day had Mass celebrated in his honor in his private chapel. (S. Iacini, *La crisi ecclesiastica italiana da Villafranca a Porta Pia* [Bari: La Terza, 1938], p. 24).

For a sketch of the the career of Count Camillo Cavour and of his relationship with Don Bosco, see the comment following the notes.

The elder brother, Gustavo (1806–1864), inherited the title of marquis. Both politically and temperamentally he was quite different from Camillo. He was also a militant and fervent Catholic.

After his wife's early death (1833), Gustavo took up

philosophy and became friendly with Father Antonio Rosmini. The priest-philosopher stayed with the Cavours when he was in Turin. Gustavo sparred with the priest-author-politician Gioberti (cf. NCE VI, 492) in the newspapers and cofounded the Turinese Catholic paper *L'Armonia*. Between 1849 and his death he served in five parliaments, often strenuously opposing his brother's policies, e.g. on church matters and on the Crimean War.

On at least one occasion Gustavo taught catechism at the Oratory while Don Bosco was showing a guest around (BM IV, 23–24).

11. Cardinal Benedict Anthony Antonucci (1798–1879) was the papal nuncio at Turin from 1844 to 1850, when the Holy See broke diplomatic relations with Sardinia. In 1851 he became archbishop of Ancona, a small city on the Adriatic coast of the Papal States. He always loved and esteemed Don Bosco.

12. In view of the relationship between this Pontiff and Don Bosco, one is surprised that his election to the Chair of Peter on June 16, 1846, passes unremarked in the *Memoirs*.

13. Cardinal James Antonelli (1806–1876) was the papal under-secretary of state at the time, and secretary of state from 1852 till his death. See NCE I, 641–642; E.E.Y. Hales, *Pio Nono* (New York, 1954); and BM IV-VII, X-XII.

14. Ceria's addition.

15. Father Carpano authored and directed the skit.

16. The order of events has been inverted. Mass and confirmation preceded the entertainment.

17. After the recent liturgical reforms, confirmation is administered within Mass.

18. Two examples of the archbishop's humor regarding the Pinardi chapel have been preserved. On this occasion he quipped sotto voce, "I must show respect for these young gentlemen and preach to them bareheaded!" Later, when he was encouraging Don Bosco's efforts to build a larger chapel, he advised him with a smile, "Make sure it's high enough so that I won't have to remove my mitre when I come to preach there." (BM III, 156) Regrettably, because of his exile he never got to come to the Church of Saint Francis de Sales.

19. The congregation of priests which Father Rosmini founded, the Institute of Charity, was active in missionary work, among other apostolates.

20. Like baptism, which it completes sacramentally, confirma-

tion requires a sponsor, who "is to see that the confirmed person acts as a true witness to Christ and faithfully fulfills the obligations connected with this sacrament" (c. 892).

21. The fact of confirmation must be entered into the official record of the church where it was celebrated and onto the individual's baptismal record in his native parish.

It is also significant that, for practical purposes, Archbishop Fransoni had recognized the Oratory as a distinct and unique parish, "the parish of abandoned youth," and confirmed his support for Don Bosco's work vis-à-vis the pastors of Turin (cf. chapters 35 and 48).

Comment on Camillo Cavour

Camillo Benso, count of Cavour (1810–1861), was still a private citizen in 1847, though one known as a proponent of economic reform. His fundamental political instincts were conservative, but he ardently opposed all forms of absolutism. The establishment of a constitutional government in 1848 opened up to him a political career.

In 1850 Massimo d'Azeglio made him minister of finance; he moved cautiously for reform until he openly supported the Siccardi Laws later that year; these laws, which eliminated some of the ancient social privileges of the Church, were bitterly fought by conservatives both clerical and lay. Pius IX recalled his nuncio, ending papal relations with Piedmont. Archbishop Fransoni's opposition was so adamant that he was imprisoned and eventually exiled.

Early in 1852 the moderate conservatives in parliament, led by Cavour, allied themselves with Urbano Rattazzi's moderates of the left to unseat the more conservative d'Azeglio. By the end of the year Cavour was prime minister, a position he held almost continually until his death. He pursued a policy of unifying Italy; winning for the nation a seat among the powers of Europe; encouraging industry, trade, and education; and separating Church and State. Shrewdness, courage, ability, and stamina were required to balance all the factions of government and society. More than a few persons felt that the premier also had a liberal amount of duplicity in his character (cf. Don Bosco's remarks, below).

Cavour's religious policy of "a free Church in a free State" brought further legislation, including some that was anticlerical and social at the same time, such as the law suppressing monasteries and seizing their vast lands. This 1855 law prompted the excommunication of all those involved in its enactment and execution. This, of course, was exactly at the time when Don Bosco was beginning to form the Salesian Society.

Sardinia's involvement in the Crimean War brought diplomatic results for Cavour, but no territorial ones. Those had to wait until the Second War of Independence in 1859, in which France helped the Piedmontese drive the Austrians from Lombardy. At the same time Cavour's agents in the small duchies of central Italy were stirring up anti-Austrian revolts and calls for annexation by Sardinia, a policy which bore full fruit in 1860.

Meanwhile, over Cavour's objections Garibaldi and his Thousand sailed for Sicily; in a matter of weeks they brought down the Neapolitan government and threatened the Papal States. Sardinia was not ready to absorb the whole of Italy; Cavour was a moderate, a gradualist. The economic and social problems of northern and central Italy offered more than enough challenge even for his genius. Nor did he wish to take on the Church again by striking at its ancient domain; he hoped a compromise could be reached by the time Italy was ready for the next unifying step.

But Garibaldi forced the count's hand, not only by taking Naples and eyeing Rome, but by supporting republicanism. If Victor Emmanuel and Cavour did not act promptly to embrace Garibaldi's gains and keep him away from Rome, a difficult situation might become impossible. So Cavour ordered the Sardinian army south, and the king followed; they checked Garibaldi by encouraging a united Italy under one king. In the process they seized the Papal States, except the province of Rome.

Thus was the unification of Italy substantially completed; only Venetia, Trent, and Istria remained under the Austrians in the northeast, and only Lazio (Rome) remained under the Pope. Victor Emmanuel II was proclaimed king of Italy in March 1861. On two separate occasions Cavour remarked in parliament that Italy would have to have Rome as its capital.

Through all of this Don Bosco was fiercely loyal to his bishop and the Pope. Yet he kept out of politics as a matter of principle. Consequently Cavour felt that he could use Don Bosco as an intermediary with the Holy See in an attempt to resolve the Fransoni problem in the spring of 1858. The attempt failed. (Francesco Motto, "Don Bosco mediatore tra Cavour e Antonelli nel 1858," *Ricerche storiche salesiane* V [1986], 3–20)

Although he was friendly with Cavour and other government officials; although they supported his work with postal exemptions, gifts of army surplus, and railway passes; although they often recommended boys to him; nevertheless Don Bosco came under suspicion as what some today would call "an enemy of the State." He and the Oratory were subjected to a repeated series of searches, and in some quarters, to lasting hostility.

Don Bosco left a memo in which he describes the various house searches. He says of Cavour:

> He often came to the Oratory. He enjoyed talking with the boys and loved to watch them in recreation. He even took part in church services; more than once he walked in our procession in honor of St. Aloysius, carrying a candle in one hand and a prayer book in the other as he sang the *Infensus hostis gloriae*. When I wished to speak with him [when he was a cabinet minister], he would refuse me an audience unless I came to dine with him. (ACS 132 Perquisizione, 2o quaderno, p. 94)

In the same memo he left an evaluation of Cavour: "The life of this famous politician is well known to history: pretty promises, courtesy toward everybody, then a stab in the back."

Toward the end of 1860 Don Bosco made one of his famous predictions of an approaching death: In the coming year a famous diplomat would die totally unexpectedly, to the shock of all Europe. Many guesses were ventured as to his identity, but Don Bosco would give no hints. No one thought of the relatively young and vigorous prime minister of Piedmont. (BM VI, 457) In fact, Cavour's health had been compromised by malaria contracted in the rice paddies of his estate years before. That, an indulgent diet, the relentless pressures of high office (he had through all these years kept the financial portfolio, and for most of them directed the foreign office, as well as the premiership), and the stress of political opposition in a parliament growing more fractious by the day, broke his health. He collapsed on May 29 and died on June 6, 1861.

The best English biographies of the great statesman are those of Thayer and Mack Smith; see also Woolf, pp. 435–467, or more briefly, Felix Gilbert et al., *The Norton History of Modern Europe* (New York: Norton, 1971), pp. 1097–1104.

The First
Boarder

*The start of the hospice • The first
boarders arrive*

While we worked to set up ways of supplying instruction in religion and literacy, another crying need became evident; it was urgent to make some provision for it. Many youngsters from Turin and migrants [were] quite willing to try to live hard-working and moral lives; but when they were encouraged to begin, they used to answer that they had no bread, no clothing, and no shelter where they could stay at least for a while. To accommodate at least some of those who in the evening knew not where to go, a stable was prepared where they could spend the night on a bit of straw.[1] But some of them repeatedly made off with the sheets, others with the blankets, and in the end even the straw itself was stolen and sold.

Now it happened that late one rainy evening in May [1847] a lad of fifteen showed up soaked to the skin. He asked for bread and shelter. My mother took him into the kitchen and put him near the fire; while he warmed himself and dried his clothes, she fed him a bowl of soup and some bread. As he ate, I asked him whether he had gone to school, whether he had family, and what kind of work he did.

"I'm a poor orphan," he answered me. "I've come from the Sesia valley[2] to look for work. I had three francs with me, but I spent them all before I could earn anything. Now I have nothing left and no one to turn to."

"Have you been admitted to first communion?"

"I haven't been admitted yet."[3]

"And confirmation?"

"I haven't received it yet."

"Have you been to confession?"

"I've gone a few times."[4]

"Now where do you want to go?"

"I don't know. For charity's sake, let me stay in some corner of your house tonight."

At this point he broke down and cried. My mother cried with him. I was moved.

"If I could be sure you weren't a thief, I would try to put you up. But other boys stole some of the blankets, and you might take the rest of them."

"Oh no, Sir. You needn't worry about that. I'm poor, but I've never stolen anything."

"If you wish," replied my mother, "I will put him up for tonight, and tomorrow God will provide."

"Where?" I asked.

"Here in the kitchen."

"You're risking even your pots."

"I'll see that it doesn't happen."

"Go ahead, then."[5]

The good woman, helped by the little orphan, went out and collected some bricks. With these she built four little pillars in the kitchen. On them she laid some boards and threw a big sack on top, thereby making the first bed in the Oratory.

My good mother gave the boy a little talk on the necessity of work, of trustworthiness, and of religion.[6] Finally she invited him to say his prayers.

"I don't know any," he answered.

"You can say them with us," she told him. And so he did. That all might be secure, the kitchen was locked, and opened only in the morning.

This was the first youngster at our hospice.[7] Very soon we had a companion for him,[8] and then others. But during that year, lack of space prevented us from taking more than two.[9] So passed 1847.

Convinced that for many children every effort would prove useless unless they were offered shelter,[10] I set about renting more and more rooms, even though the cost was exorbitant.[11]

Thus, besides the hospice, we were also able to start our school of plainchant and vocal music. Since it was the first time (1845) that public music lessons were offered,[12] the first time that music was taught in class to many pupils at the same time, there was a huge crowd. The renowned musicians Louis Rossi, Joseph Blanchi, Cerutti, and Canon Louis Nasi[13] came eagerly every evening to help at my lessons. This contradicted the Gospel dictum that the disciple is not above his teacher:[14] there was I, not knowing a millionth of what those illustrious men knew, playing the master amongst them. They came to see how the new method was applied, the same method which is practised today in our houses. In times past, any pupil who wished to learn music had to find a teacher to give him individual lessons.[15]

Notes

1. There was a stable at the east end of the ground floor of the Pinardi house (diagram in Giraudo and Biancardi, p. 157).

2. The Sesia River rises from Monte Rosa and flows 105 miles east and south, through Vercelli, and into the Po east of Casale (over forty miles to the east of Turin).

3. Again we meet late admission to first holy communion and an implied Jansenism.

4. A youngster would be taught to go to confession as soon as he reached the age of reason. Neither this sacrament nor that young age (about seven years) were closely linked to holy communion, as they are now.

5. Don Bosco's conversations with the boy and with Mama Margaret reveal to us several characteristics. First, as in his dialog with Bartholomew Garelli (chapter 28) he begins by winning a boy's confidence. Second, he comes around to what really matters, one's relationship with God. Third, his goodness is not naiveté; having been burned several times by untrustworthy young men, he has grown wary. Perhaps there is even a trace of discouragement.

6. Thus Mama Margaret began a Salesian tradition which is still observed: the "good night" talk. In his treatise on the Preventive System, Don Bosco wrote:

> Every evening after the usual prayers, before the pupils go to

> bed, the director, or someone in his stead, shall address a few kind words in public, giving advice or counsel about things to be done or to be avoided. He shall try to draw useful lessons from events which have happened during the day in the institute or outside. But his talk shall never be longer than two or three minutes. This is the key to morality, to the good running of the institute, and to success in education.

Lemoyne, himself an experienced director, says simply that this practice "yielded excellent results" (BM III, 142).

7. Don Bosco found him a job. Until winter he ate and slept at the Oratory. When his work stopped for the season, he went back to his native place, and no more is known of him. We are not so fortunate as to know his name or those of the boys who came immediately after him.

8. Don Bosco found this youngster crying, with his head against an elm tree along corso San Massimo (now corso Regina Margherita). Already fatherless, he had suffered his mother's death just the previous day. Now the landlord had thrown him out on the street, taking the furniture in lieu of unpaid rent. Don Bosco brought him home to Mama Margaret. He was a refined young lad, so Don Bosco got him placed as a shop clerk. He did well, was promoted in his job, and always proved a credit to his benefactor. Out of respect for him, the early historians of the Oratory preserved his anonymity, and now his name has been lost to us. (BM III, 143–144)

9. Some biographers, including Lemoyne (BM III, 144), have written "seven." Don Bosco wrote "two" in the original manuscript and left "two" in the copy which he revised. In the latter, however, someone unknown wrote "seven" in purple ink above the "two." The discrepancy may merely be a matter of whom one is counting: all the guests living in the house, or just those taken in without fee: see note 11, below.

10. Cf. the first draft of the Salesian Constitutions (1858), in the chapter "Purpose of This Society":

> 4. Since some boys are so neglected that, unless they are sheltered, every care would be expended on them in vain, to this end every effort shall be made to open houses in which, through the assistance of Divine Providence, they will be provided with lodging, food, and clothing. While receiving religious instruction, they will also be taught some trade or craft, as is presently being done in the hospice attached to the Oratory of St. Francis de Sales. . . . (BM V, 637)

11. As we have already seen (chapter 44, note 9), by the end of

1846 Don Bosco had rented the whole Pinardi house and had use of it all by the following March. These eleven rooms were being used as kitchen, classrooms, and rooms for Don Bosco, Margaret, and some of his helpers. Thus, the limited space for needy youths.

Don Bosco took in four paying boarders in the fall of 1847. Fathers Charles Palazzolo (see chapter 16, note 12) and Peter Ponte (1821–1892) paid thirty-five and fifty lire per month, respectively (the latter was reduced to forty the following October). During the week they went about their pastoral duties (Father Ponte was one of Marchioness Barolo's chaplains), and they helped with the Oratory on Sundays and feasts. Many such boarders found it difficult to adapt to Don Bosco's asceticism; in fact, Father Ponte moved out for a while on February 29, 1848, but that seems to have been for political reasons (see chapter 52).

The third helper was the seminarian John Baptist Bertagna of Castelnuovo (1828–1905), paying fifty lire per month. He became a teacher at the Convitto and, eventually, auxiliary bishop of Turin.

Besides these clerical helpers, in October 1847 Don Bosco brought to Turin with him a cousin, Alexander Pescarmona of Castelnuovo. Mr. Pescarmona paid Don Bosco 55.5 lire per month room and board while the boy took school lessons from Professor Joseph Bonzanino in the city (see chapter 48). The boy was to stay for three years, and his father, aware of Don Bosco's need for cash, paid the whole fee in advance.

An archival register lists the numbers of boarders at the Oratory from 1847 to 1869; Stella cautions that it is not fully reliable. The names of some of the earliest house guests are provided in another register in Don Bosco's handwriting. The former shows two boarders in 1847, one in 1848, two in 1849. The latter, which generally only gives the date of entrance, shows five for 1847, ten for 1849.

See BM III, 175–176; Giraudo and Biancardi, p. 175; Stella, *EcSo*, pp. 41, 175–176, 182, 373.

12. The date matches the stay at the Moretta house rather than the rental of the whole Pinardi premises. Don Bosco had been teaching the boys Gregorian chant and hymns since the first days of the Oratory. Now he was also teaching them to read music and sing parts, not just read the words and memorize a simple melody. On Don Bosco as music teacher, see BM III, 98–103.

13. Lemoyne gives Cerutti's first name at Joseph (BM III, 102). Canon Nasi was one of the priests who tried to get Don Bosco into the asylum.

14. Matthew 10:24.

15. Up till then, only when pupils had attained a certain proficiency in music through private lessons were they brought together to form a choir or orchestra under a conductor.

Another Oratory

In proportion to our efforts to extend our schools and provide instruction, the number of our pupils increased. On feast days, only some of the pupils could fit into the chapel for the ceremonies or into the playground for games. Then, always in agreement with Dr Borrelli, to meet this growing need a second oratory was opened in another quarter of the city.[1] For this purpose, we rented a small house at Porta Nuova on viale del Re,[2] commonly called the Avenue of the Plane Trees after the trees lining the street.

To secure that house, we had to engage in a very fierce battle with the inhabitants. It was occupied by a group of washerwomen who believed that abandoning their ancient abode would cause the end of the world. But we used a gentle approach and offered some compensation, and so a deal was struck before the belligerents reached a state of war.

Mrs Vaglienti owned that site and the play garden, which she later left in her will to Chev. Joseph Turvano.[3] The rent was 450 francs.[4] We called this new foundation the Oratory of St Aloysius Gonzaga, a name by which it is still known.*

Dr Borrelli and I opened the new oratory on the feast of the Immaculate Conception, 1847.[6] The extraordinary mob of youngsters there relieved somewhat the crowded ranks of those at Valdocco. Direction of that oratory was entrusted

---

*Today the Church of St John the Evangelist occupies the site where stood the church, sacristy, and porter's house of the St Aloysius Oratory.[5]

to Dr Hyacinth Carpano, who for several years laboured entirely gratis.[7] The same Regulations drawn up for the institution at Valdocco were adopted at the St Aloysius Oratory, without any modifications being introduced.

In that same year, with a desire of giving shelter to a multitude of children asking for it, we bought the whole Moretta house.[8] But when we looked into the work of adapting it to our requirements, we found the walls were not strong enough. Because of this, we thought it wiser to resell it, especially since we were offered a very attractive price.[9]

Then we acquired a section of land (.94 acre) from the Turin seminary.[10] This is the site where the Church of Mary Help of Christians was later built, and the building which at present houses the workshops for our artisans.[11]

Notes

1. Don Bosco consulted not only Father Borel but also the Murialdo cousins, other priests, and, of course, the archbishop (Stella, *EcSo*, p. 176; BM III, 186).

2. The Porta Nuova district took its name ("New Gate") from an entry through the no-longer-existent city wall. The area was open country with lots of trees on the fringe of the city. On a sizeable portion of empty land a few little houses were scattered. The property already swarmed with kids on Sundays. It was a good bet that the city's future expansion would be in that direction. So the site was well chosen.

   Viale del Re is now called corso Vittorio Emanuele II. The city's main railroad station, built later, is four blocks west of the oratory site.

3. Joseph Turvano, whose name comes up often in BM IV–IX, was a notary serving the Schools for the Poor, Father Cafasso, and Don Bosco, among others; a city councilor; and secretary of the Company of Mercy, a confraternity dedicated to good works.

4. The rent was reduced after the property came to Turvano: it averaged 319 lire per year between 1856 and 1858 (Stella, *EcSo*, p. 77, n. 15).

5. Don Bosco added the note to Father Berto's copy during revision. The cornerstone of the Church of Saint John the

Evangelist was blessed in 1878 and the church completed in 1882. The Salesians have charge of the parish and run a thriving youth center and school there.

6. They assembled boys there for the first time on December 8. The official opening took place on Sunday, December 19. The archbishop's letter of authorization is dated December 18.

7. Father Carpano was succeeded at the Saint Aloysius Oratory by Father Ponte, who apparently settled his differences of 1848 with Don Bosco; he was director from 1850 till about 1854. In later years two great servants of God were in charge: Saint Leonard Murialdo from 1857 to 1865, and Blessed Louis Guanella (1842–1915) from 1875 to 1878. For a brief history of this oratory, see Giraudo and Biancardi, pp. 180–181.

8. Don Bosco had been trying to get Pinardi to sell his house, but Pinardi wanted 80,000 lire, far more than it was worth or Don Bosco could afford. Father Moretta died in 1847. The house and land (.55 acre besides the house) were auctioned off on March 9, 1848. Don Bosco outbid everyone by offering 11,800 lire. He made a down payment of 601.75 lire on December 4, and 396.25 lire in interest. (Giraudi, pp. 49–50; Stella, *EcSo*, p. 76)

9. The resale took place within a year. Not only was Don Bosco offered a good price, but his own payments (see previous note) indicate that he was desperately short of cash. He could hardly afford the repairs required if he were to use the building as he had intended.

So he sold part of the house and land to James and Anthony Ferrero and to Juvenal Mo on April 10, 1849. He sold another part to Michael Nicco on June 1, 1850, and the remainder to the widow Mrs. Mary Ann Audagnotto on October 6, 1850. (Giraudi, p. 51)

Don Bosco bought back the house and land in 1875 and opened there the first oratory for girls, entrusting it to the Daughters of Mary Help of Christians. It opened in March 1876. Saint Mary Mazzarello sent seven sisters under the leadership of Sister Eliza Roncallo.

10. This was the so-called "field of the dreams" (see chapter 31), a triangular field in the angle between via della Giardiniera and via Cottolengo, across the street from the Pinardi property. It was being used as a vegetable garden at the time. Don Bosco bought it on June 20, 1850, for 7500 lire, intending to build on it.

Don Bosco had already been corresponding with Father Rosmini about the possibility of the Institute of Charity's opening a house in Turin and helping with the work of the oratories. The seminary field offered a site for a Rosminian residence as well as a larger hospice and playground area. Those discussions did not pan out, nor did Don Bosco's plans for expansion in that direction.

Financial need compelled him to sell small pieces of the lot over the next two years. He sold about half of the field in at least five parcels for a total of at least 6410.78 lire. (The sources cite five sales which do not add up to half the field.)

The remaining .48 acre was sold to Father Rosmini on April 10, 1854, for 18,000 lire. Don Bosco still owed Father Rosmini 20,000 lire at four percent interest, which he had borrowed to purchase the Pinardi house in 1851 (see chapter 54).

When Don Bosco was ready to build the Basilica of Mary Help of Christians in 1863, he repurchased the Rosminian portion of the field for 1558.4 lire. With some understatement, Lemoyne remarks that the value of the land had severely depreciated. Be that as it may, anyone who adds up the various prices which Don Bosco paid and which he received cannot doubt Don Bosco's business acumen. (He also reacquired the other sections of the field which he had sold individually in 1850–1851.)

See Stella, *EcSo*, pp. 82–85; Giraudi, pp. 112, 166, 170, 176; BM IV, 87–95; V, 20, 30–31; VII, 224–228.

11. The workshops are still there, to the left (west) of the Basilica of Mary Help of Christians: shops for mechanics, electromechanics, and the graphic arts.

❀ 48 ❀

The Revolutionary Year

*1848 • The number of artisans grows •
Their way of life • Short evening
exhortation • The archbishop grants
privileges • Retreats*

In this year, political events and the public mood presented a drama, the outcome of which nobody could foresee.[1] Charles Albert had granted the Constitution.[2] Many thought that the Constitution also granted freedom to do good or evil at will. They based this assertion on the emancipation of the Jews and Protestants, claiming as a consequence that there was no longer any distinction between Catholics and [those of] other faiths. This was true in politics, but not in matters of religion.*

Meantime, a kind of frenzy seized the minds even of youngsters; they would get together at various points in the city, in the streets and squares, believing that it was a praiseworthy to insult priests or religion. I was attacked many times at home and in the street.[5]

One day as I was teaching catechism, a harquebus shot came through the window, passing through my cassock between my arm and my ribs, and making a large hole in

---

*On 20 December 1847, Charles Albert received a petition from 600 prominent Catholic citizens, a great number of whom were clergymen.[3] They laid out their reasons for requesting that emancipation, but they attached little importance to heretical expressions concerning matters of religion which one finds in the petition. As a result, the king signed the famous decrees mentioned here.

From that time the Jews came out of their ghettos and became leading property-owners. The Protestants then broke from any restraints on their boldness; though few in number amongst us, they were protected by civil authority and did great damage to religion and morality.[4]

the wall.[6] On another occasion, a certain well-known character attacked me with a long knife in full daylight while I stood in the middle of a group of children. It was a miracle that I was able to get away, beating a hasty retreat to the safety of my room.

Dr Borrelli was also able to escape miraculously from a pistol shot, and from the blows of a knife one time when he was mistaken for someone else.

It was, therefore, quite difficult to control such aroused young people. In that perversion of thought and ideas, as soon as we could provide additional rooms, the number of artisans was increased, coming to fifteen, all amongst the most abandoned and endangered. 1847.[7]

There was a big problem, however. Because we had no workshops in our institution yet, our pupils went to work and to school in Turin, with ensuing harm to morality. The companions they mixed with, the conversations they heard, and what they saw frustrated what was said to them and done for them at the Oratory. It was then that I began to give very short little sermons in the evening after prayers with a view to presenting or confirming some truth which might have been contradicted during the day.[8]

What happened to the artisans was likewise to be lamented regarding the students.[9] Because the most advanced scholars were divided into various classes, they had to be sent to Prof. Joseph Bonzanino for grammar and to Prof. Fr Matthew Picco for rhetoric.[10] These were most distinguished schools, but going to and from was fraught with danger. In the year 1856, to everyone's advantage, workshops and classes were permanently established at the Oratory itself.[11]

At that time the perversion of ideas and actions seemed such that I could no longer trust the domestic staff.[12] As a consequence my mother and I did all the housework. To my lot fell cooking, setting the table, sweeping, chopping firewood, cutting out and making trousers, shirts, jackets, towels, sheets, and doing the necessary mending. But these things turned out very advantageous, morally speaking, for I could conveniently give the boys some advice or a friendly word as I went round handing out bread, soup, or something else.

Discerning the need to have someone come and help me

in both domestic and scholastic matters in the Oratory, I began to take some [of the boys] with me into the country and others to spend the holidays at Castelnuovo, my native country.[13] Some of them came for dinner with me, others in the evening to read or write something — always with the purpose of providing an antidote to the poisonous opinions of the day. This was done with greater or lesser frequency from 1841 to 1848. I adopted every means to pursue also my own particular objective, which was to observe, get to know, and chose some individuals who had a suitable inclination to the common life, and to take them with me into my house.[14]

With this same purpose, in that year (1848) I put it to a test with a little spiritual retreat.[15] About fifty boys gathered at the Oratory house for it. They all ate with me; but because there were not enough beds for all, some had to sleep with their own families and return to the Oratory in the morning. This coming and going to their homes risked almost all the benefit to be reaped from the sermons and instructions which are customary on such occasions.

The retreat began on Sunday evening and finished on the following Saturday evening. It succeeded quite well. Many boys for whom I had laboured in vain for a long time really gave themselves to virtuous living. Several entered religious life; others, while continuing in the secular life, became models in their regular attendance at the Oratory.[†] More will be said on this point in the History of the Salesian Society.[22]

In that same year some parish priests, especially those of Borgo Dora, Our Lady of Mount Carmel Church, and St Augustine,[23] complained anew to the archbishop because the sacraments were being administered in our oratories. When they did, the archbishop issued a decree giving us full faculties to prepare and present the children for confirmation and holy communion and [for them] to fulfill their Easter duty in the oratories, as long as they came regularly.

[†] Hyacinth Arnaud,[16] Sansoldi,[17] both deceased; Joseph Buzzetti, Nicholas Galesio; John Costantino,[18] deceased; James Cerutti, deceased; Charles Gastini,[19] John Gravano;[20] and Dominic Borgialli,[21] deceased. These were numbered amongst those who made the first retreat that year and who always showed themselves good Christians.

He renewed the faculty allowing us to hold every religious ceremony ordinarily held in parish churches. These churches, the archbishop said, will be parish churches for those young, abandoned strangers[24] as long as they are resident in Turin.

Notes

1. It was a watershed year all over Western Europe. See the introduction and, for further reading, the bibliography.

2. Uprisings during January in Palermo, Naples, and Messina compelled King Ferdinand to grant his subjects a constitution. Milan and Venice were on the verge of revolt against the Austrians. With revolutionary pressure building on all sides, Charles Albert's advisers convinced him that it would be wiser to grant a constitution than have one forced upon him.

   The Sardinian Constitution, based on the French and Belgian constitutions of 1830–1831, was issued on March 4, 1848. It legally ended absolutism in the Sardinian States and introduced parliamentary government. It is a very conservative document, with the king retaining substantial legislative as well as executive powers and all of the judicial ones. The king named the members of the senate (the upper house), and the franchise for the election of deputies (members of the lower house) was severely restricted (e.g. in the 1853 elections, one percent of the population voted; there was even one deputy chosen by seven electors [Mack Smith, *Cavour*, p. 73]).

   Though the Constitution's survival was touch and go for several years, it did survive as the fundamental law of the nation until the Republic was established after World War II.

3. Don Bosco left one note in his original manuscript and a second one in Father Berto's copy, expanding the first. To avoid repetition, we have merged them.

   On February 17 and March 29, Charles Albert issued royal decrees granting civil equality to all citizens regardless of religious beliefs. Most non-Catholics in Piedmont were either Waldensian Protestants (about 21,000) or Jews (about 7000). Catholicism remained the religion of the State.

   Marquis Robert d'Azeglio presented the petition to the king; a hundred clergymen, both diocesan and religious, had signed it. When Don Bosco was approached for his signature in October 1847, he said he would sign as soon the archbishop did (BM III, 190–191).

4. Don Bosco is referring to the Waldensians, who until then had been confined to the valleys of the Cottian Alps near Pinerolo, south and west of Turin. Their main center was at Torre Pellice, southwest of Pinerolo.

   The Waldensians were a sect founded in Lyons, France, by the merchant Peter Waldo. Beginning in 1173 by renouncing all material comforts, he and his followers took to street preaching, presenting a literal reading of the Bible. By 1179 they ran into trouble with the hierarchy. After being excommunicated, they denounced the Pope and Catholic bishops as corrupt and developed their own doctrines, e.g. that laymen and women can preach and forgive sins, prayer for the dead is useless, purgatory exists only in this life, sacraments are valid only when administered by worthy priests, oaths violate Christ's command, etc. The sect spread through southern France, northern Italy, and elsewhere. It was countered with preaching crusades, persecution, and the Inquisition at various times, and at times it was tolerated. See Kenneth Scott Latourette, *A History of Christianity* (New York: Harper and Row, 1975), I, 451–452; John P. Dolan, *History of the Reformation* (New York: New American Library, 1967), pp. 84–85; NCE XIV, 770–771.

   As it happened, the Waldensians made their Turin headquarters in Porta Nuova, near the Saint Aloysius Oratory. They preached boldly, distributed Bibles freely, assisted the poor, and opened a school. Missionary societies in Switzerland, Germany, and Britain funded them generously. They made youngsters the special objects of their proselytism. That directly challenged Don Bosco, for they not only exercised charity by offering education and public assistance, but they launched polemical attacks on Catholic doctrine and discipline. They resorted to paying boys to leave Don Bosco's oratories and come to theirs. Religious warfare between them and Don Bosco followed. (BM III, 284–288)

   On Don Bosco's ecclesiology in general, see Stella, *ReCa*, pp. 119–145; on his attitude toward Protestantism, pp. 124–131.

5. Political liberals blamed the Church (represented in Turin by a conservative archbishop and a conservative majority of the clergy) for the slow pace of political and educational reform

and even for the Austrian occupation of northeastern Italy. The emancipation of non-Catholics was regarded as a step for human dignity as well as a blow to the power of the Church. Anticlericalism began to be regarded as a litmus test of one's devotion to national unity and individual conscience. As late as 1986 there was a sign in the Waldensian church at Porta Nuova reading "Protestants and Liberty."

During the spring of 1848 large mobs were demonstrating in the streets, particularly against the Jesuits, who were the staunchest defenders of the monarchy and the ancient privileges of the Church, finally ransacking their residence and driving them into hiding; against the Convitto, which had sheltered some Jesuits; and even against the Barolo institutes, on the accusation that the marchioness was likewise harboring some of them. A mob that went for the archbishop's residence was stopped by the presence of Marquis d'Azeglio and a contingent of soldiers. The Jesuits were expelled from the kingdom, and from other parts of Italy too, soon after. (BM III, 208–210)

6. A harquebus is an ancient flintlock musket. The shot was fired over the north wall, across the twenty-six feet of the courtyard, and into the Pinardi chapel. The Pinardi building was later demolished and replaced. A sign outside the present Chapel of the Resurrection marks a window located at about the same spot as the one through which the would-be assassin fired.

   Don Bosco learned the identity of the man, who had a criminal record and apparently had been hired by political radicals. He forgave him personally when he met him some time later. (BM III, 211–212).

7. According to Don Bosco's own records, there were eight such boys in residence in 1852 and fifteen in 1853, when the hospice annex was put up (Stella, *EcSo*, p. 175; cf. chapter 46, note 11).

8. This little talk after night prayers is called the "good night" in Salesian houses. See chapter 46, note 6.

9. "Students" were the boys who were going to school, as distinguished from the "artisans," boys working as apprentices in some trade or as shop clerks.

10. Professor Charles Joseph Bonzanino (d. 1888) was a layman who later became a Salesian Cooperator. He taught the Oratory students, including those who became the first Salesians, for many years in his home at 20 via Barbaroux

(which runs between the Cittadella Garden and piazza Castello).

Father Picco (1812–1880) also maintained a long relationship with the students of the Oratory. He lived at 1 via San Agostino, next to the Church of Saint Augustine, where he taught the humanities course as well as rhetoric.

11. By then 150 boys were boarding at the Oratory. The most advanced students still went to Father Picco for their rhetoric or humanities course. Dominic Savio was one of them. (BM V, 362)

12. Don Bosco almost repeats exactly a phrase used a few paragraphs earlier. In *Cenno storico sulla Congregazione di S. Francesco di Sales e relativi schiarimenti* [A Brief History of the Salesian Congregation, and Related Explanations] (Rome: Poliglotta, 1874), Don Bosco cites a particular consequence of this "perversion." He writes:

> In that year (1848) a frenzy was worked up against religious orders and congregations, and against the clergy and all Church authorities in general. This cry of fury and contempt for religion resulted in young people's turning from morality, from piety, and hence from priestly vocations. Religious institutes were being dispersed, priests were being ridiculed, some of them were thrown into prison, and others were driven into exile. How, humanly speaking, could one ever cultivate a vocation?

Yet it was necessary in times so adverse to lay the groundwork for a new religious congregation.

> At that time, God made clearly known to me a new kind of army he wished to enlist, not from the well-to-do families, because they mostly sent their children to public schools or big colleges where every idea, every inclination to the priesthood was quickly snuffed. Those who worked with spade or hammer had to be chosen to take a glorious place among those going forward to the priesthood.

This is exactly what Don Bosco was doing at the Oratory and what he had to take care to protect from harmful influences either in the city streets or from his hired help.

One may note his comparison of his new congregation to an army. He admired the Jesuits and was much influenced by them. Even his name for the most pious devotees of Saint Aloysius — "Company" — echoes Saint Ignatius's name for his congregation, the Company of Jesus.

Reference to Don Bosco's hiring domestic help seems quite unusual. There was certainly too much work for him, his mother, and a few good women volunteers to manage, and eventually he had to hire others. Still later, when he had coadjutor brothers among the Salesians, they undertook much of this kind of work without any risk of compromising the enterprise.

13. In October 1847 Don Bosco began taking a few boys to spend a few days' holiday with him, his mother, and his brother's family at their farm in Becchi. He made this an annual practice until 1864. Originally he seems to have taken the few boys who had no place else to go for a vacation. Later, the excursion became a special treat for the best boys; as Don Bosco implies here in his memoirs, it was also a chance to discern vocations.

   These fall outings may be studied as a synthesis of Don Bosco's educational method. They embodied reason, religion, and kindness. They were a reward for exemplary students, a wholesome recreation, a learning experience, a means of preventing idleness, a chance for individual attention, and more. See the comment following the notes.

14. That is to say, almost from the very start of the Oratory, Don Bosco was thinking of forming a religious community around himself. We have already seen that he was personally attracted to the religious life (chapter 16).

15. Don Bosco pioneered the idea of retreats for young workers in Italy. The first retreat, for twenty boys, took place in 1847 (not 1848) and was preached by Blessed Frederick Albert (1820–1876), court chaplain at that time, later a parish priest at Lanzo Torinese, and founder of the Vincentian Sisters of Mary Immaculate, commonly known as the Albertines. He was instrumental in getting the Salesians to open a school at Lanzo in 1864. (BM III, 151–152; VII, 416)

16. He entered the Oratory in 1847, aged sixteen, and left in 1858. He became a secular priest and pastor of the Church of Saint Augustine.

17. Probably James Sansoldi, a shoemaker who enrolled in the Oratory chapter of the Saint Vincent de Paul Society in 1856 and still belonged in 1863 (Stella, *EcSo*, pp. 266–267, 478).

18. A paying boarder at the Oratory in 1849 (Stella, *EcSo*, pp. 176, 560).

19. Charles Gastini (1832–1902) was closely associated with the Oratory for many years. He was an apprentice barber when Don Bosco met him in 1843 and risked his neck getting

the boy's first shave. Gastini became inseparably devoted to Don Bosco. "More than once," he told Father Francesia, "Don Bosco escaped my razor looking like Saint Bartholomew" (who, according to tradition, was flayed alive). He lived at the Oratory from 1847 to May 1856. Like Buzzetti, he was counted among Don Bosco's four most promising students and studied for the priesthood. After putting aside his studies because of poor health, he became a master bookbinder. On one occasion in 1854 he and three others snuck out after the gate had been locked for the night, which did not escape Don Bosco's notice.

To Gastini we owe the idea of the Association of Past Pupils, which he suggested in 1870. He never missed a family feast at the Oratory. Known as Don Bosco's minstrel because of his excellent singing voice and his versifying, he had an original way of expressing tender sentiments. He boasted that his verses were composed in cubic meter. Those who knew Gastini could only agree with Giraudi (p. 217): "His ideas struck all who heard him. The more novel they were, the more they were appreciated and applauded."

He often repeated the refrain:

> *Io devo vivere / per settant'anni*
> *A me lo disse / Papà Giovanni*

> I'll live to be seventy / Father John told me so.

He died on January 28, 1902, one day after turning seventy.

See MB XX; Stella, *EcSo*, pp. 177, 195, 255–256; T. Bosco, SP, pp. 138–140.

20. A shopkeeper who joined the Saint Vincent de Paul Society at the Oratory in 1860 and was an officer in 1863 (Stella, *EcSo*, pp. 266–267, 477–478).

21. Don Bosco brought him to the Oratory in March 1848 (Stella, *EcSo*, p. 563).

22. Don Bosco probably meant to follow the *Memoirs of the Oratory*, which run up to 1855, with *The History of the Salesian Society*, which was being founded at that time. He never found the time to do so.

23. The parish church of Borgo Dora, to the east of Valdocco, was Saints Simon and Jude, and the pastor was Father Augustine Gattino. Our Lady of Mount Carmel Church is on via del Carmine just west of piazza Savoia (which is two blocks south of Our Lady of Consolation); the pastor was Father Charles Dellaporta. The pastor of Saint Augustine's

parish, Father Vincent Ponzati, had objected to Don Bosco's work for quite some time.

24. Don Bosco called the Oratory the parish church for the abandoned boys of Turin; now he had ecclesiastical recognition of his and their quasi-parochial rights.

Comment on the Fall Outings as a Synthesis of Don Bosco's Educational Method

For eighteen years (1847–1864), Don Bosco led a troupe of his boys to his family home at Becchi each October. While she was alive, Mama Margaret went along too. At first the boys were few: sixteen, for instance, in 1848 and twenty-seven in 1852. But by 1860 their numbers had swelled to sixty-odd youngsters, and on the last and greatest of these hikes, about a hundred went along. Fortunately, Don Bosco had seminarians to assist him from the early '50s on.

It seems that the few boys who joined Don Bosco and his mother in those first years were simply those who had nowhere else to go for a few days' vacation. Since October is the peak of the grape harvest, there would have been relatively few boys left in Turin who were in that situation. But as Don Bosco established his hospice and developed a school and shops around it, and after the First War of Independence orphaned many Piedmontese lads, he had more boys the year round. Moreover, he encouraged even those who had homes to go to either to curtail their visit to those homes or to skip them entirely. Still other students had "summer school" at the Oratory.

So by the mid-1850s at the latest, Don Bosco had quite a number of boys who might accompany him to Becchi. He selected those whose conduct and study had been most outstanding during the previous year; day students also needed their parents' testimony to good behavior.

With a small group Don Bosco would head for Becchi a few days before the feast of Our Lady of the Rosary (the first Sunday in October in those days). They would prepare things at Joseph's farm, and Don Bosco would get a day or two's "breather" himself.

The main body of trekkers departed on Saturday morning. The evening before, Father Victor Alasonatti read out the roster of the lucky ones who had been selected. Thus Don Bosco and his helpers made sure that everyone maintained his best conduct even in the few days of Don Bosco's absence, and Don Bosco showed that all the Oratory superiors were involved in the choice. Nor did Don Bosco have the difficult chore of comforting or explaining to the disappointed — there was the prefect of discipline (Father Alasonatti) right on the spot!

The immediate objective of both the saint and the boys was the annual celebration of our Lady's feast at Becchi. In 1848 Don Bosco obtained Archbishop Fransoni's permission to set up a chapel in Joseph's house. This chapel (which is still there) became the focus of a great festival for the whole town of Castelnuovo, prepared for by a novena and solemnized by the presence of the Oratory band and choir. Between the solemn religious services (which included two Masses, the rosary, litanies, and benediction), there were games; in the evening, there were festivities with skits, poetry, song, balloons, and fireworks.

In the next day or two, in the early years, the boys might do a little local hiking, play games in the farmyard, or just relax. Joseph Bosco helped very effectively with general supervision, especially while his brother was working on sermons, hearing confessions, or conducting business.

Father Cinzano, pastor of Castelnuovo, always hosted Don Bosco and his young friends for a day. The boys would visit the little town where their dear father had once gone to school, the church where he had been baptized and made his first communion. The boys provided ample entertainment and enjoyed a huge polenta.

By the mid-1850s, the outing had been extended in time to about two weeks and in locale to sites other than Becchi. Each day the boys and Don Bosco would set out for some chosen destination, making a day trip of it or sometimes an overnight. At the village, the bass drum — or the racket of the band — announced that something special was about to happen, and all the people and the pastor would assemble. Don Bosco would address a few words to them (the pastor knew in advance that he was coming, of course), gather them in church for a service, preach, and hear confessions. The Oratory band and choir provided sacred music. If it were an overnight stop, the boys entertained everyone, as at Becchi; Charlie Gastini and Charles Tomatis soon became local legends with their antics. Naturally the hosts saw that their hungry guests were well fed. In the morning Don Bosco offered Mass, usually for the deceased of the village, and there was general communion (an unusual event in parish life).

On return to Valdocco, Don Bosco unfailingly thanked his young companions for their good behavior that had edified so many people and rejoiced his own heart.

In 1861 Don Bosco announced that the outing would be especially memorable. After spending the feast at Becchi as usual, the troupe moved on to Pica, Alfiano, Casale, Mirabello, and Villafranca d'Asti in a continuous trek. At the last town they got on a train back to Turin, courtesy of a government pass. The entire outing lasted seventeen days, and sixty boys participated. In the next three years, the trips got even longer. The last one, that of 1864, involved some one hundred youngsters who spent twenty-three days on the road. This excursion took them as far as Genoa, and they used the trains quite a bit.

Don Bosco, always dressed in his cassock and dripping with sweat, walked along with a group of kids. Not even thirty of them could keep in a group. Especially in the early years, boys sometimes got so lost that some farm family would have to put them up for the night and send them on to Becchi on the morning of the great feast itself. Don Bosco entertained his immediate companions with historical, religious, or autobiographical episodes connected with the various places through which they walked, with funny stories, and with catechism lessons.

We can imagine the difficulties of marching thirty to a hundred boys to Becchi (eighteen miles from Valdocco) and lodging them there for two weeks or taking them all over the countryside for three weeks. The boys got a little pocket money from Father Alasonatti before setting out—money which they had deposited with him, according to the rules; presumably Don Bosco saw that the poorest lads had something too. At Chieri, friends of Don Bosco, especially Chevalier Mark Gonella, always met them and treated them to lunch. By the time they got to the Bosco farm around dusk, the kids were almost too tired to eat, but Joseph had a spread ready for them.

Don Bosco arranged for an extra floor to be added to Joseph's farmhouse; it became a dormitory for twenty or twenty-five of his sons when Joseph spread hay over it and gave each boy a sheet. In later years neighbors helped with the lodging, which usually consisted of their haylofts.

When the kids set out for a day's hike, someone provided them with a loaf, some cheese, and two or three apples. If they were to be away overnight, Don Bosco arranged in advance not only for lodging but for a meal to be provided by the local pastor or some other benefactor. Writing ahead in mid-September, Don Bosco asked for bread, soup, and whatever might be convenient for his hungry troops—who, as John Baptist Francesia put it, might be only a hundred but had appetites for three hundred. "Whatever might be convenient" usually included cheese, fruit, salami, and lots of polenta. Sometimes a wealthier person, a noble or a bishop, would literally "kill the fatted calf" for Don Bosco and his gang. (Part of Don Bosco's advance work was known to include "buttering up" parish housekeepers; cf. BM VI, 27–29.)

Don Bosco was not the only one with preparations to make in advance: planning the route, lining up hosts, making historical and religious notes on the sites along the way, preparing sermons. The bandmaster and choirmaster also had to rehearse their charges with both sacred and secular pieces for the church services and public entertainments that repaid the villagers for their hospitality, and the young dramatists had to prepare their skits and plays.

How did the Oratory's musical instruments and stage props make it from one village to another? By boy-power. One would think that Don Bosco would have arranged for some transport, but not so. Each bandmember had to carry his own instrument — even the bass drum — on each day's hike for the fifteen or twenty days; and several of the bigger fellows had to carry the stage props. Each boy also had his own little bundle of extra clothes (little enough, no doubt) and maybe a blanket (though the sources make no mention of any bedclothing except Joseph's sheets). While all the kids must have been glad to see the railroad station at Villafranca in 1861, none more so than the band and the actors!

That is an outline of *what* Don Bosco did. More important is *why* he did it. We can identify seven general purposes:

1. The simplest intention of the annual outing was recreational. It was a bit of vacation, a chance for the tired priest and his mother to spend a few days with their family. John and Joseph Bosco "were one in heart and soul" (BM IV, 335); and all Mama Margaret's sons and grandchildren adored her. It was a chance for fresh air, rural scenery, and lots of room for exercise for those boys who had no other family.

2. Don Bosco never took a vacation, pure and simple. In Becchi he remained the priest and apostle. He kept in close touch with Father Alasonatti and the rest of his children back in Turin. He edited the *Catholic Readings* at night. The outings themselves were pilgrimages, focused on the feast of the Holy Rosary. In his native place Don Bosco paid homage to the Madonna who meant so much to him and his sons. In the trips to neighboring towns, the hikers from Turin often celebrated other local patronal feasts as well. On the way through Chieri, the boys always visited Louis Comollo's grave. In 1857, the year of Dominic Savio's death, they began the custom of visiting his grave at Mondonio too. Thus

they honored these model youths and drew inspiration from them. The boys' affection and admiration for their deceased schoolmate Savio was so genuine that in that first year they passed up Mr. Savio's proffered refreshments to charge straight to the cemetery; when they found the gates locked, some could not wait for the key and scaled the wall. At the grave they left a tributary plaque and many tears.

Some of the boys saw the excursion as a different kind of pilgrimage. They took home bits of brick and plaster from Don Bosco's boyhood home as relics.

3. The outings were an incentive to the students and artisans of the Oratory to work hard and behave well during the school year so that they might have the privilege of being in that select group. It was a reward eagerly hoped for! It was also an inducement that Don Bosco used to encourage the boys to spend their four months' vacation with him, or at least to cut short their time at home.

4. These outings quickly became an integral part of a total educational plan and method. They capsulized that sense of God, of religion, of study, work, and apostolic venture, and of joy that Don Bosco had learned from his mother and labored to instill in his sons. These sons later looked back at those golden days with nostalgia and awe.

Don Bosco frowned on the type of vacation in which a boy returned to his native town, mixed with his former, not-very-edifying pals, heard and saw bad example from relatives, lacked an opportunity for confession — especially if Don Bosco thought that the young man might have a priestly vocation. So the fall hikes kept him in touch with these boys. They said their daily prayers, attended Mass, had him on hand for their regular confessions; he spent time with each youngster, one-on-one, advising him about his future or touching on what was in his heart. These were choice educational moments.

Outside the urban and school setting, a different kind of education could go on. The piety of the villagers edified the youths, and vice versa. Their guide helped them to see God in the beautiful nature all around them, to make a link between the sacred and the profane. Don Bosco doubted that a boy's soul could refuse God's approach when it was so gentle and pleasant. The youths could see in Don Bosco himself a continuity between prayer and play, and their prayer lives deepened. It was not uncommon for a boy waking in the middle of the night to see one of his companions kneeling in the hay, at prayer. The rapport between the boys themselves grew, as well as that between the boys and their superiors and between the boys and their benefactors.

5. Don Bosco's apostolic work on the outings was not confined to the boys. He was zealous for the people wherever he went, preaching, hearing confessions, offering religious services (usually with the pastor's assistance and always with his prior approval). Wherever he went, besides, he tried to interest pastors and concerned laity in the *Catholic Readings* so that the good effects of his visit might continue.

By 1861 Don Bosco was ready to expand his work outside Turin, and some eager offers were coming from Mirabello. So the hike served this apostolic purpose too. He led his gang there and so began the negotiations that led to the opening of a new school two years later. Later expeditions served similar exploratory purposes. The 1864 journey took him to Mornese, where he encountered Mary Mazzarello and the group of young women around her, the future foundresses of the Daughters of Mary Help of Christians.

Nor was Don Bosco the only apostle on these trips. The young men were apostles too through their singing, instrumental music, service at the altar, prayer, and public entertainments. Many boys were so attracted to the fun that Don Bosco's boys were having that they would "hook up" with the oratorians for a day of hiking, playing, and praying—and some of them hooked up permanently. The villagers who saw how Don Bosco treated these adolescents and how they responded to him grew in their esteem for priests and the Salesians.

6. Which brings us to another goal of the hikes: recruitment. What parent, seeing Don Bosco and his seminarians in action with these boys, would hesitate to send a son to the Oratory? So Don Bosco found new students; some, like twelve-year-old Dominic Savio came looking for him. In 1850 Don Bosco found another twelve-year-old, Johnny Cagliero, who was the "lord" of Father Cinzano's rectory at Castelnuovo. It was especially for potential priestly vocations that he was on the lookout. To this end he often used the feast of the Holy Rosary at the Becchi chapel as the occasion for solemnly vesting a new clerical candidate. Eleven days after moving into the Oratory as a resident student, fifteen-year-old Michael Rua was so vested in 1852; he was just one of many. Don Bosco planned these ceremonies to impress and attract the youths of Castelnuovo.

Nor was it only boys whom Don Bosco attracted; on the 1864 trip he met Father Giovanni Battista Lemoyne near Genoa.

7. Finally, Don Bosco was attentive to his benefactors, many of whom had either summer homes or permanent ones in the country. Bringing his boys to them—for lunch, of course, if not for dinner, followed by some show of appreciation through music or drama—was a marvelous expression of gratitude, as well as a way of keeping the purse strings open. These well-to-do men and women could see their charity turned into flesh and blood, so to say.

If Don Bosco could not bring the boys, he often made a little side trip himself, e.g. to his old friends the Moglias or to the De Maistres. Of course, one of his biggest benefactors was his brother. Whenever Joseph came to Turin, he brought along some produce or livestock for the poor boys of Valdocco. The boys, in turn, felt a great deal of affection and respect for "Signor Giuseppe." Indeed, sometimes Don Bosco invited him to address a few words to the boys at the Oratory (in a "good night"?), which he would do, offering some sound advice in Piedmontese dialect.

So there were many sound reasons for these trips, and they got bigger and more spectacular as the years went by. We are surprised, then, to learn that they stopped abruptly after 1864. The burden of Don Bosco's work had grown so heavy that he could no longer afford to be absent from the Oratory for so long in that fashion. We might also note that Father Alasonatti, his one truly experienced and mature helper, died in 1865. And Don Bosco himself turned fifty that year; both age and ill health were catching up with him. He continued to go to Becchi for our Lady's feast until 1870 and to take along the choir and the band, but the "golden era" had passed.

Besides BM III-VII, see Luigi Deambrogio, *Le passeggiate autunnali di Don Bosco per i colli monferrini* (Castelnuovo Don Bosco: Istituto Salesiano, 1975); Giovanni Battista Francesia, *Don Bosco e le sue passeggiate autunnali nel Monferrato* (Turin: Libreria Salesiana, 1897); idem, *Don Bosco e le sue ultime passeggiate* (Turin: Libreria Salesiana, 1897); idem, *Short Popular Life of Don Bosco* (London: Salesian Press, 1905), pp. 185–189.

Religious
Celebrations

Progress in music • Procession to
Our Lady of Consolation • Award
from the city and from the Schools
for the Poor • Holy Thursday •
The footwashing rite

The dangers to which youngsters were exposed in matters of religion and morality called for greater efforts to safeguard them. In the night school, as well as in the day program, we thought it would be good to add courses in piano, organ, and even instrumental music to those in vocal music. So I found myself as teacher of vocal and instrumental music, of piano and organ, though I had never truly been a student of them myself. Goodwill made up for everything.

Having prepared a group of the best soprano voices, we began to give recitals at the Oratory; afterwards we ventured into Turin, to Rivoli,[1] Moncalieri,[2] Chieri, and other centres. Canon Louis Nasi and Fr Michelangelo Chiatellino[3] were willing helpers in training our musicians, accompanying them, and conducting them at their public performances in various towns. Since choirs of boy sopranos with orchestral accompaniment had not often been heard up till then, and our solos, duets, and full choral renderings were so novel,[4] our music was spoken of everywhere and our singers were much sought after for various solemn occasions. Canon Louis Nasi and Fr Michelangelo Chiatellino were generally the two accompanists of our emerging philharmonic society.[5]

Every year we used to go to perform at a religious function at the Church of Our Lady of Consolation. This year we marched in procession from the Oratory.[6] The singing along the way and the music in church drew a numberless crowd of people. Mass was celebrated, holy communion received, and then I gave a short sermon suited to the occasion in the underground chapel. Finally, the Oblates of Mary[7] put a fine breakfast for us in the cloisters of the shrine.

In this way we began to overcome human respect,[8] we gathered youngsters, and we had opportunities to inculcate with the greatest prudence a spirit of morality and respect for authority and to encourage frequent reception of the holy sacraments. But such novelty gave rise to rumours.

In this year, too, the city of Turin sent another deputation composed of Chev. Peter Ropolo, Capello called Moncalvo, and Comm. Duprè[9] to assess the vague reports that were being put about. They were highly satisfied with us. When their report was sent in, an award of 1000 francs was decreed,[10] and a very flattering letter. From that year the city assigned an annual subsidy that was paid until 1878, when the 300 francs, which the judicious rulers of Turin had budgeted to provide lighting for the night school for the benefit of the sons of the people, was withdrawn.[11]

The Schools for the Poor also sent a deputation, headed by Chev. Gonella, to visit us. That work had also introduced night schools and music schools, using our method. As a mark of their approval, they gave us another award of a thousand francs.

Every year on Holy Thursday, we used to go together to visit the altars of repose.[12] But because of the ridicule — we would even say contempt — not a few of the boys no longer dared to join their companions. To encourage our young men ever more to disdain human respect, in that year for the first time we marched in procession to make those visits,[13] singing the *Stabat Mater* and chanting the *Miserere*.[14] Then youngsters of every age and condition were seen joining us along the route and racing to join our lines. Everything went off in a peaceful and orderly fashion.

That evening was the first time that we performed the ceremony of the washing of the feet. For this purpose twelve youngsters were chosen, who are usually called the twelve apostles. When the ritual washing was finished, a moral exhortation was preached to the public. Afterwards the twelve apostles were all invited for a frugal supper, and each one was given a small gift which he proudly carried home.[15]

Likewise in that year the stations of the cross were erected according to the prescriptions of the Church and solemnly blessed.[16] At each station there was a brief little sermon, and an appropriate motet was sung.

In such ways our humble Oratory continued to consolidate at the same time that grave events were running their course, events which were destined to change the face of Italian politics, and perhaps the world's.

Notes

1. A town then about eight miles west of Turin, now part of the city.

2. A small city then about six miles south of Turin, now also part of the city.

3. Father Chiatellino (d. 1901), a doctor of theology, helped in the oratories, provided funds for needy boys, and bought various publications from Don Bosco (Stella, *EcSo*, pp. 172, 379, 556, 568). See also MB XX.

4. "Gave such an impression of novelty" would probably be more accurate.

5. The second reference to the two priests is repetitious; Don Bosco added it to Father Berto's copy.

6. The year was 1848. This annual procession was continued until 1854. The church is about six blocks from the Oratory.

7. The Oblates of the Virgin Mary were founded in 1815 by Father Pius Bruno Lanteri. They work "to form an educated, young, active clergy, devoted to the Church and the Holy See, resolved to struggle against the bad press and to propagate good reading matter," to conduct parish missions, and to aid the poor (Cristiani, *A Cross for Napoleon*, pp. 105, 103). They are also foreign missionaries and teachers. The Oblates cared for the shrine of Our Lady of Consolation until 1857, when the government expelled them because of their loyalty to the Holy See.

8. In the preceding chapter, Don Bosco spoke of verbal and physical assaults on the clergy. We may presume that the boys of the Oratory were taunted too as they came and went

An aerial view of eastern Turin shows piazza Vittorio Veneto in the lower right, the Po River, the Church of the Great Mother of God to the left, and the Mount of the Capuchins at the right-center. In the background are the Turinese hills.

on Sundays, and the schoolboys as they went to their daily classes in the city. Among the schoolboys of Turin Don Bosco's stood out in their hand-me-down or military surplus clothing, which made them the objects of juvenile humor at any time, and all the more at a time of increasing anti-clericalism. Obviously the presence of hundreds of boys in procession went far to overcome those kinds of problems.

When Don Bosco speaks of overcoming human respect, he also means that one does what is right, regardless of what others say or think. For those as subject to peer pressure as adolescents are, human respect is a formidable obstacle to spirituality and morality; e.g. it could keep a lad from making his Easter duty (chapter 40).

9. All three men were members of the city council and all three later served on Don Bosco's lottery committee when he was raising funds for the Church of Saint Francis de Sales. Ropolo was an ironmonger. Gabriel Capello, a master furniture maker, may have been from Moncalvo, a town about midway between Asti and Casale in east central Piedmont. (Stella, *EcSo*, pp. 87, 625)

10. Teresio Bosco's already cited estimate of the value of the lira (chapter 1, comment) is actually placed here in his notes to the *Memoirs*. He cautions that the estimate fluctuates with the commodity being valued: the price of bread, a worker's daily wage, apartment rent, etc.

A skilled mason could make 500 lire a year; but his little apprentice mason would bring home only forty centesimi a day (about seventy lire during the whole April-October construction season). To feed his apprentices, on the other hand—and any other boarders—Don Bosco had to pay fourteen centesimi for a pound of bread. (T. Bosco, SP, pp. 76, 140) If he had ten persons to feed and each consumed a pound of bread a day, he had to spend 511 lire in a year—just for bread.

In fact, during the months October-December 1853, when there were about forty boarders at the Valdocco hospice, Don Bosco spent 1600 lire for food. In 1854, with ninety boys, he was spending from thirty-one to seventy-eight centesimi per day per boy for all expenses (food, clothing, medicine, tuition, taxes). Rent for his three oratories in 1850 amounted to 2400 lire. (Stella, *EcSo*, pp. 77–78, 201–211, 371–372)

11. In 1847 an award of three hundred lire had been made. In

1848, besides the thousand-lire award, an annual subsidy of three hundred lire was assigned. Don Bosco returns to the cancellation of this subsidy; evidently it deeply hurt him, or more precisely, prevented him from taking in some boys that he could have fed and clothed with it.

12. After the Mass of the Lord's Supper on Holy Thursday, the Holy Eucharist is removed to a side altar as a symbol of the Lord's being seized and taken away for trial and execution. This side altar, where the Lord "reposed" until the Easter vigil Mass, was elaborately decorated with candles and flowers, and pious Christians spent much of the day in prayer, keeping vigil with Christ (cf. Matthew 26:36–41). If there were several churches nearby, they would make a little pilgrimage by visiting them in turn.

After the liturgical reforms, Mass is celebrated in the evening and the Eucharist is kept at the altar of repose only until midnight. There is much more emphasis on the Mass, the footwashing, and the Lord's new commandment of love; while there is less emphasis on keeping vigil with Christ and his being taken away, the faithful are still encouraged to spend some time with him on the night of his great gifts of the Eucharist and the priesthood and of his arrest.

13. Don Bosco maintained this practice until 1866, always accompanying the boys himself. Since many of the churches in Turin were close by, it was easily done.

14. The *Stabat Mater* is a medieval Latin hymn traditionally associated with Christ's passion. The Miserere is Psalm 51, a psalm of repentance; the Church has always given it a special place in her Friday liturgy because Christ died for our sins on a Friday.

Don Bosco seems to imply that the boys sang as they went along in procession. Ceria maintains that they sang in the various churches, with the permission of the pastors (MO, p. 210).

15. The rite of footwashing, in imitation of Jesus at the Last Supper (John 13:1–11), is part of the liturgy of the Mass of the Lord's Supper. Since that Mass was celebrated in the morning in Don Bosco's time, evidently he made a separate ceremony out of it so that more boys would be able to attend.

The chief celebrant, portraying Christ, was Don Bosco himself. He washed the feet of the twelve chosen "apostles." This sound liturgical practice became a tradition in Salesian houses, as did the practice of inviting the twelve to dine

with the Salesians and giving each a little gift, e.g. a medal
or a prayer book.

16. The stations of the cross, or the way of the cross, is a popular Lenten devotion, though it may be prayed any time.
Images representing fourteen phases of Christ's passion are
set up on the church wall (or outdoors), and the faithful
meditate before each one. This may be done publicly or
privately.

A particular ritual is used in setting up and blessing the
stations. The set at the Oratory was erected on April 1, 1847,
and the first devotions performed the next day. Beginning in
1848, Don Bosco and the boys prayed the stations on the
Fridays of March. Later the pious practice was observed on
all the Fridays of Lent, a custom still kept in Salesian communities and in Catholic parishes generally.

Thirty-three
Lire for Pius IX

*1849 • The closing of the seminaries •
The Pinardi house • Peter's Pence and
Pius IX's rosaries • The Guardian Angel
Oratory • A visit from some deputies*

This year was very memorable. The war between Piedmont and Austria, begun the previous year, had shaken all Italy.[1] Public schools were suspended. The seminaries, especially those in Turin and Chieri, were closed and occupied by the army.[2] As a consequence, the diocesan clerics had neither teachers nor a place to gather. It was then, to have at least the consolation of doing what we could to mitigate these public calamities, that we rented the whole of the Pinardi house.[3] The tenants screamed; they threatened me, my mother, even the proprietor. Though great financial sacrifices had to be made, we still succeeded in getting possession of the whole building. Thus that den of iniquity, which for twenty years had been at the service of Satan, was at our disposal.[4] It embraced the whole site which now forms the courtyard between the Church of Mary Help of Christians and the house behind it.[5]

In this way we were able to increase our classes, to extend the chapel, and double our playground space. The number of young men rose to thirty.[6] But the main aim, as in fact happened, was to be able to gather together the diocesan seminarians. We can say that our Oratory house for almost 20 years became the diocesan seminary.[7]

Towards the end of 1848, political events forced the Holy Father Pius IX to flee Rome and seek refuge at Gaeta.[8] This great Pontiff had already shown us many times his customary kindness.[9] When the rumour got about that he was in financial straits, a collection was taken up in Turin. It was called *Peter's Pence*.[10] A committee composed of Dr Canon Francis Valinotti[11] and Marquis Gustavo Cavour came to the Oratory. Our collection amounted to 35 francs.[12] It was a small sum,[13] which we tried to make a bit more acceptable to the Holy Father with a message[14] that pleased him very much.

The Pope expressed his pleasure in a letter to Card. Antonucci, at that time nuncio in Turin, and now archbishop of Ancona.[15] He asked the nuncio to convey to us how much consolation he received from our offering, but even more from the sentiments accompanying it. Finally, with his apostolic blessing he sent us a parcel of 60 dozen rosaries, which were solemnly distributed on July 20 of that year [1850].[16] See the booklet[17] printed on that occasion, and various newspapers.[18] Letter of Card. Antonucci, at that time nuncio to Turin.[19]

The growing number of youngsters attending the oratories made it necessary to consider opening another centre. This was the Holy Guardian Angel Oratory in Vanchiglia,[20] near the place where, especially through the work of Marchioness Barolo, the Church of St Julia was later built.

Fr John Cocchis[21] had some years previously established that oratory with a scope somewhat like ours. But consumed by love of his country, he judged it better to teach his pupils the use of rifle and sword, put himself at their head, and march against the Austrians, which he did in fact.[22]

That particular oratory was closed for a full year.[23] When we rented it, Dr John Vola, of happy memory, was entrusted with its direction.[24] This oratory continued until 1871, when it moved alongside the parish church. Marchioness Barolo left a legacy for this need, on condition that the boys' centre and the chapel be attached to the parish, as has been done.[25]

A solemn visit was paid to the Oratory at that time by a committee of deputies and others appointed by the ministry of the interior, who came to honour us with their presence.[26] They inspected the whole place, talking to everyone in a friendly way. They then made a full report to the Chamber of Deputies.[27] This report was the subject of long and lively debate, as may be seen in the *Gazzetta Piemon-*

tese[28] of 29 March 1850. The Chamber of Deputies gave a grant of 300 francs to our boys. Urbano Ratazzi, who was then minister of the interior,[29] designated a sum of 2000 francs for us. The documents may be consulted.[30]

Amongst my pupils at last I had one who donned the clerical habit. Ascanio Savio,[31] presently rector of the Refuge, was the first seminarian from the Oratory. His clothing ceremony took place at the end of October of that year.

Notes

1. See the introduction and the bibliography.

2. Archbishop Fransoni ordered the seminaries to be shut down and the seminarians sent home early in 1848 because, despite his explicit orders to remain aloof from politics, many of the students were ardently supporting the new Constitution and war with Austria, taking part in demonstrations, wearing the revolutionary tricolor, etc. (See chapter 51, note 4.) When war came, the army needed facilities, and the seminaries were empty.

3. The previous lease had been with Soave. The new lease, at 1150 lire per year from April 1, 1849, to March 31, 1852, was made directly with Pinardi. The contract, dated June 22, 1849, was signed by Father Borel as lessee. Don Bosco, for the first time, signed as witness.

4. Although Giraudi (p. 95) and Stella (*EcSo*, p. 176) state that Don Bosco subleased the whole house in 1847–1848, Lemoyne (BM III, 429) and Don Bosco himself (here and in chapter 54) say that some tenants still remained on the ground floor till 1849. The implication, even stronger in chapter 54, is that they were prostitutes.

5. The building behind the basilica includes the Church of Saint Francis de Sales, the structure built on the site of the Pinardi house, and the hospice annex. The church, the annex, and what remains of the courtyard were once Pinardi's yard. Much of the yard between the basilica and the church was built over when the basilica was enlarged in the 1930's.

6. The number of boarders living at the Oratory.

7. Like the young students boarding with Don Bosco, the seminarians lived at the Oratory and went to school in the city. (Sections of the seminary had been left unoccupied by the

government.) Naturally Don Bosco admitted only those who had the archbishop's approval. Whoever could, paid a modest fee; the rest were kept free of charge.

Don Bosco was undoubtedly providing an invaluable service for the Church of Turin. He considered the fostering of priestly and religious vocations to be of the highest importance and rated it as one of the purposes of the Salesian Society (BM V, 637, no. 5; cf. 1984 Constitutions, article 28). In the coming years, bishops of other dioceses also boarded some of their seminarians with him. This led, unintentionally, to long and bitter conflict with two archbishops of Turin who charged Don Bosco with stealing their seminarians for his own congregation.

It is estimated that in his lifetime 2500 diocesan priests came from the Oratory or other Salesian schools — not counting men who entered religious life.

8. A city about two-thirds of the way down the coast from Rome toward Naples, within the Kingdom of Naples. The Pope stayed there from November 24, 1848, to April 12, 1850.

9. We know of only two occasions. In 1846, at Don Bosco's request he had granted faculties for three years for the Oratory to celebrate solemn midnight Mass at Christmas, a privilege normally reserved for parish churches. In 1847 he allowed himself to be enrolled among the members of the Company of Saint Aloysius.

10. In the Middle Ages, this name was given to an offering sent by Christian nations to the Holy See. On the initiative of French Catholics, the practice was revived when Pius IX was driven into exile by the Roman revolution. The Peter's Pence collection is still taken up annually around the Catholic world for the administrative needs of the Holy See and for charities which it supports.

In promoting this collection for Pius IX, Don Bosco was motivated not by a personal relationship with this particular Pope (that would develop in the future) but by a deep reverence for the Vicar of Christ, whoever he might be. This devotion to the Holy Father he made a hallmark of the Salesian spirit. See indexes to BM, and particularly BM V, 383, 635; VII, 107–109; X, 353; XIV, 461; XV, 368–369. See also 1984 Constitutions, articles 13 and 125, and the commentary on both in [Francesco Maraccani] *The Project of Life of the Salesians of Don Bosco: A guide to the Salesian Constitutions*, trans. George Williams (Rome, 1986), pp. 180–187, 899–901; Pietro

Ricaldone, "Learn to Know, Love, and Defend the Pope" (*Acts of the Superior Chapter*, no. 164, May 1951); Egidio Viganò, "Our Fidelity to Peter's Successor" (*Acts of the General Council*, no. 315, October–December 1985).

11. Canon Valinotti (1813?–1873) was from the diocese of Ivrea. When his bishop and Don Bosco cofounded the *Catholic Readings* (chapter 59), he became the business manager of the enterprise and, eventually, the center of a controversy over its direction. (BM IV–VIII)

12. The documents report the total as thirty-three lire, which was given to the collection committee on March 25, 1849.

13. From these words to "consolation he received," three sentences down, was added to the original manuscript by Don Bosco. When Father Berto copied this passage in his manuscript, he added "(and now deceased)" after "Ancona."

14. Don Bosco composed the message, which was read by one of the boys on the solemn occasion of handing over the funds collected. It was then sent along with the offering.

15. When Father Berto was copying the manuscript, he added "and now deceased" at this point. Cardinal Antonucci died on January 29, 1879 (Desramaut, *LesMem*, p. 117). The nuncio wrote to Don Bosco on May 2, 1849:

> In presenting to His Holiness ... another contribution to the Peter's Pence Fund, delivered to me ... on behalf of the committee formed for this purpose in the city of Turin, I took it upon myself to single out for His Holiness' attention the donation of thirty-three lire from your boys. I also mentioned the sentiments they expressed in presenting their contribution to the committee.
>
> In a reply dated April 18, [Cardinal Antonelli] ... informed me that the Holy Father was moved by the loving and sincere contribution of these young apprentices and by their words of filial devotion.
>
> Would you therefore kindly tell them that the Holy Father was pleased by their offering, and considered it singularly precious since it comes from the poor; he felt deeply consoled by seeing that they were already imbued with genuine reverence for the Vicar of Jesus Christ, a sign, no doubt, of the religious principles impressed upon their young minds. (BM III, 367–368)

16. The parcel of rosaries was sent on April 2, 1850, through the pontifical consulate in Genoa. The confusion prevailing in Turin at that time caused considerable delay in delivery, so that it reached the Oratory only in July. The Holy Father's gifts were handed out with great ceremony on Sunday, July 21 (not Saturday, the 20th).

17. It was a little monograph by Don Bosco with, according to the literary custom of the time, a long title: *Breve ragguaglio della festa fattasi nel distribuire il regalo di Pio IX ai giovani degli Oratori di Torino* [A short account of the feast celebrated when Pius IX's gift was distributed to the boys of Turin's oratories] (Turin: Rotta, 1850). The booklet speaks of "oratories" because the boys of the Saint Aloysius Oratory also contributed to the thirty-three lire. Even 720 rosaries were insufficient; Don Bosco had to buy more to ensure that each boy got one.

18. One article particularly worthy of note was written by Gustavo Cavour for his newspaper *L'Armonia* (no. 40, 1849). It is reproduced in BM III, 359–360.

    The Italian edition of René François Rohrbacher's (1789–1856) *Universal Church History*, after recounting some touching stories of offerings which humble persons made to help the Pope, went on to tell about a certain group of very poor artisans who had saved a bit of money daily to put together the sum of thirty-three francs, which they forwarded with a covering letter (Turin: Marietti. 6th printing, XV, 558).

19. This phrase stood in the original prior to the addition noted above (note 13). Don Bosco may have meant to have Father Berto copy out the letter.

20. Vanchiglia was the easternmost of the northern industrial zones, located in the rough triangle formed by the Dora and Po Rivers and corso San Maurizio. It

    > was a cluster of hovels whose walls, blackened by time, threatened to come tumbling down at any moment; it looked like a fortress manned by men hostile to any form of order, greedy for the possessions of others, driven by some fierce instinct to evil, ever ready to shed blood. Crime, poverty, and vice rubbed shoulders. In this neighborhood was born the notorious, feared gang of Vanchiglia [cf. BM III, 231–232]. No one dared set foot there after dark, not even the police. (BM III, 394)

    The Guardian Angel Oratory was on the property of a lawyer named Bronzino. The facilities were a shed in the vegetable garden and a rustic courtyard, which served as playground, chapel, theater, and gymnasium. (Stella, *EcSo*, pp. 71–72, n. 1; cf. BM III, 319) It was at the corner of via Tarino and via Santa Giulia.

21. Father John Cocchi (Don Bosco added an *s* to his name) was a zealous and unselfish priest, compassionate, enterprising, and patient. The Murialdo cousins worked with him, and he

enjoyed the support of Marchioness Barolo, Marquis Robert d'Azeglio, and others.

22. Without doubt Father Cocchi (and quite a few other priests) got caught up in the patriotic spirit of the hour. It was one of those epochs of history when only those who lived through it could imagine what it was like.

   On the other hand, Father Cocchi was not exactly the leader of the expedition that Don Bosco makes of him. He went as chaplain because he did not want to let the boys go alone. Those would-be soldiers numbered about two hundred. When they arrived at the front lines at Vercelli, the divisional commander would not recognize them as soldiers. In the meantime, the Austrians had routed the Piedmontese at Novara (March 23, 1849), and the youthful brigade snuck home to Turin in small groups. (BM III, 392–393)

23. After the fiasco of the oratorians' march to the war zone, their oratory stayed closed. The archbishop, sternly opposed to liberalization and unification, was content to leave it so. In any case, Father Cocchi did not return to Turin until October, and then he got involved in a new project and lacked the time and the resources to reopen the oratory (BM III, 393; cf. Giraudo and Biancardi, p. 182). By the end of 1849, Father Cocchi was forming a society of priests and laymen to work for the education of orphaned and abandoned young men by teaching them trades. This developed into the Work for Artisans [*Opera degli Artigianelli*], which eventually founded a college on corso Valdocco (see chapter 42, note 19).

   In 1851, after Archbishop Fransoni had been banished, Father Cocchi founded a new oratory in Borgo Dora — at the chapel of Saint Martin of the Mills! In later years he also turned his attention to other forms of youth ministry by opening a number of agricultural schools and schools for juvenile offenders.

   It did not take Don Bosco and Father Borel long to realize how sorely an oratory was needed in Borgo Vanchiglia. They consulted with Father Cocchi, obtained the archbishop's written authorization and the help of Father Louis Fantini, pastor of the Church of the Annunciation, and reopened the Guardian Angel Oratory in October 1850. (BM III, 393)

24. Father John Baptist Vola (1805?–1872). Father Carpano preceded him as director, transferred from the Saint Aloysius Oratory, where Father Ponte took over. He did not stay long,

nor did Father Vola. The Murialdo cousins then took charge and persevered through the problems that had discouraged their predecessors. (Giraudo and Biancardi, p. 182)

25. Marchioness Barolo provided for the building of the Church of Saint Julia (1866). Don Bosco gave title to the oratory to the pastor, and the oratory relocated and took a new name in 1871 (*ibid.*).

26. In 1849, a certain Volpato, a relative of the Gastaldis, forwarded a petition to the interior ministry, through the Senate, requesting a subsidy for the Oratory. Although he did so in Don Bosco's name, Don Bosco was not informed. Volpato worked in one of the government ministries and had advised Don Bosco to seek semiofficial government backing; Don Bosco had declined.

    The Senate appointed a committee of three senators to study the request, and they came to Valdocco one January afternoon in 1850. The three were Count Frederick Sclopis, Marquis Ignatius Pallavicino, and Count Louis Provana of Collegno. (BM IV, 12–18).

    Frederick Sclopis (1798–1878), count of Salerano, was president of the Senate, a royal counselor, a distinguished historian, and a devout Catholic. Renowned as a jurist, he served on the five-man international tribunal which arbitrated the *Alabama* case between the United States and Great Britain in 1872.

    Marquis Pallavicino (1800–1871) must have been the chairman since he filed the report with the Senate.

    Louis Provana of Collegno (1786–1861), another devout Catholic, was the younger brother of the Oratory's defender before the Turin city council (chapter 41). He served in the foreign affairs ministry between 1815 and 1825, and then moved to the education department; later he was appointed to the council of State, of which he became president in 1840 (Stella, *EcSo*, pp. 56–60).

27. The lower house of the Sardinian parliament. As indicated in the preceding note, the delegates were in fact members of the Senate.

28. The government newspaper.

29. Rattazzi (1808–1873), the anticlerical leader of the moderate left in parliament, was president of the Chamber of Deputies (1852–1853), minister of justice and cults (1853–1854), and interior minister (1854–1860). He supported Don Bosco's work, appreciating what this priest was doing for the poor.

When Don Bosco was forming the Salesian Society, the minister gave him some valuable hints on how to get around the law which suppressed religious orders (BM V, 459–562). He served two brief, unsuccessful periods as prime minister in 1862 and 1867. Don Bosco spelled his name with one *t*.

30. Especially the *Atti Ufficiali* of March 1, 1850. Marquis Pallavicino described Don Bosco as "a distinguished and zealous priest" and his institute as "religious, moral, and useful." He held that "it would be a serious loss to the whole city" if such an institution had to "suspend its work or to close down for want of a helping hand to continue such work, however incomplete it might be," as Don Bosco had done up till then.

The marquis concluded the report thus:

> Our committee believes that, to be true to itself, to the Senate which honored it with this precious charge, and to society, it should most strongly recommend to the minister of the interior to take effective steps to help such a useful and valuable work.

31. Ascanio Savio (1831–1902) came from Castelnuovo. He was one of the group of youngsters whom Don Bosco had tutored through high school level, hoping that they would stay with him and help him in the oratory work (see chapter 53). Savio's clothing ceremony took place in 1848 at the Cottolengo, the archdiocesan seminary being closed. Later he got permission to stay at the Oratory and help Don Bosco instead of living at the seminary in Chieri. In his last years Don Bosco loved to recall how much precious help this seminarian had given him. (BM III, 307–309).

The first clothing ceremony for seminarians at the Oratory took place on February 2, 1851, involving Buzzetti, Gastini, Felix Reviglio, and James Bellia. (BM IV, 161)

❦ 51 ❦

No Politics

National festivals

In those days a strange event took place which caused no little upset to our meetings. People wanted our humble Oratory to take part in public demonstrations which were being staged in cities and towns under the name of national festivals.[1] Those who took part in them and wished to make a public display of their patriotism parted their hair in the middle and let it fall in curls in the back; they wore tight-fitting jackets of various colours, and a national flag, a medal, and a blue cockade on the breast.[2] Thus attired, they went in procession singing anthems to national unity.

The chief promoter of these demonstrations was Marquis Robert d'Azeglio.[3] He sent us a formal invitation. Despite my refusal, he sent us whatever we would need to make an honourable appearance with the rest. A spot was reserved for us in piazza Vittorio,[4] amongst all the organizations of whatever name, purpose, and condition. What was I to do? To refuse was to declare myself an enemy of Italy. To acquiesce would mean accepting principles which I judged would have disastrous results.[5]

"My Lord Marquis," I answered the above-praised d'Azeglio,[6] "this family of mine, these boys who come here from all over the city, are not a corporation. I would make a laughingstock of myself were I to pretend to make my own an institution which depends entirely on civic charity."

"Exactly. Let civic charity know that this newborn work isn't against modern institutions. That will work to your advantage. Support for your work will increase. The city council and I myself will give you generous help."

"My Lord Marquis, it is my firm system to keep out of anything political. Never *pro*, never *con*."

"What do you want to do, then?"

"To do what little good I can for abandoned youngsters, using all my powers to make them good Christians in regard to religion, honest citizens in civil society."

"I understand all that," replied the marquis. "But you're making a mistake. If you persist in this principle, everybody will abandon you, and your work will become impossible. One must study the world, understand it, and shape both old and new institutions to the needs of the times."[7]

"Thank you for your goodwill and the advice you offer. Invite me anywhere that a priest can exercise charity, and you'll find me ready to sacrifice life and means. But I want now and always to remain outside politics."[8]

That renowned nobleman went away satisfied. From that day on he had no further dealings with us. After him many other laymen and priests deserted me. More than that, I was left quite alone after the incident I am now about to relate.

Notes

1. Don Bosco has backtracked to February 8, 1848, when King Charles Albert announced his intention of granting a constitution. The demonstrations followed that announcement.

2. These were the insignia of revolution. The national flag is the tricolor (green, white, and red), reminiscent of the flag of republican France. A great deal of romanticism marked the beginnings of the Risorgimento. Lemoyne wrote of it:

   > [The boys] were fascinated by the sight of young choirboys dressed in black velvet trousers and shirts, wearing felt hats adorned by tiny Italian flags. Their hair fell in curls to their shoulders, a dagger was slung at the belt, and a small shield representing Italy hung from a slender gold-plated chain on the chest. (BM III, 292–293)

   On the general climate, see Desramaut, *SpLife*, pp. 22–23.

3. Azeglio is a small town southeast of Ivrea. The d'Azeglio brothers, whose family name was Taparelli, were great Italian patriots. The most famous, Massimo (1798–1866), was prime minister (1849–1852) until unseated by Cavour and

Rattazzi. He was Manzoni's son-in-law and earned more renown as an author than as a statesman.

We have already referred to Robert (1790–1862) as the promoter of religious toleration and defender of the archbishop's palace (chapter 48, notes 3 and 5). Besides being a senator and politician, he was an art critic and director of the royal art gallery.

A third brother, Louis (1793–1862), was a Jesuit priest. He was an accomplished musician, but his main field was philosophy, which he taught for many years. He published several textbooks and treatises on political philosophy. He was an editor of the Jesuits' Roman periodical *La Civiltà cattolica*.

4. Piazza Vittorio Veneto is a great square, one end of which opens on the Po, over which the Vittorio Emanuele I Bridge leads to the Church of the Great Mother of God. In that church, modeled on the Pantheon of Rome, the city government organized a solemn ritual of thanksgiving, celebrated on February 27, 1848. The choice of that church is ironic, for King Victor Emmanuel I had erected it in thanksgiving for the defeat of revolutionary liberalism and the restoration of legitimate (absolute) government in 1815.

   King Charles Albert and the royal family were there, as well as the members of the city government; deputations from the various towns of Piedmont and from Liguria, Savoy, Nice, and Sardinia; and representatives from all the workers' guilds. This was the meeting to which Don Bosco was invited. (Nice, like Savoy, was part of the Kingdom of Sardinia until ceded to France in 1860; it was Garibaldi's native city.)

   In all, some fifty thousand people gathered in the huge square. But the archbishop refused to participate and would not allow the *Te Deum* to be sung. He did permit benediction of the Blessed Sacrament to be given. He forbade his seminarians to take part, and when they did, all decked out in the cockade of revolution, it was the last straw (after earlier clashes; cf. T. Bosco, BN, p. 173); the seminaries were closed.

5. These were the principles of political liberalism as it was then emerging. Ceria assessed Don Bosco's position thus:

   > Don Bosco sincerely loved his country. But because of his relationship and especially his frequent conversations with the archbishop, he saw what others missed: how armies, in the name of patriotism, were being aligned against the Church. So important

reasons inspired his reserve. Besides, it seemed to him that he had enough on his hands to gather abandoned youths and make good citizens out of them. (*San Giovanni Bosco nella vita e nelle opere* [Turin: SEI, 1938], p. 98)

During his life Don Bosco was deeply concerned with political matters, but not with party politics (chapter 37, note 7; chapter 45, comment). "I will never belong to a political party," he said. In his dealings with public officials (as well as with bishops and cardinals), he was a skillful politician. But when he had to deal with politicians, his interests were statesmanship, specifically the politics of Church and State, and social justice, specifically the care of abandoned youth. He entered the political arena of Church and State only when both sides pressed him and the good of souls required it. See Desramaut, *SpLife*, pp. 36–37.

Don Bosco revealed his patriotism not in flag-waving but in practice: in his willingness to mediate between the Vatican and the Italian government despite the difficulties involved and the misunderstandings risked; in his ability to distinguish the proper roles of the Church and the State and remain at the service of both; in his never-failing respect for the king (e.g. BM XV, 257–264) and government ministers; in his insistence that his work performed a public good as well as a religious one, that he was forming good citizens of Italy as well as good Christians; in the love for Italy's history, language, and culture that he showed through his study, textbooks, classroom practice, and educational outings. On his mediation, see BM VIII, 43–76, 237–242, 259–261; X, 183–245; XIII, 373–376; XIV, 72–74; and Francesco Motto, "Don Bosco mediatore tra Cavour e Antonelli nel 1858," *Ricerche storiche salesiane* V (1986), 3–20.

6. A satiric note.

7. This, of course, is exactly what Don Bosco was doing. He had run afoul of the pastors of Turin because he *was* adapting the apostolate to new times. But he refused to concede that partisan political involvement was a necessary part of such adaptation.

This has remained a firm Salesian principle, though not in as absolute a sense as previously. See the 1984 Constitutions, article 33; cf. article 31, and the commentary on both in Maraccani, pp. 312–319, 327–335; contrast that with the 1966 Constitutions, article 14, and Regulations, articles 45, 378, 386; and the evolution of those articles into the 1972

Constitutions, articles 17 and 19 (cf. Joseph Aubry's commentary, *Una via che conduce all'amore* [Turin: LDC, 1974], pp. 112–116, 121–126).

8. Bishop Jeremiah Bonomelli of Cremona (1831–1914) was a respected observer of the social issues at the turn of the century, and a moderate in the thorny issues of Church and State. In *Questioni religiose, morali, sociali del giorno* (Milan: Cogliati, 1892), I, 310, he wrote:

> One day, not many years back, I was chatting familiarly with that man of God, Father John Bosco, a true apostle of youth whose name is still held in benediction. With his characteristic simplicity and practical tact, he told me something I will never forget, in these exact words: "In 1848 I realized that if I wished to do a little good I had to stand aside from all politics. I've always kept to this policy, and so I've been able to achieve a little and avoided obstacles. Indeed, I've found help where I'd least have expected it." This rule is the fruit of experience and requires no comment.

Don Bosco saw clearly the dangers of party politics—the factionalism against which Madison warned Americans in *Federalist* no. 10. Taking one side or another would alienate some of his backers, could turn the government against him, and even risked disaster; he had just seen some of the king's favorite ministers completely disgraced.

But Don Bosco did take a stand when politics directly involved the Pope: "As a Catholic I stand by the Pope and support him unequivocally. . . . If we Catholics say we are loyal to the Pontiff of Rome, then we have to be loyal in all things" (Bonetti chronicle, July 7, 1862).

Don Bosco was well aware that the social world that encouraged political liberalism was not going to go away. Marx and Engels published the *Communist Manifesto* in London in February 1848. Don Bosco, wrote Lemoyne,

> was one of the few who understood immediately—and he said so a thousand times—that the revolutionary movement was not just a passing storm. Not all its promises to the people were unjust; many of them filled real needs. The workers demanded equality of rights without class distinction, more justice, and improvement of living conditions.

> Don Bosco [also] saw how wealth was becoming the monopoly of ruthless capitalists. Employers imposed unjust labor contracts on individual, defenseless workers, and crudely violated provisions for the Sunday rest. These abuses were bound to produce disastrous results; workers lived in misery, lost their faith, and fell prey to subversive principles. (BM IV, 55–56)

If responsible individuals and the Church did not rise to defend the dignity of the poor and the workers, others were ready to exploit them. Don Bosco was acting. Staying out of politics did not mean avoiding the real issues. (See T. Bosco BN, pp. 195–198)

See also Giuseppe Spalla, *Don Bosco e il suo ambiente socio-politico* (Turin: LDC, 1975); Stella, *ReCa*, chapter IV, "Storia e salvezza" [History and Salvation], pp. 59–100.

Another Threat to the Oratories

A particular episode

On the Sunday following the festival just mentioned,[1] at two in the afternoon I was at recreation with the youngsters. One of them was reading *L'Armonia*[2] when the priests who usually came to give me a hand in the sacred ministry appeared in a body. They were decked out with medals and cockades and carried a tricolour flag. Worse, they had a copy of a truly immoral newspaper called *L'Opinione*.[3]

One of them, a man of respectable zeal and learning, came right up to me. Noticing the boy reading *L'Armonia* beside me, he sneered, "This is outrageous! It's time we finished with this rubbish." With that, he grabbed *L'Armonia* from the boy's hand, tore it into a thousand pieces, threw them on the ground, spat on them, and stomped all over them.

Having thus freely expressed his political fervour, he stood facing me. "Now this is a worthwhile paper," he said, thrusting *L'Opinione* in my face. "This paper and no other should be read by every true and honest citizen."

His manner of speaking and acting took my breath away. Not wishing to compound the scandal in a place where good example should be given, I limited myself to asking him and his colleagues to discuss such matters in private and amongst ourselves only.

"No, sir," he answered. "No longer should anything be either private or secret. Let everything be brought into the clear light of day."

At that moment the bell called us all to church. It summoned also one of those priests, who had been charged with preaching a short sermon on morality to the poor youngsters. But on this occasion it was really immoral.[4] Liberty, emancipation, and independence resounded through the whole sermon.[5]

I was in the sacristy, impatient for a chance to speak and put an end to this disorder. But the preacher left the church immediately after finishing the sermon, and no sooner was benediction given than he invited priests and boys to join him. Heartily intoning national songs and passionately waving the flag, they marched straight to the Mount of the Capuchins. There a formal promise was pronounced not to go back to the Oratory again unless they were invited and received with all their *national* insignia.

While all this was going on, I had no way to express either my thoughts or my reasoning. But I was not afraid of anything that clashed with my duty. I let those priests know that they were strictly forbidden to come back to me. The boys then had to report to me one by one before they were readmitted to the Oratory. Everything ended well for me. None of the priests tried to come back.[6] The boys apologised, pleading that they had been misled and promising obedience and discipline.[7]

Notes

1. That would have been March 5, 1848. Since *L'Armonia* began to publish only in July 1848, evidently this event happened much later. According to Lemoyne (BM III, 291–294), a number of lesser incidents led up to the major one described here.

2. The first Piedmontese reforms, promulgated in October 1847, included the relaxation of press censorship. A proliferation of political newspapers followed. Among the first was the reform-minded *Il Risorgimento*, published by Camillo Cavour.

   L'Armonia [Harmony] was a moderate Catholic paper founded by Bishop Louis Moreno of Ivrea (1800–1878), Canon Lawrence Gastaldi, Marquis Gustavo Cavour, and Father William Audisio. After Marquis Charles Emmanuel Birago of Bische (1797–1862), Marquis Fabio Invrea, and

Father James Margotti (1823–1887) joined them, the paper became more militant, even "intransigent." Father Margotti became its guiding spirit and a major force in Turinese journalism. It ceased publication in 1859, to be replaced by *Unità cattolica* [Catholic Unity], which Father Margotti directed until his death. (BM III, 290; Stella, *EcSo*, p. 342)

3. *L'Opinione* [Opinion] was a lively and biting anticlerical paper founded in January 1848 by James Durando (1807–1894), brother of Father Mark Anthony Durando, C.M. After Durando, a veteran soldier, was given a command in the war against Austria, Massimo Cordero (1807–1879), marquis of Montezemolo, directed the paper. Durando was later a senator, government minister, and ambassador. A third Durando brother, John (1804–1869), was also a general and fought in the 1848–1849 and 1859 wars of independence and in Crimea. (Stella, *EcSo*, p. 342)

4. Don Bosco uses "immoral" in contrast to "moral" in the previous sentence. The sermon should have edified the boys; instead, it disturbed and confused them.

5. Ceria (*San Giovanni Bosco*, p. 96) writes:

> There was a universal euphoria and a mania for things new. Not a few of the clergy, intolerant of discipline or inflamed by the writings of Gioberti, or naive and deluded, let themselves be carried away on the wave of the general enthusiasm.

But before judging these priests harshly, one should consider what they were trying to do: to show that the clergy understood and supported the people's aspirations for liberty; otherwise, the enemies of religion would take the lead — as, to a great extent, in fact happened. Stella presents the problem quite well in LW, pp. 84–87.

Father Vincenzo Gioberti (1801–1852), an inactive priest, lived, taught, and published in exile from 1833 to 1848; eventually he died in exile. His *Del primato morale e civile degli italiani*, 2 vols. (Brussels, 1843), profoundly stirred Italian patriots by urging national unification under the presidency of the Pope. Gioberti recognized and upheld the importance of religion in private and public life. But the political impulse to make unification possible would have to come from Piedmont. The book's weakness was that it really ignored the problems of the Papal States and the Austrian occupation.

When he returned to Turin from exile in 1848, he immediately became involved in politics. He became president of the Chamber of Deputies and then prime minister-foreign minister for three months in 1848–1849; later he was ambassador to France (1849–1851). As a politician, he was egotistical, adventurous, and secretive at the same time — a formula for disaster.

See Harry Hearder, *Italy in the Age of the Risorgimento, 1790–1870* (New York: Longman, 1983), pp. 195–197; Arthur James Whyte, *The Evolution of Modern Italy* (Oxford: Basil Blackwell, 1959), pp. 49, 71–76.

6. Among the "liberal" priests who broke, at least temporarily, with Don Bosco at this time were Fathers Carpano, Trivero, and Ponte. The fact that Father Ponte moved out of the Oratory on February 29 would indicate a break at that point, two days after the mass demonstration in piazza Vittorio Veneto. Fathers Carpano and Ponte were both working in Don Bosco's oratories later; so the temporary breach was healed in their cases, at least. But apparently it was not in some other cases. The ever-reliable Father Borel once again stood alone with Don Bosco for a while. (Stella, LW, pp. 86, 109–110; *EcSo*, p. 176; BM III, 296–297; IV, 215–221, 254–266)

In these circumstances, Don Bosco decided to organize another retreat for his best boys, like the one of 1847, "his heart set on gathering around him a nucleus of boys truly virtuous, fit to be 'the salt of the earth' and 'the light of the world' [cf. Matthew 5:13–16] among their companions." With most of his older boys enticed away, he was able to assemble only thirteen retreatants, many of whom had also made the 1847 retreat. A new name in the list is Felix Reviglio. (BM III, 297–298; IV, 215–221, 254–266)

7. Almost every one of the older boys went with the "patriotic" priests, and so did most of the younger boys. The oratories had been drawing some five hundred youngsters every Sunday and feast day; for a few Sundays at the height of Turin's national ardor, only thirty or forty came. (BM III, 296)

Almost Alone Again

Fresh difficulties • A consolation •
Father Rosmini and the
Archpriest Peter De Gaudenzi

But I remained alone. On feast days I was obliged to begin hearing confessions early in the morning, to celebrate Mass at nine and preach afterwards; then there were singing classes and literature lessons[1] until midday. At one in the afternoon there was recreation, and then catechism, vespers, an instruction, benediction, more recreation, singing, and school until night.

On weekdays,[2] I was obliged to work during the day for my artisans,[3] and to give *ginnasio* courses to a group of about ten youngsters. In the evening, lessons in French, arithmetic, plainchant, vocal music, piano, and organ all had to be attended to. I do not know how I was able to keep going. God helped me!

A great support and a great consolation to me in those days, however, was Doctor Borrelli. That marvelous priest, though burdened with his other important duties of the sacred ministry, tried to help me every moment he could. He frequently stole from his hours of sleep to come and hear the boys' confessions. He denied rest to his weary body to come and preach to them. This critical situation lasted until I was able to get some relief from the seminarians Savio, Bellia, Vacchetta. But soon I was left without their help. For, following advice given them, they left without a word to me and entered the Oblates of Mary.[4]

On one of those feast days, I had a visit from two priests whom I think it appropriate to name.[5] At the beginning of the catechism period, I was totally occupied with arranging my classes when two clergymen arrived. They were coming with a humble, respectful bearing to commend me and seek information about the origin and system of the Oratory.

As my only answer, I said, "Would you be good enough to help me?" One I asked, "Would you come to the apse and take the big boys?" To the taller one I said, "I entrust to you this class, which is the wildest."

Convinced that they were excellent catechists, I asked one of them to give a short sermon to our boys, and the other to give benediction of the Blessed Sacrament. Both accepted graciously.

The shorter priest was Father Antonio Rosmini, founder of the Institute of Charity.[6] The other was Canon Arch-priest De Gaudenzi, the present bishop of Vigevano. From that time, both of them were always kindly disposed towards our house; in fact they were benefactors.

Notes

1. I.e., lessons in reading, writing, and correctly speaking Italian (Desramaut, *SouAut*, p. 213, n. 1).

2. Monday through Saturday.

3. In effect, Don Bosco was a one-man employment agency for his boys. He found work for them with reputable employers, worked out apprenticeship contracts (a typical example is found in BM IV, 205–206), accompanied them on their first day of work, and visited them every week at their jobs to make sure that they were being well treated and well trained and were fulfilling their responsibilities. If any were sick, he called on them at their lodgings and made sure that they had something to eat. In addition, he used those skills he had learned so long ago in Castelnuovo and Chieri: he made and mended their clothes and helped Mama Margaret prepare, cook, and serve meals for the boarders.

    Teresio Bosco (SP, p. 201) writes of this era:

    Until 1844 specific regulations governed relations between apprentices, young shop clerks, and employers in Piedmont in order to protect the young men and women and to ensure that the employers taught them their trades responsibly and did not take advantage of them.

    A royal edict of 1844, forced upon the king by the "liberals" in the name of progress, abolished these regulations. From then on, the young clerks and workers were on their own, helpless in their employers' hands (cf. Armando Castellani, *Il beato Leonardo Murialdo* [Rome, 1960], I, 468). At the age of eight or nine, they were thrown into jobs demanding twelve to fifteen hours a day, subject to abuse, scandal, and exploitation in the unhealthy environments of factories and shops.

Camillo Cavour, who favored unlicensed freedom for industry and commerce, declared in parliament in 1850, "Perhaps we are too little interested in knowing that in our mills the women and children are working almost one-third longer, if not twice as long, as they are in England" (*Discorsi Parlamentari* [Bologna, 1955], I, 302).

4. Around 1852 Ascanio Savio left Don Bosco to join the Oblates; Don Bosco predicted future problems, but he refused to listen. He became ill and had to leave the Oblates. He then became a prominent diocesan priest and was always a close friend of the Salesians. (BM IV, 342)

James Bellia (1834–1908), an outstanding singer, was one of the illustrious four first singled out by Don Bosco for special studies (1849). By the time he was sixteen, he was teaching less advanced students, as Don Bosco had hoped. He too left Don Bosco around 1852 and became a diocesan priest but remained friendly with Don Bosco. (BM III–IV; V, 382; VII, 405)

Stephen Vacchetta boarded at the Oratory at least in 1853–1854 (Stella, *EcSo*, p. 262). He joined the Oblates despite Don Bosco's prophecy that he would suffer a mental breakdown, which was fulfilled (BM IV, 342–343).

5. This was early in 1850.

6. Antonio Rosmini-Serbati (1797–1855) was a priest from Trent, a patriot, philosopher, and theologian. Ordained in 1821, he sought to reconcile Catholicism with modern thought, both scientific and political. He was a pioneer in reviving the study of Saint Thomas Aquinas. His works and letters fill some seventy-three volumes.

A man of great learning, he was also a man of genuine piety and charity. In 1828 he founded the Institute of Charity (Rosminians), a religious congregation of men, to promote education and charitable works; at one point Don Bosco seriously considered linking his work with this society so as to assure the viability of the oratories. When he began to compose the Salesian rule, he was much influenced by the Rosminians.

In his political writings Father Rosmini tried to counter the anticlericalism and anti-Catholicism that seemed to be taking over the Risorgimento. For a time he was quite close to Pope Pius IX, joining him in his exile at Gaeta. After two of his political books were condemned by the Congregation of the Index (1848), he retired from public life; the specific condemnation was lifted in 1854, but some ideas ostensibly taken from various of his works were again censured in the 1880s.

See NCE, XII, 677–679; *Encyclopaedia Britannica* (Chicago, 1981), VIII, 678–679; BM III–V.

Father Rosmini was still alive when Don Bosco wrote *La Storia d'Italia* (Turin: Paravia, 1855); so he is not mentioned in the first edition. But in the second and later editions, we can detect Don Bosco's affection for the great philosopher and man of charity:

> Antonio Rosmini came from a rich and noble family of Rovereto, a small city near Trent. . . . He was devout, and with the greatest diligence he pursued very difficult studies. . . . His great genius and his diligent study caused his teachers and his fellow students to marvel, and even then to forecast great things of him.

> When he was seventeen, he decided to become a priest. . . . Rosmini read and studied in Rovereto the major systems of philosophy then current in Italy and France. Sickened by all of them, he was inspired to try to unite reason and faith. So he studied theology. After he was ordained a priest, Pius VII urged him to devote himself to philosophy. He returned to his home town and studied with an energy and diligence that seemed prodigious.

> But the spirit of charity that he had shown from his youth remained with him in whatever he did. This was his intention in founding the Institute of Charity, popularly known as the Rosminians after their founder. . . . At Milan he published various philosophical works. After reading one of them without knowing who had written it, Alessandro Manzoni confessed, "Heaven has given a great man to Italy and to the Church in the author of this book. . . ."

> Among the many works of this outstanding philosopher and writer were some that were censured by the Church and put on the Index of Forbidden Books. For some authors this would have been cause for resentful indignation; but for Rosmini it was an opportunity to let the whole world know that his profound learning was coupled with the resolution and humility of a good Catholic. Without any hint of resentment, he answered, "With the sentiments of a son most devoted and obedient to the Holy See, I submit to the ban of the specified works purely and simply and completely, and I wish to assure the Holy Father and the Sacred Congregation of that." . . . .

> His diligent and profound study caused him to fall gravely ill in

1855. . . . Strengthened by the comforts of our Catholic religion, he died after a long illness on July 1, 1855, at the age of 58. (*La Storia d'Italia raccontata alla gioventù* [Turin, 1887], pp. 473–475)

Besides Don Bosco's respect for a benefactor and one whom he regarded as a saint, we may also observe something of his educational methods and aims: a simple style, specific details of time and place, little abstraction (e.g. concerning Father Rosmini's thought), the testimony of a great man (Manzoni), and the repetition of key ideas (study, piety, love for the Pope).

Don Bosco revered the man but kept a cool distance from his philosophy because it had been censured by Rome. This was one of the causes of his problems with Archbishop Gastaldi, who was a champion of Rosminianism (cf. BM XV). When speaking or writing to adults, even bishops, Don Bosco maintained the same ecclesial outlook that he promoted in his textbooks:

Father Rosmini proved himself to be a learned philosopher by the books he wrote, but he revealed himself to be a profoundly Catholic philosopher by his submission to the judgment of the Church. He showed his consistency by professing respect for the See of Peter in deeds as well as words. . . . I do not recall ever seeing a priest say Mass as reverently and devoutly as Rosmini. He was visibly a man of deep faith, which was the source of his love, kindness, modesty and dignified demeanor (BM XIII, 8–9, quoting Don Bosco's letters).

54

Buying the
Pinardi House

*Purchase of the Pinardi and Bellezza
houses • The year 1850*

The year 1849 was painful and sterile, even though it had cost great fatigue and enormous sacrifice. But it was a preparation for 1850, which was less turbulent and much more fruitful.[1]

Let us begin with the Pinardi house.[2] Those who had been dislodged from this house found it hard to take. "Isn't it disgusting," they went round saying, "that a house of entertainment and relaxation should fall into the hands of a priest, and an intolerant priest at that?"[3]

Pinardi, moreover, was [offered][4] a rent almost twice as great as ours. But he felt considerable remorse at getting more money by sinful means. So several times he had offered to sell [the house] if ever I wished to buy it. But his price was exorbitant. He was looking for eighty thousand francs for a building whose value must have been one-third that. God wished to show that he is the master of hearts, and he showed it here.

One feast day, while Doctor Borrelli was preaching, I was at the courtyard gate to prevent assemblies and disturbances[5] when Mr Pinardi came along.

"Hello there," he said. "Don Bosco should buy my house."

"Hello there," I replied. "Mr Pinardi should sell it to me for what it's worth, and I'll buy it at once."

"Of course I'll sell it for what it's worth."

"How much?"

"The price I've been asking."

"I couldn't think of it."

"Make me an offer."

"I can't."

"Why?"

"Because your price is excessive. I don't want to insult you."

"Offer what you wish."

"Will you sell it to me for what it's really worth?"

"On my word of honour, I will."

"Shake hands on it, and I'll make my offer."

"How much, then?"

I suggested to him, "I've had it valued by a friend of yours and mine.[6] He assured me that in its present state we ought to be discussing [a price] between 26 and 28 thousand francs. And, to close the deal, I'll give you 30,000 francs."

"Will you throw in a brooch worth 500 francs as a gift for my wife?"

"I'll give her that," I said.

"Will you pay cash?"

"I'll pay cash."

"When can we sign the papers?"

"Whenever you please."

"Two weeks from tomorrow. Payment in one installment."

"Everything just as you wish."

"A fine of one hundred thousand francs on whoever backs out."

"Amen."

That transaction took only five minutes. But where was I to get that sum at such short notice? Then began a beautiful stretch of Divine Providence.[7] That same evening, Fr Caffasso did something unusual on a feast day; he came to visit me, and he told me that a devout lady, Countess Casazza-Riccardi,[8] had entrusted him with ten thousand francs for me, to be spent on whatever I considered to be for God's greater glory. The next day a Rosminian who had come to Turin to invest 20,000 francs came to ask my advice in the matter. I proposed that they should lend it to me for the Pinardi contract.[9] In that way the sum I was looking for was put together. The three thousand francs for related costs were donated by Chev. Cotta, in whose bank the much-desired deed was drawn up.[10]

Having thus secured ownership of that building, I turned my attention to the so-called Gardener's Inn. This was a tavern where pleasure-seekers used to gather on feast days. Music from accordions, fifes, clarinets, guitars, violins, basses and double-basses, and songs of every kind flowed therefrom all day long. Indeed it was not seldom that all those sounds issued at once in concert. As only a simple wall divided our courtyard from this building, the Bellezza house, it often happened that the hymns from our chapel were confused and drowned out by the din of the music and of the bottles of the Gardener's Inn. In addition

The Bellezza house, site of the Gardener's Inn, as it appeared early in the twentieth century. Don Bosco rented the building from 1854 until he was finally able to buy it in 1884. It was razed in 1922.

there were the constant comings and goings between the Pinardi house and the Gardener's Inn.[11] One can easily imagine the disturbance this caused us, and the danger for our boys.

To free ourselves from this odious situation, I tried to buy the house, but I did not succeed. I tried to rent it, and the landlady was willing; but the tavernkeeper claimed exorbitant damages. Then I proposed to take over the whole tavern, pay the rent, and buy all the furnishings of the bedrooms, table service, cellar, kitchen, etc. By paying dearly for it all, I was able to become the manager of the premises. I changed their character immediately. In this way was destroyed the second seedbed of iniquity which up to then had existed in Valdocco alongside the Pinardi house.[12]

Notes

1. For example, in September 1850 Don Bosco arranged a week's retreat for 109 men and boys at the diocesan minor seminary at Giaveno, assisted by Father Robert Murialdo. Giaveno is a small town about seventeen miles west of Turin. The preachers were Canon Innocent Arduino (1806?–1880), the scholarly and zealous archpriest of the collegiate church in that town, Father Stephen Giorda, pastor in the village of Poirino (about thirteen miles southeast of Turin), and Don Bosco himself. The 109 participants numbered 52 boys aged sixteen or seventeen, 26 aged eighteen or nineteen, 18 young men between twenty and twenty-three years old, 6 men in their late twenties, 4 in their thirties, and 3 in their forties. The teenagers included James Bellia, Joseph Buzzetti, Caesar Chiala (who became a Salesian in 1873), Charles Gastini, Felix Reviglio, Michael Rua, Angelo Savio (one of the original eighteen Salesians and the first economer general), and seminarian Ascanio Savio. (BM IV, 78–82, 523–524)

2. As we have already seen, at first Don Bosco subrented the whole house from Pancrazio Soave. From April 1, 1849, he rented them directly from the owner. He had wanted to buy the house for quite some time.

3. Don Bosco is too delicate say directly that these last tenants were prostitutes.

4. Ceria's addition to the text.

5. From people in the street and at the Bellezza house. This was in January 1851.

6. A young engineer named Anthony Spezia (d. 1892), who lived nearby. He later designed the Church of Mary Help of Christians, donating his services.

7. Pinardi's price came down because he was fed up with the fights and other disturbances at the Gardener's Inn; the police often summoned him as a witness (BM IV, 170; cf. Stella, *EcSo*, p. 84). That did not solve Don Bosco's problem. His blind faith in God's Providence is remarkable. He hesitated not an instant in his bargaining with Pinardi. He would not spend Providence's funds blindly, but once he had done his part (getting a fair price here), he knew that God would do the rest.

8. According to the Oratory records, she was a regular benefactress of Don Bosco's work at least between 1854 and 1857 (Stella, *EcSo*, p. 379).

9. Don Bosco had not yet met Father Rosmini, but he had already written to him about possible cooperative use of the field that he had bought in June 1850 from the archdiocesan seminary (see chapter 47, note 10). When this opportunity offered itself, he hastened to suggest that they cooperate to purchase the Pinardi house, and Father Rosmini graciously agreed (letter of January 10, 1851, from Father Charles Gilardi, procurator general of the Institute of Charity, BM IV, 170–171). On January 15, 1851, Don Bosco wrote back (in part):

> Please convey my sincerest thanks to your reverend superior for all that he is doing for us. I hope that this act of charity for the greater glory of God may draw abundant blessings for him and his institute. (BM IV, 172)

Don Bosco was to pay four percent interest on the 20,000 lire; Father Rosmini advised him that it need not be paid until he asked for it. Indeed, he never asked for either interest or capital. Nevertheless Don Bosco arranged his accounts every year with Father Gilardi and finally cleared the debt.

10. Chevalier Joseph Anthony Cotta (1785–1868) was a distinguished banker, a senator, a philanthropist involved in many of the same charities as Chevalier Mark Gonella, and a major benefactor of the Oratory until his death. The related costs amounted to 3500 lire. (Stella, *EcSo*, passim; BM IV, 172)

The deed, signed on February 19, 1851, shows that Don Bosco actually paid 28,500 lire for the house and property. The purchasers were listed as Fathers John Bosco, John Borel, Robert Murialdo, and Joseph Cafasso. (BM IV, 172). Fathers Borel and Murialdo withdrew from the arrangement on January 26, 1853; that left Don Bosco and Father Cafasso joint owners and jointly responsible for the Rosminian debt. Father Cafasso gave his share to Don Bosco on October 10, 1856. (BM IV, 409; Giraudi, p. 99)

11. The only way to get to the Bellezza house was by way of via della Giardiniera, which meant there was constant traffic of merrymakers past the Pinardi house to their place of enjoyment, and their tipsy return.

12. Both moral and physical dangers to the Oratory boys were involved in the tavern's proximity. On one occasion, for instance, a couple of military officers carried their drunken swordplay to the chapel door before Don Bosco was able to intervene. (BM II, 421–422)

When the widow Bellezza categorically refused to sell her house, Don Bosco bought up the innkeeper's lease at great expense in 1853 and then arranged with Mrs. Bellezza to rent the entire building at 950 lire per year in a three-year lease through September 30, 1856. The lease was then renewed for another three years at 800 lire per year. Don Bosco sublet the house to tenants of a better character for a time; eventually Mrs. Bellezza herself moved into the house. All told, Don Bosco spent some 20,000 lire to get rid of the Gardener's Inn and its evils. (BM IV, 423–428)

Mrs. Bellezza died in 1883, and Don Bosco was finally able to buy the house and land in February 1884. Her heirs wanted 180,000 lire, but Don Bosco beat them down to 100,000. His generous French benefactor Count Louis Anthony Colle of Toulon (d. 1888) donated the money (Giraudi, p. 236; BM XV, 75–76).

The Salesians used the premises for various purposes until the house was demolished in 1922 to make room for the new workshops for the technical courses. Part of the land became a section of the playground for the festive oratory.

55

A Chapel and a Lottery

The Church of St Francis de Sales[1]

Freed from the moral vexations of the Pinardi house and the Gardener's Inn, we had to think about a more decorous church for our worship, better suited to our growing needs.[2] The old one, it is true, had been considerably enlarged; it was situated where the superiors' refectory is now (1875).[3] But it was uncomfortable on account of its capacity and its lack of height. To enter one had to go down two steps; as a result in winter and when it rained we were flooded out. In summer the heat and the bad odors suffocated us. Few feast days passed without some pupil fainting and being carried out limp. So it was necessary to start a building more proportionate to the number of youngsters, better ventilated, and more healthy.

Chev. Blachier drew up plans for what we now know as the Church of St Francis and the building that stands round the courtyard beside the church.[4] The contractor was Mr Frederick Bocca.[5]

When the foundations had been dug, the cornerstone was blessed on 20 July 1851.[6] Chev. Joseph Cotta placed the stone in position; Canon Moreno, royal almoner,[7] blessed it. The renowned Father Barrera,[8] moved by the sight of such a large crowd, stood upon a mound of dirt and improvised a marvelously opportune speech. He began with these exact words:

"Ladies and gentlemen, the cornerstone which has just been laid in the foundations of this church has a twofold significance. It is like the grain of a mustard seed destined

to grow into a mystical tree in which many boys will find
refuge; it symbolises also that this work is founded on a
cornerstone which is Jesus Christ, against which the
enemies of the faith will hurl themselves in vain."[9] Then
he proved both points, to the great pleasure of his audi-
ence, who thought that the eloquent preacher was inspired.

Here is the record. The record of that solemn occasion
was written down.[10]

Such well-publicised occasions attracted youngsters from
all over. Many turned up at all hours of the day; others
begged for shelter. That year their number passed fifty,[11]
and we began some workshops in the house; for we were
finding it ever more ruinous for the boys to go out to work
in the city.[12]

The sacred building for which we longed was beginning
to rise above ground, when I realised that my funds were
completely exhausted. I had collected 35 thousand francs by
selling some property,[13] but these disappeared like ice in
the sun. The treasury granted us nine thousand francs,[14]
but they were to be turned over only when the work was
nearing completion.

Bishop Peter Losana of Biella[15] realised that the new
building and that whole institution especially benefited the
bricklayer apprentices from Biella.[16] He sent out a circular
letter to his parish priests encouraging them to help with
contributions. The circular read thus:

Biella, 13 September 1851

Reverend and dear Father:

That devout and outstanding priest Don Bosco, inspired by a
truly angelic charity, has undertaken to bring together on feast
days as many boys as he meets, abandoned and scattered
through the squares and streets of Turin, especially in the
densely populated neighbourhoods between Borgo Dora and
Martinetto.[17] He has undertaken to provide accommodation for
them in a suitable place, so that they might enjoy honest recreation as well as Christian instruction and upbringing. Such has
been his holy zeal that the existing chapel has become too
small for their needs; in fact, it does not accommodate more
than a third of the six hundred and more boys who now flock
there. Driven by love to accomplish so much good, he has set

to the arduous task of building a church suited to the needs of his compassionate plan. He is appealing to the charity of the Catholic faithful for help with the much too heavy expenses that are entailed for its completion.

With particular confidence, then, he turns to this province and diocese through me, since of the six hundred and more boys who are already gathered round him and frequenting his Oratory, more than a third (over 200) are youngsters from Biella. Many of them he shelters in his own house and freely provides whatever they need for food and clothing, so that they can learn a trade.

Don Bosco can claim help from us, not only in charity but in justice. I ask you, therefore, Rev. Father, to bring this matter of such concern to the attention of your good parishioners, to have recourse to those who are better off, and to set aside one Sunday to take up a collection of alms for this purpose. The proceeds should be sent securely and without delay to the diocesan curia, marking clearly on the packet the amount enclosed and its place of origin.

While the children of darkness endeavour to open a temple in order to teach in it their errors, for the perdition of their brothers,[18] will the fortunate children of light not open a church in which to teach the truth for their salvation, and that of their brothers, and most of all, of their fellow citizens?

I hope, therefore, to be able to reinforce and help the undertaking of this praiseworthy man of God with the offerings that you will provide. Thus the people of my diocese will give public evidence of their enlightened devotion and gratitude for a work so holy, so useful, and indeed so necessary for our times.

I take this opportunity of assuring you again of my great esteem and affection.

Your most devoted servant,

† John Peter, bishop

The appeal brought in one thousand francs, but that was only a drop in the ocean. And so a lottery of various small prizes was conceived.[19] This was the first time that we appealed in such a way to the charity of the general public, and the project was favourably received. Three thousand, three hundred[20] prizes were collected. The Supreme Pontiff, the king, the queen mother, the queen consort,[21] and in general the whole royal court distinguished themselves with their gifts. The tickets sold out (50 centesimi each). When the public drawing took place at city hall, one individual was trying to buy a ticket; even though he offered five francs for one, there was not a ticket to be had.[22]

The plan and the rules of the lottery were:

1. Such items as objects of art or of handicraft, namely embroidery, knitwear, pictures, books, lengths of cloth, and so on, will be gratefully received.

2. Unless a donor wishes to remain anonymous, when each article is donated, a receipt will be issued describing the gift and giving the donor's name.

3. The number of lottery tickets issued will be in proportion to the value of the prizes, as provided by law, namely one-quarter of the value.

4. Tickets will detach from a counterfoil book and will be signed by two members of the committee.[23] They cost 50 centesimi.

5. All prizes will be put on public view in March, and will be left on view for at least a month.[24] Notice of the time and place of the viewing will be published in the *Gazzetta Officiale* of the kingdom.[25] The day fixed for drawing the winning numbers will also be indicated.

6. The numbers will be drawn one at a time. Should two be pulled out by mistake, they will be put back into the drum without being read out.

7. As many numbers will be drawn as there are prizes to be won. The first ticket drawn will win the item marked number one. The same for the second, and so on until as many numbers have been drawn as there are prizes.

8. The winning numbers will be published in the *Giornale Officiale*[26] of the kingdom. Presentation of the prizes will begin three days later.

9. Prizes not claimed within three months will be considered ceded to the Oratory for its own benefit.

Many of the prizewinners gladly left their prizes to help the church.[27] This proved to be an extra bonus. Though there was considerable outlay, still the net gain came to 26 thousand francs.[28]

Notes

1. In his manuscript Don Bosco numbered this chapter 17 (of his third part), omitting 16 and continuing this minor error for two more chapters, after which he dropped the numbering altogether. Ceria corrected the numbering in his edition.

2. Before beginning this project in the spring of 1851, Don Bosco made a pilgrimage to a well-known shrine to our Lady at Oropa to implore the Madonna's help. Oropa is about nine miles northwest of Biella.

3. The Pinardi shed was used as a chapel for six years. In 1852, with the opening of the new church, it became a study hall and then a dormitory. In 1856 both chapel and house were demolished to make way for a new and sturdier building; the site of the Pinardi chapel became the Salesian dining room. Here Don Bosco welcomed to his table two future Popes: Canon Joseph Sarto (Saint Pius X) in 1875 and young Father Achilles Ratti (Pius XI) in 1883. In 1927 the conversion of the dining room into the Chapel of the Resurrection was undertaken at the wish of Father Philip Rinaldi, rector major from 1922 to 1931.

4. In 1840 Chevalier Frederick Blachier was a member of the Royal Building Council with the title of designer (Stella, *EcSo*, p. 87, n. 46). Designing the Church of Saint Francis de Sales and serving on the executive committee for the lottery to pay for it seem to be Blachier's only dealings with Don Bosco. Only in 1945 did Giraudi find Blachier's plans for the new church; Ceria has used one of these as an illustration facing p. 226 of his edition of the MO, along with a sketch of the Pinardi house. The plans were presented to Don Bosco, who signs himself "Director of the Oratory for endangered youth." The plans were later altered. The new church was to measure thirty-six feet by ninety-two feet. Its cost was projected at thirty-five thousand lire.

   The plans also envisaged the eventual replacement of the Pinardi house and a wing on the far side (the future hospice annex) symmetrical with the new church.

5. Bocca had been the sponsor at the confirmation rite in June 1847 and donated fifty lire to the Oratory in July; he too served on the lottery committee (Stella, *EcSo*, pp. 87, 438, 554).

6. The first work to be done was the demolition of a couple of walls, one separating the side yard (where the church was

to be built) from the front yard, and one along via della Giardiniera, on which the church was to face (see maps 3–4 in Giraudi). This was done even before the city building department granted a permit (June 24, 1851).

During the investigations related to Don Bosco's beatification, Father John Baptist Francesia testified that as a boy of twelve he was present at the laying of the cornerstone. He remembers Michael Rua, who had just turned fourteen, preaching "a beautiful sermonette to all those present." He adds, "I liked his attractive expository style and its devotional quality, which he maintained all his life."

7. Canon Octavius Moreno (1779?-1852), called Anthony in BM IV, was a senator and was the king's official responsible for vacant church benefices. Had not Archbishop Fransoni been in exile, he would surely have performed the ceremony for his friend Don Bosco.

The archbishop had gone into voluntary exile in Switzerland in 1848. Because he had the courage to oppose civil interference in Church matters, for a time it was expedient for him to leave (cf. chapter 48, note 5). He returned within a few months. His uncompromising opposition to the Siccardi Laws led to a fine and a thirty-day jail sentence when he refused a court summons in May 1850. Having served it and been released, he was rearrested on August 7 and imprisoned in the fortress of Fenestrelle. A tribunal finally condemned him to exile for life. He settled in Lyons, where he died in 1862. Two other Sardinian bishops were treated similarly.

For opposing views of the case, see BM IV, 19–20, 42–47, 65–68, 76–77; Thayer, I, 119–126, 286–293. The most thorough treatment is M.F. Mellano, *Il caso Fransoni e la politica ecclesiastica piemontese (1848–1850)* (Rome, 1964).

8. Father Andrew Barrera was involved in the Confraternity of Christian Doctrine. Some six hundred oratory boys, plus the invited guests, heard him on this occasion. When the rosaries from the Pope were distributed the year before, he preached a "lucid, dignified" sermon full of affection for Pius IX which "held the boys' attention and stirred them to the depths of their being" (BM IV, 58–59).

9. Lemoyne gives a slightly expanded version of this preamble, an extensive passage from the body of the sermon, and its conclusion (BM IV, 193–194). Some scriptural allusions in the preamble are Matthew 13:31–32 and 21:42,44.

10. The first sentence is a marginal note in Don Bosco's original text; the second is from the copy. No such record has been found.

11. As late as 1853 Don Bosco still had only about twenty youths under his direct care, which is why he wanted to enlarge his building. After doing so, he took in about eighty in 1854. (Stella, LW, p. 115; cf. *EcSo*, p. 175)

12. Don Bosco alluded in chapter 48 to the moral risks that his boys ran in the streets of Turin. Lemoyne spells them out: "newstands peddling irreligion and immorality . . . , indecent pictures, lewd statuettes, scandalous novels, and heretical books prominently displayed in the windows of bookshops" (BM IV, 459).

    So in 1853 Don Bosco decided that it was time to set up his own workshops: shoe repairing and tailoring, for starters. He could teach these himself but soon hired reliable masters (Dominic Goffi and a certain Papino). Not only was there a moral advantage, but these practical crafts supplied needs of the household. (BM IV, 459–460)

13. Don Bosco first wrote "some of my property," then crossed out "of my." It was at this time that he sold some of the land he had bought from the seminary, among other things. The previous year he had sold the Moretta house. (See chapter 47.)

14. A ten-thousand-lire grant, to be made in three installments, came from the royal almoner's office, which was directed by Canon Moreno, by order of King Victor Emmanuel II. The king also made a personal donation of a thousand lire. (BM IV, 223–224)

15. John Peter Losana (1793–1873) was bishop of Biella from 1833 to 1873. He was charitable, progressive, and socially aware; Stella contrasts his political and social outlook with Archbishop Fransoni's (*EcSo*, pp. 88, 344; *ReCa*, p. 91). Don Bosco had various dealings with him over the years, especially in connection with the *Catholic Readings* (see MB XX).

16. Biella, about forty miles northeast of Turin in the foothills of the Alps, had fewer than ten thousand citizens in the 1850s (Stella, *EcSo*, p. 444). There is a monograph on boys from Biella at the Oratory: Basilio Buscaglia, *San Giovanni Bosco e i biellesi* (Biella, 1934).

17. I.e., across the slums of the northern industrial zone. Martinetto was the district west of Valdocco.

18. The Waldensians had already opened a chapel and lecture hall in Porta Nuova and were planning to build a church,

school, and hospital two blocks away from the Saint Aloysius Oratory. It was to counter them that in the 1880s Don Bosco built the Church of Saint John the Evangelist on the site of the oratory; there was no Catholic church in the immediate neighborhood until then.

19. Public lotteries of this sort were a favorite way of appealing to charity in Turin and had a successful history during the 1830s (Stella, *EcSo*, p. 86). The government's own lottery was an impressive institution:

> A Royal Lottery Office was established in every parish with more than 3,000 inhabitants, which meant that there were seventeen in Turin. All classes, and especially the very poorest, bought tickets for the lottery, and provided the Piedmontese government—especially in Cavour's day—with a considerable revenue. In effect the lottery supplied one of the instruments with which Piedmont was to secure the independence and unification of Italy—an instrument never mentioned in the heroic accounts of the Risorgimento. (Hearder, p. 66)

Don Bosco organized his lottery in December 1851. Long experience was to convince Don Bosco that for raising money from the public by small contributions, lotteries were the means "most suited to the times and most convenient for our needs" (Circular, January 30, 1862). Between 1851 and 1887 he organized a total of fourteen lotteries; his personal enthusiasm for them waned as time went on (T. Bosco, SP, p. 196), but he realized that they were one means by which Divine Providence wanted him to find the funds for his many projects (MB XVII, 74).

20. The exact number was 3251.

21. Victor Emmanuel II (1820–1878) succeeded his father when Charles Albert abdicated in 1849 after the disastrous war with Austria. His mother was Maria Teresa of Tuscany (1801–1855), and his wife Maria Adelaide of Lorraine (1822–1855). Their gifts are identified in BM IV, 246. Both women were pious and generous.

When the Cavour government, spurred by Interior Minister Rattazzi, was beginning to move against religious orders in 1854, Don Bosco had two dreams warning him of "state funerals at court." He wrote to the king in November 1854, urging him to oppose the laws of confiscation. The king was very upset but did not act. In January and February 1855 his mother, his wife, his newborn son, and his only brother all died, the two queens suddenly. (BM V, 111–123, 128–129, 149–160; cf. Mack Smith, pp. 79–80)

22. The drawing took place on July 12, 1852. There were no tickets to be had because some of the 100,000 issued had been lost, and others had not been returned. Seventy-four thousand were returned, grossing 37,000 lire. (BM IV, 324–325)

23. Don Bosco took great care in all his lotteries to organize different committees. Choice of the right people as promoters was the key to success. For this first lottery he brought together forty-six men promoters of various social classes and backgrounds (workers, gentlemen, priests) and eighty-six ladies of the middle class or the nobility. From this large group he chose an executive committee of twenty highly regarded gentlemen (listed in BM IV, 225–226). One member of the committee was Father Peter Baricco, deputy mayor of Turin as well as a supporter of his work. He was helpful, of course, in cutting through some of the inevitable red tape connected with the lottery. The executive committee signed the request for a government permit and, having obtained it, launched their appeal to their fellow citizens' generosity on January 20, 1852.

24. Don Bosco could hardly use Pinardi's wretched house for the public viewing. He secured permission from the war department to use a large hall behind the Church of Saint Dominic, in what had been the Dominican monastery until the government seized it. (Don Bosco did the Dominicans the courtesy of asking their permission too.) The church is at the corner of via Milano and via San Domenico, two blocks south of Porta Palazzo and one block north of city hall.

    Don Bosco published a 158-page book containing the committee's appeal, the lottery rules, and the list of prizes and their donors. It was on sale at the Marietti and Paravia bookshops for fifty centesimi.

    Many visitors came to inspect the prizes, among them the Cavour brothers. At that time Camillo was finance minister and was involved in his conspiracy with Rattazzi to topple Massimo d'Azeglio's government. Don Bosco himself gave the count a tour of the prizes. (BM IV, 252–253)

    In March 1852 twenty-year-old seminarian Joseph Buzzetti suffered a very unfortunate accident. There are two stories about how it happened. An anonymous biographer of the faithful brother tells us that Buzzetti intervened just as some thug was shooting at Don Bosco, and his left index finger was seriously damaged (Enzo Bianco, p. 49; *Dizionario Biografico dei Salesiani*). Lemoyne's account (BM IV, 253) is that Don Bosco had asked the young man and several others to sleep at the hall and keep an eye on the prizes; to scare off any would-be burglars they brought along a small pistol charged just with powder. While he was loading it one day, the powder blew, and so the finger was injured. In either case, it had to be amputated and, since at that time a dispensation would not be given for such a physical defect, Buzzetti had to give up his dream of the priesthood.

25. So Don Bosco spelled *ufficiale*. As its name suggests, it was an official record of government acts.

26. Should read *Gazzetta Ufficiale*.

27. The Church of Saint Francis de Sales.

28. Don Bosco generously gave half the proceeds to the Cottolengo Institute. The church itself was blessed on June 20. Archbishop Fransoni, who had bought a hundred tickets, wrote on July 29 to congratulate Don Bosco. Among other things he said, "Both your Oratory and [the Cottolengo], so near to each other, are a visible demonstration of God's Providence" (BM IV, 325).

56

Woe to Turin!

The powder magazine blows up •
Gabriel Fascio •
The new church is blessed

While the items were on public show, the powder magazine near the Cemetery of St Peter in Chains blew up (26 April 1852).[1] The concussion that followed was horrible and violent. Many buildings near and far were shaken, and serious damage was reported from it.[2] Of the workmen, 28 were killed. That the disaster was not even worse was due to a certain sergeant named Sacco, who at great personal risk prevented the fire from reaching a bigger supply of powder.[3] This could have destroyed the whole city of Turin. The Oratory house, which was badly constructed, suffered serious damage; the deputies sent us an offering of 300 francs to help repair it.

In connection with this incident, I would like to recall a fact which refers to one of our young artisans, Gabriel Fascio. The previous year he fell ill and was at death's door.[4] At the height of his delirium he kept saying over and over, "Woe to Turin! Woe to Turin!"

His companions asked him, "Why?"

"Because it's threatened by a terrible disaster."

"What kind of disaster?"

"A horrible earthquake," he answered.

"When's it coming?"

"Next year. Oh, woe to Turin on 26 April."

"What should we do?"

"Pray to St Aloysius to protect the Oratory and those who live in it."

It was then that, at the request of all the youngsters of our house, a *Pater*, *Ave*, and *Gloria* addressed to this saint

were added to our common morning and evening prayers.[5]
In fact, relative to the danger, our house suffered slight
damage, and there were no injuries to our boarders.[6]

Meanwhile, the work on the Church of St Francis de
Sales went on with incredible speed, and in the space of
eleven months it was completed. On 20 June 1852, it was
consecrated for divine worship with a solemnity that was
more unique than rare amongst us.[7]

At the entrance to the courtyard an arch of colossal
height was erected. On it in outsize letters was written:
*In letters of gold — we shall write on every side — may this day
live for ever.*

From every side echoed these verses which had been put
to music by Maestro Joseph Blanchi, of happy memory:

> *Sooner shall the setting sun*
> *Return to its rising,*
> *Sooner shall every river*
> *Return to its source,*
> *Than shall the memory*
> *Of this beautiful day*
> *Be forgotten amongst us.*[8]

The following words were recited and sung with ardent
enthusiasm:

> *As a bird flits from branch to branch,*
> *Goes searching for trusty shelter, etc.*[9]

Many newspapers reported this celebration.[10]

On 1 June that same year a *Mutual Aid* Society was
established[11] to stop our boys from enrolling in the so-
called Workers Society, which right from its start showed
that its principles were anything but religious.[12] One may
refer to the booklet we published; it served its purpose
wonderfully.[13] Our aid society later converted into an affil-
iated conference of the St Vincent de Paul Society,[14] which
is still functioning.[15]

The church was built but needed all kinds of furnishings. Civic charity did not let us down. Comm. Joseph
Dupré undertook to decorate a chapel dedicated to St
Aloysius and buy a marble altar which still adorns the
church. Another benefactor undertook to fit out the choir
loft, where a small organ was set up for the day boys. Mr

Michael Scannagatti[16] bought a complete set of candlesticks; Marquis Fassati[17] undertook to supply our Lady's altar and provided a set of bronze candlesticks, and later the statue of our Lady.[18] Fr Caffasso paid all the expenses incurred for the pulpit. The high altar was provided by Doctor Francis Vallauri[19] and completed by his son Fr Peter, a priest.

Thus in a short time the new church was fitted with everything needed for both private and solemn ceremonies.

Notes

1. The magazine consisted of a powder factory and three warehouses. It was located just east of Saint Peter's, not far north of the Cottolengo, and a quarter of a mile northeast of the Oratory.

2. The explosion was heard fifteen miles away (BM IV, 267).

3. The brave soldier was Paul Sacchi (d. 1884), sergeant of artillery. Though injured in the first two blasts, he risked his life to keep the flames from reaching the third warehouse, which contained eight hundred barrels of powder. The grateful city of Turin named a street in his honor along the west side of the Porta Nuova railroad station.

4. Fassio, thirteen years old, boarded with Don Bosco. He was an apprentice blacksmith. Don Bosco had predicted his death. (BM IV, 276) In some of the Oratory registers he is called Fazio (Stella, *EcSo*, pp. 177, 561). Don Bosco, still spelling his name Fascio, called him a "model of virtue" in the preface to the life of Dominic Savio (Aronica ed., p. 24; O'Brien ed., p. vii).

5. A prayer to Saint Aloysius followed by an Our Father, Hail Mary, and Glory Be remained part of morning prayers in Salesian communities until Saint Dominic Savio was canonized in 1954. At that time the prayers were simplified and a prayer to Saint Dominic replaced the one to Saint Aloysius.

6. To commemorate the grace of the Oratory's safety, Don Bosco printed five thousand copies of a most unusual picture of Our Lady of Consolation, the city, the Oratory boys, and the exploding magazine (see Ceria MO, opposite p. 236).

7. The church was completed and consecrated before the lottery was finished!

8. Lemoyne called it a "delightful motet" (BM IV, 306). Ceria had another opinion: "I hope the music was better than the verse" (MO, p. 233) — even though the verse was Don Bosco's! (BM IV, 305, 533)

9. The opening lines of an ode which Don Bosco composed to relate the adventures of the wandering Oratory before it found its permanent home at Pinardi's house. It was set to music and taught to the boys so that they could sing it in honor of their benefactors, the honored guests at the dedication of the church. (BM IV, 303) The sixteen stanzas are reproduced in BM IV, 530–532 — in Italian.

10. BM IV, 307–309, reproduces the entire report from a journal called *La Patria* [Fatherland], June 21, 1852. *L'Armonia* covered the story in its June 23 issue.

11. Don Bosco had already organized it on July 1, 1850. It was probably the first union established to look after the interests of Catholic workers. It regulations are printed in BM IV, 518–520. To join, one first had to belong to the Company of Saint Aloysius; union dues were a soldo a week, collected on Sunday. Members who fell ill received fifty centesimi a day in assistance "until their complete recovery" (regulation no. 4).

12. Piedmontese workers organized a number of mutual aid societies, starting with one among carpenters in 1822. Their purposes were to help one another in times of illness or financial difficulty and to stand together when dealing with employers. Many priests and some bishops (including Bishop Losana of Biella and the bishops of Savona and Asti) grasped the urgency of such workers' associations and supported them. (T. Bosco, *Mem*, p. 200, n. 2)

    Nevertheless, not many years later Saint Leonard Murialdo lamented, "The mutual aid societies say that they will keep young workers out of politics and are not opposed to the Catholic faith; but they propagate disrespect for priests, religious indifference, and communism" (Armando Castellani, *Il beato Leonardo Murialdo*, I, 566–567).

13. The booklet was titled *Società di Mutuo Soccorso di alcuni individui della Compagnia di S. Luigi eretta nell'Oratorio di S. Francesco di Sales* [Mutual Aid Society of various individuals of the Company of Saint Aloysius, set up at the Oratory of Saint Francis de Sales] (Turin: Speirani, 1850). Behind its title page one reads the motto, "Behold, how good and pleasant it is when brothers dwell in unity!" (Psalm 133:1). It

contains the regulations and membership form and served as the membership card. The society flourished until 1857, when it changed its form, as Don Bosco will describe next.

14. Founded by Frederick Ozanam (1813–1853) at Paris in 1833, this association of laymen and women has as its aim to serve the poor through the corporal and spiritual works of mercy. It has become a worldwide organization, with 4700 chapters in the United States as of 1988.

    The first chapter of the Saint Vincent de Paul Society in Turin was established on May 13, 1850. Don Bosco had a big hand in founding it. Some of the most prominent citizens of Turin were members, e.g. the counts of Collegno, Count Cays, and patriot-author Silvio Pellico. In 1854 there were 220 members. (BM IV, 48–51; Stella, *EcSo*, p. 477). Don Bosco frequently gave conferences to the members. These were published in book form: *The Christian Trained in Conduct and Courtesy*, trans. Silvester Adriano, ed. Margaret L. MacPherson (Paterson: Salesiana Publishers, 1956).

    In 1854 Don Bosco established a junior chapter of the society for the older Oratory boys; two years later the society's supreme council recognized the junior chapter as an affiliated unit. This was an exception to the society's by-laws, for membership was normally restricted to adults. The rules of the Oratory chapter are found in BM V, 310–311.

15. When Don Bosco wrote this last part of his *Memoirs* in 1875, the Oratory conference was still in operation, though no longer with official recognition (BM V, 311). It died out some time later at an unknown date.

16. Scanagatti was one of Father Cafasso's regular penitents; he donated 314 lire toward the church — for the candlesticks, presumably — and served on the executive committee for Don Bosco's lottery. He helped Don Bosco as either a catechist or an assistant at the boys' recreation. (Stella, *EcSo*, pp. 87, 162, 417)

17. Marquis Dominic Fassati Roero San Severino (1804–1878), his wife Mary (1824–1905), and their family were devout Catholics, very involved in public charity. They ardently supported Don Bosco, and their privileged positions at court were often useful to him. (See MB XX.)

18. This statue, which is still in its niche in the Church of Saint Francis de Sales, has a story behind it. On April 18, 1853, the solid silver, three-hundred-pound statue of the Madonna was stolen from the Church of Our Lady of Consolation. A

wooden statue was put in as a temporary replacement. Later, when a silver-plated statue was provided for the shrine, Marquis Fassati acquired the wooden one and gave it to the Church of Saint Francis de Sales.

19. One of the Oratory's medical doctors. When he died in 1856, Don Bosco, grateful for all the favors the good doctor had provided for the boys, gave him "a solemn and most devout funeral" in the Church of Saint Francis de Sales (*L'Armonia*, September 12). His son Peter (1829–1900), a good and pious priest, always remained a cordial friend of Don Bosco.

The New
Building
Collapses

The year 1852

The new church, complete with sacristy and bell tower,[1] enabled us to provide for those youngsters who wished to attend sacred services on feast days, the night school, and day classes too. But how were we to provide for the multitude of poor children who were appealing for shelter all the time? This was the more acute because the explosion of the powder magazine the year before[2] had almost ruined our ancient building. In that moment of supreme need, we decided to build a new wing on the house.[3] In order to continue using the old building, we began the new one on a site a bit apart. It stretched from the end of the present refectory to the print foundry.[4]

The builders made rapid progress.[5] Although autumn was already well along, they reached roof level. In fact, all the trusses had been put in place, all the crosspieces nailed in, and the tiles were stacked up on the beams ready to be laid down neatly. Then a torrential rain interrupted all work. Water poured down for days and nights, flowing from the beams and the crosspieces; it wore and washed away the fresh mortar, leaving the walls only of soaked bricks and stones.

Around midnight, when we were all in bed, we heard a loud rumble which became louder and more frightening by the moment. Everyone woke up[6] and, completely ignorant of what was happening, utterly terrified, wrapped in blankets and sheets, ran from the dormitory and fled in confusion with no idea where to go, with only the idea of putting distance between himself and the danger, as one can imagine. The noise and the chaos got worse. The roof framework and the tiles mixed with the wall materials as everything collapsed into ruins with a mighty roar.

Since that construction had stood against the wall of the lower, older building, we feared that everything lay flattened under the pile of rubble. But, as it proved, the only harm was the horrendous noise, which caused no personal injury.

City engineers came to inspect things in the morning. When Chev. Gabbetti[7] saw another pillar cracked at the base and leaning over a dormitory, he exclaimed: "You should go and give thanks to Our Lady of Consolation. Only a miracle is keeping that pillar up. If it had fallen, it would have buried in rubble Don Bosco and the thirty boys sleeping in the dormitory below."[8]

As the building was still unfinished, most of the loss was the builder's.[9] Our damage was estimated at 10,000 francs. The accident took place at midnight on 2 December 1852.[10]

Amid the continual sad afflictions which befall the poor human race, there is always the loving hand of the Lord to lighten our misfortunes. If the disaster had happened a couple of hours earlier, it would have buried our night school pupils. They finished their lessons at ten, and when they came out of their classrooms, about 300 of them, they used to run round the empty building under construction for half an hour or so. A little later the collapse occurred.

Not only did the advanced season no longer allow work on our ruined house to be completed; we could not even begin to rebuild part of it. In the meantime, who would provide for us in such straits? What could we do for so many boys with such limited facilities, and these half-ruined? We made a virtue of necessity. After the walls of the old church had been reinforced, it became a dormitory. We then transferred classes to the new church, which was therefore a church on feast days, a school during the week.

The bell tower beside the Church of St Francis de Sales was also built in this year. Our benefactor Mr Michael Scannagatti presented us with an elegant set of candlesticks for the high altar, which are still one of the most beautiful furnishings of this church.[11]

Notes

1. The Church of Saint Francis de Sales, the first building put up in Valdocco by Don Bosco, was the heart of Oratory life for sixteen years (June 1852 to June 1868). The reason is obvious: there boys and Salesians celebrated the Holy Eucharist every morning, gathered before It for prayer at regular times during the day, and came individually for frequent, private moments of meditation or intercession.

   Part of the old chapel served as a sacristy from 1852 to 1856, when a room in the new building that replaced the Pinardi house was turned to that purpose. A small door in our Lady's chapel gave passage from church to sacristy. In 1860 Charles Buzzetti built a sacristy on the gospel side of the church.

   The modest bell tower was built on the left side of the church between December 1852 and February 1853. Count Charles Cays bought another, louder bell to add to the small one that had been used with the Pinardi chapel. In 1929 both bells were recast into the present bell.

   Count Cays of Gilette and Caselette (1813–1882) was a leader in many of Turin's charitable associations, a close friend of Don Bosco for many years, and a member of parliament (1857–1860). His wife died in 1845; he became a Salesian in 1877 and was ordained in 1878. (*Dizionario Biografico dei Salesiani*, p. 78; Stella, *EcSo*, passim; MB XX)

2. The explosion was in April 1852.

3. As was mentioned in chapter 55, note 4, this new building project was part of Chevalier Blachier's original design when he planned the new church.

   The new building was to have three floors, an attic, a basement, and porticos. Its west end was at the east end of the Pinardi house; it began where the central stairway is today. It was to run to the wall on the east, marking the property line between Don Bosco's land and the Filippi brothers'. At that end, each story would have an additional room jutting out to the south, more or less in symmetry with the church at the opposite end of the Pinardi house. Each floor of the east-west section was to be divided lengthwise by a corridor, with rows of rooms on each side of it.

   The complete plan (including replacement of the Pinardi house) called for a main (east-west) section measuring 131 feet by 37; the north-south ell was to be 41 feet by 29; and the whole structure was to be 52.5 feet high.

When several of the boys, including John Cagliero (1838–1926), the future cardinal, objected to the narrow dimensions of the classrooms, the low ceiling in the attic (which was to be a dormitory), and other inconveniences, Don Bosco pointed to his limited means and then added that these drawbacks made it unlikely that the government would ever want to confiscate it, as it had other church property. (BM IV, 327–328)

4. What Don Bosco refers to as the refectory is now the Chapel of the Resurrection, site of the Pinardi chapel (see chapter 55, note 3). Don Bosco intended to preserve the Pinardi house, but by 1856 he changed his mind.

    In the 1870's the typecasting section of the printery was in a large ground-floor room under Don Bosco's quarters. Today the room is a gift shop.

5. The contractor was Frederick Bocca, who had done the church. Work began sometime in mid-summer and was well advanced by the time Don Bosco took fifty boys with him for a retreat at Giaveno in September (BM IV, 329).

6. As it turned out, this was not true. On the second floor of the Pinardi house, three of the seminarians (Louis Viale, Felix Reviglio, and Stephen Vacchetta) slept through the entire disaster. All together there were thirty-eight residents: boys, seminarians, Mama Margaret, and Don Bosco. One of the seminarians was Michael Rua, who had come to live at the Oratory in September 1852 and had taken the cassock at Becchi on October 3, together with Joseph Rocchietti. Among the boys were John Cagliero and John Baptist Francesia. (BM IV, 337–338, 356–357)

7. Chevalier Charles Gabetti, municipal building inspector.

8. Don Bosco's bedroom was at the east end of the Pinardi house, closest to the ruins. In one way the collapse of the building was providential. During some reconstruction work in 1928, the main walls of this first house were found to be almost entirely of stone and mortar with very little lime. As Giraudi put it, "The building which collapsed must have been built of even worse material. Divine Providence saw to the disaster so that the Valdocco Oratory might be founded not on sand, but on solid foundations" (p. 124, n. 1).

9. In more ways that one: the city's investigation found Bocca at fault and fined him. One may notice Don Bosco's sensitivity in not mentioning his name—a courtesy hardly earned by the man's incompetence and/or fraudulent behavior. In

March 1853, when it was time to resume work, Don Bosco was ordered to hire a licensed building contractor to undertake the project. (BM IV, 416; Giraudi, p. 124)

10. I.e., between December 1 and 2.

11. Don Bosco mentioned the bell tower in the first line of the chapter and Scanagatti's gift in the previous chapter.

58

Continued Growth

1853[1]

As soon as the weather permitted, we began promptly to rebuild the ruined house. Work went ahead rapidly, and by October the building was finished.[2] Because we so badly needed room, we rushed at once to move in. The room which I first took is the one which, by God's grace, I still occupy.[3] The classrooms, refectory, and dormitory were permanently established, and the number of our pupils went up to sixty-five.[4]

Various benefactors continued to look after us. Chev. Joseph Duprè at his own expense presented a marble altar rail for the St Aloysius chapel; he adorned the altar and had the whole chapel stuccoed. Marquis Dominic Fassati gave us the small altar rail for the altar of our Lady and a set of bronze gilt candlesticks for that altar. Count Charles Cays, our outstanding benefactor, prior of the Company of St Aloysius for the second time,[5] paid a long-standing debt for us, twelve hundred francs owed the baker, who was beginning to give us problems with our bread deliveries.[6] He bought a bell, which was the object of a charming ceremony. Dr Gattino, our parish priest of happy memory, came to bless it; then he took the opportunity to give a little sermon to the many people gathered from the city.[7] After the religious services, a comedy was presented which everyone enjoyed. The count also gave us a handsomely decorated baldachino,[8] which we still use, and other furnishings for the church.

With the new church thus furnished with what was essential for worship, we were finally able for the first time

The ell-shaped hospice annex was added to the Pinardi house in 1853, and Don Bosco moved into a room on the top floor (marked by a cross). In 1861 the ell was doubled in width, and in 1876 it was slightly extended. After the extension, Don Bosco took the new end rooms for his bedroom, office, and reception rooms.

to fulfill the shared desire to celebrate the forty hours devotion.[9] Though the church was poorly enough appointed, there was an extraordinary assembly of the faithful. To comply with their religious fervor and to provide all of them with an opportunity to satisfy their devotion, when the forty hours finished we followed with an octave of preaching, which was literally spent hearing the confessions of the crowds.

That unexpected attendance was our reason in the years that followed for continuing to organise the forty hours devotion with regular preaching; many people came to receive the holy sacraments and attend the other practices of piety.[10]

Notes

1. At this point Don Bosco stops numbering his chapters.

2. This is the building which extends from the central stairway up to and including the wing parallel to the Church of Saint Francis de Sales. Of the wing the only part built at this time was the part that directly faces the church, i.e. as far as the projecting pilaster before the last pair of windows on each floor. The ell was doubled in width in 1861 after the purchase of the Filippi property on the east side, and the front was extended in 1876.

3. Don Bosco took a small room on the top floor, which until 1861 served as both bedroom and office. When the ell was widened, it became his reception room — for by then he had visitors constantly — and he moved into a new room behind (to the east of) it. He moved still again in 1876 when the building was extended, so that he had a reception room, an office, and a bedroom. All of these rooms, as well as what was the boys' dormitory, are now a museum.

4. For the school year 1853–1854. By summer's end in 1854, they were up to seventy-six (Giraudo and Biancardi, p. 215). Dominic Savio entered the Oratory at the end of October 1854.

5. The Regulations for the Company of Saint Aloysius provided for its guidance "by a spiritual director, who must be a priest, and by a prior, who must be a layman." The prior was elected by the members of the company for a one-year term and could be re-elected. (BM III, 459) Lemoyne writes, "The prior was often a young man of a distinguished family. He was treated with great deference when he arrived, seated at a place of honor during the religious services, and given an ovation on leaving." (BM V, 26) He had not only oversight responsibilities but — especially later — the honor of presiding at feasts and providing some of the treats connected with them.

6. One could write a book with nothing but stories of how Divine Providence rescued Don Bosco from such situations. Many of these episodes are far more dramatic than anything he has narrated in his memoirs. For examples see BM XV, 400–401, 443. The most dramatic episode, of course, was the multiplication of breakfast rolls one morning in November 1860, right outside the Church of Saint Francis de Sales as

the boys filed out after Mass (BM VI, 453–455); a plaque on the outside wall of the church marks the place today.

7. Valdocco, though just a few blocks from the center of Turin, was beyond the old city wall and was therefore "out in the country."

8. A portable canopy carried over the Blessed Sacrament in processions.

9. The solemn exposition of the Blessed Sacrament for forty consecutive hours, with appropriate scripture readings, sermons, hymns, and silent prayer. Under current Church law, exposition is not permitted during the celebration of Mass, at least in the same church or chapel.

10. One may still witness this extraordinary piety during the festivities of the solemnity of Mary Help of Christians in her basilica on May 23–24. These celebrations draw thousands of men and women, young and old, from all over Italy.

59

The Catholic Readings

That year [1853], in March, periodic publication of the *Catholic Readings*[1] began. In 1847, when the emancipation of the Protestants and the Jews took place,[2] it became necessary to put some antidote into the hands of the Christian faithful in general, and of the young[3] in particular. From that act it appeared that the government meant only to grant freedom to those beliefs and not to harm Catholicism. But the Protestants did not understand it in this light. They produced propaganda with all the means available to them. They distributed three newspapers (*La buona Novella*, *La luce Evangelica*, *Il rogantino piemontese*)[4] and many books both biblical and nonbiblical. They gave assistance freely, found employment, supplied work, offered money, clothing, and food to those who came to their classes or attended their lectures or simply joined them at church. They used all these means to make proselytes.[5]

The government was aware of all this and allowed it to go on; with its silence it gave them effective protection. The Protestants, moreover, were organised and furnished with every means both moral and material. Catholics, on the other hand, had relied on the civil law for protection and defense up till then; they possessed a few newspapers, a few classic or learned works, but no newspapers or books to put into the hands of the working classes.

At that time, advised by necessity, I began to draw up some summaries about the Catholic Church, and then some posters entitled "Reminders for Catholics." I handed them out to both children and adults, especially at missions

Some issues of Catholic Readings *authored by Don Bosco. The top row contains lives of the Popes of the first three centuries* A.D. *At the extreme right of the middle row is an issue of* The Catholic Instructed in His Religion, *published serially in the first six numbers of* Catholic Readings *(1853). The bottom row includes the lives of Dominic Savio, Father Cafasso, and Saint Aloysius, and a tribute to the newly-elected Pope Leo XIII (1878).*

and retreats. These handouts and pamphlets were eagerly welcomed, and I had soon given away thousands and thousands of them. This convinced me of the need for some popular means of spreading knowledge of the fundamental Catholic doctrines. So a pamphlet entitled "Advice to Catholics" was printed.[6] Its aim was to put Catholics on the alert lest they let themselves be caught in the nets of the heretics. Its distribution was extraordinary; in two years it sold more than two hundred thousand copies. This pleased the good, but it enraged the Protestants, who had begun to think that they had the field of evangelization all to themselves.[7]

It was then that I began to see that the matter of preparing and printing books for the people was urgent, and I laid out plans for the so-called *Catholic Readings*.[8] When a few issues were prepared for publication, I wanted to get them printed at once. But an obstacle loomed up, as unexpected as it was unforeseen. No bishop wanted to take the lead. Those from Vercelli, Biella, and Casale refused, saying that it was dangerous to tangle with the Protestants.[9]

Archbishop Fransoni was then in exile at Lyons. He approved and recommended [the project], yet no one was willing even to undertake the ecclesiastical review.[10] Canon Joseph Zappata,[11] the vicar general, was the only one who acceded to the archbishop's request and reviewed half of one issue. Then he sent the manuscript back to me with this comment: "Take your work. I can't see my way to signing it. The cases of Ximenes and Palma* are far too recent. You challenge and take the enemy head on, but I prefer to sound the retreat before it's too late."

With the vicar general's consent, I explained everything to the archbishop. His reply was accompanied by a letter to Bishop Moreno of Ivrea,[13] asking that prelate to take under his patronage the publication I was planning and to assist it through his censor and with his authority. Bishop

---

*Father Ximenes, the publisher of a Catholic paper, *Il Contemporaneo* of Rome, was assassinated. Bp Palma, papal secy. and a writer for that paper, was done in by a harquebus shot right in the halls of the Quirinal Palace.[12]

Moreno readily agreed. He delegated his own vicar general, the canon lawyer Pinoli,[14] to act as censor, stipulating that the censor's name was not to be published.

A programme was quickly put together,[15] and the first issue of *The Catholic Instructed, etc.*[16] came out on March 1, 1853.

Notes

1. In Italian the title was *Letture Cattoliche*.

2. Emancipation was granted in 1848. See chapter 48.

3. *Gioventù*, i.e. the young of both sexes.

4. These names mean *The Good News*, *The Light of the Gospel*, and *The Cheeky Piedmontese*.

5. Don Bosco had to contend with all these activities in Porta Nuova, where the Waldensians made their headquarters.

6. *Avvisi ai Cattolici* [Advice to Catholics] was printed in Turin by Speirani in 1850. The thirty-two-page pamphlet dealt with six topics: 1. Religion in general. 2. There is only one true religion. 3. Heretical churches lack the divine character. 4. The heretical churches are not the Church of Jesus Christ. 5. A reply to the Protestant argument: "We believe in Christ and in the Gospel, and therefore we are in the true Church." 6. Protestants agree that Catholics are in the true Church.

   He later added three other topics: 1. The head of the Catholic Church. 2. Papal infallibility. 3. The advantages of defining papal infallibility. (The First Vatican Council defined this teaching as a doctrine of Catholic faith in 1870.)

   The pamphlets were printed with one of two covers: either a picture of Christ giving the keys to Saint Peter (cf. Matthew 16:13–19), or one of the papal coat of arms; below the picture was the motto, "Where the successor of Saint Peter is, there is the Church of Jesus Christ — Saint Ambrose." On the inside was written, "Our pastors unite us with the Pope, and the Pope unites us with God."

   In 1851, Don Bosco inserted "Advice to Catholics" in his new edition of *The Companion of Youth*, entitling the section "Fundamentals of the Catholic Religion."

   The third printing of "Advice to Catholics" announced the launching of the *Catholic Readings*.

7. Don Bosco sent a hundred copies of "Advice" to his former seminary professor Father John Baptist Appendini (1807–1892), who had become pastor in Villastellone and requested them. Don Bosco warned him:

> If you get involved in these booklets you're sacrificing any support you might have from *La Gazzetta del Popolo*, and maybe from others. This booklet, tiny as it is, is a nuisance to them, and they would just love to burn any copies they can get hold of. (cf. BM IV, 159)

   La Gazzetta del Popolo [The People's Gazzette] was one of the more virulent anticlerical papers that sprang up in 1848 with the lifting of censorship.

8. He first conceived the idea in 1850 (BM III, 380). It took him several years to develop concrete plans for financing the project, finding authors and translators, and attracting subscribers and other supporters.

9. The archbishop of Vercelli was Alexander d'Angennes (1781–1869); John Peter Losana was bishop of Biella (see chapter 55); the bishop of Casale Monferrato from 1848 to 1867 was Louis Nazari di Calabiana (1808–1893), the future archbishop of Milan. Events, without much delay, were to prove that their fear was well founded (see chapters 60–63).

10. Until Vatican II, books on any religious or moral topic had to be submitted to the local bishop for certification that they did not contain any opinion or teaching contrary to the Catholic faith. This was indicated on the reverse of the title page as the *nihil obstat* from the reviewer (the ecclesiastical censor) and the *imprimatur* from the bishop. Catechetical books still require such review.

11. Canon Zappata (1796–1883) had many dealings with Don Bosco, especially between 1850 and 1867, when the see of Turin was effectively vacant.

12. Both these clerics were assassinated in 1848. Father Ximenes published *Il Labaro* [The Standard], not *Il Contemporaneo* [Current Events]. Bishop Palma, one of the Pope's secretaries and the editor of *Il Labaro*, was standing near Pius IX in the Quirinal Palace during the rioting that followed the assassination of Count Pellegrino Rossi, the papal prime minister, in November 1848; when the mob began to fire on the palace, the bishop was fatally wounded. A few days later the Pope fled to Gaeta. The Quirinal Palace was the seat of papal government. (E.E.Y. Hales, *Pio Nono*, p. 98; BM III, 324)

13. Bishop Louis Moreno (1800–1878) was one of the founders of *L'Armonia*. His long relationship with Don Bosco was based on the *Catholic Readings*; unfortunately, it ended in a bitter fight over ownership. See BM IV–VIII; Stella, *EcSo*, pp. 347–368.

14. Canon Angelo Pinoli became a friend of Don Bosco and was later caught in the middle when the bishop and the saint argued over the *Readings* (BM VII, 96–97, 380; MB VIII, 375–393).

15. Don Bosco sent the prospectus to thousands of potential subscribers and other supporters, especially the bishops of Piedmont (cf. BM IV, 371, 541):

   1. These booklets will be written in a simple, popular style and their contents will deal exclusively with the Catholic faith.

   2. Each month an issue of 100 to 108 pages, or more if the topic requires it, will be published. The format, paper stock, and type font will be as in this prospectus.

   3. The subscription rate, payable in advance, is 90 centesimi per semester or 1.80 lire per year. Rates including postal delivery are 1.40 lire for six months or 2.80 lire for a year.

   4. To make it as easy as possible for any distinguished person, clerical or lay, who wishes to assist in this charitable work, the issues will be sent to them without postage charge anywhere within the Kingdom ... provided that at least 50 copies are addressed to a single center.

   5. In towns and rural centers subscriptions may be paid to agents appointed by the respective bishops, to whom we particularly recommend this work. We enclose their names and addresses.

   For a list of subscription agents in 1855, see Stella, *EcSo*, pp. 543–544. They included priests, a few bishops, and some laymen, among them Don Bosco's old friend Evasio Savio at Castelnuovo. Four of the agents were in Sardinia, which was part of the realm, and there was one each in Milan and Rome, which were not.

   To oblige Bishop Moreno, item 2 was modified to provide for two shorter issues a month, leaving the total pages at 100–108.

   Printing was done by the De Agostini Printers in Turin. The enterprise was so successful that it continued for over a hundred years, eventually changing the name *Letture Cattoliche* to *Meridiano 12* [Twelfth Meridian, i.e. the longitude of Rome]; the format had changed by then too, so that it resembled the American *Catholic Digest*.

16. The full title was *Il Cattolico Istruito nella sua Religione: Trattenimenti di un padre di famiglia co' suoi figliuoli secondo i bisogni del tempo* [The Catholic Instructed in His Religion: Discussions between a Father and His Sons according to the Needs of Our Times]. Its author was none other than Father John Bosco.

This work required six issues (March to August) for complete publication. Immediately after the August issue, Don Bosco had them bound into one volume of 452 pages. It was a popular treatise explaining why Catholicism was the true religion. According to the temper of the times, it refuted the errors and theological inconsistencies of the Protestant ministers, revealed their bad faith and the various ways in which they altered or misinterpreted the text of the Bible, faulted their manner of worship, and recounted the lives of the principal Reformers.

When Don Bosco revised the book, considerably modifying it, in 1883, he changed the title to *Il Cattolico nel secolo* [The Catholic in the World]. *La Civiltà cattolica* (1883, III, 81) called it a book "of small size but rich in sound Catholic teaching." Three years later a French edition came out, *Le catholique dans le monde* (Nice: Patronage St. Pierre, 1886).

Needless to say, this and Don Bosco's other polemical writings were tracts for his time and place, when Christians of most denominations viciously fought with one another, and Catholics and Protestants in particular gave no quarter to each other. Even in the relatively tolerant United States, there were serious anti-Catholic riots in the 1830s, 1840s, and 1850s; anti-Catholicism played a decisive role in the 1884 presidential election and was a major issue in those of 1928 and 1960.

60

Disputations
with the
Waldensians

1854

The *Catholic Readings* were warmly received, and the number of readers was extraordinary.[1] But they also aroused the anger of the Protestants. They fought back in their own newspapers and their *Letture Evangeliche*;[2] but they lacked readers. So they launched attacks of every kind against poor Don Bosco. Now one, now another would come to dispute, convinced, they said, that no one could withstand their arguments, that Catholic priests were just so many simpletons and therefore could be easily confounded.

At first they came to assault me one at a time. Later they came in pairs and finally in groups. I always listened to them, and I always recommended that they should refer back to their own ministers those problems which they did not know how to answer, and then kindly relay the answers to me. Those who came were Amadeus Bert, then Meille, the evangelist Pugno,[3] then others and still others. But they could make no headway towards getting me to cease speaking or publishing our discussions.[4] This aroused them to absolute fury. I think it good to relate some episodes on this subject.

One Sunday evening in January[5] I was informed that two gentlemen had come to speak with me. They came in and, after a long series of compliments and flattery, one of them began to say, "Good Doctor,[6] nature has favoured you with the great gift of being able to make yourself read and understood by the common person.[7] So we'd like to ask you to use this precious gift in the service of humanity and for the benefit of science, commerce, and the arts."

"At the moment," I said, "I am taken up with the *Catholic Readings*, and I intend to devote myself wholeheartedly to that project."

"It would be much better if you were to write a good book for young people on, say, ancient history, geography, physics, or geometry, but not the *Catholic Readings*."

"Why not the *Catholic Readings*?"

"Because its topics have already been dealt with over and over again by many authors."

"These topics have already been dealt with by many authors, but in learned volumes and not for ordinary people. That is precisely my aim with the *Catholic Readings*."

"But this project is of no advantage to you," they argued. "On the other hand, if you were to take on the projects which we are recommending to you, you'd gain a nice sum for the wonderful institute that Providence has entrusted to you. Here, take this advance (they were four thousand-

From 1853 to 1861 this room was Don Bosco's reception room and his office. Here he wrote or edited the Catholic Readings, *carried on a vast correspondence, composed the first drafts of the Salesian rule, met with boys and Salesians to guide their souls, received the first religious vows of the Salesians in 1859, and received visitors—including his Waldensian opponents. This is the oldest surviving photograph of Don Bosco, taken by Francesco Serra, probably in 1861.*

franc notes). And it won't be the last donation you'll get. You'll get even more."

"What's all this money for?"

"To encourage you to undertake the works we've been suggesting, and to help you with your most praiseworthy institute."

"You'll pardon me, gentlemen," I said, "if I return your money. At present I can't take on any scholarly project other than the *Catholic Readings*."

"But if a project is useless . . . " they started to say.

"If it's a useless project, why are you worrying about it? Why are you offering me this money to get me to stop?"

"You don't realise what you're doing," they persisted. "Your refusal endangers your work, exposes you to certain consequences, certain dangers. . . . "

"Gentlemen, I understand what you're trying to tell me; but I tell you clearly that when I stand up for the truth I'm not afraid of anyone. When I became a priest, I was consecrated to the good of the Church and the good of poor humanity. And I intend to continue with my weak efforts to promote the *Catholic Readings*."

"You're making a mistake." Their tone and attitude changed as they got to their feet. "You're making a mistake. You've insulted us, and who knows what might happen to you, here, and," they added menacingly, "if you leave the house, will you be sure of coming back?"

"Gentlemen, you don't know Catholic priests. While they have life they try to do their duty. If they must die because of their labour, that they would consider their good fortune and their greatest glory."

By then they both seemed so annoyed that I was afraid they were about to attack me. I got to my feet and put a chair between them and me. Then I said, "If you wish to use force, I'm not cowed by your threats. But a priest's strength rests on patience and forgiveness. Now please go."

I walked round the chair and opened the door of my room. "Buzzetti,"[8] I said, "take these gentlemen to the front gate; they're not accustomed to the stairs."

That command confused them. "We'll meet again under more favourable circumstances," they said as they left, their faces and eyes afire with indignation.

Several newspapers, especially *L'Armonia*, carried reports of this encounter.

Notes

1. In 1861 the average print run was ten thousand; in 1870, fifteen thousand (T. Bosco, SP, p. 198).

2. *Gospel Readings* was a Waldensian periodical.

3. Amadeus Bert (1809–1883) and John Peter Meille (1817–1884) were prominent Waldensian ministers, Pugno a controversialist. In 1849 Bert published *I Valdesi, ossiano i cristiani-cattolici secondo la Chiesa primitiva* [The Waldensians, or Catholic Christians as They Were in the Early Church]. Meille published the Waldensian newspaper *La buona Novella*, mentioned in the preceding chapter.

4. The *Catholic Readings*; specifically, Don Bosco is alluding to *The Catholic Instructed*, which included "discussions" in its subtitle (see chapter 59, note 16).

5. Lemoyne (BM IV, 435) and Bonetti (p. 249) maintain that it was a Sunday morning in August 1853.

6. The title "doctor," i.e. of theology, was normally reserved for those who had earned such a degree or been appointed to a prominent diocesan position. Here, the two Waldensians are either continuing their flattery or using irony because they underestimate him.

7. The reader will remember Don Bosco's youthful struggles to achieve just this ability (chapter 20).

8. Made suspicious by the attitude of the two strangers, Joseph Buzzetti and several other boarders had mounted guard in the hallway.

An Attempt on
My Life

I looked as if some group of either Protestants or Free-masons had organised a conspiracy against me.[1] I shall narrate a few short examples.

One evening, I was amidst the boys teaching school when two men called me to hurry to a man who was dying at the *Golden Heart*.[2] I went immediately, but I wanted to take some of the bigger boys with me.

"There's no need," they explained, "to bother your pupils. We'll take you to the sick man and bring you back home. Their presence might upset the patient."

"Don't worry," I replied, "my pupils will take a little stroll and then wait downstairs while I attend to the sick man."

When we arrived at the house where the *Golden Heart* was, they told me, "Wait here a minute; relax a bit while we go to let the patient know you're here."

They showed me into a ground-floor room where some good-time Charlies were eating chestnuts after their supper. They welcomed me profusely with praise and applause, and they wanted me to help myself and eat some of their chestnuts. I would not taste them, alleging that I had just finished my supper.

"Then at least drink a glass of our wine," they answered. "It won't hurt you. It comes from around Asti."[3]

"I don't feel like it. I'm not accustomed to drinking outside of meals. It doesn't agree with me."[4]

"A small glass certainly won't upset you."

With that they poured wine for everyone. But when they came to mine, they took a bottle and glass that had been put to the side. Then I understood their wicked ruse; never the less I accepted the glass and joined in their toast, but instead of drinking, I tried to put the wine back down on the table.

"You can't do that," one said. "It's offensive."

"It's an insult," another chimed in. "You can't put us off like that."

"I don't feel like, I cannot, and I will not drink."

"You'll drink it for sure!" one exclaimed as he grabbed my left shoulder. An accomplice grabbed my right shoulder and added, "We can't let this insult pass. Drink it by choice or by force."

"If you really insist that I drink, I'll oblige you. But let me go. And since I can't drink it myself, I'll get one of my sons to drink it in my place."

With this misleading remark, I moved towards the door, opened it, and invited my young men to come in.

"There's no need for anybody else to drink it, none at all!" they cried. "Never mind, then. Let's go right away to see the sick man. These boys can stay downstairs."

I certainly would never have given that glass to anybody else, but I acted as I did the better to expose their treachery in trying to get me to drink the poisoned wine.

I was then taken to a room on the second floor,[5] where instead of a sick man I discovered lying there the very fellow who had come to the Oratory to fetch me. He put up with some of my questions but then burst out laughing. "I'll go to confession tomorrow morning," he said.

I left promptly to get back to my own business.

A friend of mine made some enquiries about the people who had summoned me and about their intention. I was assured that a certain individual had treated them to a big meal on the understanding that they should try to get me to drink a little wine that he had prepared.

Notes

1. The Freemasons (or Masons) are a fraternal order whose "principles and basic rituals embody a naturalistic religion, active participation in which is incompatible with Christian

faith and practice." Some of its branches, especially in Latin countries like Italy, are "atheistic, irreligious and anticlerical." Freemasonry has been condemned by eight different Popes seventeen separate times, a condemnation which still stands. (*1989 Catholic Almanac*, ed. Felician A. Foy [Huntington, Indiana, 1989], p. 311)

Don Bosco's aim was always the good of souls. His motto, and the Salesian Society's, taken from Genesis 14:21 by way of Saint Francis de Sales, is *Da mihi animas, caetera tolle* ["Give me souls; take away the rest"]. Even his polemical writings, like the bishop of Geneva's, were inspired by moderation and charity. At the end of *The Catholic Instructed* he appealed to Waldensian ministers who might read it: "These are the words of a brother who loves you more than you think. They are spoken by one who offers himself and all he has in this world for your good."

His writings, however, enraged his opponents. In the April 1854 issue of the *Catholic Readings*, entitled *Some Interesting Current Events*, Don Bosco wrote of his Protestant adversaries:

> In publishing *Some Interesting Current Events* we must warn our readers that the Protestants have shown themselves to be outraged by my publications about them. They have shown it by their words, private letters, and even their journalism. We expected them to challenge us by pointing out various errors in what we published. But they have not done so. All their words, writings, and publications seem to consist only of insults and abuse against the *Catholic Readings* and their author. When it comes to insults and abuse, we are quite willing to grant them the victory without bothering to reply. Our greatest concern has always been never to publish anything offensive to that charity which is due to every living person. So we willingly forgive all who abuse us, and we shall avoid resorting to personalities while uncovering error wherever it may be hidden.

Don Bosco was by no means the only writer for the *Catholic Readings*; but for their first nine years (1853–1861) he averaged four titles a year, some of them (like *The Catholic Instructed*) running over two or more issues. The titles averaged 109 pages each. Over the next twenty-three years (1862–1884), however, his contributions numbered just thirty-five. At the same time (1865–1888) he was authoring or revising fifty-four other works great and small, many of them concerned with the Salesian Society. (*Dizionario Biografico dei Salesiani*, pp. 53–55; Stella, *Gli scritti a stampa di S. Giovanni Bosco* [Rome: LAS, 1977])

2. This was an inn reached through a small courtyard at 34 via Cottolengo, very close to the Oratory. Near the end of his life, Don Bosco used to point it out when he passed by and remark to the Salesians with him, "There's the chestnuts room!"

   Neither Lemoyne (BM IV, 486–488) nor Bonetti (pp. 253–256) indicates just when this episode occurred.

3. Asti, Don Bosco's native province, is famous for its wines.

4. Don Bosco was ordinarily so abstemious that we cannot conclude from his refusal of the chestnuts and wine that he suspected them at this point. But bringing some young men with him evidences an awareness of the need for caution. Since he does not tell us when this happened, we cannot be sure that it was the first of the several assassination attempts on him at this time.

5. Americans would call it the third floor.

62

Further Assaults

Attacks • *A hail of blows*

Thee attacks that I am recounting may seem like fables, but sadly, they are all too true. Many people witnessed them. Here is an even stranger attempt on my life.

One August evening[1] around six o'clock, I was standing at the fence that we had put in the Oratory courtyard, surrounded by my young men. Suddenly a cry went up: "An assassin! An assassin!" And there was a certain man whom I knew quite well and had even given assistance to.[2] He was in his shirt sleeves and was brandishing a big knife. Rushing wildly at me, he was shouting, "I want Don Bosco! I want Don Bosco!"

All of us scattered in every direction, and the intruder chased one of the seminarians, mistaking him for me.[3] When he realised his mistake, he turned and came running furiously in my direction. I just had time to beat a retreat to the stairs of the old house, and the lock to the gate was barely secured when the madman reached it.[4] He hammered, shouted, and bit at the the iron bars to open them, to no avail. I was safe inside.

My young men wanted to overpower the unfortunate man and break him apart, but I repeatedly forbade them and they obeyed me. We sent word to the police, to police headquarters, to the carabinieri. It was not till 9:30 that evening, however, that two carabinieri arrested the rogue and took him to the barracks.

Next day, the chief of police sent an officer to ask whether I would drop the charges against my attacker. I answered that I forgave that assault and all other injuries.

But in the name of the law, I demanded of the authorities greater protection for the persons and property of citizens. But would you believe it? At the very same time when I had been attacked,[5] as I was leaving the house, there was my attacker waiting for me a short distance off.

A friend of mine, seeing that I could not expect police protection, decided to speak to the wretched man.[6] "I've been paid," he was told. "If you give me as much as the others do, I'll go away peacefully." He was paid 80 francs for back rent, another 80 to book him into new lodgings well away from Valdocco, and so ended that first comedy.[7]

The second which I am going to relate was not like that. About a month after the episode just narrated, one Sunday evening, I was asked to hurry to the Sardi house near the Refuge to hear the confession of a sick woman who was said to be dying.

Because of my previous experiences, I asked several of the bigger boys to come along with me. "There's no need," I was told. "We'll accompany you. Leave these lads at their games."

This was enough for me not to go alone.[8] I left some of them in the street at the foot of the stairs. Joseph Buzzetti and Hyacinth Arnaud were on the first-floor landing[9] not far from the door of the sick woman.

I went inside and saw a woman gasping as if she were about to breathe her last. I asked the men in attendance, four of them, to move off a little so that we might speak of her soul.

"Before I make my confession," she said in a strong voice, "I want that blackguard there in front of me to take back the calumnies he has been spreading about me."

"No," one of them answered.

"Shut up!" added another, rising to his feet.

Then they all stood up from their chairs. "Yes!" "No!" "Watch it!" "I'll strangle you!" "I'll cut your throat!" These shouts, mixed with horrible curses, echoed diabolically all over the room. In the midst of that melee, the light was put out. As the din increased, a hail of blows began to be aimed over where I was sitting. I had figured out their game right away, namely to jump me. In a moment, with time neither to ponder nor to reflect, necessity became the mother of invention. I grabbed a chair, put it over my head, and as I edged towards the door under that helmet, a shower of blows from sticks fell with a tremendous racket upon the chair.

Exiting that hotbed of Satan, I flew into the arms of my young men;[10] when they heard that noise and those yells, they were determined to break in, come what may.

I had suffered no serious wound. One blow struck my left thumb, which was exposed against the back of the chair. The nail and half the tip were ripped away, so that I carry the scar to this day. The worst harm was the fright.

I never could discover the real reason for this persecution, but it seems that all these attempts on my life were intended to make me stop, they would say, calumniating the Protestants.[11]

Notes

1. Lemoyne places this episode in the section of BM IV concerned mostly with 1853; he continues the story of the deranged man with events from the spring of 1854 (IV, 488–491).

2. The man's name was Andreis, and he had once been a tenant in the Pinardi house. At this time he lived in the Bellezza house. (BM IV, 488)

3. The seminarian was Felix Reviglio (BM IV, 489; Bonetti, p. 256).

4. There was a little iron gate at the foot of the staircase of the Pinardi house.

5. About six o'clock on the evening after the assault.

6. Don Bosco's longtime benefactor, Commendatore Joseph Duprè. He did not act, however, until after still another attempted knifing, witnessed by John Cagliero. (Bonetti, p. 257; BM IV, 490)

7. T. Bosco values these 160 lire at about 650,000 lire (1986), equivalent to about $450 (SP, p. 200).

8. He had meant to bring two young men; at this point he decided that four would be better. They were Joseph Buzzetti, Ribaudi, Hyacinth Arnaud, and James Cerruti. The

last two "were so muscular and strong that they could have felled an ox." (BM IV, 491) Buzzetti, Arnaud, and Cerruti were among the boys who in 1847 made the first Oratory retreat.

9. The landing of the second floor (U.S.).

10. Lemoyne tells us that Don Bosco found the door locked, and "using his extraordinary strength he twisted and tore the lock away with one hand," the other still holding the chair over his head, just as Arnaud and Buzzetti crashed their shoulders into the door from the other side (IV, 492).

11. Sixteen-year-old John Cagliero witnessed a more explicit connection. Two men called on Don Bosco one Sunday afternoon in January 1854 while the boys were in church. The boy noticed the two and was suspicious; so he eavesdropped. After failing to dissuade Don Bosco from publishing the *Catholic Readings*, the visitors pulled pistols on him. When the conversation in Don Bosco's room grew heated, Cagliero pounded on the door, ran for Buzzetti, and came back as Don Bosco was escorting the two men out, who were flustered at being caught in the act, as it were. (BM IV, 493)

Other assassination attempts, besides those involving Grigio (next chapter), are recounted in BM IV, 494–495; XIV, 405–407. Father Margotti, editor of *L'Armonia*, suffered a violent beating in January 1856 (BM IV, 571).

63

Grigio

The grey dog was the topic of many conversations and various conjectures.[1] Many of you have seen him and even petted him. Now, laying aside the fantastic stories which are told of this dog, I will tell you plainly only what is pure truth.[2]

The frequent attacks which had been made against me made it inadvisable for me to walk to or from the city of Turin alone. In those days, the asylum was the last building on the way to the Oratory. The rest of the way was land covered with hawthorn and acacia trees.[3]

One dark evening, rather late, I was making my way home with some trepidation when a huge dog appeared beside me, which at first sight gave me a start. But he seemed friendly and even nuzzled me as if I were his master. We quickly became friends, and he accompanied me as far as the Oratory. Many other times that evening's experience was repeated. Indeed, I may say that Grigio[4] did me valuable service. Here are a few examples.

On a wet, foggy night at the end of November 1854, I was coming from the city. So as not to have a long way to go alone, I took the street connecting Our Lady of Consolation and the Cottolengo.[5] At one point along the street I noticed two men walking a little in front of me. They matched their pace to mine, quickening or slowing down as I did. When I crossed the road to dodge them, they crossed right over in front of me. I attempted to turn back but was not in time. For they suddenly jumped me from behind, keeping an ominous silence, and threw a cloak over my head. I fought to keep from getting tangled up but it was no use. Then one also tried to stuff a rag into my mouth. I was trying to shout but could no longer do so. At that moment Grigio appeared, and growling like a bear he leapt into the face of one man while snapping viciously at the other. They plainly would have to tangle with the dog before finishing with me.

"Call off your dog," they began to cry, trembling with fear.

"I'll call him off," I said, "when you agree to leave passers-by alone."

"Call him off quick," they exclaimed.

Grigio continued growling like an enraged wolf or bear. The two men took to their heels, and Grigio stayed by my side, accompanying me until I went into the Cottolengo Institute. After recovering from my scare, and refreshed by a drink which that charitable institute always seems to come up with at the right moment, I went on home with a good escort.[6]

Every evening when I had no other company, as I passed the [last] buildings I would see Grigio bound out of nowhere along the way. Many times the Oratory boys saw him. Once he was the centre of an amusing incident. The boys saw him coming into the courtyard. Some wanted to strike him, and others wanted to throw stones at him.

"Don't tease him," Joseph Buzzetti ordered. "That's Don Bosco's dog." They turned to patting and stroking him then as they brought him along to me. I was in the refectory having supper with some seminarians and priests and with my mother. They were alarmed at the unexpected sight of the dog.

"There's no need to be afraid," I said. "It's my Grigio. Let him come in."

In fact he made a wide tour round the table and came joyfully up to me. I patted him too and offered him soup, bread, and meat, but he refused all of it. He would not even sniff at what I offered.

"Well, what do you want?" I asked. He only cocked his ears and wagged his tail.

"Either eat or drink or otherwise entertain me," I concluded. He continued to evidence contentment, resting his head on my napkin as if he wanted to speak to me and tell me "Good night." Then the boys, wondering a great deal and quite happy, led him outside. I remember that I had come home late, and a friend had brought me in his carriage.[7]

The last time that I saw Grigio was in 1866[8] while I was going from Murialdo to Moncucco to see my friend Louis Moglia.[9] The parish priest of Buttigliera wanted to accompany me part of the way, and as a consequence I was surprised by nightfall only halfway on my journey.

"Oh, if only I had my Grigio," I thought to myself, "how fortunate I would be!" Having said that, I started across a field to take advantage of the last rays of light. Just then Grigio came bounding up to me, full of affection. He accompanied me for the stretch of road that I still had to travel, which was two miles.

When I got to my friend's house, where I was expected, they asked me to go round another way, fearing there would be a fight between my Grigio and the family's two mastiffs. "If they got into a fight," said Moglia, "they would tear each other to pieces."

I talked a lot with the whole family before we sat down to supper. My companion was left to rest in a corner of the room. When we had finished our meal, my friend said, "We must also give Grigio his supper."

He took a little food to bring to the dog; he looked in every corner of the room and of the house, but Grigio was not to be found. We all wondered, since neither door nor window was open, nor had the family dogs given any sign of his departure. We renewed our search upstairs, but no one could find him.

That is the last news I had of the grey dog that was the subject of so much enquiry and discussion. I never was able to find out who was his owner. I only know that the animal was truly providential for me on many occasions when I found myself in danger.[10]

Notes

1. Because of the dog's gray fur Don Bosco named him "Grigio." Art teacher Charles Tomatis, who was a student at the Oratory and saw Grigio, described the mysterious animal to Lemoyne:

> It had a truly frightening appearance. Every time she saw it, Mama Margaret would unfailingly exclaim: "Oh, what an ugly beast!" It looked like a wolf, with a long snout, erect pointed ears, and gray fur. It was over three feet tall. (BM IV, 497)

2. The story of Grigio does, indeed, sound fantastic. We should note two things right away:

   1. Don Bosco has just said that there are some "fantastic stories" being told about the dog, but he will tell only what actually happened.

   2. He was not writing for publication but for the private readership of the Salesians; he had no need to impress anyone. Several Salesians had been eyewitnesses to these events; among those who saw and petted Grigio were Joseph Buzzetti, Michael Rua, John Cagliero, and John Baptist Francesia (BM IV, 496–502; Francesia, *Vita breve e popolare*, p. 179).

3. The distance is about a quarter mile. Don Bosco uses the Italian word *bossoli* (boxwood), which is almost identical to the Piedmontese *bóssol* (hawthorn), and that is what he meant.

4. Don Bosco, aside from the first words of the chapter, calls the dog simply *il grigio*, without either the noun *cane* or capitalization of the name which he bestowed on the beast.

5. One block along via della Consolata, across corso San Massimo, and one block along via Ariosto.

6. From the front door of the Cottolengo to the Oratory was a block and a half along via Cottolengo and another block along via della Giardiniera.

7. Buzzetti recalled "that Marquis Dominic Fassati had taken Don Bosco home late that night in his coach. Having missed him, Grigio seemed to have come to assure Don Bosco that he had waited for him with his customary fidelity" (BM IV, 500).

   In 1920 an old Turinese priest, Father Philip Durando, recounted to a Salesian missionary, Father John Aliberti, how the dog appeared another time in the Salesian dining room while Father Durando was having supper with Don Bosco. (MB XVIII, 869–870)

8. Bonetti (pp. 263–264) and Lemoyne (BM IV, 496–502; VIII, 222) tell of several other incidents in which Grigio saved Don Bosco from assailants in the early 1850s or kept him company on lonely walks in the dark.

   This 1866 appearance was the last as of the time when Don Bosco was writing his memoirs (but cf. BM X, 177). In 1883, however, he saw the mysterious dog again while returning to Vallecrosia from Ventimiglia (in western Liguria!) late one evening (MB XVIII, 8). He spoke of this appearance several times in different places. One of those who heard him tell the story was his French biographer Doctor Charles D'Espiney (MB XVI, 36; XVIII, 10); another was Father Secondo Gay, pastor of Saint Silvester's Church in Asti, who testified to it on October 17, 1908, during the gathering of evidence for Don Bosco's beatification.

9. As seminarian and as priest Don Bosco cherished the Moglias and visited them frequently; he is being quite reserved here when he speaks of them.

10. Don Bosco often thought about trying to learn where the dog came from. In the end he just said, "Well, let him belong to whomever he likes, as long as he's my good friend." Henri Ghéon wrote:

    > Providence can use a dog. An angel could quite well take the form of a dog. At the very least we can assert that the animal — if animal it was — had a nose for sanctity, and would fight for it. If it was a miracle, God worked so many other miracles for Don Bosco that this one need not surprise us. (*Secrets of the Saints* [New York: Sheed & Ward, 1951], p. 358)

    It is not inappropriate that the Lord should provide a special guardian for the priest who was the special guardian of so many poor and abandoned youngsters.

    If Don Bosco has not told us all that he knew or suspected about Grigio (besides keeping silent about the other divine interventions to be mentioned in a moment), it is at least partly because he never proposed to write a complete autobiography or a complete history of the Oratory. There are, moreover, things that modesty does not permit one to write, regardless of commands.

    But Grigio appeals to our curiosity in a unique way and makes us ask about his origins. In answer to a query in 1870, Don Bosco remarked, "It sounds ridiculous to call him an angel, yet he is no ordinary dog ... " (BM X, 177). Another time, in 1883, Don Bosco was visiting the Olive family, generous benefactors from Marseilles. He told them how he had recently met his old and faithful gray friend on the road from Ventimiglia. The astonished lady of the house observed that Grigio would have to be two or three times older than dogs normally live. Don Bosco smiled mischievously. "Then it must have been Grigio's son or grandson," he suggested, evading the issue she was driving at. (MB XVI, 36)

The Salesian Sisters also claim to have experienced Grigio's protection on three occasions between 1893 and 1930 (MB XVI, 36–37)!

The Salesians feel safe in believing that Grigio sired no pups.

This seems to be an opportune place to raise a larger question, at least for those who know something more of Don Bosco than he tells us in these pages. How believable are the supernatural events connected with him? How reliable are the various sources for his biographies?

Pietro Stella has investigated some of the extraordinary charisms attributed to Don Bosco (*ReCa*, pp. 475–500). We referred at some length to Don Bosco's dreams in a comment at the end of chapter 2; he relates or mentions several of them in his memoirs, and others have turned up in the commentary.

Perhaps the most challenged instance of the supernatural in Don Bosco's life, if it actually occurred, is the reported raising to life, or resuscitation, of a deceased boy called "Charles." Stella made a forty-seven-page study of the case as a way of illustrating his historical method: *Don Bosco and the Death of Charles*, trans. John Drury (New Rochelle: Don Bosco Publications, 1985).

One may be skeptical about "Charles" or not, as one judges the skimpy evidence. Some have tried to discount all or most of the extraordinary events, as well as others (such as Don Bosco's dealings with certain great men and an occasion when he took some three hundred inmates of the Generala Prison on a day's outing without a single guard, and returned all of them in the evening). Some have discounted most of the *Biographical Memoirs* because they are barely documented and for other reasons. Ceria responded to such critics in a long letter addressed to the director of the Salesian theological school at Bollengo, outside Turin, on March 9, 1953. A translation of this letter is available in photocopy from Don Bosco Publications.

Others have said that in Don Bosco the extraordinary

became ordinary. On at least one occasion each he multiplied chestnuts (BM III, 404–406) and breakfast rolls (BM VI, 453–455); he multiplied the Holy Eucharist several times (BM III, 311–312; VI, 580–581; VII, 388–389; MB XVII, 520–521). There are well-documented instances of bilocation (BM VII, 290–291; XIV, 552–555; MB XVIII, 34–39). The examples of his predictions of deaths and other future events, his healings of the sick (at least sixty cases have been counted), his knowledge of consciences and of events happening miles away are countless and are abundantly witnessed (see MB XX under the headings *Predizioni, Guarigione, Scrutazione dei cuori, Coscienze, Cuori, Leggere in fronte,* and *Lontana*).

Postscript

POSTSCRIPT

Unfortunately the *Memoirs of the Oratory* stops with these murderous attempts and the story of the mysterious gray dog. A new phase of Saint John Bosco's life was about to begin, that of the founder. As his dreams about the future of the Oratory had foretold, his first clerical helpers and his earliest recruits (Ascanio Savio, Reviglio, Bellia, Gastini, Rocchietti) did not stay with him. But some of the lambs did grow up and turn into shepherds: Buzzetti, Rua, Cagliero, Francesia, Angelo Savio, Bonetti, and others. The Salesians are probably unique in that the founder shaped his "cofounders" right from their boyhood and did not form an association of some kind with grown men.[1]

The decade 1854–1864 were the years of founding the Salesian Society. After night prayers on January 26, 1854, Don Bosco called the young seminarians Rua, Cagliero, Rocchietti, and Artiglia to his room. It was three days before the feast of Saint Francis de Sales, and the priest proposed to the youths that they make promises to work together to perform deeds of charity toward their neighbors, that they might eventually bind themselves by vows, and that they take the name Salesians. They agreed.[2] Their practice of charity, of course, was focused on the work of the oratories (Valdocco, Porta Nuova, and Vanchiglia). Don Bosco guided them through conferences, spiritual direction, and confession. They continued their philosophical and theological studies. In the next few years their group increased, and some began to make private vows under Don Bosco's guidance.

After almost six years, Don Bosco had with him one mature and experienced priest, Father Alasonatti, and eighteen youths whom he had trained himself. In December 1859 he invited them to form a new religious congregation with him to aim "at the sanctification of each member by mutual assistance" and "to promote God's glory and the salvation of souls, especially of those in greater need of instruction and formation." For some it was really a moment of decision: "Don Bosco wants to make monks of us all!" (Besides the vocational implications, there were the political ones. The government had already expelled all the monastic orders and confiscated their property.) Impetuous

An aerial view of the Oratory in mid-twentieth century. At the center is the Basilica of Mary Help of Christians. The second dome was constructed between 1935 and 1938, when the church was enlarged. Barely visible behind that dome is the bell tower of the Church of Saint Francis de Sales. To the right of the bell tower is the building that replaced the Pinardi house in 1856, and the ell-shaped hospice annex (1853–1876). Surrounding these buildings are an oratory, middle school, ginnasio, high school seminary, technical school, parish church, publishing house, and the Salesian Sisters' oratory for girls.

Cagliero paced up and down the portico for a long time before finally deciding: "I am determined never to leave Don Bosco. Monk or not, it's all the same to me!"

When the group met on December 18, only two had decided not to come. Don Bosco, Father Alasonatti, sixteen seminarians, and one layman bound themselves by vow and formally founded the Society of Saint Francis de Sales.[3] Don Bosco had already drafted a Rule and presented it to Pius IX.

During the next ten years (1865–1875) the Salesians grew and spread. They won temporary papal approval in 1864 and final approval in 1869. After much tribulation, the Vatican approved the Rule in 1874. By then bishops and municipalities from all over northern Italy were asking Don Bosco to establish schools or oratories for them; Don Bosco and Mary Domenica Mazzarello had founded the Daughters of Mary Help of Christians; and Don Bosco was beginning to plan the Society's expansion into France and the foreign missions (which became realities in 1875).

Don Bosco the builder was at work too. By 1863 the size and scope of the Oratory had outgrown the Church of Saint Francis de Sales and he began to think of a monumental church in honor of our Lady under the relatively unknown title of Help of Christians. With his customary trust in Divine Providence, he began the work in 1864 and handed the contractor, Charles Buzzetti, the first payment: eight centesimi. But with abundant miraculous help from heaven ("Every brick represents a grace from our Blessed Mother"[4]), the church was completed and consecrated in 1868.

With similar trust, energy, and heavenly help Don Bosco proceeded to put up two more great churches in the 1870s and 1880s, one in honor of Saint John the Evangelist in Porta Nuova, the other — by papal request — in honor of the Sacred Heart in Rome (opposite the main train station).

As a young man Don Bosco had thought about going to the foreign missions. Father Cafasso, happily, discouraged him. But the dream remained. It was more than a dream, really; for the missions were the subject of many of his prophetic visions. For instance, when Cagliero was dying of typhoid in 1854 and Don Bosco was called to anoint him, he suddenly saw around the boy a crowd of dark-skinned savages from who-knows-where, and a dove fluttering over the sick boy's head. He understood that Cagliero would recover and would eventually become a missionary.[5] Other dreams seemed to show him the future fields where his sons and daughters would labor to make good Christians and good citizens.

Various requests for Salesians came from foreign lands. Don Bosco finally recognized one that answered to a dream and sent Father Cagliero and nine other priests and brothers to Buenos Aires in November 1875, with an eye to opening up missions in the vast wilderness of Patagonia. And so it happened. By 1884 Cagliero was ordained a bishop and dozens of Salesians and sisters were in Argentina, Chile, Uruguay, and Brazil.

From 1876 to 1887 Don Bosco expanded and consolidated the works which Divine Providence had entrusted to him. Realizing that lay people were critical to the apostolate in the modern world, the saint conceived another bold idea—one so bold that, when he incorporated it into his original Salesian Rule it became a major sticking point as far as the Roman Curia was concerned. That was to include laymen as full members of the Salesian Society, without vows and living at home. Anyone who wished to cooperate in working for the salvation of the young and in spreading good Christian literature was welcome! To secure the approval of the Rule, Don Bosco finally had to yield the point. But not the concept. In 1876 he brought it to reality in a different form, the Association of Salesian Cooperators. (It also included secular clergy, and indeed Pius IX asked to be enrolled as the first member.) By the end of the following year they had their own monthly magazine, the *Salesian Bulletin* (now published in a dozen languages in thirty-nine different editions). Although the Cooperators make no vows, in some sense they were the forerunners of secular institutes of consecrated lay people.

The apostle of youth's dreams continued to guide him in prophetic ways, and miraculous events became commonplace in his life. His contemporaries coveted his written and spoken word, even snips of his hair and bits of his clothing. Don Bosco exclaimed to Father Cagliero, "How wonderful is the Lord, and how immense his mercy! He chose a peasant boy of Becchi to be his instrument in performing his wonders before such a host of people."[6] In the early 1860s the Salesians at the Oratory began to document virtually everything he said and did, entrusting the results to Father Lemoyne, who himself made a habit of "pumping" the saint almost every night for stories about his youth and the early days of the Oratory. Lemoyne assembled all this, plus the testimony he gathered from alumni, benefactors, friends from Don Bosco's youth, and others, into forty-five huge volumes of raw material.

After the saint's death (January 31, 1888), Lemoyne began to edit his documents into a biography; publication began in 1898 with the first volume of the *Biographical Memoirs*. When he died in 1916, he had completed nine volumes. Fathers Amadei and Ceria finished the work in 1939 except for the index (volume XX). As was mentioned in the introduction, only the first four of these deal with the years 1815–1854, the period covered by Don Bosco's autobiography. The remaining thirty-three years of his life fill volumes V-XVIII (7980 pages) — ample evidence to how thoroughly the first generation collected anecdotes and letters and recorded events and conferences. (The nineteenth volume of the *Biographical Memoirs* covers the process of canonization, 1888–1934.)

Pope Pius XI canonized Saint John Bosco on Easter Sunday, April 1, 1934. It has been said that it was a great April Fool's joke: how Don Bosco fooled all those who thought he was crazy! Today the visitor to Saint Peter's Basilica in Rome may see his statue in the row of the saintly founders a hundred feet above the floor; it is directly above the bronze statue of Saint Peter and the medallion commemorating the pontificate of Pius IX, a fitting place for the defender of Peter's successors and friend of Pius. That, too, Don Bosco once dreamed, though without at all understanding what it meant; whoever recorded it thought it so insignificant that there are few details and no date.[7]

But the greatest monument to Don Bosco is not marble.

It is his huge family. As of March 1989, there are over 34,000 Salesian sisters, brothers, priests, and novices in thirty-three nations of Africa, twenty-five countries in the Americas, Australia, nineteen nations and colonies of Asia and the Pacific islands, and twenty-one nations of Europe. In 1989 eighty-four confreres were serving the Church as bishops, mostly in the Third World, including five as cardinals (Silva Henriquez of Chile, Castillo Lara of Venezuela, Obando Bravo of Nicaragua, Stickler of Austria, and Javierre Ortas of Spain). Tens of thousands of Cooperators and lay volunteers work alongside the Salesian religious. New branches of the family have sprung up: the Don Bosco Volunteers, a secular institute for women founded by Father Philip Rinaldi in 1917; and eight congregations of sisters founded by Salesians to carry out particular apostolic works according to the spirit of Saint Francis de Sales and Saint John Bosco. And there are, of course, the hundreds of thousands of past and present pupils — the heart of Don Bosco's family: "That you are young is enough to make me love you very much."[8]

Notes

1. See Francis Desramaut, "The Founding of the Salesian Family (1841–1876)," trans. Paul Aronica (New Rochelle, 1985); and Joseph Aubry, "The Role of the Salesians Within the Salesian Family," trans. Paul Aronica (New Rochelle, 1987), pp. 4–11.

2. BM V, 7–8.

3. BM VI, 180–183.

4. See BM VIII, 402–403.

5. BM V, 67–68.

6. BM XIV, 332; cf. X, 141.

7. MB XVII, 11–12.

8. *Il Giovane provveduto* (Turin, 1847), p. 7; quoted in Constitutions, article 14.

Appendices

APPENDIX I

Important Dates in the Life of
Saint John Bosco and Salesian History

ເononcen

August 16	1815	John Melchior Bosco is born at Castelnuovo d'Asti (now Castelnuovo Don Bosco), Piedmont.
May 12	1817	John's father dies.
	1824 or 1825	A mysterious dream reveals to John his mission from God.
March	1826	John makes his first communion.
February	1827	After repeated arguments with his stepbrother, John leaves home to live and work on the Moglia farm.
November	1829	John comes home and meets Fr. Calosso.
December	1830	After Fr. Calosso's death, John enrolls in school at Castelnuovo.
November 4	1831	John goes to Chieri, where he attends school and learns some trades and some music.
	1832	John and some friends form the Society for a Good Time.
August 4	1833	John is confirmed at Buttigliera.
	1834	Louis Comollo and John meet at school in Chieri.
October 30	1835	John enters the seminary at Chieri.
April 2	1839	Comollo dies; the next night he appears to John and other seminarians; soon after, John falls seriously ill.

June 5	1841	John Bosco is ordained by Abp. Fransoni of Turin.
November 3	1841	Don Bosco moves to Turin to take pastoral courses at the Convitto Ecclesiastico and places himself under the spiritual direction of Fr. Joseph Cafasso.
December 8	1841	Don Bosco begins the work of the Oratory with a catechism lesson at the Church of St. Francis of Assisi.
October	1844	Don Bosco leaves the Convitto; he and the Oratory move to the Refuge.
May	1845	The Oratory has to leave the Refuge and becomes the "wandering Oratory," briefly using four different sites.
September	1845	Michael Rua begins to come to the Oratory.
Fall	1845	Don Bosco and Fr. Borel begin offering night courses to young workers.
April 12	1846	Don Bosco firmly establishes the Oratory in Valdocco (Turin) on Mr. Pinardi's property.
July	1846	Don Bosco falls ill and nearly dies (pleurisy?); while he is recovering, Fr. Borel runs the Oratory.
November 3	1846	Mama Margaret moves to the Oratory.
December	1846	Don Bosco rents the entire Pinardi house and opens a full-scale night school.
April 12	1847	The Company of St. Aloysius is formed at the Oratory.
May	1847	Don Bosco takes in the first boarder at the Oratory, an orphan looking for work.
	1847	Don Bosco organizes the first spiritual retreat for boys at the Oratory.
December 8	1847	Don Bosco and Fr. Borel open a second oratory, that of St. Aloysius in Porta Nuova (Turin).

February	1848	Don Bosco refuses to get involved in popular political agitation; a crisis among his helpers follows, resulting in his resolution to form his own young assistants.
Fall	1848	Don Bosco's first seminarian dons the cassock and comes to live at the Oratory.
October 4	1848	The Boncompagni Law begins transferring authority over schooling from the Church to the State.
	1848–1849	The First War of Independence (against Austria) increases the number of orphans and causes strains on public finance.
February	1849	Don Bosco founds the journal *The Friend of Youth*, which fails after 61 issues.
April 9	1850	The Siccardi Laws abolish Church courts; Abp. Fransoni's protests lead to his banishment.
July 1	1850	Don Bosco establishes the Mutual Aid Society for the young workers of the Oratory.
	1851	Don Bosco buys the Pinardi house, begins building a new church, and begins making apprentice contracts between his boys and selected Turin tradesmen.
March 31	1852	Abp. Fransoni appoints Don Bosco "superior of the oratories" of Turin.
June 20	1852	The first real church at the Oratory is dedicated in honor of St. Francis de Sales.
March	1853	Don Bosco publishes the first issue of the *Catholic Readings*.
	1853	The first workshops at the Oratory are opened and the hospice wing is built.

January 26	1854	Don Bosco first calls his young helpers "Salesians," after St. Francis de Sales.
Summer	1854	Cholera ravages Turin; the Oratory boys distinguish themselves in their care for the sick.
October 29	1854	Dominic Savio enters the Oratory.
March 25	1855	Michael Rua is the first Salesian to make his vows.
	1855–1856	Piedmont sends 15,000 troops to support Britain and France in the Crimean War: more orphans, more public expenses, and more pressure to expel the Austrians.
May 29	1855	The Rattazzi Law suppresses religious orders in the Kingdom of Sardinia.
December 9	1855	Mary Mazzarello and other young women form the Daughters of Mary Immaculate in Mornese, Piedmont, under the guidance of Fr. Dominic Pestarino.
June 8	1856	Dominic Savio founds the Company of the Immaculate Conception.
November 25	1856	Mama Margaret dies at the Oratory.
March 9	1857	Dominic Savio dies at his home in Mondonio.
June 22	1857	The Lanza Law subjects all schools to the ministry of education; teachers have to be certified. Don Bosco acts to comply.
	1857	Don Bosco begins writing the Salesian Rule.
Feb.–April	1858	Don Bosco makes his first visit to Rome, to speak with Pope Pius IX about the Salesian Society; he mediates between Cavour and the Vatican in the Fransoni case.
January	1859	Don Bosco publishes the life of Dominic Savio.

April–June	1859	The Second War of Independence joins Lombardy to Piedmont and stimulates the annexation of central and southern Italy in 1860.
November	1859	The Casati Law completely and more strictly regulates education from elementary school to university; religion is still a required course. Don Bosco complies with its provisions.
December 18	1859	Don Bosco and the first 17 Salesians form a religious congregation.
	1860	The first Salesians are ordained priests: Frs. Angelo Savio and Michael Rua.
June 23	1860	Fr. Cafasso dies; Don Bosco delivers two eulogies, later published.
	1860–1861	Don Bosco and the Oratory, accused of conspiring against the State, are subjected to a series of house searches, which turn up nothing worse than letters from Abp. Fransoni. Some documents relevant to the Oratory's early history apparently are lost at this time.
	1861	Don Bosco sets up his own printing press and publishes the life of Michael Magone; a group of 14 Salesians under-undertakes to record everything that Don Bosco says and does.
October 20	1863	The first Salesian work outside Turin opens, a school at Mirabello with Fr. Rua as director; Don Bosco gives him guidelines which become the core of future advice to all directors.
March	1864	Work begins on the Church of Mary Help of Christians at the Oratory.
October 8	1864	Don Bosco meets Mary Mazzarello and and her friends at Mornese.
	1866	Don Bosco mediates between the Vatican and the government for the return or appointment of 45 bishops to vacant sees.

	1867	Pope Pius IX orders Don Bosco to write his *Memoirs*.
June 9	1868	The Church of Mary Help of Christians is consecrated.
	1868	Don Bosco mediates between the Vatican and the government to secure episcopal revenues.
March 1	1869	The Holy See formally approves the Salesian Society.
June	1870	Some of Don Bosco's past pupils establish the Salesian Alumni Association.
September	1870	The first Salesian house outside Piedmont opens at Alassio (Liguria).
December 7	1871	Don Bosco falls gravely ill for 50 days.
August 5	1872	The Daughters of Mary Help of Christians (Salesian Sisters) are organized with Mary Mazzarello as superior.
	1873	Fr. Borel dies; ten years of conflict with Abp. Gastaldi begin.
April 3	1874	The Holy See gives final approval to the Rule of the Salesian Society.
November 11	1875	Fr. Cagliero leads the first Salesian missionaries to Argentina.
November 21	1875	The first Salesian house outside Italy opens at Nice.
May 9	1876	The Holy See approves the Association of Salesian Cooperators and Don Bosco's work for late vocations.
August	1877	Don Bosco publishes the first issue of the *Salesian Bulletin*.
September 5	1877	The first Salesian general chapter meets for one month.
February 7	1878	Pius IX dies as the "prisoner of the Vatican"; Don Bosco is called upon to obtain government assurances of a free conclave.

February 4	1879	The Salesian Sisters move their mother-house from Mornese to Nizza Monferrato.
	1880	Leo XIII asks Don Bosco to complete the Church of the Sacred Heart at Rome and open a Salesian work in the working-class district of Castro Pretorio.
May 14	1881	Mother Mazzarello dies at Nizza Monferrato.
Feb.–May	1883	Don Bosco spends four months in France raising funds for Salesian works and the Church of the Sacred Heart.
	1884	The Salesian Sisters hold their first general chapter.
December 7	1884	John Cagliero is ordained the first Salesian bishop, for the missions of Patagonia (Argentina).
	1886	Don Bosco journeys triumphantly through Spain to raise funds for his works and the Church of the Sacred Heart.
May 14	1887	The Church of the Sacred Heart is consecrated in Rome.
November 16	1887	Salesian work in Britain opens at Battersea (London).
January 31	1888	Don Bosco dies at the Oratory in Turin. There are 773 Salesians and 393 sisters.
	1891	First Salesian works open in Africa (Algeria) and in Asia (Palestine).
	1896	Salesian works open in South Africa (Cape Town) and the U.S. (San Francisco).
	1903	The first Salesian work in Malta is founded.
	1906	The Salesians go to India under the leadership of the future Abp. Mathias.

	1911	The Holy See formally approves the Daughters of Mary Help of Christians and their Rule.
	1915	Benedict XV appoints Bp. Cagliero a cardinal.
	1917	Fr. Philip Rinaldi and some young women found the Don Bosco Volunteers, a secular institute.
	1919	Salesian work in Ireland begins at Pallaskenry.
	1922	Salesian work in Australia begins.
	1924	The first Salesian foundation in Canada opens in Toronto.
April 1	1934	Pius XI canonizes St. John Bosco.
	1940	The Salesian Pontifical University is founded at Turin (later moves to Rome).
May 24	1946	Pope Pius XII declares St. John Bosco the patron of Catholic publishers. He is also the patron of umbrella makers and of apprentices.
	1947	Pius XII canonizes St. Joseph Cafasso.
June 25	1951	Pius XII canonizes St. Mary Mazzarello.
	1951	Salesian work in the Philippines is permanently established.
June 12	1954	Pius XII canonizes St. Dominic Savio.
	1969	The Salesian Sisters move their world headquarters from Turin to Rome.
	1972	The Salesians move their world headquarters from Turin to Rome and accept two parishes on Grand Bahama Island.
October 29	1972	Paul VI beatifies Bl. Michael Rua.
	1979	Project Africa marks a new stage in Salesian missionary expansion.
May 15	1983	John Paul II beatifies the martyrs Bl. Louis Versiglia and Callistus Caravario.

| December 8 | 1984 | The Holy See approves the Salesians' renewed Constitutions. |
| September 3 | 1988 | During a visit to Don Bosco's birthplace, John Paul II beatifies Bl. Laura Vicuña, pupil of the Salesian Sisters from Argentina. |

APPENDIX II

Government in Don Bosco's Lifetime

European Monarchs

SARDINIA-ITALY
Victor Emmanuel I, 1802–21
Charles Felix, 1821–31
Charles Albert, 1831–49
Victor Emmanuel II, 1849–78
Humbert I, 1878–1900

UNITED KINGDOM
George III, 1760–1820
George IV, 1820–30
William IV, 1830–37
Victoria, 1837–1901

FRANCE
Louis XVIII, 1814–24
Charles X, 1824–30
Louis Philippe, 1830–48
Second Republic, 1848–52
Napoleon III, 1852–70
Third Republic, 1870–1940

CATHOLIC CHURCH
Pius VII, 1800–23
Leo XII, 1823–29
Pius VIII, 1829–30
Gregory XVI, 1831–46
Pius IX, 1846–78
Leo XIII, 1878–1903

AUSTRIAN EMPIRE
Francis I, 1792–1835
Ferdinand I, 1835–48
Francis Joseph, 1848–1916

PRUSSIA-GERMANY
Frederick William III, 1797–1840
Frederick William IV, 1840–61
William I, 1861–88

NAPLES
Ferdinand I, 1815–25
Francis I, 1825–30
Ferdinand II, 1830–59
Francis II, 1859–60

Prime Ministers *of Sardinia-Italy*

Count Cesare Balbo, 1848

Count Ottavio di Revel, 1848

Vincenzo Gioberti, 1848–49

Baron Agostino Chiodo, 1849

Massimo d'Azeglio, 1849–52

Count Camillo Cavour, 1852–61

Bettino Ricasoli, 1861–62

Urbano Rattazzi, 1862

Luigi Carlo Farini, 1862–63

Marco Minghetti, 1863–64

Alfonso La Marmora, 1864–66

Bettino Ricasoli, 1866–67

Urbano Rattazzi, 1867

Luigi Federico Menabrea, 1867–69

Giovanni Lanza, 1869–73

Marco Minghetti, 1873–76

Agostino Depretis, 1876–78

Benedetto Cairoli, 1878

Agostino Depretis, 1878–79

Benedetto Cairoli, 1879–81

Agostino Depretis, 1881–87

Francesco Crispi, 1887–91

Prime Ministers *of the United Kingdom*

Earl of Liverpool, 1812–27

George Canning, 1827

Viscount Goderich, 1827–28

Duke of Wellington, 1828–30

Earl Grey, 1830–34

Viscount Melbourne, 1834

Sir Robert Peel, 1834–35

Viscount Melbourne, 1835–41

Sir Robert Peel, 1841–46

Earl Russell, 1846–52

Earl of Derby, 1852

Earl of Aberdeen, 1852–55

Viscount Palmerston, 1855–58

Earl of Derby, 1858–59

Viscount Palmerston, 1859–65

Earl Russell, 1865–66

Earl of Derby, 1866–68

Benjamin Disraeli, 1868

William E. Gladstone, 1868–74

Benjamin Disraeli, 1874–80

William E. Gladstone, 1880–85

Marquis of Salisbury, 1885–86

William E. Gladstone, 1886

Marquis of Salisbury, 1886–92

Presidents *of the United States*

James Madison, 1809–17

James Monroe, 1817–25

John Quincy Adams, 1825–29

Andrew Jackson, 1829–37

Martin Van Buren, 1837–41

William Henry Harrison, 1841

John Tyler, 1841–45

James K. Polk, 1845–49

Zachary Taylor, 1849–50

Millard Fillmore, 1850–53

Franklin Pierce, 1853–57

James Buchanan, 1857–61

Abraham Lincoln, 1861–65

Andrew Johnson, 1865–69

Ulysses S. Grant, 1869–77

Rutherford B. Hayes, 1877–81

James A. Garfield, 1881

Chester A. Arthur, 1881–85

Grover Cleveland, 1885–89

Population (in millions) of Major Nations

	U.K.*	France	Italy	Austria	Germany	U.S.
1815	19.1	29.0	18.0	—	26.0	—
1820	—	30.5	—	14.0	—	9.6
1830	24.0	32.5	21.0	15.6	30.0	12.9
1840	26.5	34.0	22.4	16.6	31.0	17.1
1850	27.7	35.8	24.3	17.6	36.0	23.2
1860	29.0	36.7	25.0	19.0	38.0	31.4
1870	31.0	38.0	26.0	20.2	41.0	38.6
1880	34.8	37.4	28.4	22.1	45.2	50.2
1890	37.7	38.1	30.5	23.7	49.4	63.0

*including Ireland

APPENDIX III

Chapter Equivalencies

ເວຈວຈ

The chapter numbering of Don Bosco and the Ceria edition
compared to the chapter numbering of this English edition

Bosco-Ceria			English	Bosco-Ceria			English
Pt III	ch	1	40	Pt III	ch	13	52
		2	41			14	53
		3	42			15	54
		4	43			16	55
		5	44			17	56
		6	45			18	57
		7	46			[19]*	58
		8	47			[20]	59
		9	48			[21]	60
		10	49			[22]	61
		11	50			[23]	62
		12	51			[24]	63

*Don Bosco and Father Ceria did not number the last six chapters, nor did Fathers Barucq and Desramaut in the French edition. Father Teresio Bosco, however, did number them in the modern Italian version, though he arranged the chapter divisions slightly differently.

Bibliography

BIBLIOGRAPHY

❦❦

Publishers' Abbreviations

DBP Don Bosco Publications, New Rochelle, New York
LAS Libreria Ateneo Salesiano, Rome
LDC Elle Di Ci (Libreria Dottrina Cristiana), Turin
SEI Società Editrice Internazionale, Turin

The Memoirs of the Oratory

Bosco, Giovanni. *Memorie dell'Oratorio di S. Francesco di Sales dal 1815 al 1855*, ed. Eugenio Ceria. SEI, 1946. First published edition of the *Memoirs*, with introduction and extensive annotation by Fr. Ceria. Illustrated.

Bosco, Giovanni. *Memorie*, trascrizione in lingua corrente di Teresio Bosco. LDC, 1985. Modern Italian version of the *Memoirs* with a few notes by Teresio Bosco. There are illustrations and an appendix translated from Desramaut (see below).

Bosco, Jean. *Souvenirs autobiographiques*. Quebec: Editions Paulines, 1978. French trans. by Fr. André Barucq; contains an introduction and notes by Fr. Francis Desramaut. There are 3 short appendices from other sources, and illustrations.

Desramaut, Francis, SDB. *Les Memorie I de Giovanni Battista Lemoyne: Etude d'un ouvrage fondamental sur la jeunesse de saint Jean Bosco*. Lyons: Maison d'Etudes Saint-Jean-Bosco, 1962. Desramaut's doctoral dissertation focuses on Lemoyne's first volume, but he necessarily comments on and corrects the *Memorie dell'Oratorio* as he goes along. On pp. 115–134 he studies the text, purposes, and accuracy of DB's memoirs.

Klein, Jan, SDB, and Eugenio Valentini, SDB. "Una rettificazione cronologica delle 'Memorie di San Giovanni Bosco,'" *Salesianum* 17 (1955), 581–610. The first attempt to correct the dates given by DB and to reconcile them with other events.

Don Bosco

Auffray, Augustine, SDB. *Saint John Bosco*. Blaisdon, England: Salesian Publications, n.d. Reprint of 1930 trans. from French; one of the classic biographies. Also available in an Indian edition (Tirupattur: Salesian House, 1959), which is indexed.

Bonetti, Giovanni. *Cinque lustri di storia dell'Oratorio salesiano fondato dal sacerdote D. Giovanni Bosco*. Turin: Tipografia Salesiana, 1892. The research and recollections of one of the first Salesians; an invaluable primary source. English adaptation: *St. John Bosco's Early Apostolate*. London: Burns Oates & Washbourne, 1934; illustrated, with appendices.

Bosco, Giovanni. *Epistolario di S. Giovanni Bosco*, ed. Eugenio Ceria. 4 vols. SEI, 1955–1959. Collection of 2845 letters from archival and private sources arranged chronologically. Since 1959 many additional letters have been discovered. A new critical edition is being prepared by the Istituto Storico Salesiano at Rome.

Bosco, Teresio. *Don Bosco: Una biografia nuova*. LDC, 1979. Detailed popular biography based on the latest scholarly findings. Illustrated. English adaptation, incorporating also material from the next item, in progress.

Bosco, Teresio. *Don Bosco: Storia di un prete*. LDC, 1987. Yet another look at DB, using material published since 1979 and additional sources. Illustrated.

Caselle, Secondo. *Cascinali e contadini in Monferrato: I Bosco di Chieri nel secolo XVIII*. LAS, 1975. Ground-breaking research into the Bosco family through public documents, among other sources.

Caselle, Secondo. *Giovanni Bosco studente: Chieri, 1831–1841: Dieci anni che valgono una vita*. Turin: Edizione Acclaim, 1988. Research into the primary sources for DB's school and seminary years by Chieri's former mayor. Maps and illustrations.

Ceria, Eugenio. *San Giovanni Bosco nella vita e nelle opere*. SEI, 1941. Nice summary by the scholarly Fr. Ceria, with beautiful color illustrations by G.B. Galizzi.

Giraudo, Aldo and Giuseppe Biancardi. *Qui È Vissuto Don Bosco:*

Itinerari storico-geografici e spirituali. LDC, 1988. Detailed, scholarly guide book for visiting the places in Piedmont associated with DB. Maps, tables, illustrations.

Lemoyne, Giovanni Battista, Angelo Amadei, and Eugenio Ceria. *Memorie biografiche di S. Giovanni Bosco.* 20 vols. SEI, 1898–1939. Massive biography based on extensive primary and secondary sources, including the *Memorie dell'Oratorio* manuscripts. The last volume is an index to the entire work; there are no indexes in the individual volumes.

Lemoyne, Giovanni Battista, et al. *The Biographical Memoirs of Saint John Bosco,* trans. and ed. Diego Borgatello, SDB. New Rochelle: Salesiana Publishers, 1964–   . English edition of the above. Explanatory and cross-reference notes added; indexes in each volume; most volumes slightly abridged. 15 volumes completed through 1989.

Matt, Leonard von and Henri Bosco. *Don Bosco,* trans. Fr. John Bennett, SDB. New York: Universe Books, 1965. A popular text with 167 magnificent photographs and illustrations of the persons, places, and events of DB's life.

Molineris, Michele. *Don Bosco inedito.* Castelnuovo Don Bosco: Istituto Salesiano "Bernardi-Semeria," 1974. Details omitted or corrected from the standard biographies, with an abundance of additional background material, a genealogical table, and illustrations.

Soldà, Giuseppe. *Don Bosco nella fotografia dell'800: 1861–1888.* SEI, 1987. Detailed study of the photographs taken of DB and how they were used. Amply illustrated; bibliography.

Stella, Pietro. *Don Bosco nella storia della religiosità cattolica.* 3 vols. LAS, 1979–88. First study of DB and his work using historical-critical method; presupposes familiarity with DB's biography. Notes, bibliography, and index in each volume.

Stella, Pietro. *Don Bosco: Life and Work* and *Don Bosco and the Death of Charles.* DBP, 1985. English trans. by John Drury of vol. 1 of the above. Notes, greatly expanded bibliography, and index.

Stella, Pietro. *Don Bosco: Religious Outlook and Spirituality* and *Don Bosco's Dreams: A Historico-documentary Analysis of Selected Samples.* DBP, anticipated for 1990. English trans. by John Drury of vol. 2 of the above. Notes, bibliography, and index.

Stella, Pietro. *Don Bosco nella storia economica e sociale (1815–1870).* LAS, 1980. Critical study of DB and his work in another context. Notes, extensive tables, and indexes.

Traniello, Francesco, ed. *Don Bosco nella storia della cultura popolare*. SEI, 1987. Collection of scholarly essays with index and notes.

Don Bosco's Spirituality

Bosco, Giovanni. *San Giuseppe Cafasso: memorie pubblicate nel 1860*. SEI, 1960. Two eulogies of his mentor, with introductions by Eugenio Valentini, SDB, and Angelo Amadei, SDB, and appendices. English trans. by Patrick O'Connell: *The Life of St. Joseph Cafasso*. Rockford, Ill.: TAN, 1983; contains the two eulogies and some appendices.

Bosco, Giovanni. *Scritti spirituali*, ed. Joseph Aubry, SDB. 2 vols. Rome: Città Nuova Editrice, 1976. A broad selection from the published and unpublished writings with an excellent introduction and indexes. English trans. by Joseph Caselli, SDB: *The Spiritual Writings of Saint John Bosco*. DBP, 1984, with brief bibliography added.

Ceria, Eugenio. *Don Bosco con Dio*. Nuova edizione ampliata. Colle Don Bosco: LDC, 1946. Classic study by one of the saint's great biographers, who knew him personally. There is a somewhat rough and incomplete trans. by Hugh McGlinchey, SDB: *Don Bosco with God*. Madras: Salesian Publications, n.d.

Desramaut, Francis. *Don Bosco and the Spiritual Life*, trans. Roger M. Luna, SDB. DBP, 1979. A modern study that puts DB within the context of his times. Notes, bibliography, and index.

Lemoyne, John Baptist, SC. *A Character Sketch of the Venerable Don Bosco, Founder of the Salesian Society and the Daughters of Our Lady Help of Christians* [trans. Aloysius Trifari, SDB]. New Rochelle: Salesian Press, 1927. Trans. and abridgment of the great biographer-archivist's two-volume *Vita di Don Giovanni Bosco* (SEI, 1915).

Phelan, Edna Beyer. *Don Bosco: A Spiritual Portrait*. Garden City: Doubleday & Company, 1963. Readable, scholarly study; bibliography.

Don Bosco's Educational Method

Avallone, Paul, SDB. *Reason, Religion and Kindness: The Educational Method of St. John Bosco.* 3d ed. DBP, 1977. Clear presentation of the Preventive System.

Bosco, Giovanni. *Scritti sul sistema preventivo nell'educazione della gioventù,* ed. Pietro Braido. Brescia: La Scuola Editrice, 1965. Expert selection from a great variety of DB's writings; introduction, bibliography, indexes.

Bosco, John. "The Preventive System in the Education of the Young," and "Letter from Rome," in *Constitutions of the Society of St Francis de Sales* (Rome, 1985), pp. 246–64. These are the saint's two most systematic treatments of his educational method. Various other editions are also available in English.

Bosco, John. *Saint Dominic Savio,* trans. Paul Aronica. 2d ed. DBP, 1979. This might be considered an educational and moral treatise in biographical guise, geared toward young people in simple language. The American trans. is very readable and includes some explanatory notes and two appendices.

Braido, Pietro, ed. *Esperienze di pedagogia cristiana nella storia.* Vol. II: Sec. XVII-XIX. LAS, 1981. Scholarly exploration by various authors of the science of Christian education, including the French Oratorians, De La Salle and the Christian Brothers, and DB, among others. Notes and indexes.

Braido, Pietro, ed. *Il sistema educativo di Don Bosco tra pedagogia antica e nuova.* LDC, 1974. A series of scholarly talks from a European conference, emphasizing the modern application of the Preventive System.

Braido, Pietro. *Il sistema preventivo di Don Bosco.* Turin: Pontificio Ateneo Salesiano, 1955. Lengthy, scholarly dissertation, with notes and appendices. A 2d ed. has been published.

Cornell, Wallace L., ed. *Don Bosco: Spiritual Director of Young People.* Manila: Salesiana Publishers, 1986. Extracts from some of DB's writings which bear on his manner of guiding the young toward holiness, translated by Fr. Cornell. Contained in full are the lives of Dominic Savio, Francis Besucco, and Michael Magone; the latter two, like the first, are edifying biographies of youths of the Oratory, intended for Salesian pupils, here published in English for the first time.

Morrison, John. *The Educational Philosophy of St. John Bosco.* DBP, 1979. Analysis and evaluation by an Australian lay educator. Notes, bibliography, and index.

O'Brien, Terence, SDB. *Dominic Savio: Teenage Apostle, Saint.* New Rochelle: Salesiana Publishers, 1969. A British trans. of DB's little biography with a thorough commentary; appendix contains the dream of 1876 in which Savio appeared to DB.

Vespignani, Giuseppe. *Un anno alla scuola di Don Bosco.* San Benigno, 1932. Memoirs of a young priest who spent a year at the Oratory before going to the South American missions; he later became a member of the Superior Chapter (General Council) of the Salesians. A rough trans. [by William Kelley, SDB] was mimeographed at Newton, NJ, in the 1960s under the title *A Year at the School of St. John Bosco, 1876–1877.*

The Salesian Family

Capetti, Giselda, FMA, ed. *Cronistoria: Chronicles of the Institute of the Daughters of Mary Help of Christians.* 5 vols. DBP, 1981. English trans. of an archival history of DB's founding of the Salesian Sisters with Fr. Dominic Pestarino and St. Mary Mazzarello.

Ceria, Eugenio. *Annali della Società salesiana.* 4 vols. SEI, 1941–1951. An archival history of DB and the Salesians till 1921, of uneven quality. Index in each volume.

Constitutions of the Society of St Francis de Sales. Rome, 1985.

Giraudi, Fedele. *L'Oratorio di Don Bosco: inizio e progressivo sviluppo edilizio della Casa Madre dei Salesiani in Torino.* SEI, 1935. Amply illustrated history of the Oratory and its activities, based on archival materials; maps.

Hurley, James, SDB, et al. *Service for the Young.* Columbus, Ohio [1973]. A brief, illustrated history of Salesian work in the US and Canada; index.

[Maraccani, Francesco, SDB, et al.] *The Project of Life of the Salesians of Don Bosco: A guide to the Salesian Constitutions,* trans. George Williams, SDB. Rome, 1986. Exhaustive commentary on the renewed (post-Vatican II) Salesian Rule by 17 experts; includes notes, bibliography, and index.

Pedrini, Arnaldo, SDB. *Saint Francis de Sales, Don Bosco's Patron: St. Francis de Sales in the Times, Life and Thought of St. John Bosco,* ed. Francis J. Klauder, SDB. DBP, 1988. General survey of the influence of St. Francis on DB. Illustrations, bibliography, notes, index.

Picca, Juan and Jozef Struś, ed. *San Francesco di Sales e i Salesiani di Don Bosco*. LAS, 1986. A collection of essays on St. Francis, DB's Salesian spirituality, and the Salesian Congregation's spirituality. Notes and indexes.

Wirth, Morand. *Don Bosco and the Salesians*, trans. David de Burgh, SDB. DBP, 1982. A popularly written history, half given to DB and the development of his works, and half to the development of the Salesians after his death. Notes, bibliography, and index.

Italy in the Nineteenth Century

Aubert, Roger, et al. *The Church in a Secularised Society*. New York: Paulist Press, 1978. In-depth, scholarly treatment of the Church's relations with the French Revolution and its aftermath.

Berkeley, G. *Italy in the Making, 1815–1846*. 3 vols. The most exhaustive study of the first phase of Italian unification.

Clark, Martin. *Modern Italy, 1871–1982*. New York: Longman, 1984. One of the few studies of Italy after unification, i.e. during the last 18 years of DB's life. Part One (pp. 12–90) deals specifically with that period. The approach is social and economic as well as political. Maps, tables, notes, bibliography, and index.

Coppa, Frank J. *Pope Pius IX: Crusader in a Secular Age*. Boston: Twayne, 1979. Briefer than Hales (see below) and less sympathetic; scholarly and readable; first English biography of Pius to use the Vatican Archives. Notes, bibliography, index.

Dicastero per la Formazione. *Il Tempo di Don Bosco*. Sussidi 1 per lo Studio di Don Bosco e della sua Opera. Frascati: edizione extra-commerciale, 1986. Outline of church and secular history in Italy, Piedmont, and Turin. Maps, tables, bibliography, notes.

Gilbert, Felix, ed. *The Norton History of Modern Europe*. New York: W.W. Norton & Company, 1971. Parts IV and V offer a scholarly and convenient summary of the ages of the French Revolution, nationalism, and reform, putting DB's Italy into the European context.

Hales, E.E.Y. *Pio Nono: A Study in European Politics and Religion in the Nineteenth Century*. Garden City: Doubleday, 1962.

The first thorough biography in English (first ed., 1954) — a sympathetic one — of DB's patron, the nemesis of Italian unification. Notes, bibliography, and index.

Hales, E.E.Y. *Revolution and Papacy, 1769–1846*. University of Notre Dame Press, 1966. Sympathetic study of how the Popes coped with the dissolution of the Old Regime. Notes are minimal; appendices, thorough bibliography, and index.

Hearder, Harry. *Italy in the Age of the Risorgimento, 1790–1870*. New York: Longman, Green, 1983. Very scholarly treatment. Maps, notes, bibliography, index.

Hentze, Margot. *Pre-Fascist Italy: The Rise and Fall of the Parliamentary Regime*. London: George Allen & Unwin, 1939. A specifically political study of post-unification Italy. Notes, index.

Holt, Edgar. *The Making of Italy, 1815–1870*. New York: Atheneum, 1971. Written in a popular style; a thorough presentation of the Risorgimento. Illustrations, maps, notes, bibliography, and index.

King, Bolton. *A History of Italian Unity*. 2 vols. New York, 1899. Dated but still very useful; the most complete survey of the Risorgimento in English; anticlerical bias.

Mack Smith, Denis. *Cavour*. New York: Knopf, 1985. Highly readable, well done study of the great statesman by today's most respected English-speaking student of modern Italy. Bibliography, index. Mack Smith has also written four other major studies of the Risorgimento and its leaders.

Marriott, J.A.R. *The Makers of Modern Italy: Napoleon — Mussolini*. Oxford: Clarendon, 1931. Useful and interesting survey of the Risorgimento, tainted by a sanguine prewar view of Fascism. Bibliography, index.

Thayer, William Roscoe. *The Life and Times of Cavour*. 2 vols. Boston: Houghton Mifflin, 1911. Dated, anticlerical, but thorough. Notes and index.

Whyte, Arthur James. *The Evolution of Modern Italy*. Oxford: Basil Blackwell, 1959. DB's Italy set in political context from 1715 to 1920. Scholarly and readable. Maps, esp. of battlefields, a few notes, bibliography, and index.

Woolf, Stuart. *A history of Italy, 1700–1860: the social constraints of political change*. London: Methuen, 1979. Perhaps the best available work in which social insights and social movements receive relevant scholarly treatment.

ಐಐಐಐ

INDEXES

ಐಐಐಐ

Abbreviations Used in the Indexes

Index of Persons and Places

Index of Topics

Index of Authors and Works Cited

Amadei, Fr. Angelo (*BM* X), 6, 80, 158, 279, 295, 309, 349, 358, 424, 433–34

Ambrose, St., 404

Aquinas, St. Thomas, 94

Atti Ufficiali, 354

Aubert, Roger, xlvi

Aubry, Fr. Joseph, 288–89, 359, 434

Augustine, St., 161

Bianco, Fr. Enzo, 199, 384

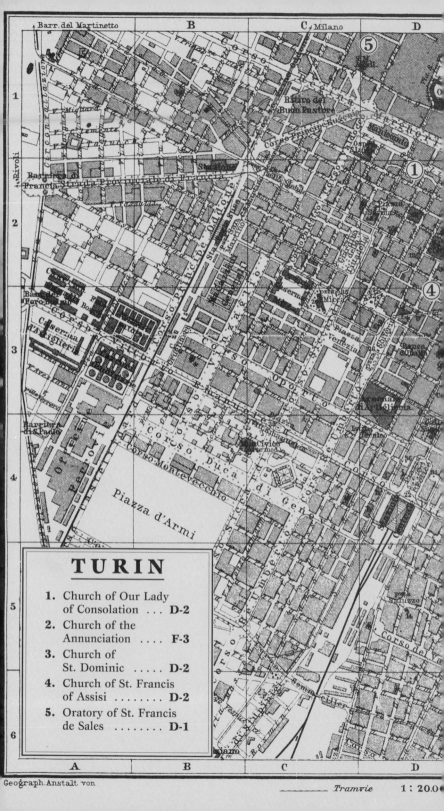

TURIN

1. Church of Our Lady
   of Consolation ... **D-2**
2. Church of the
   Annunciation **F-3**
3. Church of
   St. Dominic **D-2**
4. Church of St. Francis
   of Assisi **D-2**
5. Oratory of St. Francis
   de Sales **D-1**

Geograph. Anstalt von

Tramvie   1 : 20.00